International Law
and
Ethnic Conflict

International Law and Ethnic Conflict

EDITED BY

David Wippman

Published under the Auspices of the
American Society of International Law

Cornell University Press · *Ithaca and London*

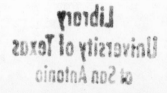

First published 1998 by Cornell University Press.

Printed in the United States of America

Cornell University Press strives to utilize environmentally responsible suppliers and materials to the fullest extent possible in the publishing of its books. Such materials include vegetable-based, low-VOC inks and acid-free papers that are also either recycled, totally chlorine-free, or partly composed of nonwood fibers.

Library of Congress Cataloging-in-Publication Data

International law and ethnic conflict / edited by David Wippman.
        p. cm.
Includes index.
ISBN 0-8014-3433-5 (cloth : alk. paper)
1. International law   2. Ethnic relations.   I. Wippman, David, 1954–   .
KZ1255.I58   1998
341—dc21   97-33557

Cloth printing   10 9 8 7 6 5 4 3 2 1

Contents

Part II   Institutional and Policy Responses to Ethnic Conflict

Contributors

NATHANIEL BERMAN is Professor of Law at Northeastern University School of Law.

LEA BRILMAYER is the Benjamin F. Butler Professor of Law at New York University Law School.

ABRAM CHAYES is Felix Frankfurter Professor of Law Emeritus at Harvard Law School and a former legal adviser to the U.S. Department of State.

ANTONIA HANDLER CHAYES is a senior adviser of the Conflict Management Group in Cambridge, Massachusetts, and a former undersecretary of the U.S. Air Force.

LORI FISLER DAMROSCH is Professor of Law at Columbia University School of Law.

TOM FARER is the Dean of the Graduate School of International Studies at the University of Denver and a former president of the Inter-American Commission on Human Rights of the Organization of American States.

DIANE F. ORENTLICHER is Professor of Law at American University's Washington College of Law.

MICHAEL PLATZER is Head of the Operational Activities and Advisory Services of the U.N. Crime Prevention and Criminal Justice Division.

STEVEN R. RATNER is Professor of Law at the University of Texas Law School.

DAVID J. SCHEFFER is U.S. Ambassador at Large for War Crimes Issues and a former senior adviser and counsel to the U.S. Permanent Representative to the United Nations.

ANNE-MARIE SLAUGHTER is Professor of Law at Harvard Law School.

FERNANDO R. TESÓN is Professor of Law at Arizona State University College of Law.

RUTH WEDGWOOD is Professor of Law at Yale Law School and the director of the Project on International Organizations and Law at the Council on Foreign Relations.

DAVID WIPPMAN is Associate Professor of Law at Cornell Law School.

Acknowledgments

This volume had its origins in a workshop on international law and ethnic conflict held at Cornell Law School in November 1995, part of a series of workshops organized by professors Valerie Bunce and Shibley Telhami on the subject of ethnic conflict.

Funding for the workshop was provided by the Carnegie Corporation of New York, the U.S. Army War College, and Cornell Law School. In addition, several programs at Cornell provided invaluable assistance in organizing and sponsoring this project: the Berger International Legal Studies Program of Cornell Law School, the Peace Studies Program, and the European Studies Program.

John Oakley, as project coordinator, provided invaluable advice and assistance at all stages of the project. Theodore Schultz and Leslie Smith provided essential research support, and Kathleen O'Rourke and Linda Majeroni offered critical logistical support for the organization and conduct of the November conference. Special thanks to Pamela Finnigan for shepherding the manuscript through all its various permutations.

In addition to the authors, other conference participants made valuable contributions to the discussions of the various chapters in this volume: John J. Barceló III, Colonel David Crane, Colonel William Doll, Valerie P. Gagnon, Milton Esman, Captain Warren Reardon, Judith Reppy, and Shibley Telhami. These comments proved extremely helpful to the authors, particularly to me, as the editor of the volume.

Finally, I am grateful to the staff of Cornell University Press for excellent editorial suggestions and timely production, in particular to Roger Haydon, for helping guide this project through the publication process.

D. W.

International Law
and
Ethnic Conflict

Introduction: Ethnic Claims
and International Law

David Wippman

The end of the cold war has seen a series of profound changes in the
international system. Three changes are of particular significance for this
book. First, the end of the U.S.-Soviet rivalry accompanied, and in some
respects facilitated, a proliferation of virulent ethnic conflicts. Many of
these conflicts erupted in the former Soviet Union and Eastern Europe as
political entrepreneurs latched onto ethno-nationalism as an organizing
principle and a vehicle to political power. But similar conflicts also
emerged or intensified in many other countries around the world, with
truly catastrophic consequences. Second, the immediate corollary to the
end of bipolar competition was the beginning of new possibilities for
great power cooperation in international organizations, the Security
Council in particular. Though the potential for such cooperation has often
been overstated, the fact remains that in recent years the U.N. and other
international organizations have displayed a far greater ability and willingness to intervene in what might previously have been considered the
domestic affairs of member states. This change, coupled with the extraordinary destructiveness of contemporary ethnic conflicts, has spurred ever
increasing demands for greater involvement by international organizations. Third, the collapse of socialism as an alternative to the liberal democratic capitalism promoted by Western states has accelerated a shift in
international norms pertaining to the legitimacy of state power and external intervention in internal affairs. The international legal system is
increasingly less statist in its orientation; states and international organizations display a substantially greater willingness to insist on democratic
governance as a prerequisite for international legitimacy and at least a

nascent willingness to value human rights over territorial integrity in exceptional circumstances. The purpose of this book is to consider the application of international law to ethnic conflict in light of these inter-related trends.

Admittedly, ethnic conflict is not, per se, an ordinary or natural category for legal analysis. In keeping with its Westphalian underpinnings, international law tends to compartmentalize issues pertaining to armed conflict along state lines. As a result, armed conflicts are typically characterized and analyzed as international, internal, or mixed, with important consequences turning on the distinctions. In legal theory, the ethnic character of such conflicts is generally of little importance. Similarly, the recognized actors in international law include states, governments, peoples, minorities, and individuals but only rarely ethnic groups, and then typically as an aspect of another category. Ethnicity may be a characteristic of a minority, or it may serve as part of a group's claim to be a people entitled to self-determination, but membership in an ethnic group is not by itself a basis for asserting particular claims under international law.

Nonetheless, virtually all of the central issues arising out of ethnic conflict implicate key aspects of international law and, from a lawyer's standpoint, should be regulated by international law. At its core, ethnic conflict tends to center on competing claims to territory and the exercise of state power. From Bosnia to Tajikistan, from Abkhazia to Sri Lanka, ethnic groups seek greater political power for their members in ways that range from demands for independence to enhanced political participation within existing states. Because the conflicts that arise in connection with these demands call into question the legitimacy of states and governments, they go to the heart of international law. The issues raised by ethnic conflict, and regulated to a greater or lesser extent by international law, include the legitimate basis for statehood and the exercise of state power; the extent to which external actors should take cognizance of, and perhaps even demand acceptance of, claims by substate groups to exercise political power domestically and internationally; the political, social, and cultural rights of groups and individuals; the role that international organizations can and should play in responding to ethnic conflicts; the compatibility of particular conflict management strategies with individual rights; the circumstances and manner in which force may be used to support or oppose claims advanced by ethnic groups; the nature and implications of citizenship; and the rights and responsibilities of outside actors in dealing with refugee flows, humanitarian catastrophes, and reconstruction of ethnically torn polities.

These are the issues the chapters in this book address. Because ethnic conflict potentially implicates virtually all of public international law, it is impossible to be truly comprehensive in a single volume. The goal of this volume is instead to consider some of the principal issues associated with ethnic conflict within the general framework of international law. To set the stage, I consider in this introduction some of the definitional issues that inevitably surround discussions of ethnic conflict and then seek to set out in general terms the legal framework within which readers can locate subsequent chapters.

I. The Nature of Ethnic Conflict

International lawyers have long struggled to achieve consensus on the definition of the "peoples" entitled to self-determination and the "minorities" entitled to protection under international human rights norms. No consensus has emerged in large part because the terms attempt to fix for international law purposes aspects of group identity that are inherently contextual and forever subject to change. As a result, international legal instruments commonly ascribe rights to peoples and minorities without defining those terms, trusting in the ability of the relevant actors to apply them as appropriate in any given case.

Similar problems arise in attempts to define the ethnic groups that make for ethnic conflict. This is not surprising because all three definitional categories—peoples, minorities, and ethnic groups—are closely related and to a large extent overlap.[1] Political scientists, sociologists, anthropologists, historians, and lawyers have offered a broad range of definitions, none of which is universally accepted but most of which share certain key elements from which a working definition adequate for present purposes may be derived.

Two related elements in particular characterize most definitions of ethnicity: belief by members of the group in a common origin or descent and a sense that the group shares a common culture that distinguishes it from the society at large. The belief in a common origin affords the psychological basis for strong intragroup loyalties of the sort that characterize extended kinship networks. To a greater or lesser degree, members of ethnic groups tend to see themselves as bound by ties of blood that require members to render assistance to each other in their dealings with outsiders. The belief in a common origin is typically reinforced by the presence of various ascriptive markers of identity, which enable group members and outsiders to distinguish each from the other. Such markers include but are not limited to language, physical characteristics associated with race, religion, and distinctive cultural practices. The second principal

[1] *Cf.* Ian Brownlie, *The Rights of Peoples in Modern International Law*, in THE RIGHTS OF PEOPLES 5 (James Crawford ed., 1988) ("references to 'nationalities', 'peoples', 'minorities', and 'indigenous populations'—involved essentially the same idea").

characteristic of ethnicity, the notion of a shared culture, extends beyond particular cultural practices and includes a sense among members of the group that they share a common history and that they form a natural community. For members, participation in the cultural life of the group is central to their sense of personal identity. Perceived threats to the viability of the group's culture are taken as threats to individual members of the group and may provoke a violent reaction.

Broadly defined, then, groups that cohere around a belief in a common origin and a shared culture, and that are large enough to transcend the possibility of familiarity through face-to-face interactions, may be considered ethnic groups. It is fashionable now to argue that, in reality, such groups constitute what Benedict Anderson so evocatively termed "imagined communities." The insight behind the phrase is that the boundaries between ethnic groups are often fluid, that their histories are often based on myth as much as on fact, and that their members' belief in a common origin that diverges sharply from their neighbors' may be mistaken. There is considerable truth to the view that ethnic identity is a malleable and socially constructed phenomenon: ethnic boundaries may shift over time; ethnic groups may be mistaken about their history and ancestry; ethnic divisions can be "created, accentuated, reduced or destroyed" by outside events; and, over the long term, ethnic groups can be constructed and deconstructed by patterns of migration, conquest, and assimilation.[2] But ethnic groups cannot be created out of whole cloth, though some have tried. There is something real at the core of ethnic identity that renders ethnic affinities resistant to the leveling influences of modernization and that provides a solid base for intense, even passionate, collective action and political mobilization in ways that may appear irrational to outside observers.[3]

It is this capacity for communal solidarity and political mobilization that renders ethnic affiliations different from other kinds of group identifications and leads many authors to regard ethnic groups as "primary" and "natural" and to consider other forms of association as secondary.[4] The strength of ethnic cleavages tends to preempt competing sources of political loyalty, at least in instances in which group members perceive a threat to the group's culture or position in society. Thus, apparently dormant ethnic cleavages often surface violently during periods of state collapse or transition.[5] For the same reason, ethnic ties, unlike other bases for

---

[2] Robin M. Williams, Jr., *The Sociology of Ethnic Conflicts: Comparative International Perspectives*, in 20 ANNUAL REV. SOC. 49, 51, 58 (1994).

[3] *Id.* at 57–58.

[4] Antony Anghie, *Human Rights and Cultural Identity: New Hope for Ethnic Peace?* 33 HARV. INT'L L. J. 341, 345 (1992).

[5] *Id.*

group affiliation, can form a seemingly natural basis for attempts to establish independent political communities.[6]

Ethnic conflicts of the sort that are the subject of this book arise when two or more ethnic groups within a state compete for economic and political goods, which may include territory, political power and offices, or access to resources controlled by the state. In extreme cases, ethnic conflict manifests itself as a demand by an ethnic group for a state of its own. More commonly, though, ethnic groups make lesser demands, which may range from insistence on participation in the political life of the state on terms of equality with other groups to affirmative measures, such as special language and education rights, to demands for limited autonomy within the state.

Of course, not all multiethnic states experience ethnic conflict, at least not at a level sufficient to attract international attention. Ethnic pluralism is thus a necessary but insufficient condition for the outbreak of ethnic conflict. The triggers for such conflict must be located elsewhere. While no one theory can adequately account for all incidences of ethnic conflict, most have their roots in "objective conditions such as economic deprivation, discrimination, [or] loss of political or cultural autonomy."[7] These conditions create grievances that can be exploited by ethnic entrepreneurs to mobilize ethnic groups for political action.[8] The form that political action will take and the likelihood that such action will succeed depend on a host of variables, which include the size of the contending ethnic groups; their strength and distribution; the resources available to them; the history of their prior interactions; the extent to which the groups are interdependent; the depth of the grievances at issue or the extent of the preferences claimed; the role and structure of political parties within the state; the presence or absence of cross-cutting or mutually reinforcing cleavages along class, religious, or other lines; and the attitude and involvement of outside states.[9]

Whatever its causes, ethnic conflict is often violent, protracted, and resistant to settlement. By conservative estimates, at least 11 million people have been killed in such conflicts since 1945; many estimates are much higher.[10] Because only a handful of states even approximate ethnic homogeneity, ethnic conflict is potentially a problem for virtually all countries. Certainly, numerous ethnic conflicts blight the contemporary landscape, in countries as diverse as Azerbaijan, Bosnia, Rwanda, Sri

---

[6] CLIFFORD GEERTZ, THE INTERPRETATION OF CULTURES 261 (1973), quoted in *id.*

[7] Williams, *supra* note 2, at 72.

[8] *Id.*

[9] *Id.*

[10] *Id.* at 50.

Lanka, and the Sudan. In some cases, as in Cyprus, ethnic conflict has persisted at varying levels of intensity for decades.

Liberal theory once predicted that ethnicity would gradually diminish and eventually disappear as a significant political force under the homogenizing influence of modernization.[11] The assumption was that "in the wake of economic development and nation-building, ascriptive loyalties would lose their social function and gradually wither away."[12] Painful experience demonstrates, however, that ethnic affinities will not disappear any time soon, a fact many liberals find problematic. In general, liberals view ethnic solidarities with suspicion. At the extremes, they see a broad competition between civic nationalism and ethnic nationalism; between cosmopolitan, inclusive, liberal democratic visions of the ideal polity and narrow, exclusivist, authoritarian notions. They point to ethnic cleansing in Bosnia and mass murder in Rwanda as the not surprising outcome of attempts to organize states on ethnic lines. Liberals favor broad political participation of all those within the geographic boundaries of a given state, regardless of their ethnic identity. They reject claims to status based on ascriptive characteristics rather than on merit. They regard romantic notions of the significance of community as essentially irrational bases for political action, and they believe that individual liberties and rights should take precedence over group interests and claims.

In recent years, however, many political theorists, especially communitarians, have challenged some of the central tenets of the liberal orthodoxy. Echoing earlier romantic notions of the importance of culture and group, communitarians claim that liberal theorists underestimate the centrality of ethnicity and communal affiliation to personal identity. In their view, liberal theory falsely treats individuals as wholly autonomous agents when in reality individuals are part of a larger community and culture that give meaning to the choices individuals make. Communitarians tend to be sympathetic to claims for group rights and the affirmative protection of group cultures, even at the expense of individual rights.

International law has never wholly resolved the tension between these two broadly opposing views of the importance of group identity.[13] As the dominant paradigm for many years, liberal theory has exercised a strong influence on the international law norms that pertain to state formation, group claims, and individual rights. To a large extent, international law in these and related areas has "assimilated [the] cosmopolitan, liberal vision

---

[11] See MILTON J. ESMAN, ETHNIC POLITICS 17–18 (1994) (noting that modernization in fact tends to "reinvigorate" rather than supplant ethnic solidarities).

[12] Id. at 12.

[13] Cf. Martii Koskenniemi, National Self-Determination Today: Problems of Legal Theory and Practice, 43 INT'L & COMP. L.Q. 241, 250 (1994).

of states" and "disdained ethnic particularity as an organizing principle
. . . emphasizing instead republican virtues of civic equality."[14] But at the
same time, international law has never wholly overlooked the competing
claims of romantic and communitarian visions of the political good. The
last few years in particular have witnessed a strongly renewed interest in
protecting the rights of ethnic communities and their members. That interest is manifested in a variety of recent human rights instruments that
emphasize the importance of preserving the cultural integrity of ethnic
communities and of enhancing their members' opportunities for meaningful participation in the governance of the states of which they are a
part.

II. The International Law Framework

The recent surge of ethnic conflict highlights the importance of these
perennial debates over the place of ethnic communities in the international order. Unfortunately, the international community has yet to develop a
principled or fully coherent political or legal response to ethno-nationalist
claims. Separatist claims in particular have produced a confused and
confusing international reaction. On the one hand, most states and international and regional organizations routinely condemn exclusivist ethnic
separatism, reject the use of force as a tool to alter existing international
(and even internal) boundaries, and demand respect for the principle of
territorial integrity. On the other hand, the international community has
nonetheless reluctantly accepted, and in some respects ratified, the forcible reconfiguration of states in Ethiopia and the former Yugoslavia.

For international lawyers, the challenge now is "to rethink the most
fundamental norms of our craft" in order to devise appropriate legal
responses to the competing claims of states, ethnic groups, and individuals.[15] In particular, international lawyers must continue to debate the
meaning and scope of self-determination, the distinction between peoples
and minorities and the rights of each, and the proper role of outside actors
in shaping the future of political communities.

A. Sovereignty and Self-Determination

At the core of any international legal response to ethnic conflict lie two
fundamental legal norms of doubtful compatibility: the right of states to

[14] Diane Orentlicher, *Separation Anxiety: International Responses to Ethno-Separatist Claims,*
23 Yale J. Int'l L. 1 (1997).
[15] Thomas M. Franck, *Postmodern Tribalism and the Right to Secession,* in Peoples and
Minorities in International Law 4 (Catherine Brölmann, René Lefeber & Marjoleine
Zieck eds., 1993).

preserve their territorial integrity and the right of peoples to self-determination. Notwithstanding much recent discussion about the erosion of state sovereignty, the international system for the most part still retains its state-centric focus, and the right of states to control and preserve their territory free from external interference remains the central feature of that system. At the same time, the right of peoples to shape their own political destiny and to choose the boundaries of their political allegiance now constitutes a fundamental norm of international law, perhaps even a peremptory norm. Insofar as that norm entails a right to independence for substate groups, it stands in direct opposition to the norm of territorial integrity.[16] The central problem for international law, then, is to reconcile these two apparently conflicting norms.

1. The Origins and Evolution of Self-Determination

Self-determination achieved prominence as a political principle at the time of the French Revolution. Fundamentally, it was a principle of democratic self-governance, with two major aspects: first, it implied that the people within a state should have the right to form their own government free from external interference; second, it implied that a state's inhabitants should not be transferred from one state to another without their consent, a not uncommon practice at the time.[17] During the course of the nineteenth century, German cultural nationalists lent a different aspect to the principle of self-determination by invoking it in support of claims that each nation, understood as an "authentic" political and cultural community, should have its own state.[18] The democratic and romantic features of self-determination have been uncomfortably intertwined ever since.

Both understandings of self-determination, but especially the romantic one, played a significant role in the political and territorial adjustments that followed the end of World War I. At the Versailles peace conference in 1919, the victorious allies, led by Woodrow Wilson, proclaimed their intention to redraw the map of Europe in at least partial accord with prevailing notions of self-determination. In practice, this meant that the allies considered the distribution and interests of ethnic groups when drawing or revising boundaries for the new and the defeated states emerging from the breakup of the Austro-Hungarian and Ottoman empires. Where politically feasible and consistent with the allies' strategic interests, boundaries were drawn along ethnic lines; where national groups could not be accommodated with their own states, they received

---

[16] Whether the two are actually in opposition depends on one's interpretation of self-determination. See Lea Brilmayer, Secession and Self-Determination: A Territorial Interpretation, 16 YALE J. INT'L L. 177 (1991).

[17] See Orentlicher, supra note 14.

[18] Id.

special protections under League of Nations' auspices through adoption of the minorities treaty system. In a few instances, the allies sponsored plebiscites to enable particular populations to choose their sovereign, the reverse of the historical practice of allowing sovereigns to transfer territories and their populations at will. Thus, Versailles represents a significant effort to give at least partial effect to the notion that ethnic groups form natural communities entitled to some measure of political independence or protection and, to a lesser extent, to the notion that peoples should control the destiny of the territory in which they live rather than the other way around.

But despite broad rhetoric about the need to respect self-determination as a governing political principle, the allies made no attempt to universalize that principle. There was no thought of granting autonomy, much less independence, to "nations" outside the territory or control of the newly created or defeated states. In particular, the allies made no move to relinquish their colonial possessions, although the colonial territories of the defeated empires were transformed into mandates for supervision and eventual disposition by the victors. Moreover, there was no effort to create a generally applicable system of minority rights. The minorities treaties applied only to states whose boundaries were created or reshaped as part of the Versailles settlement.

Further, even though self-determination was often invoked as a principle of general application, it was never intended to legitimate a right of secession from established states. This point is clearly stated in a 1921 decision by the Commission of Jurists established by the League of Nations to settle a dispute between Finland and Sweden over demands by inhabitants of the Aaland Islands that they be allowed to separate from Finland and merge with Sweden. The jurists rejected the notion that self-determination constituted a legal right as distinguished from a political principle; in particular, they denied that it constituted a legal right to dismember an existing state.[19] In a subsequent report, a League-appointed Commission of Rapporteurs agreed with the Commission of Jurists in language that reflects the longstanding assumed incompatibility between self-determination as a principle authorizing secession and territorial integrity as a right of states and explains the traditional basis for giving priority to the latter: "To concede to minorities, either of language or religion, or to any fractions of a population the right of withdrawing from the community to which they belong, because it is their good wish or pleasure, would be to destroy order and stability within States and to inaugurate anarchy in international life; it would be to uphold a theory

[19] Report of the International Committee of Jurists Entrusted by the Council of the League of Nations with the Task of Giving an Advisory Opinion upon the Legal Aspects of the Aaland Islands Question, LEAGUE OF NATIONS OFF. J., SPEC. SUPP. No. 3, at 5 (1920).

incompatible with the very idea of the State as a territorial and political unity."[20]

Although both commissions went on to suggest that secession might be justifiable as a remedy of last resort in states that failed to respect minority rights, the more absolutist denial of any right to secession, driven by concerns over the stability of existing states, characterized the prevailing approach to national self-determination in international law during the interwar period, and it continues to drive contemporary approaches to self-determination questions.

Nonetheless, international law governing self-determination shifted substantially after World War II. During the postwar period, self-determination gradually made the transition from a political principle to a legal right. The impetus behind the transformation was the evolution of human rights norms in general and the need to create a legal vehicle for decolonization in particular.

In 1950, the U.N. General Assembly recognized for the first time "the right of peoples and nations to self-determination."[21] In its 1960 Declaration on the Granting of Independence to Colonial Countries and Peoples, the General Assembly defined self-determination as a right to political independence for peoples subject to alien or colonial domination.[22] The 1970 Friendly Relations Declaration, adopted by consensus, solidified self-determination as a right of subjugated peoples to decolonization, whether through the choice of independent statehood or "any other political status freely determined" by the inhabitants of the territory involved.[23]

In shifting from a political principle to a legal right, self-determination thus metamorphosed from a principle for state formation along ethnic lines to a principle of independence for all the inhabitants of colonial territories.[24] Self-determination retained its secondary association with popular sovereignty insofar as decolonization was assumed to be consistent with the wishes of colonial populations. But self-determination during the decolonization era was not understood to encompass any right to democratic governance in the newly independent states or elsewhere.

Limiting the application of self-determination to decolonization had the advantage of constraining the right's destabilizing and anti-statist potential. But conceptually, this limitation, sometimes referred to as the saltwa-

---

[20] The Aaland Islands Question: Report Submitted to the Council of the League of Nations by the Commission of Rapporteurs, League of Nations Doc. B7.21/68/106 at 28 (1921). For a thoughtful analysis of both commissions' reports, see Nathaniel Berman, *"But the Alternative Is Despair," European Nationalism and the Modernist Renewal of International Law*, 106 HARV. L. REV. 1792 (1993); Orentlicher, *supra* note 14.

[21] G.A. Res. 421 (V) (1950).

[22] G.A. Res. 1514 (1960).

[23] G.A. Res. 2625 (XXXV) (1970).

[24] *See* Orentlicher, *supra* note 14.

ter doctrine for its requirement of geographic separation between colony and metropolitan power, was hard to defend. Colonialism is not the only, or necessarily the worst, form of domination. At the same time, though, states retained their strong dislike for anything that might seem to legitimate secession. That dislike appeared in the resolutions and declarations mandating decolonization in the form of strong language denying that anything in those resolutions could be construed to authorize the violation of a state's territorial integrity. The separation of a colony from the colonial power of which it was nominally a part was justified on the theory that a colony already had a legal "status separate and distinct from the territory of the State administering it";[25] thus, there was no real violation of territorial integrity.

While this rationale neatly confined the secessionist aspect of self-determination to colonies in Africa and Asia, the powerful attraction of self-determination as a broader political ideal proved impossible to contain in that limited compass. As early as 1966, self-determination was formally defined as a right of all peoples in the two principal international human rights covenants. Ever since, international lawyers have debated both the identity of the "peoples" entitled to exercise the right of self-determination and the scope of the right.

2. Contemporary Approaches to Self-Determination

Various strategies have been suggested to permit broad application of self-determination without encouraging secession. One option is to limit the groups entitled to claim self-determination. In its most common form, this approach entails redefining "peoples" to mean all of the people within the boundaries of an existing state. The strategy builds on the fact that decolonization brought independence to colonial territories but not to substate ethnic or political communities within those territories. In practice, this redefinition of peoples turns self-determination into the obverse of the principle of nonintervention; the people of a given territory are entitled to choose their own political system and practices free from outside interference. A variation on this strategy insists that self-determination includes an internal as well as an external component and that it therefore mandates democratic governance within states as well as freedom from meddling by foreign states.[26]

An alternative strategy acknowledges that self-determination is a right of peoples, not states, and that it must apply to substate groups, not simply to all inhabitants of a given state. This strategy focuses not on the

[25] Friendly Relations Declaration, *supra* note 23.
[26] *See* Thomas M. Franck, *The Emerging Entitlement to Democratic Governance*, 86 AM. J. INT'L L. 46 (1992).

identity of the rights holders but on the appropriate means of implementing the right; it seeks to confine the impact of self-determination by characterizing it as a variable right with different consequences in different circumstances. Under this approach, substate ethnic groups might be entitled to claim self-determination, but in the exercise of that right they may have to settle for autonomy, enhanced political participation, or other protections short of independent statehood, depending on the extent to which their legitimate interests can be accommodated without disrupting the territorial integrity of their home state. This approach lends flexibility to the right of self-determination but also renders it highly uncertain in application.

In practice, the international community has yet to settle on any single version of self-determination. All of the interpretations I have noted and more coexist within contemporary international law, with different actors invoking different aspects of the principle as convenient. The normative confusion generated by this state of affairs is evident in the divergent invocations of self-determination in the context of the breakup of the Socialist Federal Republic of Yugoslavia. In that case, self-determination was claimed variously to justify the central government's use of force to preserve the federal state, the republics' claims for independence, demands for democratic governance and respect for minority rights within the republics turned states, and the separatist claims of minority ethnic communities within those new states.

Confronted with the fait accomplis of Yugoslavia's disintegration, the Badinter Commission, the arbitral body entrusted with the task of sorting through the tangle of legal claims surrounding the breakup of Yugoslavia, found it easiest to decide what self-determination is not. Noting that "international law as it currently stands does not spell out all the implications of self-determination," the commission declared that "whatever the circumstances, the right to self-determination must not involve changes to existing frontiers at the time of independence . . . except where the States concerned agree otherwise."[27] Accordingly, the commission rejected the separatist claims of Serbs in Bosnia and Croatia. It went on to suggest, however, that in the context of Yugoslavia's collapse, self-determination affords each individual a right to "choose to belong to whatever ethnic, religious, or language community he or she wishes."

Although the commission's analysis leaves much to be desired, its reluctance to countenance secession does reflect the predominant sentiment of the vast majority of states. At the same time, the commission's effort to link self-determination with the right to choose one's ethnic affiliation reflects the continuing sense that, subject to the overriding importance

---

[27] Conference for Peace in Yugoslavia Arbitration Commission, Opinion No. 2 (1992).

placed on preserving territorial integrity, ethnic groups are entitled to some recognition of their communal identity.

B. Minority Rights

In considering the rights of ethnic communities within the newly created states of Bosnia and Croatia, the Badinter Commission placed great emphasis on the importance of affording them "every protection accorded to minorities" under international law.[28] This focus on minority rights reflects a longstanding tendency in international law to diffuse the anti-statist tendencies of self-determination by channeling claims based on group identity into the narrower confines of minority rights. Where "peoples" may be entitled to a state of their own, "minorities" can claim only the right to equal (and, in some instances, preferential) treatment within existing states.

This tendency to rely on minority rights as an alternative to self-determination dates back at least to the Versailles settlement and the minorities treaties it provided for nationalities denied a state of their own. It appears again in the Commission of Jurists' report on the Aaland Islands dispute. Although rejecting the islanders' claim to full self-determination, the commission noted that a "compromise" amounting to "an extensive grant of liberty to minorities" might be the best way to deal with such claims.[29]

After World War II, though, interest in the recognition and protection of minorities as collectivities declined in favor of the protection of individuals through adoption of universal human rights norms. This trend was driven by the increasing dominance of political liberalism and a lingering hostility to claims made by Nazi Germany on behalf of German minority populations residing in other countries. The adoption of the Universal Declaration of Human Rights in 1948 reflected the prevailing belief in individual rights and equality as a sufficient basis for the protection of the legitimate interests of members of minority groups. In this postwar paradigm, a bright line was drawn between self-determination and minority rights. Colonial peoples could opt for self-determination and protect their collective interest in freedom from external domination through the formation and administration of their own state; minorities within states could claim only the protections afforded by individual human rights norms, which were supposed to foster the tolerance and pluralism deemed adequate for protection of minorities' interests.

Until recently, most major human rights instruments paid little or no attention to minorities per se. The principal provision dealing with minorities appears in Article 27 of the International Covenant on Civil and

---

[28] *Id.*
[29] Jurists' Report, *supra* note 19, at 5–6.

Political Rights. Article 27 provides that "persons belonging" to ethnic, religious, or linguistic minorities "shall not be denied the right, in community with other members of their group, to enjoy their own culture, to profess and practice their own religion, or to use their own language." Although recognizing the communal aspect of ethnic identity, Article 27 affords only limited protection to minority groups and then only by means of the protection accorded to the individual members of those groups. The collectivity itself has no legal status under the covenant or under most other international human rights instruments.

In the last few years, however, interest in the recognition of limited collective rights for ethnic groups as an alternative to self-determination has revived.[30] In 1992, for example, the General Assembly adopted the Declaration on the Rights of Persons Belonging to National or Ethnic, Religious, and Linguistic Minorities.[31] The declaration insists that states should both protect and promote the group identity of ethnic and other minorities within their borders and ensure that members of such minorities have adequate opportunities for participation in the political, economic, and cultural life of the state. Although still couched primarily in the rhetoric of individual rights, the declaration and other even more recent instruments reflect the growing sense that the protection of ethnic communities may be essential to the "political and social stability of the States in which they live."[32] Theories of nation building, with their emphasis on forging a common national culture and identity, are out of fashion. Induced assimilation is no longer viewed as essential to a unified state; instead, it is seen as an incitement to ethnic unrest. Ethnic separatism and conflict are now often viewed as responses to discrimination and exclusion from full participation in the dominant society; pluralism, diversity, and broad political participation are cited as the antidote. From this perspective, individual rights and a focus on nondiscrimination are vital but not sufficient; in practice, they tend to promote assimilation as members of minorities become part of the dominant culture in order to advance their economic or social position within the larger society. To forestall the decay of minority cultures and communities, and the backlash that decay invites, affirmative protections for minority culture, language, and political status may be needed.

Once again, minority rights are seen as an alternative to full self-determination, as a less complete but less destructive means to satisfy the demands of communal affiliation. As the Commission of Jurists observed in connection with the Aaland Islands dispute, self-determination and minority rights "both have a common object—to assure to some national

30 *See, e.g.*, Koskenniemi, *supra* note 13, at 256.
31 Annex, G.A. Res. 47/135 (1992).
32 *Id.*

Group the maintenance of its social, ethnical or religious characteristics."[33] The underlying assumption is that by giving members of ethnic
and other minorities the ability to maintain their group identities, they
will feel no need for—and have no right to—states of their own.

From this it follows that membership in an ethnic group by itself still
carries no right to self-determination in the traditional sense of a right to
independence. But theoretically, at least, such a right might be justified if a
state is unable or unwilling to protect the rights of minorities within its
territory. As the Commission of Jurists put it more than fifty years ago,
secession might be an appropriate "last resort when the State lacks either
the will or the power to enact and apply just and effective guarantees" for
the protection of minorities.[34] The penultimate paragraph of the 1970
Friendly Relations Declaration, which limits the priority of territorial integrity over self-determination to states "possessed of a government representing the whole people belonging to the territory without distinction
as to race, creed, or colour," might be read in a similar fashion.[35]

Still, contemporary international law does not yet acknowledge a right
of secession, even as a last resort, though many commentators have suggested it. Moreover, the trend toward recognition of collective rights for
minorities is both limited and controversial. States still fear, with some
justification, that enhanced minority rights, especially collective rights,
will institutionalize differences among groups within society and foster
internal divisions rather than national unity. As a result, states tend to
approach the regulation of minority rights in an ad hoc and pragmatic
fashion, seeking to find the right balance between the interests of subnational communities and the interests of the state as a whole.[36] International protections remain tentative. There is as yet no general international
law right to cultural integrity for minority groups, although the trend is in
that direction. Rights of political participation are expanding but are still
limited and ill defined. In Europe, there is a strong trend toward according minorities special language rights wherever feasible, including the
right to receive public services and education in the dominant language of
a particular region, but that trend has made only limited headway in other
parts of the world.

As was true at the end of World War I, international insistence on
strong minority protections is greatest in the reconfigured and newly
emerging states of Central Europe and, to a lesser extent, of the former

[33] Jurists' Report, *supra* note 19, at 6.
[34] *Id.*
[35] Friendly Relations Declaration, *supra* note 23. To date, though, this provision has been
invoked primarily as a justification for the assertion of claims to majority rule against white
minority regimes in countries such as South Africa and the former Rhodesia.
[36] *See* Koskenniemi, *supra* note 13, at 266.

Soviet Union. Once again, minority rights are seen as a means to moderate demands for communal autonomy in states in which political and strategic considerations militate against granting full self-determination to substate communities. It is no coincidence that the European Community insisted, at least rhetorically, on strong protections for minority rights as a precondition to recognition of new states on the territory of the former Yugoslavia and Soviet Union.[37] Similarly, it is no surprise that all of the various peace plans for Bosnia included substantial protections for ethnic minorities.

Unfortunately, much of the current insistence on minority rights is a case of too little, too late. It either follows large-scale intercommunal violence or comes too late to avert it. Moreover, there is considerable doubt about the efficacy of minority rights to prevent or mitigate conflict in at least some deeply divided societies. Not all demands for group autonomy are premised on discrimination or threats to a group's cultural survival. In some cases, such demands stem from efforts of the dominant group to preserve or enhance an already privileged position within society, from regional turmoil or external interference, or from various other causes not amenable to resolution through simple adoption of minority rights agreements. In any event, when large-scale interethnic violence does erupt, it clearly calls for a response beyond simple exhortation to respect the rights of minority groups. In many cases, an effective response may require coercive external intervention, with all the legal, philosophical, and practical problems that go with it.

C. Intervention and the Use of Force

As a formal matter, international law treats internal conflict as a matter of domestic jurisdiction, something to be decided by the people of the affected state in keeping with their right to order their own affairs as they see fit. International law does not prohibit revolution, civil war, or ethnic conflict. International law does place some constraints on the conduct of hostilities, but that body of law is incomplete and uncertain in its application; while it affords some protections to noncombatants in civil strife, it is much less fully developed than the complex body of humanitarian law applicable to interstate conflicts.

Although international law does not prohibit civil war, it does restrict foreign intervention in such conflicts. It is generally accepted that foreign states may assist recognized governments in their efforts to suppress

[37] *See* Declaration of the European Council on the Guidelines on the Recognition of New States in Eastern Europe and the Soviet Union, issued on December 16, 1991, attached as an annex to U.N. Doc. A/46/804 (December 18, 1991).

limited rebellion or civil strife. By contrast, foreign states may not ordinarily assist rebel forces without violating the sovereignty of the affected state. If rebel forces, by dint of their own efforts, achieve a degree of organization and battlefield success sufficient to threaten the overthrow of the incumbent government, most states consider aid to either side in the conflict to be a violation of international law. In such cases, "[f]or a foreign state to support, with 'force,' one side or the other in an internal conflict, is to deprive the people in some measure of their right to decide the issue themselves. It is, in terms of article 2(4), a use of force against the political independence of the state engaged in civil war."[38]

In practice, of course, foreign intervention in internal conflicts seems to be the rule rather than the exception. Ethnic conflicts are particularly susceptible to external interference because in many cases neighboring states count numerous kin to one or another of the warring factions among their population. In the struggle over Bosnia, for example, both Serbia and Croatia actively supported their ethnic kin.

Such interventions violate the affected state's autonomy and threaten to transform an internal conflict into a wider, international conflict. As a result, the international community almost invariably has an interest in taking steps to contain the conflict. That interest is typically heightened by the devastation such conflicts commonly unleash and by the associated transboundary consequences, which often include substantial transborder refugee flows, arms trafficking, and violence by ill-disciplined, roving combatants.

The magnitude of the human suffering generated by ethnic conflicts and the threats they pose to regional peace and security routinely result in calls for external intervention. Most states continue to oppose unilateral action, even when it can be characterized as a genuine humanitarian intervention, for fear that the grant of such a license to intervene would be too easily abused. As a result, most demands for action are addressed to international organizations, the United Nations in particular.

The basic legal framework for such intervention is well established. If the parties to the conflict consent, the U.N. (or any other sufficiently motivated party) may supply peacekeepers to assist the parties in implementing whatever agreements they reach concerning the termination of hostilities and the reconstruction of the country. If one or more of the major warring factions objects to any external intervention, the U.N. may choose to exercise its coercive powers under Chapter VII of the U.N. Charter, so long as the Security Council determines that the conflict poses a threat to international peace.

[38] Oscar Schachter, *International Law: The Right of States to Use Armed Force*, 82 MICH. L. REV. 1620, 1641 (1984).

In recent years, the U.N. has invoked its Chapter VII powers to respond to a number of predominantly internal conflicts in countries such as Somalia, Iraq, Bosnia, and Rwanda. In the process, the Security Council has clearly expanded the traditional understanding of a threat to international peace and security, leading some international lawyers to question whether the council exceeded its legal authority to intervene in at least some of these cases. As a practical matter, however, it is clear that the council has broad discretion to determine whether a particular conflict presents a threat to international peace sufficient to warrant external military intervention. It is also clear that the council has not chosen to exercise anything like the full extent of its legal authority in responding to recent ethnic conflicts. Although political consensus within the council on the desirability of intervention in any given case is now possible, it is still difficult to achieve. One or more parties may have the sympathy of a veto-wielding state, making it difficult to agree on a course of action acceptable to the council as a whole. Further, most states remain reluctant to commit U.N. forces, much less their own, to military conflict in states in which the intervenors have no vital national interest. Moreover, many states, including Russia and China, are reluctant to set too many precedents for intervention in internal chaos for fear such precedents might someday return to haunt them.

Political concerns of this nature are exacerbated by philosophical doubts about the appropriate course of action to take in a given conflict. In general, the U.N. remains extremely reluctant to take sides, preferring instead the role of honest broker. This preference is consistent with still-prevalent notions of state autonomy and the view that any externally imposed solution is likely to be unstable and short-lived.

To make matters worse, the U.N. suffers from severe financial and resource limitations. Without greater support from its members, the U.N. cannot play a major role in more than a few conflicts at any given time. As a result, it must choose from among numerous possible missions and opt for strategies that may be within its means but inadequate to the task at hand. Similarly, the U.N. must entrust substantial responsibilities in the conflict management field to regional organizations and individual states with an interest in the outcome of the conflict (and the potential for bias that goes with it) sufficient to warrant their involvement.

These conceptual and practical difficulties have prompted widespread debate over both the norms and the institutional structures governing the use of force in internal conflicts, especially ethnic conflicts. At the same time, the limited utility of force as a tool for managing civil strife has prompted equally widespread debate about the norms and institutional practices most conducive to peaceful and consensual settlement of such conflicts. All of the issues raised above are considered in some detail in subsequent chapters of this volume.

III. An Overview of the Book

The chapters that follow are divided into two parts. Part I deals with general conceptual, philosophical, and legal issues arising out of efforts to apply international law to ethnic conflict. Part II considers the kinds of policies the international community may wish to promote when faced with ethnic conflict and the institutional competence of various international organizations to pursue those policies.

Nathaniel Berman begins Part I with a call to historical awareness. He analyzes the history of international legal responses to ethno-nationalist claims, the barriers to consensus on issues such as the identity of peoples and minorities, and the role international law plays in constructing group identity. He concludes by delineating the contours of a new international law of nationalism.

The next two chapters, by Lea Brilmayer and Fernando R. Tesón, consider the moral significance of ethno-nationalist claims and the normative implications of international law's treatment of those claims. Brilmayer argues that the existing international law system is premised in part on the need to respect the demands of national groups for communal autonomy but notes that the institutional principles that have developed to protect and regulate communal autonomy now exist and apply independently of the reasons underlying their creation. She then considers, but ultimately rejects, the argument that these institutional principles should yield to more direct means of furthering communal interests whenever the two conflict. Tesón argues that international law should not accord ethnic groups special group rights over and above currently recognized individual human rights simply by virtue of the fact that ethnic groups share particular racial, linguistic, or cultural traits. Instead, he argues that group rights can only be justified by other considerations, such as the need to escape state oppression or the right to vindicate prior historical title to a given territory.

In Chapter 4, Steven R. Ratner tackles a related problem: how should the international community respond to demands by substate ethnic groups for revisions in state boundaries? Ratner argues that the norm of *uti possidetis*, which required new states emerging from colonial domination in Africa and Asia to adhere to the boundaries they held at independence, does not and should not govern contemporary cases of state dissolution or secession. Instead, Ratner argues, international law should encourage states emerging from the wreckage of countries such as the former Yugoslavia to adopt boundaries that will maximize the prospects for stability and democratic governance within and among the new states.

Part I concludes with a chapter by Anne-Marie Slaughter. This chapter is designed to serve as a bridge between the two parts of the volume and to illustrate some of the connections between the chapters in each part. Slaughter examines the tensions between individual and group rights and between legal and political responses to ethnic conflict apparent in many of the chapters in this volume. In light of these tensions, she explores the ways in which the spectrum of responses to ethnic conflict both reveals and reinforces fundamental changes in the international legal order. In doing so, she highlights the emergence and legitimation of an "ideal polity" as a prescription for both internal and international peace.

Part II begins with two chapters assessing the mandates, capabilities, and legal authority of international organizations in responding to ethnic conflict. David J. Scheffer's chapter focuses on U.N. interventions in ethnic conflict. He examines the different ways in which the U.N. engages in ethnic conflicts, ranging from hortatory pronouncements to military intervention, and the evolving legal bases for each form of engagement. Antonia Handler Chayes and Abram Chayes then consider what international and regional organizations other than the U.N. can really do to prevent and manage ethnic conflict. They identify the relative strengths and weaknesses of some of the principal international organizations currently involved in dealing with ethnic conflicts and suggest ways in which their conflict prevention and management efforts could be enhanced.

My own chapter analyzes an approach to ethnic conflict pursued with increasing frequency by the U.N. and other international organizations: internationally brokered political settlements that seek to preserve the territorial integrity of deeply divided states by sharing power among the principal ethnic groups within those states. I argue that on balance such settlements are usually preferable to other alternatives for settling ethnic conflicts and that they should be considered an appropriate means to give effect to emerging norms governing political participation in plural societies.

The next three chapters in Part II consider the extent to which international law protects individuals and groups from organized violence in ethnic conflict and ways in which the law should be altered to respond more effectively to such violence. In Chapter 9, Ruth Wedgwood asks why international law prohibits the recourse to force as a means to settle disputes between states but not within states. She argues that international law should extend the prohibition on force contained in Article 2(4) of the U.N. Charter to civil wars and that international organizations should assist in the implementation of the corollary obligation to settle disputes peacefully. Lori Fisler Damrosch then considers the scope of and ambiguities associated with the existing legal prohibition of genocide and the reasons for the international community's failure to prevent and punish genocide, notwithstanding its status as a crime under international law. She goes on to suggest ways in which a satisfactory definition of genocide can be matched with more effective mechanisms for enforcement. In Chapter 11, Michael Platzer considers an issue that arises in all cases of large-scale ethnic conflict: how to respond to the needs of international refugees and internally displaced persons. Platzer argues that despite recent innovations, such as the development of a doctrine of temporary protection, contemporary international law in these areas often serves as an inadequate substitute for broader political solutions.

In Chapter 12, Diane F. Orentlicher considers the obverse side of some of the issues raised earlier by Brilmayer and Tesón. Instead of analyzing the claims of ethnic groups against their state, she considers whether states may have obligations to individuals long resident on their territory and, in particular, whether states may effectively denationalize members of particular ethnic groups. In discussing the new citizenship laws adopted by Latvia and Estonia, Orentlicher argues that, although existing law gives governments broad discretion to determine who is entitled to citizenship, the trend in international law is toward recognition of a presumptive entitlement to citizenship based on habitual residence in a territory, in accordance with a territorial/civic rather than an ethnic conception of nationality.

Our study of international law and ethnic conflict ends with an essay by Tom Farer. Farer begins by contrasting the methodology of the authors represented in this volume with the approaches commonly used by the Realists and Positivists of an earlier generation of international law scholars. He then organizes the chapters into four general positions and ends by urging adoption of a syncretic approach to ethnic conflict, one that "attempts to balance the interests of the contending parties consistent with the imperative of respect for basic human rights."

PART I

*Ethno-Nationalism
and Legal Theory*

1

The International Law of Nationalism: Group Identity and Legal History

Nathaniel Berman

[It sometimes appears] as if there were fashions in international law just as in neckties. At the end of the first World War, "international protection of minorities" was the great fashion. . . . Recently this fashion has become nearly obsolete. Today the well-dressed international lawyer wears "human rights."
            —J. L. Kunz, *The Present Status of the International Law*
                    for the Protection of Minorities (1954)

How could the self-determination granted to the Algerians in 1962 have been refused to the German population who in 1938 had been living in Czechoslovakia for [only] twenty years?
            —Georges Bonnet, Dans la Tourmente, 1938–1948 (1971)

Although it has no national minorities on its territory, France [is] conscious of the importance of this question for many participating States. . . .
            —French CSCE Delegate (1991)

The rules that govern intelligible identity . . . operate through *repetition*. . . . [T]he subject is a consequence of certain rule-governed discourses that govern the intelligible invocation of identity. . . . "[A]gency," then, is to be located within the possibility of a variation on that repetition. . . . There is no self prior . . . to its entrance into this conflicted cultural field.
            —Judith Butler, Gender Trouble: Feminism
                    and the Subversion of Identity (1990)

I. Introduction: Discontinuous History, Shifting Identities

A "veritable international law of nationalism" is emerging in the post–cold war period, a body of theory and practice that has an uneasy rela-

I thank Marie-Claire Belleau, Jerry Frug, David Kennedy, Duncan Kennedy, Hope Lewis, and Lucy Williams for their comments.

tionship to its own deeply troubled history.[1] A vast amount of work has gone into the reestablishment of this field of international law: theoretical clarification of legal terms designating the protagonists of nationalist conflicts (such as "nations," "peoples," and "minorities"), doctrinal specification of rights like self-determination and cultural autonomy, drafting of innovative general conventions, deployment of policy packages on particular conflicts, and philosophical debate about nationalism's cultural meaning. At the same time, a sense of historical déjà-vu seems pervasive: the past few years have seen the striking resurgence of forgotten nationalist conflicts as well as legal notions that once seemed relegated to subordinate status, such as international minority rights.

Nonetheless, doctrinal and policy discussions often seem quite divorced from historical reflection. This striking disjunction between the sense of uncanny historical repetition and the concern for appalling current exigencies often leads to both the misinterpretation of history and the impoverishment of current doctrine and policy. The conventional portrayal of past legal responses to nationalism as piecemeal adumbrations that need to be developed into a coherent system is symptomatic; it ignores the fact that past efforts have themselves taken comprehensive and systematic form. Conventional accounts ignore the discontinuities in the history of the international law of nationalism: rather than a smooth process of customary law "ripening," this history has been one of construction, denunciation, rupture, and resumption. These discontinuities make history a rather embarrassing guest at the policy-proposing feast, while making policy proposers seem like well-intentioned naïfs at the table of historical wisdom.

In contrast to conventional, linear approaches, I define an international law of nationalism as a *historically contingent* array of doctrinal and policy options for deployment by a contingent embodiment of international authority on nationalist conflicts whose protagonists are designated by a contingent set of legal categories. The historical discontinuities between the various incarnations of the international law of nationalism may be tracked through the discontinuities in the international projections of international and nationalist identity. In order to build an account of a particular nationalist conflict, international law projects onto the protagonists a set of historically contingent categories—states, nations, peoples, minorities, religions, races, indigenous peoples, individuals, and so forth—a set whose elements and valorizations have changed over time. In addition, legal analyses of nationalist conflict always identify a state, group of states, or institution as the "international legal organ," as em-

---

[1] I paraphrase Judge Petrén, who, in 1975, wrote of the crystallization of a "veritable international law of decolonization." Western Sahara Case, 1975 ICJ 12, 110 (Advisory Opinion of October 16).

bodying the authority of the international legal community. These projections identify the general roles that international law provides for the protagonists in its accounts of specific nationalist dramas; they may, accordingly, be referred to as "protagonist-positions" ready to be filled by particular groups, states, or institutions in particular contexts.

The determination of the set of protagonist-positions and the manner of their application are informed by cultural projections that have often been contested within given periods and have dramatically changed over time. Yet the study of the international law of nationalism demonstrates a more complex imbrication of doctrinal, policy, and cultural contingencies than does this elementary Legal Realist insight about the relative indeterminacy of formal categories. Rather, it shows the crucial role that the construction of separate domains of doctrine, policy, and culture has played in the history of this field. In particular, the understanding of some problems as "cultural" upon which "law" can be deployed is itself a contingent feature of international legal history that has played different roles in different periods.[2] Even the decision whether to call this field the "international law of nationalism" or "international law and ethnic conflict" requires one to take a position in international and local struggles with highly charged histories.

Moreover, nationalists often form their self-understanding, as well as their self-presentation, in response to their understanding of international legal categories. Nationalists everywhere have internalized, resisted, adapted, or denied the identities projected by international law because of those identities' cultural meanings, legal implications, or tactical consequences. In performing, transforming, and deforming these internationally projected identities, nationalists reshape their meaning and may even thereby redirect the general course of the international law of nationalism. Focusing on the contingency of the identity-constitutive elements of the international law of nationalism thus brings out its culturally constructive, as well as contentious, dimension.

Ignoring this dimension often gives rise to indeterminate arguments between those who would see a given international action as simply imposing the international community's interests or values and those who would see it as demonstrating deep empathy with the nationalist protago-

---

[2] On the relationship between the construction of "culture" and the legitimation of Western dominance, see, e.g., Samir Amin, *Imperialism and Culturalism Complement Each Other*, 48 MONTHLY REV. 1 (1996); Antony Anghie, *Francisco de Vitoria and the Colonial Origins of International Law*, 5 SOC. & LEGAL STUD. 321 (1996); Annelise Riles, *Aspiration and Control: International Legal Rhetoric and the Essentialization of Culture*, 106 HARV. L. REV. 723 (1993); Nathaniel Berman, *Modernism, Nationalism, and the Rhetoric of Reconstruction*, 4 YALE J. L. & HUMAN. 351 (1992); Lila Abu-Lughod, *Writing against Culture*, in RECAPTURING ANTHROPOLOGY 137 (Richard Fox ed., 1991). *Cf.* JAMES CLIFFORD, THE PREDICAMENT OF CULTURE 10 (1988) ("Culture is a deeply compromised idea I cannot yet do without.").

nists. For example, Western plans for Bosnia, all involving some form of partition, have been characterized as the ratification of Serb aggression by outside powers acting on cultural stereotypes, on the one hand, and as the compassionate striving for ethnic reconciliation through delicately balancing the protagonists' desires, on the other. In contrast to such dichotomies, an emphasis on law's culturally constructive dimension shows how the legal projection of internationalist and nationalist identity serves *simultaneously* to legitimate international power *and* to construct a possible field for principled humanitarian action. *No* formulation or deployment of a plan for a conflict like Bosnia is possible that does not project a contestable set of identity positions onto the conflict's protagonists; the worth and effectiveness of any particular plan will depend on the manner of the reappropriation and redeployment of these projections by those protagonists. These projections, such as those of coherent, unitary, and stable ethnic identities able to serve as the basis for a partition plan, may be resisted by some of the protagonists as a violent imposition, be embraced by others as conforming to their self-image, and impel still others to transform their meaning through political struggle.

International power and principle do not "belong to two different planes."[3] Rather, the power of international law to shape the identity of the protagonists of such conflicts cannot be separated from even its principled activities to remedy them. The tenacity of hackneyed oppositions in international debate—idealism and realism, law and politics—reflects a failure to understand this dynamic.

Relating legal discontinuities to contingent projections of identity highlights the significance of the different postures international law has taken in relation to nationalist conflict. Three of the most important of these postures may be called theoretical or doctrinal formalism, policy pragmatism, and cultural activism. The relationship among these postures may be schematized as follows:

(1) *Formalism:* When a group makes a claim against a sovereign state, international law first determines whether the claims transcend the state's domestic jurisdiction and then determines whether the group meets the criteria defining a people, minority group, collection of individuals, or another legal category; finally, balancing rights claims with other relevant legal factors, international law may provide the right to self-determination, minority rights, individual human rights, or other legal remedy.

(2) *Pragmatism:* Confronted with ethnic, nationalist, etc., tensions, international policymakers propose legal frameworks to international authority and local parties embodying policies able to satisfy as many of the compet-

---

[3] E. H. CARR, THE TWENTY YEARS CRISIS 93 (1951).

ing interests as practicable; shedding formalist determinism for functional-
ist flexibility, the policymaker can explore how various legal techniques
would work in particular situations.

(3) *Cultural activism:* International law plays a culturally constructive role
in shaping nationalist identity and thus in altering the course of nationalist
conflict; international law's culturally differential projections also inform its
own formalist and pragmatic analyses; at various times, international lawyers have overtly embraced, implicitly pursued, politically opposed, or tactically transformed such cultural activism.

Of course, I have intentionally simplified and exaggerated the differences
among these three postures, for we are all formalists, pragmatists, and
cultural activists. It would be more accurate to speak of formalist, pragmatic, and cultural aspirations that all international lawyers share: all seek
to provide general normative criteria, to formulate workable policies to
remedy particular problems, and to consider the effects of their cultural
proclivities.

Yet the form and relative valorization of these postures have undergone
dramatic historical transformations. Cultural activism, for example, was
explicitly celebrated by most international lawyers in relation to Africa
and Asia as recently as the interwar period in the guise of the "civilizing
mission"; this activism overtly framed doctrinal and policy options. During the later phases of the cold war, policy pragmatism predominated,
with formalism seen as an outdated rigidity that pragmatism sought to
transcend and cultural activism seen as an allegation of imperialism that
pragmatism sought to disprove. Since 1989, cultural activism has resur-
faced in both affirmative and critical forms: the former in the resurgence
of explicit cultural projections by lawyers and policymakers, most notoriously in talk of a "clash of civilizations," and the latter in the effort to
render explicit, and therefore contestable, the cultural functions of international law and policy.

This chapter considers the critical potential of an emphasis on the cultural dimension in discussing formalism and pragmatism. It rejects the
way the formalist aspiration for doctrinal generalization implies that
groups existed before the categories that would subsequently be applied
to them; similarly, it rejects the way the pragmatic aspiration for neutral
policy implies that those categories can be deployed purely tactically to
manage preexisting interests. Rather, I argue that groups' identities and
tactics come to be defined by themselves and by international authorities
in response to a cultural conjuncture partly constructed by those very
categories. Yet I also explore the way the construction of a realm of "cultural" problems—a construction that has taken widely divergent historical forms—has shaped and legitimated different kinds of international

power. The chapter thus contributes to showing how the international "construction of the cultural" enables us "to see the cultural not as the *source* of conflict—*different* cultures—but as the *effect* of discriminatory practices—the production of cultural *differentiation* as a sign of authority."[4]

Descriptions of the history of minority rights can illustrate the relationship between these postures. For example, the most recent edition of *Oppenheim* briefly notes pre–World War I efforts, reviews the interwar system in some detail, declares that minority protection was "subsumed" in the post–World War II concern with individual rights, and discusses the relevant postwar documents.[5] It concludes by adding that "[i]n some instances minorities might be a sufficiently cohesive group to constitute a 'people' enjoying the right to self-determination now recognised in several international instruments."[6] A faultless performance in the genre of the treatise, *Oppenheim*'s discussion could also be viewed as a typical product of the pragmatic posture. It frustrates our formalist aspirations, for its analytical modesty seems unacceptably question begging: what does *subsumed* assert about the state of customary law; how can *sufficiently cohesive* be applied to particular cases? From a cultural perspective, *Oppenheim*'s seamless chronological account elides the controversies that marked each period and the ruptures that lie between periods. Its recourse to phrases like *subsumed* and *sufficiently cohesive* smoothes over always conflictual processes both among and within the legal, political, and cultural domains.

Another recent commentator is rather closer to the cultural perspective when he writes that between World War II and 1989, the "problem of minorities was occulted: it was a practically taboo subject."[7] Yet he fails to explore the relationship between this description and the linear processes normally demanded of customary international law. For example, customary law concepts like *ripening* and *desuetude* do not evoke the phenomenon suggested by highly charged, and therefore more apt, terms like *occultation* and *taboo*. Nor does he reflect on how the link between nationalism and taboo might participate in the history of Western projections of fears and fantasies about "occult" cultures, projections that have played crucial roles in the international law of nationalism.

The rest of this chapter provides an overview of the structure and history of the international law of nationalism alternative to the kind of account exemplified by *Oppenheim*. Part II explores some illustrative ways

---

[4] HOMI K. BHABHA, THE LOCATION OF CULTURE 114 (1994).

[5] ROBERT JENNINGS & ARTHUR WATTS (EDS.), OPPENHEIM'S INTERNATIONAL LAW 973–77 (9th ed. 1992).

[6] *Id.* at 977.

[7] Paul Tavernier, *A Propos de la Convention-Cadre du Conseil de l'Europe pour la Protection des Minorités Nationales,* 100 RGDIP 385 (1995). (All translations are mine unless otherwise noted.)

in which international law has projected its own identity and that of nationalist protagonists in several historical periods. Part III examines the justification of change in the international law of nationalism through illustrative arguments about continuity and discontinuity with previous historical periods. Throughout, I show how this field has been structured by discursive and practical movement between internationalism and nationalism, power and principle, "law" and "culture."

II. THE PROJECTION OF INTERNATIONAL AUTHORITY AND GROUP IDENTITY

> . . . I cannot but express the conviction that the German Government . . . will never accept as satisfactory . . . any solution which does not comply with the principle of a State of nationalities as opposed to a national State in which the Sudeten will continue to be treated as a minority and not as a Staatsvolk ("State nation").
>
> —Sir Neville Henderson (1938)

> [The presidency] considers it especially important that selective application of principles be avoided. The principle of self-determination e.g. cannot exclusively apply to the existing [Yugoslav] republics while being deemed inapplicable to national minorities within those republics.
>
> —Dutch E.C. Presidency (1991)

Comprehensive approaches to nationalist conflict have been embodied in a series of legal regimes over the last century and a half. One can distinguish at least five major incarnations of the international law of nationalism during this period: (1) pre–World War I management of the disintegrating Ottoman Empire, whose high point was the 1878 Treaty of Berlin;[8] (2) post–World War I disposition of the defeated and dissolved empires, whose milestones include the 1919 Peace and Minority Protection Treaties,[9] the 1923 Geneva Convention on Upper Silesia,[10] and, in a kind of coda, the 1947 Palestine Partition Resolution;[11] (3) the 1930s revision of the Versailles settlement, symbolized by the 1938 Four-Power Agreement on Czechoslovakia;[12] (4) the decolonization decades, epitomized in the 1960 General Assembly Resolution 1514, the "colonial declaration of independence"; and (5) post-1989 efforts, such as the European Framework Convention for the Protection of National Minorities,[13] the

---

[8] 153 CTS 170 (1878).

[9] *E.g.,* the Versailles Treaty, 225 CTS 188 (1919); Polish Minority Protection Treaty, 225 CTS 412 (1919).

[10] German-Polish Convention Concerning Upper Silesia, May 15, 1921, *reprinted in* GEORGES KAECKENBEECK, THE INTERNATIONAL EXPERIMENT OF UPPER SILESIA 567 (1942).

[11] G.A. Res. 181, 2 U.N. GAOR 131 (A/519) (1947).

[12] *Reprinted in* II DOCUMENTS ON BRITISH FOREIGN POLICY 627 (3d ser. 1938).

[13] *Reprinted in* 34 I.L.M. 351 (1995).

1991 Draft Convention on Yugoslavia,[14] and the 1994 Washington[15] and 1995 Dayton[16] agreements on Bosnia. These documents echo each other in remarkable ways: the proposals for former Yugoslavia, for example, employ every technique (self-determination, minority protection, regional autonomy, citizenship rights, international tribunals, and so on) developed in the preceding two centuries; in their encyclopedic range, they resemble the Upper Silesia and Palestine plans. This list is deliberately heterogeneous, selective, and, particularly with the inclusion of 1938, directed against seamless narratives of legal evolution and conventional distinctions between "legal" and "political" approaches.

The leading protagonist-positions that we use today to analyze nationalist conflicts—states, nations, peoples, minorities, individuals—have been part of the international law of nationalism at least since the nineteenth century. International law appears to have created a small set of stable protagonist-positions by which stunningly disparate conflicts have come to be framed over five continents for almost two centuries. Of course, one might bemoan the paucity of legal imagination, the forcing of the diversity of human conflict into a small set of categories. Yet for good or for ill, this power of international law to effectively frame the terms in which such disparate conflicts have been understood both internationally and locally seems quite astonishing.

Nevertheless, we should beware of taking this appearance at face value: a protagonist-position (for example, "minority group") that may be important in one period (such as 1878) may be subordinated or absent in a subsequent period (such as 1960) and may live again in a still later period (such as 1996). Indeed, we may distinguish different periods of the international law of nationalism by their distinctive cast of protagonist-positions. As a result, a group that understood itself in one way at one time may come to understand itself, or at least to present itself, in another way in a subsequent period because of the shifting value given to the legal protagonist-positions. The Arab-Israeli conflict provides a rich example of the ways in which groups shift their performance of their identities due to changes in the international projection and valorization of protagonist-positions: at various times, it may have been either culturally persuasive, legally dispositive, or tactically useful to perform group identity as a "religion," a "minority," a territorial "people," a transfrontier "nation," a "people not yet able to stand by themselves under the strenuous conditions of the modern world,"[17] a "provisional government," and so forth.

[14] Treaty Provisions for the Convention, U.N. Doc. S/23169, Annex VII at 36 (1991).

[15] Proposed Constitution of the Federation of Bosnia and Herzegovina, reprinted in 33 I.L.M. 740 (1994).

[16] General Framework Agreement for Peace in Bosnia and Herzegovina, reprinted in 35 I.L.M. 75 (1996).

[17] Versailles Treaty, art. 22, 225 CTS 188, 203 (1919).

Attempts to resolve uncertainties about group identity through definitional formalism or policy pragmatism thus often appear arbitrary in the
face of the dynamics of nationalist conflict. Such conflicts always involve
turbulent political and discursive processes in which the protagonists'
identity and interests change in their own or others' eyes. Such transformations can affect both the international and nationalist sides of the equa-
tion. An institution or group of states may shift from being recognized as
the representative of universal legal principle to being perceived as a
partisan powerbroker and vice versa; particular groups may shift from
the status of a "nation" to that of a "minority" or a mere collection of
"persons" and vice versa. In the first fifty years of the twentieth century,
for example, the Sudeten Germans successively occupied the positions of
a part of the Hapsburg *Staatsvolk* prior to 1914, one of the legion of national claimants at the Paris Peace Conference in 1919, an internationally
protected minority in the 1920s, a self-determination aspirant in the early
1930s, an agent of a foreign power in the late 1930s, a part of a majority
group in 1938–45, and a group of expelled refugees after 1945; at each
stage, the legitimacy and impartiality of international legal authority was
also contested. Each of these transformations came about through both
discursive and political-military conflict. One could trace an equally complex transformation of the identity and tactics of the Balkan national
groups during the twentieth century.

In the next two sections, therefore, I explore arguments about the shifting identity and status of international authority and of group identity.

A. International Authority

The Treaty of Berlin must be presented . . . as a law of necessity, imposed by the
superior exigencies of European peace. . . . And you, for whom a conciliation
treaty is inadequate, who want a victory treaty, do you hear the cannon and the
hail of bullets carrying away the human victims over there in Bosnia?
—Benoit Brunswik, LE TRAITÉ DE BERLIN, ANNOTÉ ET COMMENTÉ (1878)

Justifications of international authority involve the claim of an institution or group of states to embody general legal principles, transcending
partisan power. Comprehensive international settlements almost always
rest on an explicit assertion that the international community seeks to
resolve nationalist conflicts in light of its responsibility for a general
peace. The persuasiveness of such assertions rest on historically and culturally contingent projections about the identity of international authority
rather than solely on their formal rigor or pragmatic feasibility; these
projections construct the juxtaposition between the international "legal"
community and the nationalist "cultural" Other that has played a decisive
role in establishing international authority. While the surprisingly endur-

ing general form of this juxtaposition highlights the structural continuities in the history of justifications of international authority, the shifts in its constitutive projections mark the historical discontinuities and the fierce debates about particular deployments of international power.

The preamble to the recent European Framework Convention for the Protection of National Minorities carefully balances the supranational interest in unity and continental peace, sovereign prerogatives, and minority rights.[18] This careful contemporary drafting seems designed to avoid the rather more piquant formulations found in the convention's predecessors, in which the tension among such elements is readily apparent to today's readers. Examples of such tension may be found in assertions of international authority in the late nineteenth century, the Versailles system, and the revisionist thirties.

The 1878 Treaty of Berlin was the most systematic nineteenth-century attempt to condition international recognition of new states (such as Serbia) on minority group protection as well as to impose such protections on an already existing state (such as the Ottoman Empire). The treaty thus embodied a forceful assertion of international authority; for example, it "finally broke with the diplomatic fiction" of portraying Ottoman concessions on minority rights as "emanating from the Sultans' initiative."[19] The treaty's distinctive assertion of international authority comes in the preamble's declaration that "les questions soulevées en Orient" are to be settled "dans une pensée d'ordre Européen."[20] This Europe/"Orient" dichotomy, which the treaty clearly presents as equivalent to that between universal legal reason and particularistic cultural passion, shows the way in which the position of protagonists can shift over time. Today, of course, an overt identification of universal legal reason with Europe would be viewed by many as a dubious, or perhaps ironic, assertion. The transformation of "Europe" from a universal to a particularist protagonist-position is a familiar, if still contested, historical process; yet as we shall see, the Europe/"Orient" distinction still can provide a guiding thread through much of this topic.

The Permanent Court's declarations of international legal supremacy in the interwar minority protection system are less jarring than the 1878 Europe/"Orient" juxtaposition but no less assertive of international authority. In 1923, for example, the court asserted international authority to define both states and national minorities by focusing on the simultaneity of the rebirth of Poland and of its obligations under the Minority Protec-

---

[18] See note 13 supra. The preamble states: "Considering that the aim of the Council of Europe is to achieve greater unity between its members. . . . Being resolved to ensure . . . the effective protection of national minorities . . . , respecting the territorial integrity and national sovereignty of states . . . "

[19] BENOIT BRUNSWIK, LE TRAITÉ DE BERLIN, ANNOTÉ ET COMMENTÉ 34 (1878).

[20] 153 CTS 170, 172 (1878).

tion Treaty—on the fact that the peace treaty, which recognized the Polish state, and the Minority Treaty were "signed on the same day."[21] The court concluded that Polish sovereign rights were on a legal as well as temporal par with its minority protection obligations. The definitions of "Poland" and its "minorities" were governed by a new international legal order that took priority over them both; no Polish law could "interfere" with these obligations.[22] The court in this way rejected the Polish argument that minorities in Poland could only be defined and thus placed under international protection once Poland had decided who its citizens were; rather, international law would determine the composition of both the Polish citizenry and its minorities. And just as the 1878 identification of Europe with universal authority would be challenged today, so Poland had described the League of Nations in 1923 as a mere "contracting Power" without "universal competence" over minority rights.[23] Moreover, Poland and other states that were to be bound to the minority protection system had objected to its implication that they were nations "of inferior civilization."[24]

The 1938 Czechoslovak crisis provides a disturbing, and disturbingly consistent, variant of this pattern. The Note transmitting the Anglo-French proposals to the Czech government declared that the two Great Powers had decided that "the further maintenance within the boundaries of the Czechoslovak State of the districts mainly inhabited by the Sudeten Deutsch cannot, in fact, continue any longer without imperilling the interests of Czechoslovakia herself and of European peace. . . . [B]ecause th[e] cause [of peace] is common both to Europe in general and to Czechoslovakia herself they have felt it their duty jointly to set forth the conditions necessary to secure it."[25]

This statement follows in the pattern of the two earlier examples: the assertion of international authority to resolve nationalist conflict through imposing conditions on a sovereign to satisfy the national claims of a minority group in the interest of European, as well as local, peace. In this case, the disjunction between general and particular interest is glaring: the (highly contestable) claim of saving general European peace at the expense of a dispute in a "faraway country between people of whom we know nothing."[26] Yet it is striking that the Note's rhetoric is not exceptional but is made available by an established pattern from which it is, *in*

---

[21] Polish Nationality Case (Advisory Op. No. 7), P.C.I.J. (Ser. B.) at 13–16 (1923).

[22] *Id.*

[23] German Settlers Case (Advisory Opinion No. 6), P.C.I.J. (Ser. C.), No. 3, Vol. I, 458, 462 & 467 (1923) (Speech of Count Rostworowski).

[24] *See* Memorandum by M. Paderewski (June 15, 1919), in X LA PAIX DE VERSAILLES 129, 130 (1932); Letter of Nik. P. Pachitch, for the Delegation of the Serb-Croat-Slovene Kingdom (August 1, 1919), in *id.* at 259, 262.

[25] The Anglo-French Proposals Presented to the Czechoslovak Government on September 19, 1938, *in* CORRESPONDENCE RESPECTING CZECHOSLOVAKIA, SEPTEMBER 1938 at 8, 9 (1938).

[26] Address of Prime Minister Neville Chamberlain to the British Nation, September 27, 1938, *reprinted in* 20 LA SOCIÉTÉ DES NATIONS: REVUE DOCUMENTAIRE 283 (1938).

form, hard to distinguish. Of course, the 1938 Czechs were subjected to a wholly different order of coercion to come to terms than the 1919 Poles. Nevertheless, it should be remembered that some of the Polish Minority Treaty provisions were also simply to be "dictated to Poland."[27]

In Part III I will discuss in greater depth the way in which the relationships between such instances have been historically portrayed. The point here is that neither formalist criteria nor pragmatist exigencies can fully account for the degree of persuasiveness of such assertions of international authority. Arguments about the identity and stature of that authority depend on variations on a repeating rhetorical structure that itself has enduring cultural power yet also shifts historically in tandem with shifts in its constitutive projections. This perspective does not deny that one can and perhaps should be persuaded by arguments that posit vast differences between the European Powers in 1878 Berlin, 1919 Paris, 1938 Munich, and 1995 Strasbourg. One can, for example, be persuaded that the 1919 Allies were a legitimate embodiment of international authority fit to intervene on behalf of Polish minorities, whereas the four Powers assembled at Munich to deal with the Czech minorities were unworthy powerbrokers. Such persuasion comes not at the level of the general structure but of its contingent cultural and political projections; more crucially, such persuasion depends on the projections that construct the contingent form of the juxtaposition of a legally supreme "international community," on the one hand, and battling particularist nationalisms, in the guise of an "Orient," a "civilizational inferior," or a "faraway people," on the other. Persuasion is made possible *both* by the structure's relative stability *and* by its contingency—its institution by, and ongoing reliance on, variable projections. The lack of international backing for three years to "impose a settlement" in Bosnia partly reflected the failure of such a settlement's proponents to make culturally persuasive arguments about the international community's stature rather than merely debate about formal legal competence or pragmatic tactical capacity.[28]

B. Group Identity (or, What Is a Nation?)

> The Plebisicite always seems to me to be the devil, and as likely to precipitate as to prevent.
> —Viscount Halifax (1938)

If we now turn to the dynamic role of international law in relation to groups, the transmutation of "nations" into "minorities" or "persons",

---

[27] *See* Note by M. Sonnino for the Council of Four (June 17, 1919), in X LA PAIX DE VERSAILLES, *supra* note 24, at 134.

[28] *See, e.g.,* DAVID OWEN, BALKAN ODYSSEY 105 (1995).

and vice versa, we find a multilayered imbrication of culturally and historically variable projections. I will focus on three contingent aspects of such projections: (1) the projection by international law of non-European peoples as "civilizationally" distinct from European peoples and as "developmentally" ranked among themselves; (2) the projection of distinctions among *European* peoples on the basis of cultural rank; and (3) the instability and mutability of the meaning of the legal categories—that is, their transformation through their reappropriation and redeployment by nationalists. While some may assert that the first two kinds of culturally differential projections could be eliminated through legal generalization, the cultural perspective contends that there are *no* distinctions between protagonist-positions like "nations" and "minorities" that are not produced through such contingent and contestable projections. Ostensibly neutral formalist or pragmatist approaches can only proceed either by provisionally holding steady, affirmatively acting to deny, or implicitly taking rigid partisan positions on contestable cultural projections.

1. The Europe/Non-Europe Dichotomy

In the twentieth century, the international legal version of the Europe/non-Europe dichotomy has taken a variety of forms, from the violent to the subtle. Perhaps the most familiar overt example of cultural projections framing the legal definition of groups was the Versailles settlement's disparate treatment of the European and non-European possessions of the war's defeated and collapsed empires. While the settlement provided self-determination for many European peoples and minority protection for others, it provided the Mandate system for non-European peoples—those peoples "not yet able to stand by themselves" and who, therefore, needed to be entrusted to the tutelage of "advanced nations" as a "sacred trust of civilisation."[29] This distinction, which no internationalist would make so overtly today, was justified with formal and pragmatic arguments made possible by the construction of a realm of civilizational difference and the projection of particular cultural traits on non-European peoples.[30]

Such distinctions remained entrenched throughout the interwar period, though at times they were contested to a greater or lesser degree. For example, the Italians sought to disarm criticism of their invasion of Ethio-

[29] League of Nations Covenant, Versailles Treaty, 225 CTS 188, 203 (1919).
[30] See, for example, this almost unreadable passage in the extremely influential preparatory memo by Jan Smuts, *The League of Nations: A Practical Proposal* (1918), *in* DAVID HUNTER MILLER II, THE DRAFTING OF THE COVENANT 23, 28 (1928): "[T]he German colonies in the Pacific and Africa are inhabited by barbarians, who not only cannot possibly govern themselves, but to whom it would be impracticable to apply the idea of self-determination in the European sense."

pia in 1935 through manipulating Ethiopia's anomalous position as both African and sovereign; by using the rhetoric of the Mandate system, the Italians responded to League of Nations criticism in terms of Versailles' own distinctions between "civilized" and "uncivilized" peoples.[31] A group of distinguished French intellectuals published the "Manifesto for the Defense of the West," which asserted that defense of Western "culture" required supporting the invasion of Ethiopia.[32] In response, another group attacked the invasion with the "Manifesto for the Respect of International Law," protesting against the "abuse" of the idea of the "West" and its "culture."[33] Consider also that one expression of Western outrage at the 1939 German declaration of a protectorate over Bohemia and Moravia was that it was an impermissible contamination of European by non-European protagonist-positions: Germany had turned the Czech lands into a "white protectorate," enacting the "first German colonial statute for a white and civilized nation."[34]

Article 22 of the League Covenant, the Mandate article, pursued the process of cultural differentiation further, explicitly making legal distinctions *among* non-European peoples depend on their cultural dignity. The status of Mandated Territories ranged from "provisional recognitions of independence" with temporary Mandatory tutelage to indefinite administration by the Mandatory Power as "an integral portion of its territory." The amount of control by the Mandatory Power depended on a people's "stage of development" and "remoteness from the centres of civilisation."[35]

International lawyers might contend hopefully that such embarrassments lie safely in the past: surely no contemporary document would make such invidious distinctions. And, indeed, decolonization brought with it attrition in the number of protagonist-positions. The categorical call of the 1960 General Assembly Resolution 1514 for self-determination for "all peoples" entailed a rejection of an entire range of protagonist-positions distinctive to colonialism and the Mandate system. These protagonist-positions had been used to evaluate the relative merit of nationalist claims. For example, at the 1900 meeting of the Institut de Droit International, international lawyers had discussed whether the permissibility of third-party intervention to support or oppose self-determination claims might

---

[31] *See, e.g.,* Charles Rousseau, *Le Conflit Italo-Éthiopien (Ch. III)*, 45 RGDIP 53, 60–62 (1938).

[32] Manifeste pour la Défense de l'Occident, *in* LE TEMPS, October 4, 1935. The signatories ranged from the right-wing Charles Maurras to the Catholic intellectual Gabriel Marcel.

[33] Manifeste pour le Respect de la Loi Internationale, *in* LE POPULAIRE, October 5, 1935. This manifesto's signatories ranged from the leftist Louis Aragon to Henri de Montherlant, an equivocal figure later compromised during the Occupation.

[34] EUGENE V. ERDLEY, GERMANY'S FIRST EUROPEAN PROTECTORATE: THE FATE OF THE CZECHS AND SLOVAKS 15, 41 (1942).

[35] Versailles Treaty, art. 22, 125 CTS 189, 203 (1919).

depend on whether the claimants were Europeans seeking to "reconstitute a nationality"[36] or were "savage countries or countries outside of Christendom."[37] Resolution 1514's categorical language rejected the kind of protagonist-positions that had made such discussions possible. Similarly, the resolution explicitly rejected the protagonist-position of the Mandate system's "peoples not yet able to stand by themselves."[38]

The purging of the colonial taint from the letter of international law through the generalized language of Resolution 1514 seemed to displace the onus of any differential treatment from law to residual political or cultural bias that could eventually be eliminated. Yet the evident hyperbole of Resolution 1514 and the persistence of differential projections in the "political" domain showed the untenability of this generalization and displacement. Resolution 1514's hyperbole should be seen not as a failed attempt at doctrinal generalization but as an effective intervention in a particular legal-historical conjuncture, that of decolonization. The resolution's exclusion of the kind of differential cultural projections embodied in the Mandate system was a condemnation of the way cultural discourse had functioned in international law prior to decolonization—specifically, the invidious effect of the projection of different kinds and degrees of "civilization." Yet anticolonialism's exclusion of an overt cultural discourse in law contributed to the persistence of this discourse, freed from critical legal scrutiny, in other institutions and disciplines. Since 1989, Resolution 1514's generalization and displacement have given way to a new willingness to make overt cultural judgments. For example, those seeking to reestablish activist international authority have proposed reviving some form of trusteeship, proposals that appeared in various guises in debates about Cambodia, Bosnia, Somalia, and Haiti.[39] At the same time, those critical of ostensibly neutral formalist and pragmatic discourses have sought to explicate the cultural functions of international action and inaction.

The purpose of this analysis of historical projections about non-European peoples is thus not simply to saddle international law with the guilt of its colonial past. Rather, it should teach us to examine the contingent and contestable projections deployed through today's putatively general doctrines and neutral policies, just as we have learned to discern the differential projections deployed through the legal practices of the past. More fundamentally, it should teach us that the function of cultural

---

[36] *Procès-Verbal des Séances du 7 Septembre au 8 Septembre, in* 18 ANNUAIRE DE L'INSTITUT DE DROIT INTERNATIONAL 183 (M. Pierantoni) (1900).

[37] *Id.* at 185 (M. Kebedy).

[38] "Inadequacy of . . . preparedness should never serve as a pretext for delaying independence." G.A. Res. 1514, 15 U.N. GAOR at 1273, 1274, U.N. Doc. A/PV.947 (1960).

[39] *See, e.g.,* Gerald B. Helman & Steven R. Ratner, *Saving Failed States,* 89 FOREIGN POL'Y 3 (1992).

discourse is both protean and ambivalent. The projection of the civilizational Other in the Mandate system legitimated disparate application of legal principles, while providing some opening for legal criticism of colonialism. The explication of today's cultural projections can show how new configurations of international authority are constructed; it can also make available for discursive and political contestation the contingent projections framing the technocratic discourse still often used in debate about the deployment of international power.

2. Distinctions among Europeans

Although subject to less critical analysis than the Europe/non-Europe dichotomy, the projection of cultural differences among *European* peoples has been of great historical importance and has reemerged today. I have elsewhere argued that this kind of distinction played an implicit role in legal justifications of the arms embargoes on Spain in the 1930s and Bosnia in the 1990s.[40] Other forms of intra-European distinctions have long concerned dichotomies between Eastern and Western Europe, often centering on the implications of the word *national* to describe the protagonist-position "minority group."

A telling example of such intra-European distinctions was provided by the opening statement of the French delegate to the CSCE Meeting of Experts on National Minorities: "Although it has no national minorities on its territory, France, conscious of the importance which this question has for many participating States and of many populations, is ready to participate in the elaboration of conclusions which would be inspired by these ideas and to give them its accord."[41] The dividing line lies between those states "which have been constructed, founded, assembled through a slow economic, social, cultural, and political process" and those "where the entanglement of peoples remains extreme and is the sometimes recent reminder of tumultuous upheavals."[42] In short, the French delegate projects the problem of minorities onto other states; or, more specifically in the European context, he projects it *eastward*. France will participate in the elaboration of norms, norms for *others*. To be sure, one could linger long over the complicated justifications that a French speaker would give for the statement that France has no "national minorities." At the end of this dalliance,

[40] Nathaniel Berman, *Between "Alliance" and "Localization": Nationalism and the New Oscillationism,* 26 N.Y.U. J. INT'L L. & POL. 901 (1994).
[41] Discours d'Ouverture de M. Bernard Dejean de la Batie, Chef de la Délégation Française, CSCE Meeting of Experts on National Minorities, July 2, 1991, at 10. France has always maintained that it has no minorities within the meaning of Article 27 of the Covenant on Civil and Political Rights. *See, e.g.,* PIERRE-MARIE DUPUY, DROIT INTERNATIONAL PUBLIC 157 n. 2 (2d ed. 1993).
[42] Discours d'Ouverture, *supra* note 41, at 3.

one might even be persuaded that the superior magnetism of French culture has succeeded in assimilating those who might have become "national minorities" in lesser cultures. Or perhaps not. In either case, the French position shows how the affirmation or denial of an identity like "national minority" requires contentious cultural exclusions and inclusions.

Such controversies about the "nationalness" of minority group identity have long played a crucial role in European discussions. Indeed, a decisive moment in the 1919 debates over the legal projection of the European minorities concerned the use of the adjective *national* and the related question of collective rights. The early drafts of the Polish Minority Protection Treaty would have protected Poland's "several national minorities"; these minorities would also have been recognized as "distinct public corporations" and would, among other things, have had a right to proportional representation in all state elective bodies.[43] The final version of the treaty, however, suppressed the word *national* from the definition of the protected minorities, replacing it with the phrase "persons who belong to racial, religious, or linguistic minorities"; collective rights were deleted except in certain provisions relating to education.[44] The 1919 suppression of the term *national* and the focus on "persons who belong to" rather than the groups themselves include in their progeny the familiar formulation of Article 27 of the Covenant on Civil and Political Rights.

Significantly, the Permanent Court gave more extensive recognition to collective identity in the *Greco-Bulgarian "Communities" Case*, involving Balkan population exchange, than in other minority protection cases.[45] The court attributed its evaluation of these "communities" to the importance of collective identity in "Eastern countries."[46] This cultural "tradition"[47] meant that the treaty at issue should not be interpreted in accordance with those who saw it primarily as safeguarding "individual rights."[48] The court consequently declared that the existence of the protected Balkan "communities" was rooted in their members' "sentiment of solidarity" rather than in the law of the territorial sovereign.[49] International supremacy over state law was thus grounded through the projection of a collectivist "Eastern tradition," which could only be safeguarded internationally.

[43] Draft Clauses for the Protection of Minorities in Poland (Miller draft; April 29, 1919), *in* X LA PAIX DE VERSAILLES, *supra* note 24, at 12, 14.

[44] 225 CTS at 417.

[45] Greco-Bulgarian "Communities" Case (Adv. Op. No. 17), P.C.I.J. (Ser. B) (1930). *See* Nathaniel Berman, *"But the Alternative Is Despair": European Nationalism and the Modernist Renewal of International Law*, 106 HARV. L. REV. 1792, 1842–58 (1993).

[46] "Communities" Case, *supra* note 45, at 21.

[47] *Id.*

[48] "Communities" Case, Discours Prononcé par M. le Professeur Verzijl (Bulgarie), P.C.I.J. (Ser. C.), 69, 89 (1930).

[49] "Communities" Case, *supra* note 45, at 22.

The reappearance of the term *national* in recent documents like the U.N. Declaration on the Rights of Persons Belonging to National or Ethnic, Religious, and Linguistic Minorities[50] and the European Framework Convention for the Protection of National Minorities[51] may indicate a shift in international attitudes. Alternatively, it may indicate that the term *national minority* has lost the legal meaning, as well as some of the political and cultural charge, that accompanied it in the first decades of the century.[52] In any event, the controversies that attended the earlier use of the word *national* have certainly not been resolved.[53] Moreover, recent documents differ among themselves. The U.N. declaration and the European Framework Convention stress individual rights.[54] By contrast, the various proposals for former Yugoslavia, including the 1991 Draft Convention for Yugoslavia and the Washington and Dayton Agreements (documents for the "East"), formalize the role of nationalist identity in their institutional proposals.

3. Instability and Mutability

The competing cultural projections that produce conflict over the determination of the set of protagonist-positions persist in struggle over their interpretation and deployment, frustrating attempts at stabilization through formal definition or pragmatic functionalization. The 1919 debate about the "nationalness" of minorities, for example, was understood not only as opposing states to minorities generally but also as opposing two different cultural conceptions of group identity—those of Western and Eastern Europe.[55] Yet the suppression of the word *national* in the Polish treaty was not necessarily viewed by all concerned as the end of the matter. Some Eastern European Jews who sought recognition as "national minorities" felt that the "demands of the Jews . . . 'may be called ethnic

[50] *Reprinted in* 32 I.L.M. 911 (1993).

[51] *See* note 13 *supra.*

[52] Thus, one commentator on the European Convention declares that the term *national* in "national minority" refers not to the "nationalness" of the minority but to the fact that the group is a minority on the "national territory" of the state in which it resides. Heinrich Klebes, *The Council of Europe's Framework Convention for the Protection of National Minorities: Introduction,* 16 Hum. Rts. L.J. 92, 93 (1995). If Klebes is right, then the convention intends the phrase in the opposite sense from the interwar usage. The Explanatory Memorandum on the Convention notes that it was "impossible to arrive at a definition" of the phrase and, therefore, it "was decided to adopt a pragmatic approach." *Explanatory Memorandum on the Framework Convention, in id.* at 101, 102. *Cf.* the Report of the CSCE Meeting of Experts on National Minorities, *reprinted in* 30 I.L.M. 1692, 1696 (1991) ("[N]ot all ethnic, cultural, linguistic, or religious differences lead to the creation of national minorities".).

[53] *See, e.g., Commentary on the Provisions of the Framework Convention,* 16 Hum. Rts. L.J. 102, 103 (1995) ("no collective rights of national minorities are envisaged").

[54] *See, e.g., id.*

[55] *See* Oscar Janowsky, The Jews and Minority Rights, 1898–1919 at 264–360 (1933); C. A. Macartney, National States and National Minorities 280–86 (1934).

rights in the language of western Europe; the word 'national' was not essential as long as the thing was secured.'"[56] For such interpreters, the treaty provision should be read ironically, at the expense of both the drafters and of other Jews who sought to use the treaty to promote their own, non-nationalist, definition of Jewish identity. These nationalist protagonists seemed to announce their intention to strategically play the formal, pragmatic, and cultural levels against each other: they would seek to advance their cultural self-understanding through a pragmatic retreat on the formal definition in order to secure their view in other forums. If this ironic reading had been generally known, it might have reinforced Polish trepidations about the treaty; Paderewski, for example, had objected that it would "transform the Jews into an autonomous nation."[57]

Paderewski had also warned of "the migratory capacities of the Jewish population, which so readily transports itself from one State to another."[58] He might have been more genteel had he pointed to the danger of their reading capacities, their ready "transportation" of textual meaning from literality to ironic reversal. Paderewski warned the Western Powers that they could not simply project the "national" problem eastward; the Jews' "migratory capacities" meant that they "will claim elsewhere the national principles which they would enjoy in Poland."[59] Paderewski thus was paradoxically arguing against distinguishing Eastern and Western Europe in *law* by appealing to the Western Europeans' fear of contamination by Eastern European *cultures*. He hoped the Westerners would adopt legal generality precisely as a method of maintaining cultural separation: legal neutrality in the service of xenophobia and racism.

If Paderewski seemed concerned with the Jews' wily cosmopolitanism, the Yugoslavs worried more about their minorities' cultural primitivism. The Yugoslav representative argued that "[i]n view of the fact that owing to their intellectually and politically backward condition, a large proportion of the minorities in our state might be prompted to misinterpret these clauses, it is necessary for the Conference to declare that it is not at all a case of privilege but of the protection of rights."[60] In this argument, it was "intellectual backwardness" that posed the danger of the interpretive instability of the minority protection treaty. If cosmopolitans were feared due to their deliber-

---

[56] JANOWSKI, *supra* note 55, at 300.

[57] Memorandum of M. Paderewski, *supra* note 24, at 129, 132. Both proponents and critics of the minorities treaties discussed the "danger" that they would grant minorities, particularly the Jews, the status of a "State within the State." *See, e.g.*, Annex (B) to Eighth Meeting, Second Report (May 13, 1919) in X LA PAIX DE VERSAILLES, *supra* note 24, at 42, 45.

[58] Memorandum of M. Paderewski, *supra* note 24, at 129, 133.

[59] *Id.*

[60] Letter of the Serb-Croat-Slovene Delegation (November 5, 1919), in X LA PAIX DE VERSAILLES, *supra* note 24, at 359, 362.

ate efforts to transmogrify their "minority" status, primitives were viewed as prone to naïvely exuberant exaggerations of its subtly restricted meaning.

Both the Polish and the Yugoslav arguments rested on the twin notions that the minorities' self-understanding would be transformed by the possibilities they discerned in the legal categories and that this understanding could in turn transform the international meaning of the categories. This instability seemed to be particularly dangerous in the case of the protagonist-position "minority," which has always stood between that of individual citizenship and "nationhood." The delegates of the two new states sought to prevent giving their "minorities" the sense that the shift from the status of "individuals" to that of "minorities" could continue even further along the spectrum, all the way to "nationhood."

Discussions like those described in this section indicate the complexity of attempting to provide definitive criteria for distinguishing among protagonist-positions. Discursive and political transformations often shift groups across a range of identities and back again. A full spectrum shift, which some groups have traversed in its entirety, could be described thus: "nations" or "peoples" arise to claim self-determination because their submersion in a non-national state excludes expression of their national identity; "national minorities" arise to claim collective minority protection because national states exclude their cultural identity; "persons who belong to ethnic, religious, or linguistic minorities" arise to assert individual rights because "national" cultures (majority or minority) exclude expression of their individuality. Or vice versa: "persons" may unite to form "national minorities" because the availability of that legal category may enable them to understand their own cultural or political alternatives in a new, more collective, way; "national minorities" may form "nations" or "peoples" because of the possibilities opened up by those categories; and, finally, "nations" or "peoples" may form states because sovereignty is the legal and cultural signifier of full participation in the international community. And there are many other variations, both directional and motivational, of such movements up and down the scale of identity. Attempts to stop the movement along the scale, such as the Polish or Yugoslav effort to give a restrictive meaning to the word *minority,* involve contentious cultural projections that cannot be definitively stabilized by doctrinal fiat or pragmatic management. Moreover, all such attempts depend on a contestable construction of a cultural realm, whose contingent form makes possible their efforts to restrain, facilitate, or transform identity.

III. History Continuous and Discontinuous

As for the Palais des Nations, . . . there are excellent facilities for a conference, with the capacity to expand quickly to absorb numerous delegates and then contract down to a small secretariat. Yet, sometimes, as I wandered at night through the deserted art deco halls, I felt haunted by the 1930's and wondered whether Yugoslavia would do to the UN what Abyssinia did to the League of Nations.
—Lord Owen, BALKAN ODYSSEY (1995)

As I have noted, today's discussions of nationalist conflicts are marked by a radical disjunction between technocratic urgency and historical déjà-vu. This sense of both the inevitability and incongruity of analogies to past events itself partakes of a tradition. Past phases of this tradition, however, have involved thickly textured arguments about continuity and innovation rather than stark compartmentalization between historical precedent and current exigencies. It is a tradition in which past texts have been continually reread in a manner modifying, preserving, transforming, or reversing their earlier meaning. If today's disjunction between historical and programmatic discussions seems both theoretically and normatively inadequate, rereading these earlier discussions can teach us much about our own implicit fidelity to, and rupture with, the past. To illustrate this method, I will briefly examine texts from three transitional moments in the international law of nationalism: the Versailles period (1919), the revisionist late 1930s, and the pre-decolonization early 1950s.

Debates about the relative propriety of different periods' assertions of legal competence over nationalist conflict always involve competing views about the proper configuration of elements such as power and principle, idealism and realism, law and politics. These arguments can only be studied by close examination of particular texts, showing both the elaboration of competing configurations and the way they construct a realm of cultural difference to justify or refute the "legality" of legal innovation.

A. 1919

The provisions of the World War I peace treaties for dealing with nationalist claims in Eastern and Central Europe remain the most systematic deployment on a vast region of the various legal techniques for dealing with nationalism. The system's place in international legal history is ambivalent: international policymakers have rejected it as outdated due to its ultimate collapse, yet they constantly seem to be struggling to imitate it, particularly in their most ostensibly updated, cutting-edge efforts. At its inception, the Versailles system was itself debated both in terms of its continuities with nineteenth-century precedents and of its creative legal innovations; given the similar current ambivalence toward the legal past, the 1919 debates, particularly those concerning the minority protection treaties, warrant close analysis.

"In the first place, I would point out that this Treaty does not constitute any fresh departure."[61] With these words, Clemenceau launched into his historical argument to overcome Paderewski's objections to the Polish Minority Protection Treaty. Clemenceau focused on arguing that the treaty embodied specifically legal norms, both because of its continuity with past practices and its distance from their "political" aspects.[62] Thus, he asserted that "[i]t has long been the established procedure of the public law of Europe that when a state is created or even when large accessions of territory are made to an established state, the joint and formal recognition by the Great Powers should be accompanied by the requirement that such State should, in the form of a binding international convention, undertake to comply with certain principles of government."[63] The precedents to which Clemenceau referred were all drawn from the nineteenth-century minority protection guarantees that were made conditions of international recognition of the states detached from the Ottoman Empire; this "established procedure" was epitomized in the 1878 Treaty of Berlin.

On first reading, Clemenceau thus seemed to present legal history as a smooth evolutionary process. He treated the nineteenth-century agreements as worthy precedents, even though not wholly purified of the appearance of improper Great Power interest. The nineteenth-century agreements were "open to the criticism" that they could give the Great Powers a pretext to intervene impermissibly in the affairs of the states with minority obligations.[64] The new treaties, therefore, "differ[ed] in form" from their predecessors, placing the guarantees in the hands of the League of Nations rather than the Great Powers.[65] This change, coupled with judicial review, would complete the move from a "political" to a legal system.[66] This continuity and discontinuity with the past seems no more problematic than the familiar riddles implicit in the "ripening" metaphor in the evolution of customary law.

Clemenceau's ironic relationship to his precedents, however, begins to emerge when we read his argument in light of the letter from Paderewski to which he was responding. Paderewski had declared that "[t]he Polish nation has not forgotten that the dismemberment of Poland was the con-

---

[61] Letter Addressed to M. Paderewski by the Conference (Clemenceau Letter) (June 24, 1919), *in* X LA PAIX DE VERSAILLES, *supra* note 24, at 160, 161.

[62] *Id.* For related arguments about the League Covenant, *see* David Kennedy, *The Move to Institutions,* 8 CARDOZO L. REV. 841 (1987).

[63] Clemenceau Letter, *supra* note 61, at 161.

[64] *Id.* at 162.

[65] *Id.*

[66] *Id.*

sequence of the intervention of foreign Powers in affairs concerning her religious minorities, and this painful memory makes Poland fear external interference in internal matters of state more than anything."[67] Paderewski cited this history to ground his protest against the minority protection system's infringement of Poland's "sovereign rights."[68] He argued that this insult to the Polish state was "equivalent to regarding the Polish nation as a nation of inferior standard of civilization."[69] Clemenceau's recourse to precedents drawn from the recognition of the Balkan states in the nineteenth century thus might have confirmed Paderewski's worst fears: that Poland was being treated as "Balkan" in the pejorative sense, its internal affairs associated with the perennial "questions soulevées en Orient." A comparison between the treatment of Polish and Czech minority issues by the peace conference would have confirmed this view.[70] Beneš, unlike Paderewski, convinced the Commission of New States and Minorities that his new country should be viewed as a Western European society.[71]

For Paderewski, both the continuities and discontinuities with the past worked to delegitimate the new treaty. The current representatives of international legal authority were potentially new versions of the ignoble protagonists of past Great Power interventions who used minority rights as a cover for political interest; conversely, the high dignity that Poland now merited was being wrongly downgraded to that of states who were viewed as not quite real, not quite up to the level of other European states. Paderewski presented the relation between the Minority Protection Treaty and earlier precedents as a mocking parody. The low figures of the past were being incongruously dressed in noble costume; the sainted martyr from the past was being unfairly cast as a reprobate sinner. Furthermore, it sought to simultaneously use the present and the past to legitimize each other: the current international authority would use its high legal dignity to ennoble that of the past retrospectively, while looking to the past for the source of its own legitimacy. For Paderewski, by contrast, linking the League with the Great Powers of the past only heightened the danger of the League's reenactment of the latter's unpalatable role; similarly, casting the newly sovereign Polish nation in the same subordinate role as the Poland so easily dismembered in the past offended its contemporary dignity.

Clemenceau's portrayal of the role of the Great Powers, like his portrayal of Poland, also involved a complex and ironic response to Paderewski's

[67] Memorandum of M. Paderewski, *supra* note 24, at 129.

[68] *Id.*

[69] *Id.* at 130.

[70] *See, e.g.,* Report No. 3: Czechoslovakia (May 21, 1919), *in* X LA PAIX DE VERSAILLES, *supra* note 24, at 61.

[71] *See id. See also* Beneš's Note on the Regime of Nationalities in the Czecho-Slovak Republic (May 20, 1919), *in id.* at 53.

fears. For Paderewski, the only way to purge international authority of the taint of impermissible political bias was precisely by heightening that authority through generalizing minority protection duties, making them "obligatory for all states belonging to the League."[72] In response, Clemenceau declared: "The Principal Allied and Associated Powers are of opinion that they would be false to the responsibility which rests upon them if on this occasion they departed from what has become an established tradition. In this connection I must also recall to your consideration the fact that it is to the endeavors and sacrifices of the Powers in whose name I am addressing you that the Polish nation owes the recovery of its independence."[73] Clemenceau thus coupled his assertion of the Allied and Associated Powers' responsibility to the legal "tradition" with a reminder of Poland's material dependence on them: it is on the support of "these Powers" for the League that "Poland will to a large extent depend for the secure possession" of its territory.[74] This assertion, that Polish sovereignty was an expression of a just claim to national self-determination, on the one hand, and attributable to the power of the Allies and therefore subject to their conditions, on the other, was enshrined in the first lines of the Polish Minority Protection Treaty ("[w]hereas the Allied and Associated Powers have by the success of their arms restored to the Polish nation the independence of which it has been unjustly deprived"). The repeated stress on this point was an ironic commentary on the disclaimer of the treaty's "political" dimension; according to the logic of Clemenceau's argument, if the move from the Great Power guarantee to that of the League was incomplete, so was the move from "politics" to "law." It suggests rather more continuity with precisely the purportedly negative features of the nineteenth-century system than the rest of Clemenceau's argument would allow.

A close reading thus shows how both statesmen presented complex claims about the new system's continuity and discontinuity with its predecessors. Clemenceau's argument seemed on first reading to assert a gradual evolution from Great Power politics to international law, while Paderewski's argument seemed like a traditionalist clinging to sovereign political prerogatives. Yet more careful analysis shows how Clemenceau sought to preserve the political elements of the nineteenth century system in his emphasis on Allied power, while Paderewski insisted on a fuller evolution from politics to law. Similarly, in drawing parallels between the Paris and Berlin conferences and between the restoration of Polish sover-

---

[72] Memorandum by M. Paderewski, *supra* note 24, at 131. Poland ultimately would suspend its participation in the minority protection system over the issue of generalization. *See* Declaration of Polish Delegate Beck to the League Assembly, LEAGUE OF NATIONS O.J. Spec. Supp. 122 at 42 (1934).
[73] Letter Addressed to M. Paderewski, *supra* note 61, at 161–62.
[74] *Id.* at 162.

eignty and the settlement of exotic Balkan matters, Clemenceau promoted the continued extension of international supremacy where Paderewski would have required rupture in deference to Polish nationalism; yet in refusing to extend international scrutiny to all League members, the Allies continued the deference to Western European sovereignty where Poland demanded an innovative generalization of international supremacy. Finally, Paderewski sought to use historical precedent to demonstrate the minority protection system's demeaning cultural activism and thus to debunk its impartial legal pretensions; Clemenceau, implicitly embracing the history of Western European cultural activism, asserted that the tradition of imposing special obligations on the Central and Eastern European states legitimated the legal dignity of the current treaty. The two statesmen's opposed configurations of nationalism and internationalism, power and principle, continuity and discontinuity thus hinged on the contestation of internationalist cultural activism and the projection of cultural difference among European nations.

B. 1938

If 1919 is remembered in conventional legal histories as the moment of transition from a political to a legal conception of the international law of nationalism, 1938 is remembered as the reverse. Just as the former narrative must be rethought, so must the latter. The haste, yet inexorability, with which the irredentism of the 1930s is mentioned in the opening passages of many writings on international minority rights indicates the unresolved, traumatic role of the events evoked by "Munich" in the international law of nationalism; while this irredentism is generally cited to explain the eclipse of minority rights, it is never clear how new proposals meet the problem.

To be sure, pragmatists may seek to reassure us that the 1938 Four-Power Agreement in Munich was merely a case of misjudgment, however grave. For such an interpretation, the non-fascist powers simply erred in the way they weighed the national claims of the Sudetendeutsche and German state interests against the national claims of ethnic Czechs, the multiethnic claims of many Czech citizens, and Czechoslovakia's state interests: excessively deferring to a powerful state, erroneously weighing competing ethnic claims. Yet the agreement and the period debate cannot be so easily dismissed as an aberration either doctrinally or pragmatically. Munich haunts the international imagination today because of its consistency with the enduring structural elements of the international law of nationalism. Although cold war invocations of Munich have been thoroughly criticized, the lack of examination of its significance for minority rights (the purported substance of the dispute) has allowed its uncritical deployment in current debate about nationalist conflict.[75] Munich has been cited vehemently during the wars in the Balkans.[76] The current resurgence of minority rights requires that we explicitly grapple with the 1930s events that contributed so decisively to their long occultation.[77]

It is often said that Munich was a "reverse Versailles," the final undoing of the interwar regime, the transformation of Europe from a "pluralist" to a "hegemonic" system.[78] By contrast, historian A. J. P. Taylor declared (ironically?) that Munich "was a triumph for all that was best and most enlightened in British life"; the "offence redressed at Munich" was the "subjection of three million Germans to Czech rule," a violation of the principle of "equal justice between peoples."[79] These conflicting views may be seen as a debate about the justice and practicality of the protagonist-position "protected minority," to which the Sudetens were "subjected." The buildup to Munich was replete with British and French statements critical of the "minority" protagonist-position, at least in the context of the Sudetens' dynamically shifting self-understanding. Thus, British mediator Lord Runciman described the transformation of Sudeten aspirations from "some degree of home rule" within Czechoslovakia to the demand for the "full right of self-determination."[80] He sympathetically declared that it "is a hard thing to be ruled by an alien race," particularly when many Sudetens considered the Czechs to be cultural inferiors.[81] This transformation of Sudeten identity, which garnered decisive international support in 1938, illustrates the ambivalences toward the "minority" protagonist-position and the role of the construction of a realm of cultural identity and competing projections of cultural difference.

The Munich Agreement itself, *when read out of context,* is shocking precisely because of its familiarity, its consistency with its predecessor

[75] *See, e.g.,* GÖRAN RYSTAD, PRISONERS OF THE PAST? (1982).

[76] Most strikingly, it was evoked in 1991 by the Yugoslav defense minister, who compared the secession of Slovenia to that of the Sudetenland (LE MONDE, July 20, 1991); by the Venezulan delegate during the 1993 Security Council debate on the arms embargo in an eloquent comparison of Izetbegovic with Edouard Beneš (U.N. Doc. S/PV.3247, June 29, 1993, at 128–31), a comparison also evoked by Izetbegovic himself; and by Jacques Chirac in 1995, who compared the Western treatment of Bosnia with the treatment of Czechoslovakia by Chamberlain and Daladier (THE INDEPENDENT, July 17, 1995). David Owen's defense of the European role in Bosnia often seems obsessed with the "too many false analogies" drawn with "Europe in the 1930's and 1940's." OWEN, *supra* note 28, at 366.

[77] I explore the international legal and cultural implications of the Munich settlement in greater detail in *Beyond Colonialism and Nationalism? Ethiopia, Czechoslovakia and "Peaceful Change,"* 65 NORDIC J. INT'L L. 421 (1996).

[78] Otto Feinstein, *Conflict at Munich: Pluralism vs. Hegemonism, in* APPEASING FASCISM 19 (Melvin Small & Otto Feinstein eds., 1991).

[79] A. J. P. TAYLOR, THE ORIGINS OF THE SECOND WORLD WAR 189 (1961).

[80] Letter of Lord Runciman to Neville Chamberlain, September 21, 1938, *reprinted in* CORRESPONDENCE RESPECTING CZECHOSLOVAKIA, SEPTEMBER 1938 at 3 (1938).

[81] *Id.*

treaties.[82] Indeed, read paragraph by paragraph, it seems to defer to earlier treaties rather than to "reverse" them. Its first three paragraphs recall the Treaty of Berlin in providing for the conditions under which an incumbent sovereign must evacuate territories under nationalist dispute.[83] The fourth paragraph's provisions for the transfer of "predominantly German" areas evoke the thirteenth of Wilson's Fourteen Points, which called for the establishment of Poland on territories with "indisputably Polish populations."[84] The fifth paragraph evokes provisions of the Versailles Treaty in its call for a plebiscite in territories to be determined by an international commission and occupied by "international bodies" until after the plebiscite.[85] Indeed, it practically *cites* the Versailles Treaty in its declaration that the plebiscite will be held under the "conditions of the Saar plebiscite," a Versailles-ordained event.[86] The sixth paragraph vests the final determination of frontiers in an international commission, in line with similar expert bodies under Versailles auspices.[87] Its seventh paragraph echoes Versailles's Article 91[88] in its granting of the right of option "into and out of the transferred territories."[89] Finally, two months after Munich, the Czechs and Germans concluded an agreement to protect their respective "national minorities."[90] The agreement, envisioning a mixed German-Czech commission with possible direct representation of the minorities' themselves, echoed similar arrangements after the partition of Upper Silesia.

A reverse Versailles? For the Germans, we should speak, rather, of a parodic Versailles—a mocking imitation of international legal texts whose substance the Germans sought to destroy, a destruction achieved at Munich through a variation on those very texts. For the British and French, the situation is more complicated. Whatever the subjective intentions of Daladier and Chamberlain, the appeal of the agreement lay in part in the way it seemed to preserve and yet transform the cardinal

---

[82] Four-Power Agreement on Czechoslovakia, *supra* note 12.

[83] *Compare, e.g.,* Treaty of Berlin, art. 1 (XI), 153 CTS at 177.

[84] Woodrow Wilson, *The Fourteen Points Address* (1918), *in* 45 THE PAPERS OF WOODROW WILSON 536, 539 (Arthur S. Link ed., 1984).

[85] Compare the provisions for the Upper Silesia plebiscite and International Commission, Versailles Treaty, art. 88 & Annex, 225 CTS 188, 237–40.

[86] Versailles Treaty, art. 49, 225 CTS at 215.

[87] *See, e.g.,* Report of the Committee of Experts Appointed to Study the Frontier to Be Laid Down between Germany and Poland As the Result of the Plebiscite *in* GEORGES KAECKENBEECK, THE INTERNATIONAL EXPERIMENT OF UPPER SILESIA 552 (1942).

[88] 225 CTS at 240–41.

[89] This provision was further elaborated in a Czech-German treaty on citizenship and option, *reprinted in* II REICHSGESETZBLATT 896 (1938).

[90] The agreement is reprinted in XII DOCUMENTS DIPLOMATIQUES FRANÇAIS 798 (2d ser. 1938); *see also* HUBERT RIPKA, MUNICH: BEFORE AND AFTER 269 (1939, trans. Ida Sindelkova & Edgar Young, 1969).

Versailles principles.[91] I have argued elsewhere that this desire to pre-serve-and-transform the Versailles principles produced a "parodic/ real-ist" destabilization of international discourse.[92] Yet many contemporaries viewed the relationship of the Munich Agreement to Versailles as a "rip-ening", an implementation of principles imperfectly adhered to in 1919. Such an argument was made possible by the adherence to the form of the international law of nationalism: the assertion of international authority in the cause of peace, the impositions on sovereignty, the combination of "objective self-determination" (expert determination of ethnic borders) and "subjective" self-determination (the plebiscite principle), with their supplements of the rights of citizenship, option, and minority protection. The ultimate in legal discontinuity, the dismemberment of Versailles-cre-ated Czechoslovakia, could be justified by some as a reconfiguration, rather than a rejection, of the Versailles principles.

That this interpretation, *in context*, was horribly, murderously, wrong goes without saying. Yet Munich should neither be used to reject an international law of nationalism nor be dismissed as a now-irrelevant aberration. There is no history of the international law of nationalism without Munich: it endures both as one of the possible variants of the legal structure and as a crucial turning point in its history. Allegations of new "Munich sellouts" are made possible by the structural affinity of that settlement with legal tradition; in particular, they are made possible by the ambivalence of the international law of nationalism, the tension and potential for crossover between its internationalism and nationalism, its power and principle. Rejections of such allegations are made possible by the contingency of that structure, its institution through contingent projec-tions of cultural difference that may legitimate or delegitimate particular assertions of legal authority. The persuasiveness of the claim of the "injus-tice" of "subjecting Germans to Czech rule" lies in complex projections of cultural identity, difference, and hierarchy in relation to the contending groups as well as the international authorities who did the "subjecting." If international law is serious about resurrecting minority rights, as in the EU's conditions on recognition of new states, it must be prepared to meet the objections to which they are vulnerable.[93] The powerful interference with sovereign prerogatives involved in the imposition of minority rights must be openly justified; the cultural objections raised against the limita-tion of certain peoples to minority status rather than full nationhood must be confronted; the technical ability of international law to enforce the

[91] For examples of such French opinion on both left and right, *see* YVON LACAZE, L'OPIN-ION PUBLIQUE FRANÇAISE ET LA CRISE DE MUNICH 309–29, 439–52 (1991).

[92] *See Beyond Colonialism and Nationalism? supra* note 77.

[93] European Community, Declaration on Yugoslavia and on the Guidelines on the Recog-nition of New States, *reprinted in* 31 I.L.M. 1485 (1992).

protections must be assured. No assertions of international authority are innocent of power, culturally neutral, or safe from co-optation by abhorrent forces: they may, nonetheless, be required.

C. 1938 and Decolonization

Munich marked a rupture in the international law of nationalism, initiating the postwar "occultation" of minority rights and the general denigration of interwar legal conceptions. After World War II, "no one proposed to revive the dead letter of the minorities treaties."[94] Most observers assumed that something like the Czech experience would be the inevitable result of such a legal regime.[95] The distinctive blend of international authority and nationalist desire epitomized in minority rights thus could not be resurrected after the war. Rather, they became disjoined from each other. On the one hand, the concern for nationalist desire came to take the form of a right to self-determination redefined as independence within the colonial borders of the non-European possessions of European powers. On the other hand, internationalist aspirations were channeled into doctrines and institutions to protect individual human rights; minority protection survived only in the pallid Article 27 of the Covenant on Civil and Political Rights. This disjuncture between deference to nationalism and assertion of internationalism was the fate of the international law of nationalism during the decolonization decades.

Yet conventional accounts of the post–World War II period often omit a transitional period during which some invoked the interwar period to justify a new international law of nationalism on the basis of a rejuvenated systematic vision. In 1953, for example, one distinguished commentator declared that the "superior interests of the international community" gave it the right to evaluate critically nationalist claims.[96] He asserted that "specialists of public law condemn the nationalist phraseology according to which every national claim should be accepted."[97] The two main criteria for evaluating such claims would be whether granting them would advance "democracy" and "civilization." Thus, a people living in a democratic state would not be able to join a nondemocratic state, nor would a people living in a "State of a high degree of civilization" be allowed to join a "State of illiterates."[98] The latter case would be condemnable "in the

---

[94] William E. Rappard, *Vues Rétrospectives sur la Société des Nations*, 71 RCADI 117, 187 (1947-II).

[95] *Id.* at 185. *See also* J. L. Kunz, *The Present Status of the International Law for the Protection of Minorities*, 48 AM. J. INT'L L. (1954).

[96] Boris Mirkine-Guetzévich, *Quelques Problèmes de la Mise en Oeuvre de la Déclaration Universelle des Droits de l'Homme*, 83 RCADI 255, 347–48 (1953-II).

[97] *Id.* at 334.

[98] *Id.* at 349.

name of culture as much as that of democracy."[99] The dismemberment of Czechoslovakia was used as a central argument for critical scrutiny of nationalist claims, particularly those of the colonized peoples.[100] This proposal thus reasserted international competence to judge nationalist claims in light of superior values; it combined new ideas about human rights and democracy with interwar ideas about cultural difference and internationalist supremacy.

This kind of comprehensive approach to nationalism, in which international authority would have the competence to rank national claims according to cultural judgments, was not to win out during the decolonization decades. Rather, one particular element of the international law of nationalism, decolonization within colonial borders, was to prevail against such a revival of comprehensive deployments of the gamut of doctrinal and policy options. Another key element in the old international law of nationalism, minority protection, was delegitimized due to the anticolonial stress on unconditional sovereignty as well as to the "lessons of Munich." Nationalist claims were thus divided into two groups: claims that merited full self-determination, to which international law must defer (that is, decolonization), and those not meriting full self-determination, in relation to which international law would be largely irrelevant.

Thus, in the immediate postwar period, Munich had become the terrain of competing interpretations. This debate opposed those who used it as an argument to evaluate every self-determination claim in the name of internationalism to those who used it to turn self-determination into a formal right applied to formally defined cases. The gradually developing anticolonial consensus gave victory to this latter interpretation and, together with cold war competition, gradually suppressed all explicit legal discussion of cultural status in the old sense. For many anticolonialists, a formalist approach to self-determination and sovereignty was the only way to bring an end to the imperial deployment of both flexible pragmatism and cultural activism. This emphasis on decolonization and its delegitimization of internationalist supremacy over nationalist claims made impossible a systematic approach in the manner of either the late nineteenth century or the interwar period.

[99] Id.
[100] Id. at 337–49.

IV. Conclusion: A New International Law of Nationalism?

Religious freedom does not only affect the Jews; in imposing it on Serbia as a condition of its independence, the Treaty equally provides it for the Muslims. The territories attributed by the Congress to Prince Milan give him a great number of Muslims who will have to become Serbian citizens, in law and in everyday life. This will be, in our view, the best way for Serbia to fulfill its destiny.
                 —Benoit Brunswik, LE TRAITÉ DE BERLIN, ANNOTÉ ET COMMENTÉ (1878)

In the first place, it is altogether remarkable to observe that the Arbitration Commission, established in the framework of the Peace Conference for Yugoslavia, . . . has not hesitated . . . to classify minority rights in the superior category of peremptory norms of international law (*jus cogens*).
                 —Pierre-Marie Dupuy, DROIT INTERNATIONAL PUBLIC (1993)

During the early 1990s, a conventional metaphor to describe resurgent nationalist tensions was "the thawing out of nationalism from the Communist freezer," yielding old antagonisms in particularly horrible and diseased form. Perhaps the end of the cold war's freezing of the old international law of nationalism might similarly be said to have led to the reemergence of the categories and approaches of that law—although presumably in reformed, rather than diseased, shape. The analysis presented in this chapter suggests some explanations for today's "altogether remarkable" resurrection of minority rights other than such question-begging metaphors.

The end of the cold war has facilitated the emergence of a new comprehensive international law of nationalism due to its revival of the central features of previous comprehensive approaches: a vigorous sense of international legal authority, the availability to that authority of the entire range of doctrinal and policy techniques, and the construction of a realm of cultural difference that both legitimates and informs the deployment of international power. The first feature follows from the rather familiar point that the end of the cold war has transformed the structure of international authority. Although the exuberance of the immediate post-1989 period has evaporated, the notion of a relatively unified international authority has persisted. Thus far, the international legal community has not been divided along ideological lines like those of the 1930s or the cold war. Such a relatively unified international authority has been an indispensable premise of all comprehensive approaches to nationalist conflict: some institution or group of states must be able to occupy the position of "international legal organ" in whose name power and principle can be asserted.

Second, the decline of the anti-imperialist stress on formal deference to a formal version of self-determination and sovereignty has made it possible for internationalists to consider systematically the array of techniques for settling nationalist conflict. The new reassertion of international authority thus makes possible options such as the imposition of minority rights. Minority rights, always a good barometer of the state of the international law of nationalism, are associated with the strong internationalist assertion of the right to impose conditions on new states formed in acts of national self-determination—and, therefore, such rights were relegated to the back burner during the heyday of anticolonialist suspicion of the principledness of international power.

Finally, explicit affirmations and contestations of cultural activism have reemerged in debates about the deployment of international power. Proponents and critics of international cultural activism have clashed in debates about new forms of trusteeship and "failed states," in the highly culturally charged debate about Bosnia and the "Sarajevo ideal," in the debate about cultural relativism and universal human rights. The legitimation of international authority through the construction of a realm of cultural difference has been contested in the critique of end-of-history liberal-triumphalism and its more ominous twin, the "clash of civilizations." The birth pangs of a new, systematic international law of nationalism may be heard in these debates in which cultural discourse plays a variety of shifting and politically ambivalent roles.

The comprehensive frameworks embodied in documents such as the 1991 Draft Convention on Yugoslavia and the 1995 Dayton Agreements are some of the most advanced expressions of the new international law of nationalism, made possible by the three developments I have discussed. This return to comprehensive frameworks does not mean that the deep ambivalences structuring this field—internationalism and nationalism, power and principle—have been resolved. Each of the new comprehensive documents is subject to competing interpretations; each interpretation involves contestable projections of cultural difference as well as contestations of the role of culture as a legitimator of international action.

As in the past, the new international law of nationalism is a terrain of discursive and political struggle, not a set of doctrinal definitions or neutral pragmatic solutions. As a commentator on the 1878 Treaty of Berlin wrote: "[The Treaty] represents all the solutions or purported solutions which the eastern crisis [la crise orientale] has provoked in people's spirits. The Treaty has an advantage over criticism: criticism seeks only the victory of one solution over the others . . . while the Treaty of Berlin, incorporating all opinions, . . . provides to each the means of peacefully working for its definitive victory."[101] This passage may be viewed as an early example of the approach pursued in this essay, that of understand-

---

[101] BRUNSWIK, supra note 19, at ix.

ing doctrinal and policy analyses in light of their projection of cultural fears and fantasies. Nationalism has always appeared to the international imagination as an exotic, frightening, and fascinating stimulus to legal creativity; the international law of nationalism has always furnished a terrain of conflict in which the construction of a realm of cultural difference and competing projections of international and nationalist identity have played a crucial role. Yet if we have learned to be wary of the Western- and Eurocentric version of this relationship, if we have abandoned expressions such as "la crise orientale," we should not delude ourselves into thinking that we have acceded to the rationalist utopia of pure doctrine and neutral pragmatics. Asserting such transcendence simply means that the cultural imagination will continue to operate implicitly, if not unconsciously. The refusal of cultural discourse may serve to reject the oppressive form it has taken, most egregiously in colonialism; it may also mask the cultural projections deployed through ostensibly neutral doctrine and policy.

The new international law of nationalism, like its predecessors, will not take the form of complete theoretical and doctrinal generalization or fully neutral technocratic policy but that of a new set of persuasive practices, implicating contestable and contingent projections. It will be a resumption of a tradition whose record embodies both the noblest and basest efforts of international community. The reemergence of an international law of nationalism makes possible both concrete humanitarian efforts and the necessity to scrutinize a whole range of cultural and political projections uncritically, or unconsciously, deployed by previous generations. It is not possible to decide a priori whether a new international law of nationalism should be embraced or resisted, whether today's conditions continue to demand anti-imperialist assertions of strict respect for sovereignty, make palatable the revival of cultural activism, or facilitate vigorous international action that can realize the noblest aspirations of both while avoiding their oppressive dimensions. Yet the history of the international law of nationalism demonstrates that it is simply not possible to construct a neutral approach innocent of differential cultural projections and unimplicated in the partisan imposition of power. Rather, the legacy of international law's troubling efforts to engage with nationalism should be the vigilant awareness of the possibilities and dangers implicit in all the approaches and the willingness to deploy them tactically to prevent the horrors that have, more often than not, followed even the noblest of legal dreams.

2

The Institutional and Instrumental Value of Nationalism

Lea Brilmayer

The chapters in this volume deal with nationalism in many of its possible manifestations: historical, legal, political, and others. Most are descriptive or analytical; this chapter, however, is normative. It deals with the moral judgments we make about nationalist behavior. Nationalism has something of a bad odor these days. This is not surprising considering the human misery that nationalist conflicts have caused around the world. But recently, nationalism has also had its share of academic philosophers riding to the rescue. Several excellent articles and at least one justly applauded recent book attempt to provide nationalism with respectable liberal credentials, and there has for a number of years been a vigorous literature suited to mounting a more communitarian defense.[1]

Several articles of my own dispute what I see as a common philosophical understanding of the moral issues that nationalism raises.[2] This chapter builds on the arguments there, but it does so in a way that tries better to recognize what these other accounts contribute to our general views on nationalism. I do not ultimately think that these philosophical accounts

---

[1] The literature is enormous, so I refer to only a few of the sources. The book is YAEL TAMIR, LIBERAL NATIONALISM (2d ed. 1995); among the articles taking a liberal approach to the problem is Avashaim Margalit & Joseph Raz, *National Self-Determination*, 87 J. PHIL. 439 (1990).

Among the more communitarian authors that have addressed nationalism or related topics, the most important may be Michael Walzer, Michael Sandel, and Will Kymlicka. *See, e.g.,* WILL KYMLICKA, LIBERALISM COMMUNITY AND CULTURE (1989); Michael Walzer, The National Question Revised (Tanner Lectures, 1989); MICHAEL SANDEL, LIBERALISM AND THE LIMITS OF JUSTICE (1982).

[2] *See The Moral Significance of Nationalism*, 7 NOTRE DAME L. REV. 7 (1995); *Secession and Self-Determination: A Territorial Interpretation*, 16 YALE J. INT'L L. 177 (1991).

should govern our evaluation of what nationalists do, and I remain convinced that they overlook what is and ought to be the most important set of normative considerations. But taking a closer look at these other accounts provides a better understanding of what precisely is at stake.

The usual philosophical approaches seem to look for justifications of a particular kind. They seem to assume that, for nationalist actions to be morally justifiable, they must be explainable in terms of some value advanced by having nations, which are assumed to be groupings of human beings that are homogeneous with regard to culture, ethnicity, language, religion, or some other factor. Recognition of the claims of nationalists is treated as instrumental to the achievements of these other values, which I refer to as "communal values." The question then becomes, what values are these? Why is it desirable to promote groupings that are homogeneous in this respect? The primary philosophical challenge of nationalism is that it seems prima facie inconsistent with liberalism, which celebrates diversity, individual autonomy, and pluralism. The challenge is to explain why homogeneity in the relevant respect (whether language, culture, race, or whatever) entitles one to particular resources: usually, but not invariably, a territorial state of one's own.

It is possible, though, that the fact of homogeneity plays no important part in the moral argument, that a national group's entitlement (or lack of entitlement) to the resource is independent of its degree of homogeneity. If this is the case, then there is no apparent inconsistency with liberalism to explain. The question is merely whether the group in question is entitled to the resource that it wants on the grounds of whatever independent basis it offers as a justification for its demands. Just as a corporation's rights might not be a function of the fact that it is a corporation (because the rules of contract or tort law apply to corporations and other legal persons roughly equally), so, too, may the claims that nationalists make on behalf of their states not be a consequence of nationhood. An earlier article tested the limits of this argument, which I called "the irrelevance hypothesis," and concluded that nationalist claims are indeed largely independent of the fact that that they are made on behalf of nations, although there are some interesting and important potential exceptions.[3]

This chapter returns to the problem of why we might look for value in grouping the human race into national communities. The simplest version

---

[3] The article is *The Moral Significance of Nationalism, supra* note 2. Of the exceptions that I consider, two of the more interesting are that independence might be thought inalienable when possessed by nations (so that even after voluntary confederation, complete independence would always be recoverable) and that, when the merits of an argument for independence are unclear, the burden of proof might fall on the party opposing the rights of the nation.

of the standard philosophical argument just described (to the effect that recognizing nationalist demands furthers communal values) will be referred to as the "instrumental" explanation of nationalism. But there is another and (to my mind) more convincing way to look at nationalist demands, which also relies on the value of grouping the human race into nationalist communities. We might turn to nationalist values at the institutional level as a source of reasons either to create an international system based on nation-states or to retain the one we have. After making the commitment to an institutional arrangement of this sort, and choosing principles to regulate it, we might then turn our back on the underlying reasons for choosing this arrangement. In resolving particular disputes as they arise, we might consult instead our institutional principles. The principles would create or fortify entitlements that have a more or less independent existence from the reasons for creating or retaining an international system based on nation-states. Communal values would figure in at the institutional rather than the direct instrumental level.

If this scenario is accurate, then it explains why two rather different descriptions of what is going on are both appealing. It would explain both why nationalists feel that their group is entitled to some particular thing independent of its national status and why it somehow matters to liberals and communitarians alike that national flourishing is something to be promoted. The institutional explanation, therefore, incorporates elements of both the standard philosophical account of nationalism and my criticisms of those accounts. It does raise the philosophical question, however, of whether we really want to entrench institutional norms to such a great degree that their underlying value justifications are completely irrelevant in deciding particular cases. In response to these doubts, I will consider a third position, one of defeasible institutional entitlements. If this approach were adopted, then we would normally consult institutional principles in resolving disputes but on the grounds that doing so would in most cases further instrumental values. In those unusual cases where the instrumental and institutional analyses pointed in different directions, the instrumental values would trump institutional entitlements.

After spelling out these three interpretations in greater detail, I will return to the question of how we should evaluate the things that nationalists do and argue that an institutional interpretation is preferable to one relying on instrumental reasoning, whether it is directly instrumental or based on defeasible entitlements. Nationalist behavior, in other words, should not primarily be evaluated with reference to the communal values that the institution of the nation-state promotes, except at the point where institutional arrangements are created.

I. The Instrumental View

What characterizes nationalism, in contemporary popular imagination, is its vitriol and blood. That is what Americans see on television when reports on Serbia or Chechnya are shown. "Ethnic cleansing" is the phrase we probably most associate with nationalism. Whether perpetrated through violence (as when Muslim civilians are rounded up or killed in Bosnia) or through legal strategem (as when Russians are denied citizenship rights in their formerly occupied Baltic provinces), the effects of national sentiment that we see today are largely unpleasant.[4]

Taking the longer (and more discerning) view, however, philosophers have also found that national sentiment has its more attractive side. Often it moves otherwise rather ordinary people to extraordinary feats of generosity and sacrifice. And there is no denying that some of the historical movements understood as nationalistic had entirely legitimate objectives: the decolonization movement, for example. This more attractive side of nationalism has led philosophers to search for what might be its best defense and to try to sort out the instances of nationalism that should be encouraged from the instances that must be condemned. The challenge of this project is a consequence of the way that nationalism's better side seems so intimately connected with its worse. It is precisely the desire to differentiate between fellow nationals and outsiders that accounts for both. The desire to promote the interests of fellow nationals is what leads to generosity and heroism; the desire to do this selectively (not promoting comparable interests of others) is what leads to discrimination and exclusion. The general philosophical response to this puzzle starts by asking what positive values national sentiment promotes.

The answer to that question has followed roughly these lines. Human beings can only truly flourish in communities that have some more or less secure existence. People need community to develop the kind of personal ties that lead to familial and romantic love, professional satisfaction, friendship, intellectual stimulation, and creative fulfillment. Shared practices and cultural traditions shape our identities and give us a sense of belonging. Thus, it is natural for us to want to draw together into more or less distinct communities with some historical continuity and with the ability to differentiate our fellow members from outsiders.

---

[4] I should add that, in my own view, the fact that disputes are vitriolic or bloody (or have unpleasant consequences) does not automatically mean that the actions of nationalists are unjustified. Although I will not argue the point here, I believe that most of the efforts to discourage Russian nationals from remaining in the Baltic states after they regained their independence were justifiable, even though they involved a certain amount of vitriol and unpleasantness. My point here is merely that the unpleasantness of nationalist conflict has captured the attention of the media.

Community sentiment translates into national sentiment because only certain sorts of political entities have the power to shape their destiny. If national sentiment includes a strong desire that one's nation have a state of its own (and this is commonly thought to be an identifying characteristic of nationalist thought), then this desire can be explained in terms of the fact that, without the international recognition that states are given, the community cannot maintain its distinctiveness. Without the right, for example, to control immigration, a community is at risk of dilution and assimilation; without the power to tax and spend, the community cannot support its cultural practices through the establishment of schools, museums, and popular entertainment. The desire for community therefore finds natural expression in the desire for a state with internationally acknowledged status and a state power equal to what other nations have. National sentiment is justifiable in terms of promotion of the value of community, which is central to fulfilling human life.

At this point, the argument faces a fork in the road. Those who are comfortable with community as a foundational concept—they might be called "communitarians"—will be roughly satisfied with the sort of thing that has been already said, although it will have to be articulated more fully and persuasively. Liberals, however, may want to press the logic further because for them community is not a foundational, but a derivative, good. Not only will they want to emphasize the value of community to individual human beings, but they will want to reconcile it with the values of individual autonomy and choice.[5] It is not so clear how best to do this because communities generally (and national communities in particular) are not typically formed through the exercise of autonomous choice. Generally, one becomes part of a historically situated community through the accident of birth. One is an American, Israeli, or Cambodian because of where one was born and who one's parents were, coupled with one's upbringing in the relevant (American, Israeli, or Cambodian) culture and traditions.

This fact presents challenges but not necessarily insurmountable ones. As Yael Tamir has emphasized, while nationality is typically acquired at birth and through upbringing, it is not entirely immutable. There is an element of choice in that one can change one's nationality or one can decide to retain the nationality one has. The fact that nationality is difficult to change is not fatal to this argument; that simply makes it an important choice, a commitment that cannot be undertaken on a whim. Choosing to learn to play the violin or to raise bonsai are also difficult and long-term

---

[5] YAEL TAMIR, LIBERAL NATIONALISM, *supra* note 1, is the most fully developed effort to reconcile nationalism with liberalism along these lines. *See* especially her chapter 2, *National Choices and the Right to Culture*. The few short remarks here, understandably, do not attempt to do justice to her arguments.

enterprises, but part of what makes both valuable is that they are not easy and do not come quickly. Having a good marriage is not inconsistent with choice and autonomy as long as one has made the choice to be married, and getting married five times or with little forethought is not a sign that one is more autonomous than the person who marries only once or with great deliberation.

While there are important philosophical issues at stake in the decision whether to follow the liberal or the communitarian path, the differences will not matter much for present purposes. What the two approaches have in common is that recognition of nationalist claims is justified in instrumental terms. A nation should get what it wants (usually a state of its own, although sometimes something less, such as more limited political autonomy) because it is a community of the appropriate kind and because granting the nation what it wants will contribute to that community's flourishing. In either case, it is an important ingredient of the argument that national self-determination promotes the underlying values that human beings receive from political communities. National self-determination, in other words, is to be supported because it is instrumental to what might be called communal values.[6]

In addition, under either of these two interpretations, whether a nation is entitled to what it wants would depend on whether those criteria are satisfied. An attraction of both the communitarian and the liberal understanding of the value of nationalism is that both apparently help us to differentiate between those exercises of national sentiment that are morally defensible and those that must be condemned. Both identify positive aspects of nationalism without giving way to its more violent and exclusivist tendencies. Neither excuses hatred or the desire to humiliate; and presumably even where nationalism's positive values of commuity are at stake, neither would allow the indiscriminate employment of all available means of pursuit, such as torture, rape, or genocide. Nationalism is justifiable only when it serves the values of community and when the means that it employs are morally within bounds.

While this view has its merits, there are nonetheless several aspects of it that should give us pause. These relate to the fact that the value that it assigns to national self-determination is purely instrumental. The appeal of this instrumental approach lies in its ability to distinguish between those manifestations of nationalism that merit support and those that do not. But the way that it makes this distinction is somewhat out of touch

---

[6] When I use the phrase "communal values," therefore, it should not be understood as privileging the communitarian version of the instrumental argument over the liberal one. Liberals, also, might believe in the promotion of communal values; it is just that they will do so out of a belief in the moral worth of individuals and out of the belief that communal values can be reconciled with values of individual autonomy.

with what nationalists seem to be claiming. Of course, this may simply show that some of the things that nationalists are claiming are things that they (and their nations) are not entitled to. Before concluding as much, though, we ought to take a closer look at three ways that this instrumental justification does not fit current sentiment.

First, often the groups that make claims, and even characterize these claims as nationalistic, do not seem to be communities in the relevant philosophical sense. It is evident that groups need not be linguistically, culturally, ethnically, or religiously homogeneous to make nationalist demands. Particularly during the decolonization period, the groups demanding national independence were often quite diverse along all of these lines. Certainly there was no test for homogeneity; and while the group was not perfectly homogeneous, it had been deemed to be homogeneous enough. The question seems not even to have been raised; no such standard was even brought to bear, and no other criteria for community seem to have been applied, either. While some observers objected that the colonies should not be granted independence because they were not politically mature enough for self-governance, or because practically speaking the new states would be unmanageable, no one objected in principle because they lacked the relevant indicia of a community.[7]

Second (and similarly), there is a gap between national self-determination and the communal values that it supposedly promotes because there are ways to promote community other than to allow independent statehood. In particular, regional autonomy within existing state borders, national language schools, subsidies for the national arts, and so on might be successful at encouraging community sentiment without the necessity of redrawing international borders. Yet in many, if not most, such cases, these alternatives would be deeply unsatisfying to the claimants (and at least in the case of decolonization, would seem quite morally unsatisfying to the rest of us as well.) The similarity to the point first raised is that, if nationalist movements must be justified by reference to instrumental values, then nationalist movements that are not sufficiently well suited to promoting those values need not be recognized. This is true either when the movement in question does not actually promote community (because it is itself internally fragmented) or when there is some alternative to statehood that would promote community almost as well and perhaps at lower cost.

Third, the instrumental explanation we have given does not very well

[7] Perhaps it would be argued that what matters is not whether the entity demanding self-determination is a community at this point in time; what matters (from the instrumental point of view) is whether over the long run it is going to become a community. If so, then providing it with a state will promote communal values. While there is a valid point along these lines, it remains the case that this test has never been employed either.

account for the fact that nationalists typically have a particular piece of territory in mind when they demand statehood. This third point is really a corollary of the second. If there are other ways to provide for a flourishing community that are at least as good from the instrumental point of view, then the particular claim that the nationalist is making need not be granted. If regional autonomy or separate language schools would do as well, then independent statehood is not necessary; this is the second point, namely that different *types* of remedies might work. But if offering separate statehood in some other location were an option, this also would undercut the nationalist claim to separate statehood on what the nationalists see as their historic homeland. If we could offer the Palestinians (or Serbians or Chechnyans) a piece of uninhabited land elsewhere on the globe, they would have no good reason not to take it.

Of course, there are practical objections to this argument. A first objection is that rarely does some other plot of land exist that presents a practical option for resettlement. But even if in many cases there is no other plot of land for resettlement, there will often be a possibility of giving the nationalists only a part of what they want. A fraction of the land that they claim might be adequate as a practical matter to found a flourishing cultural community, yet such an offer of compromise is unlikely to be welcomed with enthusiasm. A second objection is that there are likely to be certain cases where the argument can be made from a cultural point of view that a particular piece of ground is unique. Jerusalem and Sarajevo are cases in point. It may be that, to preserve Israeli or Palestinian culture, one must give it access to Jerusalem; to preserve Bosnian Serb or Bosnian Muslim culture, one must give it part or all of Sarajevo. The fact that competing claims can be made on both sides of the argument (Israeli and Palestinian, Serb and Muslim) suggests, however, that there must be more to the story of resolving nationalist claims than deciding whether they are central to cultural flourishing; for there must be ways to decide how competing claims to unique and necessary cultural resources are to be adjudicated.

Perhaps these problems are to be resolved purely and simply by asking what division of the land in question will best promote communal values and then letting the territorial chips fall where they may. Philosophers may think so. But this is unlikely to satisfy nationalists. The difference between the philosophical account under consideration and most actual nationalist sentiments is roughly as follows. In the philosophers' view, recognition of nationalist claims is a means to an end. Nationalist claims are not right or wrong independently and in their own right. They are right or wrong only insofar as they further some particular other goal (in particular, the goal of community flourishing). According to the nationalists themselves, however, they should not have to show that, if they are given what they want, it will further these other values. It should not matter that they are not a community in the philosophical sense, or that some solution other than national statehood would do as good a job of promoting community, or that statehood on some other (or smaller) piece of land would do as well. In their eyes, they are entitled to what they claim independently of whether it would do anyone, or anything, or any value any good. From this point of view, part of the very nature of the claimed entitlement is that it need not be justified by reference to any other values.

Compare such a description of nationalist claims to the posture of a legal claimant who comes to an adjudicator seeking compensation from someone else who (it is claimed) has done him or her wrong. Say, for instance, that a plaintiff in a torts case demands compensation on the grounds that the defendant negligently manufactured a product that injured her. If the court asked the plaintiff to show that she was going to put the money to some good use (or to a better use than the defendant would put it), this would be failing to respond to her claim that she has an entitlement that need not be justified on other, instrumental, grounds. If she is correct that she has a valid legal claim, then she should get the money regardless. If she is incorrect, she should not get the money; again, this is regardless of the fact that awarding her a judgment would promote some other, instrumental, value. Nationalists, similarly, feel that they are entitled independently, whether or not granting them what they want would happen to further other values that the world recognizes. The peoples of the Baltic states felt that they were entitled to independence because they had wrongfully been annexed fifty years earlier by the Soviet Union. The Serbs of Bosnia have similar beliefs, as do the Palestinians (and the Israelis before them.)

Of course, to say that this is how nationalists see their claims is not to show that they are right; perhaps they are wrong, and the instrumental account is correct. (It is also, needless to say, not the same as saying that they are right on the merits of the particular claims they make; that must be independently decided.) In two earlier articles, I offered reasons for thinking that the nationalist version of the debate has the better of the argument, that these independent claims are what we ought mainly to be considering when we ask whether nationalist demands are justified.[8] In evaluating what nationalists do, we should ask both whether their nation is entitled to the thing that they demand for it and whether the means that they employ to gain their ends are legitimate under the circumstances. Both questions can be posed independently of whether the entity raising the claim is a nation or whether giving the entity what it wants will

[8] See *The Moral Significance of Nationalism,* and *Secession and Self-Determination, supra* note 2.

promote national flourishing. We will return to the choice between these two ways of interpreting nationalist conflicts in the final section of this chapter.

But first we should face another issue: why has there been so much attention to communal flourishing, if not because nationalism is instrumental to achieving it? If the argument against an instrumental account of nationalism is correct, does that mean that all the talk about communal values is irrelevant? Not necessarily. There is another way to view the matter that also makes communal values crucial, though at a different level. Instead of seeing community as giving instrumental value to nationalist sentiment, we might understand communal values as providing a foundation for the institutions that create the entitlements that nationalists claim. According to this view, the institution on which nationalists rely in making their independent claims to entitlements is territorial sovereignty, and their entitlements are largely based on arguments of corrective justice.

II. THE INSTITUTIONAL VIEW

The institutional and instrumental views of nationalism have in common that both explain nationalism in terms of its contribution to communal flourishing. They differ over whether to consult communal flourishing directly in deciding the legitimacy of particular nationalist claims. The institutional interpretation of nationalism is content to retire communal values from service once they have served their purpose in setting up institutions; particular cases are then resolved by consulting the institutional principles that create institutional entitlements. To make the institutional account more plausible, we need to say something more about what entitlements nationalists think they have and how these can be explained in terms of existing legal and political institutions in the international setting and in terms of the promotion of communal values. The entitlements that nationalists claim are largely territorial and historical.

That they are generally territorial is evident. The claims generally take the form of a demand for a territorial state of the sort that the international system will recognize (or, at a minimum, for greater regional autonomy, which is also a territorial claim, although a more diluted one). Thus, during the decolonization movement the nationalists fighting for independence sought to establish territorial nation-states with status equal to the colonial powers. Nigeria, Ghana, India, and Pakistan (to name just a few) sought recognition as politically independent territories. This is not to say that no demands were made that could have been met in some other way. There were a few colonies that merely wanted greater political autonomy while remaining a politically subordinate entity within the

British Commonwealth. And certainly there were complaints about deprivations of human rights that could have been remedied through means other than territorial independence (say, by giving inhabitants the right to vote in the elections of the colonial power or by taking measures to eradicate racial discrimination). But by and large the evil that the decolonization movement sought to remedy was unjust territorial annexation, and the remedy that was sought was a return to the inhabitants of political sovereignty over the colonial territory.

The same is true of other nationalist movements. In the Baltic states, the thrust of the nationalist movements was to regain political sovereignty that had been wrongfully extinguished by Stalin's annexation. In northern Sri Lanka, Kashmir, and the former Yugoslavia, nationalists fight to gain political control over territory that (in their view) they have been wrongfully denied. Nationalists fought the United States–supported South Vietnamese army and the South African–supported regime in Namibia. In all of these cases, the goal was consolidation of political control over a particular piece of land.

The point that it was a particular piece of land is an important one. We just noted that a purely instrumental interpretation of nationalism, which assigns it moral value only if its objective is the flourishing of national culture, does a poor job of explaining why some particular piece of land is uniquely important. It is entirely plausible, as liberal philosophers have claimed, that culture often necessitates sufficient public space to engage in the sorts of activities that people find culturally worthwhile: arts and entertainment, political discussion, and intellectual debate.[9] But why do nationalists seem so committed to the chance to do these things in one particular place? And if one offered to give them half the land they claimed (assuming that it was large enough to stage such activities), why would they feel this to be insufficient? The reason is that they believe the land in question is already theirs—that this particular piece of land is already theirs—rather than being something for the international system to allocate in whatever way will best promote the general flourishing of cultures.

If the objects of these claims are territorial, then the basis for them is typically historical.[10] Ask a nationalist why he or she feels entitled to the particular piece of land he or she claims, and you will probably get a historical account. It may relate to colonial conquest, or to wrongful an-

[9] This is one of Yael Tamir's points. See chapter 3 of LIBERAL NATIONALISM, supra note 1, especially pages 69–77.

[10] Tamir disputes the claim that nationalist claims are essentially historical by pointing out that there are some groups that have suffered historically but are not entitled to states of their own—for example, women and gays. Id. at 82–83. But this does not follow logically, for the position that some historical injustices (namely, nationalist ones) call for a territorial remedy cannot be refuted by saying that there are some that do not. It is only territorial historical wrongs—wrongful takings of territory—that call out for such a remedy, and my argument is that nationalist claims typically assert such a territorial historical wrong.

nexation, or to an illegitimate influx of outsiders that threatens the political control of the indigenous group, but it will probably be based on arguments about corrective justice. Nationalists know that in our present international system, historical pedigree is essential to claims to land. So Israelis and Palestinians offer their competing accounts of what was going on in a certain piece of territory around the turn of the twentieth century and in the decades that followed; Japanese and Korean historians dispute whether the annexation of Korea (about the same historical time) was voluntary; and Serbs, Muslims, and Croats disagree about who was right and wrong during the last few centuries of warfare in the area that came to be known as Yugoslavia.

As with the characterization of nationalist disputes as "largely" over territory, it is best to describe them as "largely" founded on historical arguments about corrective justice. Many elements come together in these passionate debates. A dispute that is largely territorial, such as the Japanese annexation of Korea, can also have monetary (or other) aspects—for instance, if monetary damages (or an apology) is sought. A dispute that is largely based upon corrective justice, such as decolonization, can also have an element of avoiding further political injustice in the future. What links these mixtures of elements? An important part of the reason that nationalists feel that a remedy is morally appropriate is a sense of entitlement that follows from a historical violation of territorial sovereignty. History and the territorial claims that only history is thought capable of establishing are conceived to be essential to the claims that nationalists make on their nation's behalf.

Note that, if such a claim exists, it will not matter whether the group in question is homogeneous along linguistic, cultural, religious, or ethnic lines. The newly freed colonial nations were notoriously diverse in these respects, and no one thought that this created principled objections to their claim to freedom. The unity that might be needed as a practical matter to fight successfully for independence (or to govern afterward) can be a consequence of the existence of a claim, because a product of shared historical injustice, rather than its source. The group in question, in many cases, did not exist prior to the historical wrong. It should not be a surprise that it has been difficult to pinpoint precisely what features characterize nationalist movements; for neither language, culture, nor any of the other supposedly identifying features is something that nationalistic movements universally possess. It is generally acknowledged that there is a large subjective element in whatever ties a national movement together; what matters is that fellow nationals feel like they are part of the same nation. Benedict Anderson's phrase "imagined community" has proven popular in efforts to express this subjectivity.[11] But even if this is subjec-

[11] BENEDICT ANDERSON, IMAGINED COMMUNITIES (1983).

tive, it is not *entirely* subjective. Nationalists do not just imagine that they share something; they actually do. What they share commonly arises out of shared history and, in particular, what they perceive as historical injustice.

If we attempt to push this inquiry one step further, we might ask why history should matter. Why, after all, should rights to territory be explainable in terms of historical pedigree? My object here is not to give an answer to this problem (which is probably fortunate, considering the difficulty of the question) but to make some observations about the sort of answer we might think is successful. A successful answer would probably have to do, at least in part, with the rights of people who have lived on a particular piece of land to continue to do so and to continue to regulate their affairs free from outside interference. It would combine elements of reasoning about community (such as those I have outlined in speaking of the instrumental justification for nationalism) with elements of reasoning about historical continuity and sense of place. Historical rights to territory somehow vest; and it is reasonable to think that they need to vest if values of community are to be preserved.

In short, the entitlements that nationalists are ultimately relying on are grounded in a system of territorial sovereignty for international states, and this system itself can be explained in terms of its value to human community. Territorial sovereignty provides the historical continuity that communities need to flourish. But it must be territorial sovereignty over time; it cannot be completely renegotiated every time some new and potentially worthwhile community makes a claim that it, too, needs a state. Existing groups with existing territorial claims must be entitled to continue to exist and exercise authority over their land. This is not to say that land can never, under any circumstances, change hands or that wrongful changes cannot ever acquire legitimacy of their own over time. The regime of territorial sovereignty for states has developed principles that limit changes, though; and while no one claims that these are adequately protected by existing legal institutions, there is substantial consensus about the proper moral view of territorial aggression in its most straightforward manifestations.

The existence of principles of territorial sovereignty explains why nationalists feel entitled to particular pieces of land, and it does so in a way that is consistent with the logic of communal values.[12] There are other

12 It also underlies the particularization of political obligation itself; for as A. J. Simmons has pointed out, political obligation cannot be explained solely by the substantive justice of a state. If it could, then everyone would have an equal obligation to support all equally just states. *See generally* A. J. SIMMONS, MORAL PRINCIPLES AND POLITICAL OBLIGATIONS (1979); on the connection between this problem and territoriality, see my JUSTIFYING INTERNATIONAL ACTS, chap. 3 (1989). Which state one has an obligation to support is a function both of where one happens to be located when one acts and what community one is a member of (which is

ways that territorial claims might be philosophically grounded. One might accept something like the labor theory of value and believe that groups come to have rights to land by "mixing their labor with it"—by using their labor, in other words, to improve upon it. Such an explanation would build on the analogy between ownership of property and sovereignty over territory. Or one might accept some religiously based theory of sovereignty rights, or one might develop another theory altogether. The point I am making here is not that the only way to justify regimes of territorial sovereignty is through reference to communal values; the point is merely that institutional explanations are not at war with community values. Community can play a role in making nationalist arguments by giving reasons for having a system of territorial entitlements. In accepting such a scheme, one is relying on these values in the justification for a particular set of regulatory institutions, which nationalist arguments could then be framed by reference to.

The analogy to ownership of property is, in fact, illuminating. One might, analogously, justify the institution of property in terms of its value to human flourishing (on the grounds that the ability to own a house, or personal effects, or artistic creations, or professional implements creates opportunities for personal identity creation that would not otherwise exist). But this does not mean that disputes over who owns what have to be governed by direct reference to those values. Once the institution of property is recognized, it can itself provide the principles for allocating property and for deciding what to do in case of conflict. One would not ordinarily decide who should own a particular piece of art by asking who will most appreciate it but by asking about principles relating to ownership.[13] Institutional questions would control, questions shaped by the contours of the system of private property in the particular political, moral, and legal climate in which one found oneself. Is there a contractual right? Does one of the parties claim through inheritance? If the work in question was stolen, did the present possessor come to have the artwork in good faith? And so on. Such questions would be resolved by reference to institutional entitlements even though in particular cases an argument

---

itself, as I have argued, a function of the fact that communities have historic ties to particular pieces of land). What matters here about the way the logic runs is that, while community plays a part in grounding the system of entitlements, it does not play an immediate and direct part in adjudicating particular disputes. Particular claims and counterclaims are, instead, evaluated by reference to the principles established to protect the vested rights that the community depends upon.

[13] This is not to say that there is anything morally outrageous or logically inconsistent about a system in which art is allocated on such a basis, only that most systems of private property do not take this position. The point is that the institutions of private property may reflect a desire to make it possible for people to own works of art that they will appreciate immensely yet may not allocate individual works of art on that basis as a case-by-case matter.

could be made that some other allocation would better suit the underlying purposes of human flourishing through property ownership. The existence of institutional principles would make the institution opaque to what the underlying value justification might seem to require in a particular case.

There are many issues raised by this account of nationalism (just as there are many issued raised by analogous accounts of individual property). One very important one is whether complete opacity is ever really called for. Might there not be cases where the underlying values themselves are so compelling that they warrant an exception to the principles and direct recourse to the underlying values instead? If the institutional principles are themselves only instrumental to the underlying values, then, although it would usually serve the values best to follow the principles, there might be exceptions. This issue resembles the familiar problem of whether consequentialist justifications of rules of ethics are really watertight. Won't exceptions be justifiable in those unusual cases where the desirable consequences outweigh the desirable consequences of sticking to the rules? The same question can occur with an account of territorial sovereignty that purports to create institutional entitlements by reference to other, communal, values.

In an interesting way, exactly this question may account for some failures to join issue in particular current nationalist disputes. The special case of Israel pits a certain set of territorial claims (those held by today's Palestinians) against another (those held by the Israelis). There are two ways to understand the dispute. The first sees the dispute as a conventional one about historical pedigree according to the usual principles of territorial allocation. One would then consider who had been on the land, for how long, during what period of time, and how long ago.

But one can also introduce an additional factor: the claim that, unless Israel were given a state of its own, in its unique circumstances its people seemed likely to be completely annihilated. This argument changes the nature of the dispute, for arguments of need are not the usual sort in establishing territorial claims. Adding this argument to the rhetoric of the conflict presents the problem of whether to consult directly instrumental communal values of the sort we have already described. As an instrumental argument, it raises all of the problems that we have already described with justifying nationalist struggles in instrumental terms; there might be other ways to satisfy the instrumental objectives, instrumental objectives do not entitle one to a particular piece of territory, and so forth. Most important, those who think that they have entitlements resist having those entitlements taken away on instrumental grounds. Palestinians respond, therefore, that instrumental considerations about communal protection for the Jewish people are extraneous to the merits of the dispute;

that if something needs to be done to create the state of Israel, it should not be done at their expense. These are arguments for continuing to respect the usual entitlement rules and for not disrupting the rights that (in the Palestinian view) these usual rules of territorial sovereignty create. The Israeli and Palestinian arguments are importantly different in kind; the former appeals to instrumental values directly, while the latter rests on institutional entitlements.[14]

As this example illustrates, there is room for considerable disagreement over whether (and, if so, how commonly) to consult the values of community flourishing directly. At one end of the spectrum, we might use them only once, in setting up the principles, and then retire them forever. At the other end, we might employ them as a matter of first resort. Someplace in between would fall the position that the underlying values should only be consulted when there is an ambiguity or gap in the institutional principles so that there are no entitlements to upset. Also in the middle, but importantly slanted toward the instrumental point of view, would be the position that the institutional point of view presented the point of departure for analysis but that in case of conflict the instrumental values should be more important. This is similar to a standard of defeasible entitlements, to which we will turn in a moment. To say that nationalist claims might be founded indirectly on values of communal flourishing because they might be founded on entitlements that are justified in terms of those values does not provide an answer to the question of how seriously to take those institutional entitlements when they come into conflict with the values themselves.

So we still need to consider the question of how opaque to make the institutions we create. Perhaps nationalists are wrong in thinking that the justice of their cause should be determined by reference solely to these rules. Perhaps such rules, and the entitlements they seem to establish, should not be granted any entrenched moral status; perhaps these entitlements ought always to be subject to renegotiation according to whether they promote the value of community flourishing directly. The difference between the argument that nationalist claims should be resolved by reference to nationalist entitlements and the argument that nationalism is at most instrumental to communal values may, therefore, be a disagreement about the proper degree of institutional entrenchment. Nationalists typically seem to take institutional entrenchment, and entitlements, quite

[14] This is not, of course, to say that there are not other sorts of arguments for the Palestinian and Israeli positions that do not fit this mold. Either side might appeal to religious principles, or the Israelis might argue that their opponents forfeited all territorial rights by declaring war on the Israeli state just after it was founded, or the Palestinians might claim that Israeli human rights abuses result in forfeiture of whatever claims Israel had, and so forth. My claim is only that there are ways in which some of the arguments made on the opposing side can be seen as fitting into the pattern I describe.

seriously. So, for that matter, does the position I have staked out in earlier articles. But perhaps they (and I) are wrong. That question is next on the agenda.

III. Defeasible Entitlements

If we were to try to reconcile the institutional and the instrumental views of nationalism, we might do so by employing an approach based on defeasible entitlements. These would be entitlements only of a prima facie sort, in the same way that "rules of thumb" are only prima facie rules. They guide action in many or most cases, but they really only summarize what the more compelling underlying values require. Whenever those values depart from what the entitlements (or the rules of thumb) provide, the underlying values govern rather than the entitlements. National territorial sovereignty would then provide a general set of principles that would in most instances give the same result as directly protecting communal values, but these principles of national territorial entitlement would have no more than instrumental value. They would be wholly derivative and subject to defeasance whenever the two sets of values came into conflict.

There are real practical attractions to following the route just described, to assigning national territorial rights a purely derivative status. On the one hand, it recognizes that territorial sovereignty will often be a positive force toward fostering community: first, because it gives groups historical continuity; second, because a regime of territorial rights discourages destructive fighting over the right to possession of land. On the other hand, it stops short of offering full entitlements; and the reasons that this is attractive are particularly vivid in light of contemporary events, when the costs of seeing things in terms of national territorial entitlements are so vivid. Some of the most unattractive aspects of nationalist conflict may be related to the fact that participants are motivated by their sense of their own entitlements to do things that from any other point of view seem quite appalling. Placing entitlements in a secondary status, as subject always to the overriding values of human community, promises to make nationalism more philosophically presentable. Indeed, it is easy to interpret the current philosophical interest in reducing nationalism to underlying communal values as partly motivated by a general need to domesticate nationalism, to counteract its most vicious tendencies by focusing on those aspects that are philosophically more tractable.

So we need to say more about why an approach based on defeasible entitlements has these virtues. As I just suggested, it seems entirely plausible that a substantial part of the viciousness of current national battles is traceable, in practice, to the righteousness that typically characterizes both sides of the dispute. Partly this is because entitlements are an all-or-nothing matter. If you are convinced that you are in the right, then your opponents must (in your view) be in the wrong. The fact that they are behaving wrongly suggests that they are malicious. And if they are in the wrong, and malicious, then you need not listen to their evidence or arguments. You certainly do not need to take their interests, fears, or desires into account. And there is no reason to consider compromise, for you would be giving up something to which you were entitled in order to get back nothing more than that to which you were already entitled.

The very notion of entitlements puts a problem in its most emotional light. This is true in two ways. First, when one side is actually entitled, or feels entitled, then there is almost a moral obligation not to bow down to injustice. This is true even when there seem to be practical reasons for compromise; emotional commitments to the justice of one's cause make it impossible to settle disputes. When one's entitlements are absolute, to compromise is a sign of weakness. This is more true when injustice to fellow nationals is alleged than when the motive is vindication of one's own rights. One is entitled to compromise one's own just claim; there is no shame in deciding that vindication is not worth the price. Indeed, compromise of one's own interests can be an act of generosity. When the sacrifices and interests of one's fellow nationals are at stake, however, compromise seems the act of a traitor. The logic of group behavior, when combined with the rhetoric of entitlements, is potentially both poisonous and explosive.

Second, phrasing things in terms of entitlements makes it all the more likely that a group will mistakenly conclude that it is actually in the right. In a case where compromise is called for, right and wrong seem a question of degree. An error one way or the other does not matter so much. When one senses keenly that matters of justice are involved, however, one becomes unwilling to risk an error that compromises principles. One looks with care for every evidence of injustice, for every slight or wrong. A moral understanding of the question that encourages those involved to see things this way makes matters worse, it can be plausibly argued, because it discourages close self-criticism and encourages a romantic and narcissistic idealization of one's nation's claims.

In gauging the impact of the rhetoric of entitlements we should not, of course, make the mistake of assuming that only one set of motivations is at work and, in particular, that the motivations of the elites are the same as the motivations of those who bear the burden of the conflict. There are often differences—both in terms of access to information and in terms of political motivation—between those who lead and those who follow. But we do not have to assume that the elites are honestly motivated by a sincere concern for what they genuinely believe to be their entitlements to worry about the rhetorical impact of nationalist framing of a conflict. Indeed, the concern for the impact of nationalist rhetoric should be particularly great given the possibility of differences of motivation and information. It is easier to manipulate public images and the factual beliefs of those who are called upon to fight if the problem can be framed in terms of justice and injustice. The emotionality of a discourse of entitlements combined with the sense that compromise is an affront to justice make the general population more vulnerable to cynical manipulation by elites.

Indeed, there have been circumstances when cynical leaders have taken advantage of exactly this dynamic in manufacturing popular support for policies that are disastrous in terms of both national interests and human rights.[15] By committing injustices, those in control can provoke reprisals that then seem to justify the retaliatory acts one had been planning all along. Seeing things in terms of justice, injustice, and entitlements—instead of toleration, forgiveness, and compromise—encourages an infinite chain of retaliation and retribution. One might well want to think twice before encouraging the use of the language of sovereign entitlements in the nationalist context or giving it one's philosophical blessing.

All of these points may be particularly important when the subject of the entitlements is territory. Territorial rights are vivid in a way that few other things are. Land is tied to blood, because it is both the land of one's ancestors and (as a source of food and a place to live) the land of one's descendants. It is also absolutely central in the quest for military security; for even in an age of ballistic missiles, most wars are fought "on the cheap," and the more usual weapons are land mines, guns, and so forth. Certainly it is possible to kill and die for less tangible prizes, such as the right to practice one's religion (or the chance to impose one's religion) or for vengeance for past abuses. But it is harder to villify one's opponents if one expects to have to live with them afterward. The logic of territoriality suggests that one can afford to do this because, if one wins and either exterminates one's enemies or drives them out, one does not have to live with the untoward consequences of their hatred for you.

Now, there is an important response to this line of argument that needs to be addressed. The fact that people may abuse a concept of territorial entitlements does not mean that the notion of entitlements should be abandoned; instead, the solution seems to be to provide better ways of determining the moral entitlements to territory that actually exist. Justice and injustice do not cease to matter just because some people misunderstand what they consist of. While it is true that cynical individuals may manipulate popular opinion by appealing to a misplaced sense of griev-

---

[15] I thank Chip Gagnon for emphasizing the importance of this point.

ance, and that individuals may on their own be carried away by an inflated view of what they see as their entitlements, these objections do not mean that entitlements and justice are not real or that we should alter our ways of thinking. Instead, the proper remedy is to create a forum in which all sides of the issue can be aired fully and dispassionately. What is needed, in other words, is an appropriate institutional setting for making and recognizing national sovereignty claims. In such a setting, untoward passions could be diffused, and calm and reasoned investigation of territorial entitlement claims would be encouraged.

Certainly, if national territorial sovereignty is to continue to have the place in popular political imagination that it currently does, it would be highly desirable to have opportunities for balanced and sensitive consideration of the moral claims that national groups make. The problem with this line of reasoning lies not in any theoretical lack of philosophical appeal but in the practical impediments to its implementation. One difficulty is that providing a forum for the airing and calm consideration of national sovereignty claims is not likely to recommend itself to established states that are fighting nationalist movements. Often they are not particularly amenable even to negotiations or discussions about putting an end to conflict, even though such discussions do not require them to concede that they have violated someone else's rights. How are they likely to feel about a forum for discussing the right and wrong of the matter? There seems to be little incentive for an existing government to commit itself to impartial adjudication of whether it has violated the entitlements of the national groups that oppose it.

This is a specific example of a rather general point.[16] The international system, as it is presently constituted, is not well situated to pursue corrective justice. The mechanisms of international law and politics that currently exist are reasonably well adapted to facilitating compromise and implementing solutions that are beneficial to all parties in a dispute. This is a substantial achievement and should not be underestimated. But if nationalist disputes are seen to be based on claims of corrective justice, international law will not have much to do that is useful in solving them. The particular mechanisms that international law has at its disposal do not include the ability to force actors (and, in particular, state actors) to go along with things that are intrinsically not in their interests.

National territorial claims are likely to be particularly difficult for the international system to resolve. Whenever a dispute is essentially zero sum, it will be difficult to resolve from an international legal point of view due to the inability of international law to compel reallocation of re-

---

[16] For a more general discussion of this point, see my *International Justice and International Law*, 98 W. VA. L. REV. 611 (1996).

sources from one party to another as opposed to facilitating mutually beneficial solutions. Territorial disputes, however, present the most intractable of cases because each piece of territory is unique. In situations where corrective justice can be achieved through some form of financial compensation, there is at least the possibility that contribution from the international community at large might alter parties' perception that whatever goes to one of them comes out of the pocket of the other. The Camp David peace accords, for example, were possible because the United States was willing to commit itself to substantial financial assistance to both participants. Such willingness on the part of outside parties is not relevant where territory is at issue. There is only a fixed amount of territory in the world; and more to the point, with nationalist claims the claim is precisely for a particular piece of nonfungible land.

Thus, we cannot avoid the fact that, if national disputes are conceived in terms of territorial entitlements, they are likely to be emotional, brutal, and invulnerable to the well-intentioned efforts of the international community to solve them. If the ugliness of today's nationalistic conflicts is a direct consequence of the fact that the participants see the conflicts in such uncompromising terms, then it would be genuinely an advance if we could look beyond our current habits of conceptualization to understandings that were more supportive of compromise and mutual reconciliation. The "best" understanding of nationalism might be one that not only highlights the most morally defensible aspects of nationalism but also leads to the most morally desirable state of world affairs. The fact that seeing things in terms of corrective justice leads to violence while seeing things in terms of the underlying community values (with, at most, a defeasible commitment to national territorial rights) leads to reconciliation and tolerance might be what really matters, even if nationalists themselves are convinced that territorial entitlements are the real issue. To put it another way, philosophical condemnation of nationalist rhetoric may lead to a morally second-best solution compared to a first-best solution of effective implementation of international corrective justice; but given that the only realistic alternative is a far distant third (namely, incessant and inhumanly bloody conflict), it is perhaps the solution that should be philosophically supported.

There may indeed be substantial room for mutually beneficial accommodation if the single-minded quest for corrective justice is abandoned and nationalist claims are reconstructed in terms of something closer to defeasible or prima facie entitlements. Yael Tamir, for one, has addressed some of the parameters of such a reconstruction.[17] The object would be to create greater opportunities for national self-determination in the cultural

---

[17] See LIBERAL NATIONALISM, *supra* note 1, at chap. 7, especially pages 150–67.

sense by letting go of the assumption that self-determination must be expressed territorially and in the form of a traditional international state. Letting go of this assumption would open the way to other forms of national self-expression. These might include greater political autonomy within existing territorial states (regional self-governance) or various forms of support for private or semiprivate cultural groups that do not possess formal law-making authority (schools, churches, museums, popular entertainment centers, and so forth). Devolution of political and legal power might end either by the current nationalist challenger having equal status with the currently dominant group or with the current challenger continuing on in some sort of minority status but with special rights and protections. The hope would be that offering either some degree of legal and political autonomy or some support for national culture would satisfy national aspirations in a way that stops short of full international statehood.

Regardless of whether the resulting political structure is hierarchical or equal, and regardless of what special political protections or economic subsidies are provided to the minority group, what differentiates this vision from one based on territorial entitlements is that, from the entitlements point of view, it necessarily provides either too much or too little political and cultural autonomy for the nationalist challengers. It is too much autonomy if the nationalist group in question did not, in fact, have a good claim to independence; for a political structure was set up on land properly owned by the dominant group even when the formerly subordinate group lacked a good entitlement. It is too little autonomy if the challengers were, in fact, entitled to full independent statehood; for they ended up with something less. Exactly how much too much, or how much too little, depends upon the degree of autonomy provided and how the challenger group's new status compares to the status of the formerly dominant group. But precisely the distinguishing feature of such an approach is that those entitlements would not provide the measure of the political and cultural autonomy to be delivered.

Yet a group's legitimate historical interest in the territory that it claims might still be considered a defeasible entitlement whether that group was a state or a nonstate nationalist challenger. A state's territorial status in the international legal system would be secure so long as it was not challenged by a nationalist group seeking greater autonomy, whether cultural or political. At the point that a challenge was raised, its continued status as a traditional territorial state would be put in question. At that point, it would not automatically be the case that devolution would occur. As we have already recognized, there is considerable value in continuity of existing territorial political units, even if one's first priority is the furtherance of the values of community. The existing state order does, after all, contin-

ue to have instrumental value; it simply fails to provide an airtight entitlement against the onslaught of nationalist claims that also are based on
community values. The proper response when a nationalist challenge is
raised, then, would be a case-specific inquiry into whether community
values are better served by maintaining the existing political order or by
dividing political authority and requiring greater support for cultural
autonomy.

It may be that close cases would have to be decided according to a
presumption in favor of the existing order, and in that sense territorial
states would still be privileged entities. But their degree of privilege
would be considerably diminished. The status quo would be entitled to
nothing more than presumptive status. Conversely, the historically legitimate claims of nonstate nationalist challengers would likewise not be
given conclusive weight; they, too, would have to justify their claims in
terms of the ability to further the underlying community-based values. To
rise to a level of international political recognition, nationalist claims
would have to be founded on their instrumental value in promoting morally cognizable group cultural solidarity.

IV. The Problem with Defeasible Entitlements

An approach based on defeasible entitlements, it might be said, is nothing more than an instrumental calculation decorated with the trappings of
entitlement. In an important sense, this is so; for when instrumental values and entitlements come into conflict, the instrumental values always
win. Yet if it effects mutually beneficial compromises, promotes tolerance,
discourages retaliation and retribution, defeats national prejudices, and at
the same time protects the most important underlying values—communal flourishing—this seems an unbeatable combination. No doubt it
would be difficult to implement, considering the resistance it would face
from the protectors of the statist status quo, but who could deny its
attraction in theory? The chief problem that I want to raise with an approach based on defeasible entitlements is that it does not square with
other aspects of the international political system.

The problem arises from the fact that what nationalists demand is nothing more nor less than that their claims should be judged in the same way
that corrective justice claims, generally, are judged. They are not asking
(in their own view) for any special consideration just because they are
fighting on behalf of a nation as opposed to some other sort of international entity. They dispute the apparent premise in international law that they
are entitled to nothing simply because of the fact that they are not internationally recognized states. What they seek is something that is already

granted to certain other sorts of political groupings, namely the territorial sovereignty rights based on corrective justice that recognized states would have.

Any response to their demands that is based on the premise that territorial sovereignty is itself not fully justified—that there should be only defeasible territorial rights, always subject to reexamination in light of community values—must therefore take a position on whether territorial sovereignty will still be the norm in other sorts of international disputes. If the logic I have outlined about reducing territorial sovereignty to at most a prima facie claim is actually convincing, then it should be just as convincing in other areas. Thus, for example, border disputes between neighboring countries or the moral justifiability of attempts to roll back illegitimate conquest would have to be resolved on the basis of the same argument about underlying communal values. It would be easier to deny nationalists what they are demanding if in fact they are claiming something special by virtue of their national status, as philosophers seem to be assuming—if, for example, they argue that linguistic or cultural homogeneity entitles them to more than what other sorts of groups are getting. But to deny their territorial entitlements on the ground that absolute entitlements should not exist, when territorial entitlements generally are still recognized as compelling, is more difficult to explain. There are several possible responses to this challenge.

The first would simply be to concede the point. Some philosophers might be perfectly content to do away altogether with any absolutist notions of territorial sovereignty and entitlement. Territorial entitlements are something of a philosophical embarrassment anyway; there currently exists no really good explanation for territorial sovereignty, and the institutional view I have outlined presents nothing more than the barest hint of what an adequate explanation might look like. In addition, territorial sovereignty is often used toward bad ends, such as to bar international scrutiny of domestic human rights abuses or to deny entrance to refugees. Why not just pay the price of philosophical consistency and admit that no groups of any kind have anything more than defeasible entitlements?

One reason is that it is not entirely clear that the logic about underlying communal values can be contained so easily, limited to cases where we might wish to do away with territorial sovereignty. A large part of the argument applies to all sorts of claims based on corrective justice because it amounts to a rejection of entitlements in favor of instrumental reasoning. If this is the price to pay for employing defeasible entitlements in the nationalist context, then it is a high one.

In addition, consistency on this issue is a trifle utopian. Today's political actors are not, to put it mildly, about to do away with the territorial state system. More to the point, if one were willing to be utopian, why favor this solution over other utopian ones? If one's solution does not need to be practical, then the problems become much easier regardless of which analysis of nationalism one adopts. Yes, of course, one can maintain that nationalists are not entitled to an internationally sovereign state if one decides in effect that no group is entitled to an internationally sovereign state either. As long as we are willing to imagine quite radical solutions, however, we could as well start planning for a world court that could adjudicate territorial entitlements and solve the whole problem within a more traditional corrective justice framework. Why not just decide that the problem would be solved if only there were a world government?

The second approach would probably be the preferred one, then: to try to find some way to explain the selectivity of applying the instrumental logic, with its notion of defeasible entitlements, only to nationalist claims. Here, two related questions arise. First, to which claims are we to apply the notion of defeasible entitlements and to which a more absolutist approach based on corrective justice? What, in other words, is the domain of defeasible entitlements? Second, what is the justification for treating the two sets of cases differently? Obviously the answer to this second question is dependent on the answer to the first, for the justification for different treatment will turn in important ways on how the line between the two different categories is drawn.

With regard to the question about proper domain, it is not entirely clear what proponents of different treatment would suggest. It is not clear, in other words, what disputes philosophers see as falling into the nationalist category. The question is difficult; for while some very traditional territorial disputes between existing states might be referred to as nationalistic, it is not clear that we would want to approach them instrumentally rather than in terms of corrective justice. Was the dispute between Argentina and Great Britain over the Malvinas/Falklands a nationalist dispute? What about the border dispute between Ecuador and Peru? Should either be approached from within a purely instrumental framework?

International law has a rough answer to this question. Disputes between states are, usually, treated differently from disputes between nonstate actors or between a state and a nonstate actor. By and large, national groups that are not also state actors receive distinctly second-class status (what that means, actually, is usually that they receive nothing). Thus, there is a general lack of international legal support for secessionist movements. The virtue of this solution is its relatively clarity; it is at least clear, for the most part, which type of case is which.[18] But that may be its only virtue. It is unlikely to have much appeal to those who are thinking of the

---

[18] It would not be correct, of course, to assume that no problems of categorization will arise. There are difficulties at the margin. Is the Vatican a state? Is Taiwan a state? And so forth.

morality (as opposed to the legality) of the question; for it is unattractively statist, and its statism cannot be defended on communitarian grounds because the state in question may resemble a community less than the national movement currently challenging it does. The position is also unlikely to go far in terms of facilitating compromise and conflict resolution, for it offers little to nationalists to induce them to lay down their guns.

Perhaps philosophers have not addressed this question of domain because they take it as obvious that nationalist disputes are truly distinctive. Nationalist claims are ones that are made on behalf of culturally, linguistically, or ethnically homogeneous entities and that rely in some way on the fact of homogeneity in arguing for their claim. Yet as I have already argued, many if not most nationalist claims do not fit this pattern. National groups are often culturally, linguistically, or ethnically diverse. And frequently the claims that they make are indistinguishable in content from the claims to corrective justice that would be made by other sorts of entities: they do not make homogeneity central to the argument, even when homogeneity exists. In both nationalist and other sorts of disputes, the parties may be homogeneous or diverse, and the merits of both sorts of claims may be indistinguishable. Thus, treating the domain of defeasible entitlements as being disputes that are nationalist in this sense leaves a lot of corrective justice claims intact.

The inability to distinguish between the two sorts of cases exacerbates the second issue, namely the question of justification. If the parties and the merits are virtually the same regardless of whether a dispute is classified as nationalistic or not, then why do they receive such different treatment? The problem is compounded by the fact that in some circumstances defeasible entitlements are more generous and in some circumstances they are less generous. As I have said, from the point of view of corrective justice, defeasible entitlements either provide too much (where corrective justice would provide no remedy at all) or too little (where a full corrective justice remedy would otherwise be appropriate). It would be hard enough to explain why nationalist challenges are always treated more favorably by virtue of the fact that they are nationalistic, or why they are always treated less favorably. But what is the explanation for the fact that they sometimes get a more generous reception and sometimes a less generous one?

Assume, for example, that we take seriously the notion that the point of recognizing nationalist claims is to promote the sort of cultural flourishing that is possible only in culturally homogeneous groups. The domain of the defeasible entitlement logic, then, would be culturally homogeneous national groups. If one assumes that otherwise such groups will be entitled to nothing, then perhaps this makes sense. By virtue of the fact that a group is culturally homogeneous, it will receive something when it would otherwise have been given nothing at all. The fact of cultural homogeneity, then, adds to the strength of a group's claim. But when one considers that a group might otherwise have a claim to full corrective justice, it does not seem an unalloyed benefit to qualify for augmented cultural rights. A group would actually lose its moral right to make a corrective justice claim by virtue of the fact that it is culturally homogeneous. This seems exceedingly odd.

Perhaps one solution might be that the claiming group gets the higher of the two remedies it is qualified for. If it is culturally homogeneous but has no corrective justice claim, then it only gets defeasible entitlements. If it has a corrective justice claim, then that is what it should, morally, be awarded. If it is diverse and has no argument based on corrective justice, then it gets nothing. While this has some appeal because it seems maximally to preserve the rights of groups challenging the status quo, it completely undercuts any chance to garner the hoped-for benefits of moving to a system of defeasible entitlements. Because there is still an option to continue to fight for a corrective justice remedy, groups will still engage in overheated rhetoric, villify their opponents, commit human rights abuses in the name of what they see as their entitlement to territorial sovereignty, and so forth.

All of this seems rather puzzling until one remembers the backdrop against which nationalist claims first started to receive legal and political recognition. At the end of World War I, there existed virtually no formal recognition of any international legal and political rights for nonstate actors. National groups that did not have their own states, at that point, would have been left with nothing without some protection on the grounds of their nationhood. If one takes this extreme statism as the starting point, then defeasible entitlements would be a clear advantage; at least national groups would be entitled to something. One could then say that this entitlement came about because the groups were homogeneous in the relevant sense. Or to put it another way, rhetoric about national self-determination that highlights homogeneity can be understood as an effort to claim for a national group a watered-down version of the rights of territorial states. The basis for the claim to these watered-down rights is that these groups are, essentially, watered-down states. Ordinarily they would have nothing because they are not states; but because they are homogeneous, they are quasi states, so they get quasi sovereignty entitlements—that is, defeasible entitlements.

But a line of argument that makes sense as a practical compromise given a world in which the only way to get something is to argue that you are "like" a traditional state is headed for some very deep philosophical water. As a philosophical matter, there is no reason to start with the

premise that nonstate actors get nothing. This is particularly true considering that nonstate actors can have moral claims based on corrective justice. One cannot avoid the worry, therefore, that a nation with a corrective
justice claim will be shortchanged by being limited to a defeasible entitlement. The fact that a nation is more statelike than certain other sorts of
groups does not explain why they are entitled to less than a full corrective
justice remedy.

The problem with defeasible entitlements is that, no matter what their
appeal, they are radically different from the ways in which we normally
think about territorial sovereignty and corrective justice. We are willing to
take this solution seriously in the context of nationalist disputes only if we
don't take nationalist disputes very seriously. The reason we don't take
them very seriously is, perhaps, because at some level we buy into the
idea (encouraged by international law) that nationalists have no right to
anything at all; therefore, offering them anything (even watered-down
entitlements) is better than nothing.

But nationalists do not see things this way. Like any other persons who
are fighting for what they think is just, they tend to compare their situation, and the compromises that are offered to them, with what they think
that they are entitled to. From this perspective, defeasible entitlements—
based on an instrumental view of what national claims are all about—is
completely unsatisfactory. Nationalists buy into the international system
of territorial sovereignty in very important ways. What they seek is, precisely, the benefits that it provides. Something less is not likely to satisfy
their claims.

Nor, I am suggesting, should it. If territorial sovereignty is a good thing,
and if corrective justice is worth pursuing, then both are good and worth
pursuing in all areas of international politics equally. Law may, perhaps,
make compromises with practicality, and in this sense it is not surprising
that international law does not purport to grant strong entitlements to
groups that challenge the statist status quo. But international morality
should shoulder the job of identifying ideals. In the present context the
ideal is to recognize and promote the cause of corrective justice and to
differentiate between nationalist claims that are based on justice and those
that are based on prejudice, self-interest, or misunderstanding. Unless
and until we are ready to abandon those ideals more generally, they are
the ideals that we should turn to in evaluating the normative worth of
nationalist claims.

3

Ethnicity, Human Rights, and Self-Determination

Fernando R. Tesón

Should groups defined by traits such as race, language, religion, or shared history (ethnic traits) receive special group rights over and above recognized human and democratic rights? Examples of such special group rights are the right of a minority to veto legislation; the right of a group to enjoy preferential status with respect to language (such as the enforcement of French in Québec) or religion (such as the right of aboriginal populations to enforce establishment of their religion in their territory, notwithstanding the separation of church and state in the state at large); the right of a group to have greater autonomy than other groups in the state (such as an ethnic province in a federal state that has more autonomy than a nonethnic one); and the strongest right of all, the right to sovereign statehood. In this chapter I argue that groups should not enjoy such prerogatives *merely by virtue of the fact that they possess some common ethnic trait.* Group rights, including self-determination, are justified (when they are justified) by other considerations, such as the need to escape injustice or the vindication of a legitimate territorial title. I will examine and critique standard justifications of self-determination and special group rights and offer some alternative suggestions.

I. The Nationalist Thesis

The nationalist argument for self-determination makes two claims. First, groups entitled to self-determination are identified by nonvoluntary factors; second, as a matter of right, political and ethnic boundaries must coincide.[1] The nationalist thesis seems to be implicit in the broad language of the applicable international instruments, at least if *peoples* are defined as ethnic groups.[2] This view has a suspect pedigree because it is directly anchored in an organicist theory of the nation, in a definition of the nation as distinct from the state. This line of thought is quite old and has been given various versions of varying degrees of plausibility. But its flaws are quite obvious and have already been pointed out by commentators.[3]

The first is the difficulty associated with the definition of *people* or *nation*. If a people (nation) is defined by reference to shared history, there is the problem of historical discontinuity. History is ever changing, and different groups participate in the history of a nation or state (not to mention the epistemological difficulties of choosing, say, political history over social, economic, or other kinds of history as constitutive of the social identity of the nation in question). If a people is instead defined by reference to ethnicity, then multiethnic states lack legitimacy because the association of their citizens is not based on the cultural traits that the nationalists favor. The same objections apply to definitions based on language, religion, and similar factors.

But the most devastating objection against the nationalist thesis is its potential for exclusion of, and hostility toward, those persons that do not possess the ethnic trait. For ethnic identity as a political normative principle has a double face. In its kind face, the principle seems to stand for inclusion and vindication of some lofty cultural trait of which the members of the group are proud. But in its unkind face, the principle endorses ethnic homogeneity. And this can only be achieved, as Gellner puts it, if the group "either kills, expels, or assimilates all non-nationals."[4] Many kinds of evil practices, from Nazi genocide, to Turkey's massacres of Armenians, to modern ethnic cleansing have been committed in the name of the nationalist principle understood in this way, and the connection is far from being coincidental. If I believe that my race is the foundation of the bonds of citizenship, I will not feel a strong political obligation toward those persons who, though living in the same territory, have a different race. From that view to the view that I do not have any moral obligation to them and can therefore treat them as means to my ends, as things, there is only one small step.

One could go even further and suggest, with Gellner, that the very concept of nation is spurious because the ideology of nationalism en-

---

[1] *See* ALLEN BUCHANAN, SECESSION: THE MORALITY OF POLITICAL DIVORCE FROM FORT SUMTER TO LITHUANIA AND QUEBEC 48 (1990).

[2] G.A. Res. 1514, art. 2 (1960); International Covenant on Civil and Political Rights, art. 1, 999 U.N.T.S. 171 (1967); International Covenant on Economic, Social, and Cultural Rights, art. 1, 993 U.N.T.S. 3 (1967).

[3] *See, e.g.,* BUCHANAN, *supra* note 1, at 49–50.

[4] ERNEST GELLNER, NATIONS AND NATIONALISM 2 (1983).

genders nations, not the other way around. Thus, languages and cultures are invented and reinvented selectively to justify particular political arrangements.[5] For those reasons, it is hard not to agree with Allen Buchanan's view that the pure nationalist principle, notwithstanding its popularity in some circles, is one of the least plausible arguments for self-determination and group rights. The moral costs of implementing the principle (understood in this way) are prohibitive.[6]

II. THE COMMUNITARIAN THESIS

The defense of a group right to self-determination need not, however, reach the extremely illiberal conclusions of nationalism. Some writers have tried to explain self-determination by appealing to more reasonable and moderate notions of community, ones that do not completely lose sight of the moral ends served by states and nations. This more moderate view, communitarianism, still places moral value in the group as something distinct from its individual members and regards collective rights as irreducible to individual rights. The best effort in this regard is contained in an article by Avishai Margalit and Joseph Raz.[7] Their thesis can be summarized as follows: the right to self-determination is grounded in the wider value of self-government. Self-government, however, is justified not as an end in itself but instrumentally—by reference to the well-being of a self-governing group's members. Only certain groups (called "encompassing groups") have the right to decide whether or not the group will be self-governed. Encompassing groups are those that meet a list of more or less stringent communitarian requirements. Thus, the group must have a common character and a common culture that encompasses many, varied, and important aspects of life. The ability of the group's members to lead a meaningful life will be seriously reduced if they are denied access to these features of communal life. Characteristics of encompassing groups include mutual recognition and self-identification by members of the group through those nonvoluntary features shaped during a relatively long period in the group's history. In short, groups that qualify are those that have pervasive cultures where the value of self-identification for members of the group is crucial to their individual well-being.[8]

Margalit and Raz add some important qualifications to this definition. When a group qualifies, it can exercise the right to determine whether it

---

[5] *Id.* at 55–56. He adds: "The cultural shreds and patches used by nationalism are often historical inventions."

[6] *See* BUCHANAN, *supra* note 1, at 48.

[7] Avishai Margalit & Joseph Raz, *National Self-Determination*, 87 J. PHIL. 439 (1990).

[8] *Id.* at 442–47.

will be self-governed (for example, form an independent state), but that decision must be made with regard to not only other interests of members of the group but also the interests of minorities within the group and the interests of outsiders. Because self-determination is instrumental, the case for it is sensitive to counterarguments relevant to its justification.[9] For example, if a group seeks political autonomy and, along with legitimate reasons, the members of the majority intend to oppress minorities or women, then their case is fatally undermined.[10] Similarly, self-determination loses its moral force if it is sought for the wrong reasons, such as controlling certain economic resources. (Katanga is an example.)[11]

With respect to the manner of exercising this right, Margalit and Raz conclude that, because decisions about self-government are usually irreversible, they should require more than a mere majority vote: there should be an overwhelming majority of members of the group wishing to pursue self-government.[12] Finally, the authors claim that the right to self-determination is not reducible to liberal notions of political consent because "[self-determination] is a group right, deriving from the value of a collective good, and as such opposed in spirit to contractarian-individualistic approaches to politics or to individual well-being."[13]

This view of self-determination is thus a mixed one. By asserting that the value of self-government is purely instrumental, Margalit and Raz reject the nationalist approach to self-determination. As we have seen, the nationalist view treats individual rights, interests, and well-being as derivative of, and consequently subordinated to, the original notion of community. While Margalit and Raz reject this approach by focusing instead on the value of self-government for the individual well-being of members of the group, they still believe that the issue of self-determination is independent of other issues of political morality. In this sense, their view closely resembles that of Michael Walzer, for whom communal integrity takes precedence over other matters of political morality, even though it is ultimately a function of the rights and interests of individuals.[14]

On balance, I believe Margalit and Raz's model is predominantly communitarian and not liberal for two reasons. First, the traits that define an encompassing group (and one thus entitled to self-determination) are largely nonvoluntary, as I have indicated. This naturally undermines liberal insistence on consent and the honoring of individual preferences as the bases of political institutions. Second, and related, self-determination

---

[9] *Id.* at 451.

[10] *Id.* at 459–60.

[11] *Id.* at 459.

[12] *Id.* at 458.

[13] *Id.* at 456–57.

[14] *See* Michael Walzer, *The Rights of Political Communities, in* INTERNATIONAL ETHICS 165, 181 (Charles R. Beitz, Marshall Cohen, Thomas Scanlon & A. John Simmons eds., 1985).

is a group right and as such is linked to notions of collective, not individual, good. This is reflected in the fact that it is the group's collective will that counts, not individual opinions or objections to self-government.

The moderate communitarian view attempts to reconcile liberal intuitions linked to the inherent worth of individual human beings with the undeniably communitarian thrust that underlies the concept of self-determination—the foremost group right, the group right par excellence. I suggest, however, that the authors' concessions to communitarianism are unnecessary and that the seemingly unsolvable dilemma of group rights can be explained within the framework of liberal political theory. In addition, their argument unduly neglects the question of territorial rights and, in doing so, fatally begs the question of determining the appropriate democratic unit—that is, the unit that is entitled to create an independent state.

The first problem with the communitarian argument is connected with the claim that goals and relationships, essential for individual well-being, are culturally determined. For the authors, "familiarity with the culture determines the boundaries of the imaginable," thus making all possible choices by individuals culturally confined. Culture is what provides the context for meaningful choice. What this means is that the prosperity of the culture is important for the well-being of the group's members. According to Margalit and Raz, "[i]f the culture is decaying, or if it is persecuted or discriminated against, the options and opportunities open to its members will shrink."[15] But this premise, essential to the argument, is problematic.[16]

The Kantian tradition, as well as other versions of the liberal tradition, provide alternative explanations of rational choice where persons choose to pursue cultural values, rather than being predetermined by them. In other words, for Kantian theory, choices by people in a culture (for example, to participate in the group's religion) count only if they are in some sense voluntary. In the words of John Rawls, the ideal society is one that comes "as close as a society can to being a voluntary scheme."[17] An important assumption of liberalism is that we can detach ourselves from any particular communal practice: we are able and must be allowed to evaluate, revise, and eventually reject cultural practices.[18] An emphasis on nonvoluntary foundations of the bonds of citizenship runs counter to

[15] Margalit & Raz, *supra* note 7, at 449.

[16] There is a voluminous literature devoted to this debate between liberals and communitarians. The best liberal response is, in my view, WILL KYMLICKA, LIBERALISM, COMMUNITY, AND CULTURE (1990). *See also* DEREK L. PHILLIPS, LOOKING BACKWARD: A CRITICAL APPRAISAL OF COMMUNITARIAN THOUGHT (1995).

[17] JOHN RAWLS, A THEORY OF JUSTICE 13 (1971).

[18] *See* KYMLICKA, *supra* note 16, at 50–51.

the liberal ideal that the democratic community cannot be based merely on force but on some form of consent. Perhaps consent is simply our ability to revise and reject what is given to us from birth. Even on this weak definition of consent, membership in a culture is, for the Kantian, chosen by the individual, not imposed upon her. This foundational disagreement between liberals and communitarians is a much discussed topic today, and I will not attempt to address it fully here. I shall confine myself instead to showing where the communitarian position leads to problematic or counterintuitive results with regard to the issue of self-determination and special group rights.

Consider Margalit and Raz's discussion of the decay of cultures. There are two possibilities according to them: a culture may be persecuted, or a culture may decay on its own. The first case poses no need to resort to group rights. If members of a group are persecuted or discriminated against, then this is simply a violation of individual rights for which liberal theory has a sufficient answer without any need to resort to collective rights. The solution may very well be to recognize a legal right to self-determination for the group, but this will occur not because the group has a pervasive culture or because there is an independent moral status of the group above and beyond that of individuals but simply because their human rights are violated and they may be justified in seeking their liberation through special group rights, even perhaps secession.

On the other hand, what does it mean to say that the culture is decaying (as opposed to being persecuted)? That the culture is decaying means simply that its members do not care much about the culture, that they voluntarily choose social arrangements and rituals other than those constitutive of the original culture. The culture of the group is decaying not because the majority discriminates against the group but because many of its members (say, its youth) prefer another (perhaps more cosmopolitan) culture. But if this is the case, what can be the argument for coercively preserving the culture—for example, by recognizing greater autonomy from the larger unit so that the group leaders can impose the culture by law? Presumably, the idea here is that the culture needs to be preserved and that this can only be achieved through self-determination and self-government. But there are problems with this suggestion. For one thing, if the culture is decaying as a result of people's voluntary choices, preservation of the culture is not likely to be assured by self-government because people will likely continue making the same choices. (Canadian sovereign independence doesn't make Canadians less inclined to buy American goods or listen to American music.) If this is the case, the only way for the new sovereign government to preserve the culture is by the use of state power aimed at frustrating people's choices. So self-determination or special group rights as a solution to a culture's spontaneous decay often will lead to the adoption of laws aimed at thwarting voluntary choices by members of the group in a manner inconsistent with their autonomy. Self-determination and special group rights in such cases may thus lead to unduly repressive policies.

A possible argument in favor of preserving the culture in cases of spontaneous decay draws from the literature on the provision of public goods.[19] Sometimes, it is argued, people make individual choices unaware that the result of others' making similar choices is not something they would want if they could express the preference for such a collective result. For example, I am a Latin American but speak to my sons in English for reasons of convenience. If somebody asked me, "Do you want Spanish to be preserved in the Latino community?" I'd say yes. Because, however, the only way in which Spanish is going to be preserved in the Latino community is if people like me speak in Spanish to their children, there is an inconsistency between my individual choice (speaking in English) and my preferred result for the group (that Spanish be preserved). Perhaps I am just unaware of the consequences of my individual choice, in which case I will choose differently once I am made aware of those collective consequences. Or perhaps (more likely) I hope to free-ride on the other members of the group: I don't believe that my speaking Spanish will make a difference because I am confident that all the other Latinos will do, collectively, whatever is necessary to preserve the language in the community.[20] So I can obtain the benefits of the public good in question (preservation of the Spanish language) without incurring the costs. But if everyone does the same thing, then there will be no Spanish spoken—that is, no public good provided.[21]

If this is the case (so the argument goes), then we are confronting a case of market failure. Because of partial ignorance and free-riding problems, the collective result is not what the majority (or even perhaps all) of the members of the group want for the group. In specialized language, "the failure of the group to cooperate to produce a collective good may be collectively, but not individually, sub-optimal from the point of view of self-interest."[22] The time has come, it is then argued, for coercive interven-

---

[19] For a representative collection of essays, see THE THEORY OF MARKET FAILURE: A CRITICAL EXAMINATION (Tyler Cowen ed., 1988).

[20] On free riding, see the sharp article by Garrett Cull, *Moral Free Riding,* 24 PHIL. & PUB. AFF. 3 (1995).

[21] A public good, such as, let's suppose, the linguistic identity of a community, is defined as one that exhibits the characteristics of nonexclusiveness (that is, it cannot be privately supplied because suppliers cannot exclude people who don't pay) and nonrivalry (that is, one person's consumption of the good does not lessen the amount of it available to others).

[22] Cull, *supra* note 20, at 4.

tion: the government needs to have special powers to correct the market failure. Sartorius describes this view well:

> The strong hand of government will typically be required to lead individuals to make decisions whose collective effects will be mutually advantageous rather than mutually detrimental. The power to tax is, in this view, the power to compel individuals to contribute to the purchase of public goods that they would not be motivated to purchase for themselves. The power to make and enforce laws backed by coercive sanctions is, in this view, the power to provide individuals with reasons to act in ways that satisfy the general schema. If everyone (or a sufficiently large number of people) acted that way, everyone would be better off.[23]

In the case of spontaneous decay of pervasive cultures, the communitarian argument is that self-determination and even secession might be needed to empower a government that will correct the market failure and enact into law the preferences for the public good (preservation of the culture) held by members of the culture. Coercion is needed to prevent defection, which in turn is caused by the lack of assurance against defection by others. Thus, the public goods argument presumes the legitimacy of helping people do what they want to do (preserve the culture) but cannot do without the government's help.[24]

This is a sophisticated argument, and its appeal rests on the fact that it relies on the idea of rational choice. The argument, however, encounters serious difficulties. One is that it assumes without proof that force can be justified as a solution to the public goods dilemma.[25] It does not follow from the fact that there is a public goods dilemma (which is essentially a prisoner's dilemma) that it is morally justified to use governmental coercion to supply the public good in question. Why? The interests that different people have in a public good can vary widely. In particular, "that a good exhibits characteristics of nonexclusiveness and nonrivalry in consumption does not guarantee that a given person has an interest in it."[26] Some people simply don't care about the public good in question. It is true that if all cared, then it might be justified to use coercion to do away with free riding. In this case, because every member of the community would like to see the good produced (the language preserved), all of them will be more than happy to have the state prevent defection (which in turn occurs

---

[23] ROLF SARTORIUS, THE LIMITS OF LIBERTARIANISM 104–5 (1980).

[24] See DAVID SCHMIDTZ, THE LIMITS OF GOVERNMENT: AN ESSAY ON THE PUBLIC GOODS ARGUMENT 82 (1991).

[25] Here I follow closely David Schmidtz. Id. at 82–107.

[26] Id. at 83.

for prisoner dilemma type of reasons). But surely there are those who refuse to contribute simply because they don't want the good, and the prisoner's dilemma analysis mistakenly assumes those people don't exist.[27]

This objection shows that there is both a false premise and a non sequitur in the public goods argument. The false premise is that all members of the group want the public good in question as their first preference, that they would gladly contribute to the good only if all others would do the same. As we saw, this assumption is false because there are honest holdouts. The non sequitur is to say that, because a good is public, government intervention is justified in order to supply it. In fact, defenders of group rights need an independent justification to force some people (the honest holdouts) to help pay for other people's projects. The public goods argument alone fails to justify special governmental powers or group rights.

At any rate, the public goods argument sounds strange because of the difficulty in discerning structures of preferences different from the ones expressed in the political market. If someone acts on an individual preference that, if universalized, would corrode the group's culture, then can we say that she also has the preference that the culture not be corroded? It seems that she can't have her cake and eat it too: whatever people's motives (including but, as we saw, not limited to free riding), they are presumably aware of the alternatives and prefer to do those things that collectively result in the demise of the culture. Why, then, enforce the counterfactual choice that the agent decided *not* to make? Again, I suspect that those who make the market failure argument have decided in advance that the collective goal is worthy so that the true reason to favor that goal does not really depend on the existence of the market failure.

The gist of the liberal position is that, in principle, a free society must privilege individual choice and that arguments to the contrary carry the burden of proof. A liberal regards a group's cultural symbols as important insofar as the members themselves regard those symbols as important. An ethnic group does not have a right that its culture survive if a majority of its members do not want it to survive. So if a majority discriminates against a culture (this, by the way, is a misnomer: only individuals can be discriminated against), then that majority violates the right to equal treatment of the members of the culture. If, on the other hand, the culture is decaying spontaneously, it is hard to see how that fact would justify special group rights or secession from a liberal state.

The final problem with the communitarian thesis is that it unduly neglects the territorial issue: self-government over a territory implies title

---

[27] Schmidtz calls these the "honest holdouts." *Id.* at 84.

over that territory within which it seeks self-government. Therefore, appeal to the nonvoluntary communitarian traits that, according to Margalit and Raz, define encompassing groups cannot resolve the question of self-determination. A group may be encompassing and have a pervasive culture yet lack title over the territory within which it seeks self-government. If this is so, then the group is not entitled to self-determination. This view has been forcefully advanced by Lea Brilmayer, and to it I now turn.

III. THE TERRITORIALIST THESIS

Lea Brilmayer has argued that, contrary to conventional legal analysis, secessionist claims (and, I add, other claims for group autonomy) involve, first and foremost, disputed claims to territory. Group traits emphasized by communitarians, such as ethnicity, simply serve to identify the people making the territorial claim. As a result, the strength of a separatist claim "does not depend primarily on the degree to which the group in question constitutes a distinct people."[28] Claims to territory do not flow automatically from ethnic distinctiveness, and oppression of the group can be remedied by eliminating such oppression (perhaps through revolution), not by granting permission to set up a new state.[29] Brilmayer encourages secessionist groups to make their territorial claims explicit instead of subordinating them to the current self-determination rhetoric (a right of peoples to govern themselves).[30] The territorial approach focuses on the history of the dispute rather than on whether the secessionists are "a people." According to Brilmayer, the standard account of self-determination fails to appreciate that secessionists (and other groups seeking lesser forms of political autonomy) typically seek to remedy historical wrongs.[31] Under this interpretation, "a different set of questions must be addressed in order to evaluate the merits of a separatist movement": a territorial approach to secession and special group rights focuses not on factors such as whether the group considers itself a people or whether they have the same race or language but on territorial equities. Typical questions then are, How immediate was the historical wrong? How alive has the claim been kept? Are there new settlers? Has there been adverse possession? How serious was the wrong—that is, was the territory conquered, or was the settlement gradual instead?[32] Brilmayer concedes that the answers to these questions aren't any easier than the answers to the

[28] See Lea Brilmayer, *Secession and Self-Determination: A Territorial Interpretation*, 16 YALE J. INT'L L. 177, 178 (1991).
[29] Id. at 188.
[30] Id. at 189.
[31] Id. at 191.
[32] Id. at 197–201.

questions posed by the traditional approach, but at least, she concludes, these are the right questions.

Brilmayer's argument is an important contribution to solving the puzzle of self-determination. Moreover, her view gets some support from the leading case on self-determination: the Western Sahara advisory opinion.[33] One of the issues in that case was whether Morocco or Mauritania had title over the Western Sahara. The International Court of Justice concluded that they did not and that for that reason the principle of self-determination was applicable.[34] *A contrario sensu,* a finding of title would have legally prevented the people of Western Sahara from voting themselves into independence.[35] The court's view, therefore, is very close to Brilmayer's: a determination of the status of the territory is a determination of title, not merely of wishes.

Brilmayer's analysis is incontrovertible—as far as it goes. The territorial analysis proves that having a valid territorial title is an important factor in the evaluation of self-determination claims. But a government exercises its authority over both territory and people. Thus, although the territorial argument rightly draws our attention to the neglected territorial issue, it goes too far if it means that having the territorial title (difficult to show as that may be) is a *sufficient* justification for special group rights, including secession. In other words, while Brilmayer is absolutely right in criticizing both the consent and communitarian versions of self-determination with their misplaced emphases on personal factors, the justification of legitimate political authority involved in ethnic disputes must, under liberal theory, go beyond matters of territorial title. Moreover, it is also doubtful that a valid title is a necessary condition for recognizing special group rights, for there may be cases where recognition of such rights is the only viable way for ethnic groups to escape serious forms of oppression. Under the primacy of individual human rights presupposed by the Kantian thesis, the urgency of escaping oppression where revolution is unavailable may justify special group rights, even secession, notwithstanding the absence of title to the territory at issue.

The reverse is also true: self-determination for the purpose of violating human rights is illegitimate. Suppose that the people in one of the territories that is now part of Russia wish to secede. Suppose further that the secessionist leaders intend to create a rigid dictatorial state founded on the restoration of the principles and practices of Stalinist Marxism. Let us assume that the group has a valid territorial title founded in a legitimate historical grievance against Russia. Under the thesis defended in this chapter, the issue of human rights takes precedence over the territorial

[33] 1975 I.C.J. 12.
[34] *Id.* at 68.
[35] Judge Dillard expressly rejected this implication in his concurrence. *See id.* at 122.

title. The government of Russia has a moral obligation to protect the citizens of the territory (who, until the secession is consummated, are under Russian jurisdiction) against the abuses that can be reasonably expected under the planned Stalinist regime. The territorialist approach would have to disregard the question of human rights in favor of the question of territory, and that seems questionable from a moral stand-point. The reason is that governmental power is both authority over terri-tory and authority over people; and just as the communitarian and consensual views neglected the former, the territorial view neglects the latter. This problem does not disappear simply because a majority of the citizens of the territory have voted to secede because oppression cannot be legitimized by majority vote. The issue can be put differently: a liberal does not merely ask, "Is this territory yours?" Rather, the liberal follows the question with a second one: "And just what do you intend to do in that territory?" Territories are loci for rights, and land rights are instru-mental to justice. (I examine the concept of territorial justice later in this chapter.)

IV. THE LIBERTARIAN THESIS

The foregoing discussion has shown that both the communitarian and territorial views fail to take fully into account important concerns. The communitarians do so by overemphasizing group traits over individual rights and preferences, the territorialists by overemphasizing title to terri-tory over human rights. But what about the view that there ought to be an (almost) unlimited right for groups to organize themselves as they see fit, even to secede? According to this view, people ought to have an unlim-ited right freely to establish whatever political associations they wish to establish, including sovereign states. Harry Beran has defended such a view,[36] and Judge Dillard seems to have adhered to it in his separate opinion in the Western Sahara case.[37] For Beran, a right to secession follows from liberalism's commitment to freedom and popular sover-eignty. Because liberalism regards the justified civil society as that which comes as close as possible to being a voluntary scheme, people ought to be

---

[36] Harry Beran, *A Liberal Theory of Secession*, 32 POL. STUD. 21 (1984). I read Christopher Wellman as proposing a similar view: "*any* group may secede as long as it and its remainder state are large, cohesive, and geographically contiguous enough to form a government that effectively performs the functions necessary to create a secure political environment." Christopher H. Wellman, *A Defense of Secession and Political Self-Determination*, 24 PHIL. & PUB. AFF. 142 (1995). Thus, for this author the freedom to secede is normatively preeminent, and it is limited only by pragmatic reasons (size and so on).

[37] 1975 ICJ 122 ("It is for the people to determine the destiny of the territory and not the territory the destiny of the people.").

able freely to choose their political associations.[38] But states are not and should not be immutable, so "a commitment to the freedom of the self-governing choosers to live in societies that approach as closely as possible to voluntary schemes, requires that the unity of the state itself be voluntary."[39] As a result, liberalism must grant "territorially concentrated groups" the right to form their own state.[40]

Beran is right that under liberal theory, *some* form of consent is the basis of political obligation.[41] As the previous discussion shows, however, even if the liberal premises are accepted, the view neglects the territorial question. What does Beran mean by "territorially concentrated" groups? This cannot mean groups in the communitarian sense, for what matters are people's voluntary choices, not involuntary group traits such as ethnicity. As Lea Brilmayer has shown, the fact that the group living in a territory wishes to secede does not mean that it can lawfully take the territory. Government by consent does not include a right to opt out but merely requires a right to democratic participation.[42] Because Beran's argument neglects the issue of territorial title, it begs the question of how to define the group entitled to self-determination: secessionists will answer that their group is the relevant one, members of the larger unit that theirs is. So it seems that Beran does not resolve this question unless by "territorially concentrated groups" he means groups that have the title to territory. If so, his argument is identical to Brilmayer's: if a group owns the territory and wishes to secede, it should in principle be allowed to do so.

There is another problem with Beran's thesis. We saw that, for him, the right of unlimited secession follows from the ideas of popular sovereignty and freedom. Yet to be consistent with the conception of freedom he espouses, Beran has to require unanimity in order to secede (or to establish a group right). Otherwise, the majority in the group would be establishing a new authority over the dissenters within the group. And why can't they in turn exercise a right to secession? Again, the expression "territorially concentrated groups" is suspect. If such entities have the right to self-determination, so do subgroups and so do individuals. Thus, "popular sovereignty" is not very useful if we have not identified the populus. Even if we have, popular sovereignty does not sit well with individual freedom (unless unanimity is secured).

This failure of consent-based arguments brings out a very important point about the relationship between self-determination and liberal prin-

[38] Beran, *supra* note 36, at 25.

[39] *Id.*

[40] *Id.* at 26.

[41] For a brief discussion of the general problems with the view, see BUCHANAN, *supra* note 1, at 71–73.

[42] Brilmayer, *supra* note 27, at 185.

ciples. There is a tradition in liberalism that places emphasis on people's actual preferences and actual consent. Understandably, for such a view there is a temptation to have a presumption in favor of self-determination because, in some sense, political autonomy is wanted by people and must therefore be honored. But a different liberal tradition, the Kantian tradition, honors rational preferences, not just any preferences. Under that tradition, the justified constitution is the one to which people will rationally agree, and that constitution is one that protects human rights. Therefore, government by consent is government to which every rational citizen would agree, one where every individual can consider himself a co-legislator. This suggests that the presumption might well be against self-determination for a group in a liberal state where no past injustice has been committed against the group. Certainly, the mere possession of an ethnic trait could not by itself justify special group rights or secession in the absence of injustice.

V. POLITICAL INJUSTICE

A. Violation of Human Rights

The first justification for special group rights (and, in appropriate cases, secession) exists when those who inhabit the region are subject to serious injustice, and other remedies (say, democratic remedies) are unavailable. What counts, however, as a serious injustice? Here writers differ. Allen Buchanan treats as injustices the violation of group rights,[43] the need to prevent genocide,[44] and the need to escape what he calls "discriminatory redistribution."[45] Yet there is one more obvious form of injustice: the serious violation of individual human rights, even if it does not reach genocidal proportions. Oppression may be directed against the group as such or against all the citizens of the state. In either case, the government has lost its legitimacy, and citizens have a right to do those things that are necessary to free themselves from oppression. An important proviso, however, is that other means of redress (and, in extreme cases, revolution) must be unavailable. It may be that the persecuted group cannot enlist a sufficiently large number of votes (or revolutionaries) or even that the majority in the state acquiesces in the human rights violations. In such cases, it should matter little whether or not the group has a legitimate historical grievance over the taking of territory, although if it does, its case will, of course, be strengthened. Brilmayer objects that the remedy for

---

[43] See BUCHANAN, *supra* note 1, at 40.
[44] *Id.* at 64–67.
[45] *Id.* at 38–45. Under "rectifying past injustices," Buchanan includes the territorial argument suggested by Brilmayer.

mistreatment is better treatment, not secession.[46] If peaceful reform or violent revolution within the state cannot achieve better treatment, however, then special group rights, and sometimes secession, are morally preferable to the preservation of the unity of a state that countenances oppression. The right to self-determination is thus derivative of the right not to suffer injustice but not independent of it. As a recent commentator put it, "citizens have only a right not to be treated unjustly, not a primary right to political self-determination that permits secession in the absence of injustice."[47] But when the right of self-determination is triggered, it trumps the state's so-called right of territorial integrity.

Two other forms of injustice have been put forth as possible justifications for self-determination and special group rights. But as I will discuss, both prove inadequate on closer analysis.

B. Discriminatory Redistribution

The second alleged form of injustice is discriminatory redistribution, which may be defined as "taxation schemes or regulatory policies or economic programs that systematically work to the disadvantage of some groups . . . in morally arbitrary ways."[48] According to Buchanan, discriminatory redistribution can occur even when the state respects both individual rights and group and minority rights, including the right to democratic representation. This form of injustice may call into question the legitimacy of existing political authority with regard to the group that is being victimized. This, however, is dubious grounds for self-determination and special group rights. If no rights are being violated, then all the group can complain about is that they ended up losing in the democratic process. If so, either they have title to territory, or they do not. If they do, their will should by itself suffice to enable them to establish their state on that territory. If they do not have title over the territory, then their claim is no different from the claim of any other group that ends up losing in the democratic process: the farmers, the auto industries, the homeless, and so on. In other words, a disadvantaged group's claim that it is the victim of discriminatory redistribution is tautologically true of any economic program adopted in a democratic political system that respects individual rights and abides by the strictures of democratic fairness. If the state is just in the liberal sense (and, again, this may be hard to determine), then there is no residual claim of injustice by those whose interests (not rights) have been thwarted in the democratic process. Here the remedies should be democratic, and there seems to be little merit in the suggestion that, if the

[46] See Brilmayer, *supra* note 27, at 188.
[47] See Wellman, *supra* note 36, at 157.
[48] See BUCHANAN, *supra* note 1, at 40.

group has an ethnic identity, then it should be given a special shield against adverse democratic decisions. To be sure, if our liberal theory of justice mandates economic redistribution, and if the laws of that country do not provide for such redistribution, then people who live in a territory and who happen to be the victims of that economic injustice may be entitled to self-determination in order to escape the injustice (just like any other case of violation of human rights). In other words, a violation of economic rights that cannot be redressed through the democratic process or by other means may leave no alternative but the creation of some form of political autonomy. Of course, it is not enough that the region be economically disadvantaged in a general sense (for example, southern Italy); rather, the economic arrangements must fail to satisfy the minimal requirements of liberal justice for the majority of the people who inhabit the territory, and self-determination (special group rights, political autonomy, or secession in extreme cases) must be the only realistic remedy to that injustice.

C. Violation of Group Rights

We are left, then, with two possible forms of political injustice: the violation of individual rights and the violation of group rights. Are group or collective rights, however, a distinct category within liberal theory? Some distinguished writers, such as Allen Buchanan and Will Kymlicka, think so. In their view, liberal theory has unjustifiedly neglected group rights and should therefore be reformulated to make room for them. I believe, however, that group rights do not have a place in liberal political theory and that what many call group rights should instead be defined as social policies or collective goals.

Collective or group rights have three characteristics.[49] First, they are ascribed to groups, not to individuals. Second, they can only be exercised collectively or on behalf of the collective (usually through some mechanism of political representation). Finally, the good secured by the right will be available to all or most members of the group. Thus, for example, the right of a group to preserve its language (as distinct from the individual right to speak the language of one's choice) is a right that is exercised on behalf of the group by its representatives—say, by enacting the laws necessary to preserve the group's language. In addition, the good secured by the right, namely the preservation of the group's language, will be available to all members of the group, including its future members.

As a preliminary matter, there are some rights that look like group rights but are not. Sometimes a claim of collective right can be understood

[49] *See id.* at 74–75.

as shorthand for a claim advancing individual rights or benefits or interests for the individuals that belong to the group in question. For example,
a claim that women should enjoy equal opportunity to run for office is
simply a claim about each individual woman's right to run for office
under the same conditions as men. This is not a right that the collective
entity "women" have, but a right belonging to each individual woman.
The only collective aspect of this individual right is that the right holders
are identified by their having certain characteristics—in this case, physical
characteristics—that not all human beings possess. Even in cases where
the asserted right is not one related to formal notions of equality, it can
still be analyzed or reduced to a cluster of individual rights or benefits.
Suppose someone asserts that Latinos have a right to receive preferential
treatment for government jobs. What this means is that each individual
Latino has the right to receive such preferential treatment. This kind of
right is collective in the obvious sense that the way to identify its holders
is through group membership, but it will still be the case that the right of
the group can be properly reformulated without any loss of meaning, in
terms of individual rights. Any such right may or may not be plausible or
defensible, but its analysis does not create problems other than those
encountered in the analysis of individual human rights.

Defenders of group rights, however, do not have these cases in mind.
Some collective rights, we are told, cannot be analyzed in terms of individual rights.[50] A collective right is conceived as a right to realize some
state of affairs that, it is thought, can only be a group attribute. Take, for
example, the right to language preservation. Such a right, we are told, is
necessarily held by the group, by the community. It does not seem appropriate to disaggregate this collective right into individual linguistic rights.
Nor does such a right seem to depend on individual preferences of the
members of the group.

I believe that the attempt to vindicate group rights alongside individual
rights is misguided. In particular, the contention, defended by Will Kymlicka, Allen Buchanan, and others, that liberalism can accommodate
group rights is problematic. For what their proponents call group rights
are really instances of social policies that they believe should prevail over
claims of individual rights. I do not attempt to demonstrate here whether
or not in a particular instance it is morally justified to secure a collective
goal (be it called group right or social policy) that is partially inconsistent
with individual rights. Rather, my point is that the meaning of the word

[50] For an excellent discussion of the conceptual distinctions inherent in collective rights,
see WILL KYMLICKA, MULTICULTURAL CITIZENSHIP 34–48 (1995). While I agree with Kymlicka's distinction between internal restrictions and external protections, and, as the text
demonstrates, I also share his skepticism about the former, I am less optimistic about his
contention that the liberal tradition can accommodate group rights with ease.

right in the expression "collective rights" is different in crucial ways from the meaning of the same word when talking about individual rights. In fact, it is precisely the opposite.

Let us start with a definition of rights that is typical of deontological liberalism—the one suggested by Ronald Dworkin.[51] Under liberal theory, to say that someone has a right to X is to say that he has a moral reason to effect X that, at some point, trumps the pursuit of social utility or other collective or aggregative goals. The justification for upholding the right is thus found in a principle that predates the assertion of the right and outweighs other arguments, especially prospective utilitarian arguments. Sometimes, of course, the collective goal may prevail over the right in question; but for a claim to be called a right it has to have *some* threshold value where it trumps other considerations—in particular, the pursuit of the general welfare.[52] If this definition of rights is accepted, we cannot call just any claim that competes against an individual right also a right. Suppose we recognize that people have the right to free speech but that this right can be limited for pressing reasons of national security. We can say, rhetorically, that society has a right to national security, but according to the theory under consideration that would be inaccurate. What we say is that individuals have the right to free speech but that the threshold value of that right, high as it is, doesn't allow it to prevail against the social policy of urgent national security. Another technical way of describing the difference is that rights are individualized, nonaggregative, and distributive, while social policies are nonindividualized, aggregative, and nondistributive.

I would like to focus on the following questions: are group rights genuinely deontological (trumping rights) in the sense that individual rights are deontological? Or are they instead simply social policies that sometimes prevail over individual rights? It will help if we focus on a concrete example: the so-called collective right to preserve a language, such as the collective right of Québec to preserve the French language in that Canadian province. The argument for recognizing that right might run as follows: the community of Québec has a distinctive character (in the sense explained by Margalit and Raz), and one of the distinctive features is that its members speak French in a largely English-speaking country, Canada. Because the preservation of French is crucial to the endurance of Québec as a distinct community, the Québécois authorities should be allowed to enact legislation mandating, say, the exclusive use of French in public places. This (so the argument goes) is a matter of right for the community of Québec, but it is a collective right, not an individual one. As such, the

[51] *See* RONALD DWORKIN, TAKING RIGHTS SERIOUSLY xi–xii, 90–100 (1978).
[52] *Id.* at 92.

right concerns a collective good—that is, a good that, if secured, will be available to most or all members of the community. The implementation of this right is delegated by the group to an agent, the provincial government, through a mechanism of democratic representation.

The first question to ask is, Who is the right asserted against? In other words, who (if anyone) has the corresponding obligation? The answer, of course, is more complex than the answer we would give to a similar question concerning an individual right. Because the right to the preservation of the indigenous language is a collective right, it has a double dimension: internally, the community asserts the right against the dissenters within Québec—that is, against those who want to speak English in public places.[53] Externally (and for defenders of collective rights this is perhaps the most important dimension), the right is asserted against higher centers of authority—for example, the central government of Canada.[54] This is tantamount to saying (so the argument suggests) that Québec is asserting its right against Canada, group against group. To use Dworkin's metaphor, the right to Québec's language preservation trumps the interest of Canada to, say, have a multilingual system.

This analysis, however, is highly misleading. When closely examined, the exercise of the collective right of preservation of French in Québec is nothing more than an attempt to grant powers to the provincial government to thwart individual rights that Canadian citizens would normally have. Suppose the democratic lawmakers in Québec enact legislation imposing French in all public places, banning the use of other languages. It wouldn't matter how many people wanted to speak English because the government would be enforcing a right that pertains to the nation. The dissenters would have lost a right to free speech that they would normally have had in the absence of the restricting legislation. So internally, a collective right is simply a prerogative or carte blanche granted to governments to thwart rights or preferences that individuals would have except for the existence of the collective right. The so-called collective right to language preservation is a power granted to the government to impose restrictions on the speech of dissenters within the group. Now, such restrictions might or might not be morally justified, all things considered. But why are they even called a collective right? The original meaning of *rights* was that they constituted barriers against the government; they were deontological restrictions on the pursuit of the general welfare. Why not simply say that there is a greater collective interest (language preservation) that prevails on these facts over freedom of speech?

[53] This is what Kymlicka calls "internal restrictions." *See* KYMLICKA, *supra* note 50, at 35–48.
[54] This is what Kymlicka calls "external protections." *Id.* He wants to downplay the internal coercion presupposed by group rights and emphasize the external aspect. But it is hard to think of many group rights that do not involve a claim by the group leaders to restrict the individual rights of the group's members.

A possible answer by supporters of group rights is to emphasize the external dimension of the right in question. In our example, the collective right of Québec to preserve the French language is asserted against the Canadian government. Because the Québécois are a minority in Canada, their group right is a deontological restriction on the wishes of the Canadian majority represented by the Canadian government. So (the argument concludes) the group right has a trumping threshold just as the individual right has a trumping threshold against the pursuit of social policy. This symmetry, however, is only illusory. For the interest of the Canadian government (which represents, indeed, the majority) is simply to protect the individual right to speak English that individuals would normally have under the Canadian Constitution. The federal government is, one would assume, the guarantor of individual rights, and its interest in not seeing the Québécois legislation enacted is simply the interest in protecting Canadian citizens against unconstitutional majoritarian encroachments upon their rights. The argument that Québec has a collective right to speak French that trumps the contrary interests of the Canadian government is exactly like the argument made by some Southern states in the United States some decades ago to the effect that state's rights (that is, state legislation mandating racial segregation) ought to trump the pursuit of racial equality by the federal government. The point here is that not just any claim can be called a right, and not just any claim can be called a policy. The collective interest in protecting individual rights is not just another policy in the Dworkinian sense. And the social policy of language preservation is not another right held by the community that is qualitatively equivalent to the individual right that the policy purports to suppress.

So on a classic liberal analysis of the concept of right, collective rights are not rights but aggregative social policies considered particularly weighty by their supporters. Collective rights lack the deontological bite, as it were. Why do many people, then, defend the idea of collective rights? The reason might be simply rhetorical. The rhetoric of rights is extremely powerful. As many have pointed out, to say that a certain claim is a matter of right is to give the most powerful moral reasons in favor of that claim. Rights talk is the heaviest artillery of our moral arsenal. In the light of this usage, those who advocated an expansion of governmental power (such as the one exemplified by Québec's collective right to language preservation) had considerable difficulty in justifying those proposals because liberals would insist that, in most cases, individual rights may not be lightly sacrificed in the pursuit of social policies. From the standpoint of rights-based liberalism, the burden of proof is always on those who advocate the primacy of a social policy over the (individual) right with which it competes. So defenders of expanded governmental power decided to avail themselves of the persuasive, emotional connotations of rights language. The situation would no longer be described as right versus policy, where the burden would be on those who favor the policy, but rather as right versus right—the (individual) right of free speech versus the (collective) right of cultural preservation, where presumably there would be no burden of proof on either side. If we look at international law, we see that most of the so-called third-generation human rights are assertions of increased governmental power at the expense of individual freedoms.

Collective rights in this internal sense, then, reveal a different face: they are assertions of communal power to cancel individual rights—what Kymlicka calls "internal restrictions."[55] Once again, I am not claiming that the linguistic question in Québec should be resolved in favor of individual freedom of speech and against attempts to impose the French language. Nor am I claiming that strong prudential considerations, such as the need to manage conflict, may not justify the establishment of special group rights, such the consociational arrangements discussed by David Wippman in this volume. It may well be that these are cases where the social policy is urgent enough to outweigh the individual rights with which the policy competes. The claims on behalf of the community are claims to limit individual rights, and the clash must be decided, like all moral matters, on its merits. What I am claiming is, first, that those communal claims cannot be called rights in the same sense that liberal theory defines rights; and, second, that for that reason the establishment of such arrangements should be subject to a high level of scrutiny to make sure that they do not impinge too much on traditional human rights, including the right to political participation. For liberals, the burden of proof is on those who purport to deny the individual right; and while the decision to call these arrangements group rights may be ultimately a verbal preference, such a linguistic decision should not strengthen the merits of the claim.

Is self-determination, however, different? Someone may concede the accuracy of the foregoing analysis with respect to many group rights yet suggest that self-determination (the right of a group to govern itself) has a different status. In that case the issue is one of entitlement to enter into a new social contract and, in the case of secession, to opt out of an existing one. Unlike the examples usually given of group rights, this one does not necessarily entail canceling individual rights. In addition, it seems to have a powerful external dimension because the right is asserted against a political authority that previously had jurisdiction over the group. Yet one could ask why the right to self-determination is different from the liberal individual right of free association. Why not simply hold that people have an individual right to associate freely with others and to agree to create their own government structures? If such a view were accepted, the right of self-determination would no longer be a group right, except in a purely

---

[55] See id.

derivative sense: to say that the group exercised its right to self-determination would be to say that individuals have freely chosen to associate with one another and to create their own institutions—a political contract.

But supporters of the idea of group rights object by pointing out that it is absurd to suggest that there is an unlimited right of individuals to associate themselves in this way. We need a theory of groups, they suggest, in order to know which groups qualify. And the only way out of this is a communitarian theory of groups such as the one suggested by Margalit and Raz: the only groups entitled to associate themselves and form a new state are those that display a series of relatively stringent communitarian traits—that is, those that exhibit pervasive cultures. This objection, however, can be overcome once we realize that the question of self-determination has a crucial *territorial* component. As we saw, the liberal can reply by maintaining his free association approach and adding the requirement that the group that wishes to create its own independent government must have a valid title to the territory in which it wants to exercise this right (so long as the group respects the legitimate expectations of others). I now turn to an examination of territorial injustice as the basis for special group rights, including secession.

VI. Territorial Injustice

Another justification for self-determination rests on a group's claim of territorial title. This, as we saw, was first suggested by Brilmayer and adopted by Buchanan in his analysis of secession. Certainly, the need to redress an unjust territorial taking provides a good justification for self-determination rights for an ethnic group, on the condition that the group itself intends to observe human rights. If it does not, then its title to territory (being instrumental to the just exercise of political power) does not provide a sufficient justification for self-determination because the group intends to deprive citizens of their rights. On the other hand, a group escaping oppression is justified in seeking political autonomy whenever revolution or other means of political reform are unavailable, even if they do not have a title. So title to territory is a sufficient justification for self-determination only in the case of a liberal group's seeking autonomy within a liberal state. In other cases, the preservation and protection of human rights should take precedence.

But what exactly does it mean to say that a group has title over a territory? There are several possibilities. The first is to say that people who live in a territory have title over it. But this cannot be right. Certainly, to put forth an autonomy claim, the claimants must have a territory available; and in most cases it will be the territory where they live. But this is surely different from the question of title. The inhabitants of California do not have title to California just because they live within its confines. The federal claim is that California is first and foremost U.S. territory and that for that reason California may not seek autonomy or secede. Those who oppose secession always argue that people who live in a territory may not lawfully take it. The Russian government, for example, argues that Chechnya is part of Russia as a matter of territorial sovereignty. The secessionist Chechnyans, on the other hand, claim that the territory at issue was unlawfully annexed by Russia. Presumably they do not consider themselves entitled to secession just because they live there. So while living in a territory may be a physical precondition for most self-determination claims, it is not dispositive of the question of title.

A second alternative is to derive territorial sovereignty from private property. A group has title, under this view, when its members hold legitimate titles of property over land that, when added together, constitute the group's title over the territory as a whole. This approach seems consistent with libertarian theories of natural property rights. Property rights are antecedent to government, and the latter's authority is created to protect them. But this view misconstrues the notion of territory. The rights of a group over a territory is not the sum of private property rights but the locus of the exercise of authority derived from the social contract. This holds even if we accept, for the sake of argument, that the libertarian explanation of the state is adequate. According to a libertarian view, individuals create the state to fulfil minimal functions of protection against crime and external enemies.[56] Thus, for example, the government's authority over my private land is superimposed over my property right to the same land.

Another possibility is to draw from the international law principles regarding title to territory. According to customary international law, there are several ways in which a state can lawfully acquire title, but peaceful and uninterrupted occupation is, with some exceptions, as good as title.[57] Customary law has also developed the notion of critical date—that is, the date on which the question of title was crucial. This is in most cases the date when the dispute arose between two states about sovereignty over the territory. The critical date is important for assigning legal weight to acts of sovereignty that occurred after that date. In general, critical date analysis considers the period leading up to the critical date as the most important to deciding title. Acts of open and peaceful display of sovereignty in the period leading up to the critical date are, therefore, decisive for the determination of which state has title over the territory in dispute. Can this analysis help to decide questions of self-determination?

The main problem with customary international law is that it is only

---

[56] *See generally* ROBERT NOZICK, ANARCHY, STATE, AND UTOPIA (1974).

[57] For the classic statement of the theory of acquisition of territory, see Island of Palmas Case (Neth. v. U.S.), 2 Rep. Int'l Arbitral Awards 829 (M. Huber arb., 1928).

relevant to disputes between states. Because self-determination involves claims by groups that are not states, international law regarding title is of little help. For example, it is obvious that the Soviet Union exercised open acts of sovereignty in Chechnya over a long period of time. This sovereignty was accepted by other states, but it does not help us solve the issue of whether or not the territory was unjustly taken from the Chechnyans. Thus, international law is helpful in interstate territorial disputes; but because of its traditional emphasis on state sovereignty, it begs the question of the justice of states' takings of land that belongs to groups that are not states.

Nonetheless, an analogical use of some international legal concepts such as critical date may help. For example, a relevant question is whether or not the Chechnyans were an independent state, or on their way to becoming one, at the time when the Russians took over the territory. Another relevant question is whether the Chechnyans consented at the time to become part of Russia. Under critical date analysis, events leading up to the critical date will be the most important for determining title. For example, the critical date in the Chechnya dispute would be in principle the date when the Russians annexed the territory. But if an event occurred a long time ago, the group's claim will be weakened. In other words, the more recent the unjust territorial taking, the stronger the claim will be. Here, considerations of political stability affect territorial claims. This seems to be analogous to the insistence of customary law on occupation and display of sovereignty. In short, the international law principles may be useful provided that they shake off their statist bias and take into account instead territorial claims of substate groups.

Yet another possibility is to analyze territorial injustice as a form of unlawful usurpation of power. What does it mean to say that a group (say, Latvians) has title over the Latvian territory? Perhaps what we mean is this: there was in the past a government in Latvia that was, in some sense, legitimate. At some point, the Soviet army invaded and forcibly replaced that sovereign with a new one. The change of sovereign would be analogous to an unconstitutional change of power. To say that Latvians have a title over the territory is to say that the group (Latvia) has a right to restore the original sovereign over the territory. But what if the original sovereign was itself morally illegitimate (that is, a tyrannical regime)? It seems odd to persist with the thesis of unlawful usurpation, for the old sovereign would not be any more legitimate than the new one.

I do not choose among these different possibilities. It is sufficient for the argument in this chapter to accept that groups may have a collective title over land determined, perhaps, by long occupation. After all, it does make sense to say, "The Armenians have lived in this territory, Armenia, for a period long enough to create a title so that, whether or not they form a separate state, it is their territory."

The foregoing discussion suggests that there are three factors to be considered in the moral evaluation of self-determination claims. The first is the moral urgency to escape serious political injustice against a group. In this case, self-determination, autonomy, group rights, and even secession may be the only viable forms of political reorganization to end the injustice. The second is the need to remedy past territorial injustice against the group (along the lines suggested by Brilmayer). Political injustice occurs when members of a group are denied human rights, territorial injustice when the group's governance over the territory has been forcibly replaced by outsiders. The third factor is the need to take into account the legitimate interests of third parties—in particular, of people in the parent state. How these three factors are to be weighed against the legitimate expectations of the remainder state cannot be determined by any fixed formula. Some consequences follow, however:

(1) Liberal principles of justice act as deontological constraints on self-determination claims.

(2) Ethnic groups are never morally entitled to create a despotic state.

(3) The establishment of group rights (and other forms of group autonomy) cannot take place at the cost of the violation of the rights of members of the group.

(4) Conversely, self-determination (including secession) as the only viable means to escape oppression is justified.

(5) The exercise of the right of self-determination and secession must take into account the legitimate interests of third parties—in particular, of the parent state. Those legitimate expectations of third parties, however, should always involve either moral concerns (such as a fear that larger autonomy for the group would impair the democratic institutions in the parent state) or strong prudential concerns (such as a danger that larger group autonomy will jeopardize a vital food supply).

The reasons usually given by international lawyers to oppose secession and self-determination, such as the need to respect the territorial integrity of the state, are suspect. There is no right to territorial integrity independent of the legitimacy of the state that rules over that territory, and there is nothing that is inherently morally important in keeping the territory together. Here as elsewhere, traditional international law is highly anthropomorphic: because the preservation of bodily integrity is morally important, lawyers assume that preservation of the body of the state, the territory, is equally important. Similarly, there seems to be something intrinsically sobering about the death of a person (even of one who deserves to die), but there is nothing intrinsically wrong with the death of a state (think about East Germany). A person has inherent dignity, while the state is simply a form of political organization. The life of a state is entirely dependent on the rights and interests of the people who populate it. The state is not a person, and the territory is not a body. A territory is the locus of political organization and thus the space where persons exercise their moral rights. A society needs a territory, but it does not follow that a specific territory is required by principles of justice.

While the recognition of collective rights carries real dangers of restrictions on people's freedoms, nothing in this chapter precludes the establishment of legal group rights or other forms of group autonomy for weighty pragmatic or prudential reasons, such as the need to avert ethnic conflict.[58] What I have tried to show is that, while legal collective rights may sometimes be an appropriate remedy, they are never required by justice. They are not supported by principled, deontological reasons nor by the popular public goods argument. There are no moral collective rights—at least none that are consistent with rights-based liberalism.[59]

The issue of ethnic identity and the rights associated with it raise profound questions about our commitment to freedom and equality. An assertion of group rights founded in common race, religion, or language challenges liberalism's commitment to universality and its emphasis on human commonality. Equal rights of citizenship are, for liberals, color-blind (and language-blind and so on). The assumption behind the political relevance of ethnic identity is that there is a right to be governed by members of one's own race (or language and so on). But that cannot be right, notwithstanding rhetoric to the contrary. If a government is morally legitimate under liberal principles, why should it be important that the officials "look like me"? Colonialism was wrong not because the ruler of the colony was white. Rather, the government was morally illegitimate because it did not respect human or democratic rights and had been established for the purpose of subjecting the inhabitants of the colonies to political and economic exploitation. These are liberal-individualistic reasons to condemn colonialism. The recognition of special group rights and self-determination is linked to, and dependent on, the imperatives to respect human rights and promote social justice. Only to the extent that ethnicity is linked to political or territorial injustice may ethnic groups legitimately claim special rights.

[58] See the penetrating essay by Horacio Spector, *Communitarianism and Collective Rights*, 17 ANALYSE & KRITIK 67, 88 (1995). Spector's position is quite close to the one defended in this chapter.

[59] *See id.* at 79–82. Spector makes the following powerful point: "[Individual] autonomy is especially important because it involves the exercise of second-order capabilities which tell us whether a preference we have is appropriate or not, compatible or incompatible with our nature. . . . And it is this rational ability that the communitarian weakens or replaces directly by the preference of her community (or its authorities)." *Id.* at 82.

4

Ethnic Conflict and Territorial Claims: Where Do We Draw a Line?

Steven R. Ratner

The foregoing analyses of ethnic conflict under international law all recognize explicitly or implicitly that the most intractable ethnic conflicts of the late twentieth century center upon, in the words of Georges Scelle, the "obsession du territoire."[1] Those struggles involve claims by groups for greater control over land; and they typically seek, and with some frequency have now achieved, secessions and breakups of states or in some cases arrangements within a state affording significant autonomy. But no appraisal of, or set of solutions to, this challenge can be complete without consideration of the logical follow-up question: how do we draw a line allocating territory?

At the core of the legal debate over the territory of new states or autonomous regions is the concept of uti possidetis. In its original Latin form, uti possidetis was an edict that the praetor would issue to two parties claiming ownership of real property, granting provisional legal possession to the possessor during the litigation.[2] Despite these origins as a provisional remedy, by the nineteenth century international law had bestowed upon uti possidetis a seemingly more permanent consequence: that states

I greatly appreciate comments from Hans Baade, Gregory Fox, Mark Gergen, Jeffrey Herbst, Samuel Issacharoff, Douglas Laycock, Alexander Murphy, Jonathan Pratter, Peter Spiro, and Jay Westbrook. This chapter is a condensed version of *Drawing a Better Line: Uti Possidetis and Borders of New States*, 90 AM. J. INT'L L. 590 (1996).

[1] Georges Scelle, *Obsession du Territoire*, in SYMBOLAE VERZIJL 347 (1958).

[2] W. W. BUCKLAND, A TEXT-BOOK OF ROMAN LAW FROM AUGUSTUS TO JUSTINIAN 734 (Peter Stein ed., 3d rev. ed. 1963); JOHN BASSETT MOORE, COSTA RICA–PANAMA ARBITRATION: MEMORANDUM ON UTI POSSIDETIS 5–8 (1913). The edict became summarized in the phrase *uti possidetis, ita possidetis*: "As you possess, so may you possess."

emerging from the decolonization process would presumptively inherit the colonial administrative borders that they held at the time of independence. It governed much of the determination of the size and shape of the states of former Spanish Latin America beginning in the early 1800s as well as imperial Africa and Southeast Asia from the 1950s. The relevance of uti possidetis today seems confirmed by the practice of states during the dissolution of the former Soviet Union, Yugoslavia, and Czechoslovakia, as the world community sanctified the former internal administrative lines as interstate frontiers.[3]

Reliance upon uti possidetis during the post–cold war breakups has stemmed from three arguments or assumptions. First, uti possidetis reduces the prospects of armed conflict by providing the only clear rule in such situations, without which new states will fall prey to irredentist neighbors or internal secessions. Second, because a cosmopolitan democratic state can function within any borders, the conversion of administrative borders to international borders is as sensible as any other approach and far simpler. Third, uti possidetis is asserted as a rule of international law mandating conversion of *all* administrative boundaries into international borders. This rule emerged during the decolonization period but would apply by logical extension to the break-up of states today—a view most significantly elaborated by the esteemed commission advising the European Community on legal questions associated with the breakup of Yugoslavia.[4]

However compelling these views seem, the easy embrace by governments of uti possidetis and the suggestion that it is now a general rule of international law to govern the breakup of states lead to two distinct and dangerous spillover effects. First, a policy or rule that transforms all administrative borders into international boundaries creates a significant hazard in the name of simplicity and finality—namely the temptation among ethnic separatists to divide further the world along more administrative lines.[5] If the Republic of Georgia's new borders must coincide with those of the former Georgian Soviet Socialist Republic, are not the future Republic of Abhazia's equally clearly those of the former Abhaz Autonomous Soviet Socialist Republic? Would the Québécois consider secession so readily if the new state had borders different from those established by Canada and the United Kingdom for the purpose of integrating Quebec into the Dominion?

---

[3] *See, e.g.*, S.C. Res. 713, preambular para. 8, September 25, 1991, U.N. SCOR, 46th Year, Res. and Dec., at 42, 42–43, U.N. Doc. S/INF/47; Charter of the Commonwealth of Independent States, June 22, 1993, art. 3, 34 I.L.M. 1279, 1283 (1995).

[4] *See* Conference on Yugoslavia, Arbitration Commission Opinion No. 3, January 11, 1992, 31 ILM 1499 (1992).

[5] *Cf.* Hurst Hannum, *Self-Determination, Yugoslavia, and Europe: Old Wine in New Bottles*, 3 TRANSNAT'L L. & CONTEMP. PROBS. 57, 69 (1993).

Second, the extension of uti possidetis to modern breakups leads to injustices and instability by leaving significant populations both unsatisfied with their status in new states and hardly assured of political participation there. By hiding behind inflated notions of uti possidetis, state leaders avoid engaging the issue of territorial adjustments—even minor ones—central to the process of self-determination. In the case of Yugoslavia, for example, although uti possidetis hardly caused the eruption of armed conflict, states' assumption of its applicability from the outset prevented any debate over the adjustment of boundaries and limited the universe of possible borders to one.[6] This meant endorsement of frontiers that left those people on the "wrong" side of the border ripe for ethnic cleansing. Any theory of justice in these matters, such as that set forth by Lea Brilmayer in her chapter, must take into account the justice of borders.

I. LEGAL CONTOURS OF THE PRINCIPLE

As developed by states to respond to the decolonization of Latin America, Africa, and Asia, uti possidetis can be summarized as follows.

First, state practice lends support for regarding uti possidetis as a customary norm requiring states to presume the inheritance of colonial borders unless, as occurred in relatively few cases, the colonial state(s) or other decision maker had determined otherwise. Most new states in these regions inherited their colonial borders without alteration and, in cases of disputed boundaries, typically agreed to settle them through reference to uti possidetis.[7] Uti possidetis also appears in numerous domestic constitutions in Latin America;[8] in the Organization for African Unity's 1964 Cairo Resolution as reflecting the trends within Africa at that time;[9] and, by implication, in the U.N.'s 1960 Declaration on the Granting of Independence to Colonial Countries and Peoples.[10] The World Court has stated in dictum in the *Frontier Dispute* case (Burkina Faso/Mali) that uti possidetis is a "general principle" and a "rule of a general scope" in the case of

[6] *See* DAVID OWEN, BALKAN ODYSSEY 33–34 (1995) ("The refusal to make [Yugoslavia's internal] borders negotiable greatly hampered the EC's attempt at crisis management . . . and subsequently put all peacemaking . . . within a straitjacket that greatly inhibited compromises.").

[7] *See, e.g.,* Treaty of Arbitration, Guat.-Hond., July 16, 1930, art. V, *in* Honduras Borders Case (Guat./Hond.), 2 UNRIAA 1304, 1322 (1933); Special Agreement, Upper Volta–Mali, September 16, 1983, preamble, *in* Frontier Dispute (Burkina Faso/Mali), 1986 ICJ 554, 557 (December 22).

[8] *See, e.g.,* Constitution of the State of Venezuela, September 22, 1830, art. V, 18 BRIT. & FOREIGN ST. PAPERS 1119 (1833).

[9] Resolution on Border Disputes, 1964, *in* BASIC DOCUMENTS ON AFRICAN BOUNDARIES 360, 361 (Ian Brownlie ed., 1971).

[10] G.A. Res. 1514 (XV), para. 4, U.N. GAOR, 15th Sess., Supp. No. 16, at 66, 67, U.N. Doc. A/4684.

decolonization.[11] Although evidence of opinio juris among states is lacking, these trends lend some support for the existence of a norm of regional customary law in Latin America and Africa, if not a general norm, that regards uti possidetis as a default rule in the decolonization context.[12]

Second, uti possidetis does not prevent the emergence of different borders during decolonization. In a significant number of situations, the states emerging from colonial rule did not assume their pre-independence borders.[13] Single colonies also split at independence.[14] Moreover, states have agreed in *compromis* to accept borders deviating from uti possidetis in certain circumstances.[15] Uti possidetis was not, then, a uniform practice by or obligation upon colonial powers—although the General Assembly has sought to limit those states' ability to divide a colonial territory unilaterally during the independence process.[16]

Third, uti possidetis does not bar postindependence changes in borders carried out by lawful means. It is not a norm of jus cogens and precludes neither changes in borders nor even the creation of new states by mutual consent.[17] In Latin America, for instance, Gran Colombia, the United Provinces of the Río de la Plata, and the United Provinces of Central America dissolved into separate states.[18] Later dissolutions included the Federation of Mali (after Senegal's departure) and the Federation of Ma-

---

[11] 1986 ICJ at 565. It has never adjudicated whether uti possidetis was a norm of customary law because, in the border disputes it has heard, both parties have stipulated that their boundary would be determined according to borders in effect at the time of independence.

[12] See Affaire des Frontières Colombo-Vénézuéliennes (Colom./Venez.), 1 UNRIAA 225, 229 (1922) (dictum that uti possidetis of 1810 is law for the states "by virtue of a general South American theory"); Beagle Channel Arbitration (Arg./Chile), 52 ILR 98, 124–25 (1977); IAN BROWNLIE, AFRICAN BOUNDARIES: A LEGAL AND DIPLOMATIC ENCYCLOPAEDIA 11 (1979) (customary effect in Africa for "those states which have unilaterally declared their acceptance of the principle"); ROSALYN HIGGINS, PROBLEMS AND PROCESS: INTERNATIONAL LAW AND HOW WE USE IT 123–24 (1994).

[13] See Northern Cameroons, 1963 ICJ 15, 21–25 (December 2); A. RIGO SUREDA, THE EVOLUTION OF THE RIGHT OF SELF-DETERMINATION 151–63, 199–202 (1973) (Togo and Kuria Muria); MICHLA POMERANCE, SELF-DETERMINATION IN LAW AND PRACTICE: THE NEW DOCTRINE IN THE UNITED NATIONS 19–21 (1982) (absorption of various enclaves).

[14] See POMERANCE, *supra* note 13, at 19–21 (Belgian Rwanda-Urundi and British Gilbert and Ellice Islands).

[15] See, e.g., Gámez-Bonilla Treaty, Hond.-Nic., October 7, 1894, art. 2(6), *in* Arbitral Award Made by the King of Spain on 23 December 1906 (Hond. v. Nic.), 1960 ICJ 192, 199–200 (November 18) [hereinafter King of Spain]; Beagle Channel, 52 ILR at 132–33; Indo-Pakistan Western Boundary (Rann of Kutch) Case (India/Pak.), 50 ILR 2, 470 (1968). See also King of Spain, 1960 ICJ at 215 (refusing to regard uti possidetis as overriding compromis giving arbitrator authority to consider other factors).

[16] Frontier Dispute, 1986 ICJ at 653 (sep. op. Luchaire); IAN BROWNLIE, PRINCIPLES OF PUBLIC INTERNATIONAL LAW 135 (4th ed. 1990). See also GA Res. 49/18, U.N. GAOR, 49th Sess., Supp. No. 49, vol. 1, at 17, U.N. Doc. A/49/49 (1994) (calling on France to return Mayotte to the Comoros Islands).

[17] HIGGINS, *supra* note 12, at 123–24; Hurst Hannum, *Rethinking Self-Determination*, 34 VA. J. INT'L L. 1, 55–56 (1993).

[18] See generally HUBERT HERRING, A HISTORY OF LATIN AMERICA 260–91, 434–37 (1955).

laysia (after Singapore's expulsion).[19] The 1975 Helsinki Final Act did not rule out peaceful border adjustments in Europe (however unlikely) but only banned changes through force.[20]

Fourth, uti possidetis does not override other, nonconsensual considerations arguing for a different border. Both the Vienna Convention on the Law of Treaties (1969) and the Vienna Convention on Succession of States in Respect of Treaties (1978) support this view with respect to those boundaries determined by treaties—that is, those separating colonies of different European powers—by specifically refraining from adopting the maintenance of such boundaries as a rule of conventional law.[21] Thus, uti possidetis is agnostic on whether or not secessions or breakups *should* occur and is not simply the legal embodiment of a policy condemning them.[22] It would not purport to render unlawful the changes in the borders of Pakistan and Ethiopia as a result of the creation of Bangladesh in 1971 and Eritrea in 1993, although it might suggest that the borders of the new states should coincide with those of East Pakistan and the former Ethiopian province, respectively.

As for the extension of uti possidetis to the breakup of states, the trend of states to transform existing borders in the cases of Yugoslavia, Czechoslovakia, and the USSR suggests some movement toward normative expectations as endorsed by the Badinter Commission. But the history is brief, and opinion remains divided.[23]

II. Uti Possidetis and the Function of Boundaries

The true subjects of uti possidetis, of course, are boundaries themselves; and internal and interstate boundaries, in fact, serve highly different pur-

---

[19] See Malcolm Shaw, Title to Territory in Africa: International Legal Issues 213–14 (1986); Frank N. Trager, *The Federation of Malaysia: An Intermediate Failure? in* Why Federations Fail: An Inquiry into the Requisites for Successful Federation 125, 143–50 (Thomas M. Franck ed., 1968).

[20] Conference on Security and Cooperation in Europe, Final Act, August 1, 1975, principle III, 14 I.L.M. 1292, 1294 (1975) (parties regard frontiers as "inviolable" and will refrain from "assaulting these frontiers") [hereinafter Helsinki Final Act].

[21] See Reports of the International Law Commission, U.N. Doc. A/6309/Rev.1, *reprinted in* [1966] II Y.B. Int'l L. Comm'n 169, 259, U.N. Doc. A/CN.4/SER.A/1968/Add.1 (on limitations of Article 62 of 1969 convention); Report of the International Law Commission on the work of its twenty-sixth session, U.N. Doc. A/9610/Rev.1, *reprinted in* [1974] II Y.B. Int'l L. Comm'n, pt. 1, at 157, 201, U.N. Doc. A/CN.4.SER.A/1974/Add.1 (part 1) (on limitations of Article 11 of 1978 convention).

[22] See Gregory H. Fox, *Self-Determination in the Post–Cold War Era: A New Internal Focus?* 16 Mich. J. Int'l L. 733, 751–52 (1995) (reviewing Yves Beigbeder, International Monitoring of Plebiscites, Referenda and National Elections: Self-Determination and Transition to Democracy [1994]).

[23] *Compare, e.g.,* Alain Pellet, *Note sur la Commission d'Arbitrage de la Conference Européene pour la Paix en Yougoslavie,* 37 Annuaire Français de Droit International 329, 342 (1991) (norm of custom) *with* Hannum, *supra* note 17, at 55 (extension of uti possidetis is "dubious").

poses. Governments establish interstate boundaries to separate states and peoples, while they maintain internal borders to unify a polity. The line-drawing exercises in each case seek efficiency and simplicity, but for opposing purposes.[24] These differences, in turn, render uti possidetis a profoundly illogical way of determining the borders of new states.

As for international boundaries, although they historically sought to ensure the physical preservation of a state from its neighbors, today they serve the important function of limiting the territorial jurisdiction of states. A simple line determines which state can, subject to international law, prescribe and enforce laws and policies relating to the full range of attributes of persons and property, whether citizenship, taxation, or educational opportunities.[25] When those governing a state look internally, their concern is not on protection and separation but on binding together or managing separate areas as a whole.[26] They create or accept subdivisions because of the need to devolve some authority to, or tolerate some decision making at, subnational levels. That devolution will range from a federal structure (such as Switzerland) to greater concentration at the national level (such as France), but even the unitary state will likely have some administrative lines. While these lines may end up fragmenting the state in certain situations (for example, in federal entities through different regimes of local laws), the state's ultimate goal remains unity.[27]

Some administrative boundaries predate the current cultural landscape.[28] Others were drawn as states expanded into territories lacking inhabitants of the governing nationality, as is the case of much of the straight-line boundaries of the American and Canadian West and Australia.[29] Just as possible is the prospect that the central government has drawn or reconfigured the borders or part of them for the express purpose of preserving the unity of the state, including in response to centrifugal forces. The central and peripheral elites might need to forge a national

[24] Cf. Land, Island, and Maritime Frontier Dispute (El Salvador/Honduras, Nicaragua intervening), 1992 ICJ 351, 388 (September 11) (noting conversion into international borders of boundaries "intended originally for quite other purposes").

[25] See Aegean Sea Continental Shelf Case (Greece v. Turk.), 1978 ICJ 3, 35–37 (December 19); Milan Sahović & William W. Bishop, The Authority of the State: Its Range with Respect to Persons and Places, in MANUAL OF PUBLIC INTERNATIONAL LAW 311, 316 (Max Sørenson ed., 1968).

[26] Richard Hartshorne, The Functional Approach to Political Geography, 40 ANNALS ASS'N AM. GEOGRAPHERS 95, 104–10 (1950).

[27] See RONAN PADDISON, THE FRAGMENTED STATE: THE POLITICAL GEOGRAPHY OF POWER 19 (1983).

[28] S. WHITTEMORE BOGGS, INTERNATIONAL BOUNDARIES: A STUDY OF BOUNDARY FUNCTIONS AND PROBLEMS 28–30 (1940). These would include those corresponding to ancient lines of control that far antedate the establishment of the particular state, such as the case of many English counties, or those corresponding to old land grants of a colonial power, such as the original thirteen U.S. states.

[29] See, e.g., FRANKLIN K. VAN ZANDT, BOUNDARIES OF THE UNITED STATES AND THE SEVERAL STATES 228–58 (1966) (Western United States).

identity, whether through obliteration of territorial units with competing sources of loyalty or compromise with those units to ensure their respect for the unity of the greater polity. Or they might simply try to draw lines to permit governmental agencies, at the national or substate level, to divide up national responsibilities more efficiently.[30]

Thus, numerous states have created, abolished, and redrawn internal boundaries as part of the nation-building process, including Canada, France, and Britain.[31] The Soviet Union determined the number and borders of the union and autonomous republics with the explicit goal of national unification, at first taking into account the ethnodemographic composition of these territories but during Stalin's years according to a philosophy of divide and conquer.[32]

Moreover, from the perspective of the ordinary resident of a state, the administrative border itself—even in the case of federal systems—has completely contrasting implications for daily life compared to interstate borders. While school systems, sales taxes, much private and public law, and even official language may differ on either side of the internal border, it stands apart from the international border by the ease with which it may be crossed. This porosity may prevail at the interstate level for states that have eliminated obstacles to crossborder movement, but most typically retain the right to search and prevent movement into their territory of undesirable persons or goods.[33]

To apply uti possidetis during the formation of new entities thus involves a change in the overall function and image of the boundary, with two deleterious results. First, it seems reasonable to posit that in those situations where states are breaking up, the process of forging new national identities in the successor states will result in a special significance for the borders. The very forces that propelled the creation of the new state are likely to cause it to erect barriers—to people, goods, and even ideas—against its neighbors. The international border between Croatia and Serbia, or the Czech Republic and Slovakia, is thus not merely legally distinct from the previous interrepublican border; the change in its status has clear consequences for the people and governments of those two states.[34] In Michael Walzer's words, these boundaries give a "dimension"

---

[30] See PADDISON, supra note 27, at 49–55.

[31] See Mary Janigan, The Roots of the Struggle: A Turbulent Past Haunts Quebec, MACLEAN'S, November 25, 1991, at 26; ROY E. H. MELLOR, NATION, STATE, AND TERRITORY: A POLITICAL GEOGRAPHY 139–46 (1989).

[32] ROBERT J. KAISER, THE GEOGRAPHY OF NATIONALISM IN RUSSIA AND THE USSR 107–12, 409–11 (1994).

[33] See, e.g., European Community Council of Ministers Directive No. 64/221, February 25, 1964, 1963–1964 O.J. SPEC. ED. 117 (restrictions of persons within free-trade area on limited grounds of public policy).

[34] See Philip Sherwell, Neighbors on the Borderline: New Boundaries Rekindle Old Fear, SUNDAY TELEGRAPH (London), January 3, 1993, at 15.

of "physical space" to the rights and common life on each side of them.[35]

When the boundary lines assume this new significance, their location becomes even more critical. While many internal lines will make optimal international borders because they historically define a distinct community whose unity and identity override other concerns (such as Scotland or Bavaria), other considerations and scenarios also abound. Groups separated by administrative lines within one state may well prove able to protect their interests through influence at the central level; but they would not wish to tolerate separation in different states, whereupon they could lose that power.[36] Economic efficiencies irrelevant when adjacent communities were separated only by administrative lines may become important when the border is now an international frontier.[37] And military establishments integrated across administrative lines face constraints during dissolution.[38]

The second deleterious result is that conversion of administrative lines to international boundaries disregards the interconnection between the internal borders and the efforts to forge national unity in the old state. As I have noted, internal boundaries are often drawn for the purpose of uniting the state, not with the possibility of secession in mind. Thus, when the contract among the territorial units or between those units and the center, or the center's master plan for unity, is violated through secession or collapses through disintegration, why assume that one of its core elements—the location of the internal borders—must remain unchanged? Rather, the breakup of the state calls into question the parties' original bargain premised on the continuity of the whole state.[39] In the case of Canada, secessionists seek to have their cake and eat it too—to secede and take with them the land given to Québec in order to keep it in Canada.[40]

---

[35] MICHAEL WALZER, JUST AND UNJUST WARS 55, 57–58 (2d ed. 1992).

[36] LEE C. BUCHHEIT, SECESSION: THE LEGITIMACY OF SELF-DETERMINATION 29–30 (1978).

[37] See, e.g., ALEXIS HERACLIDES, THE SELF-DETERMINATION OF MINORITIES IN INTERNATIONAL POLITICS 61–62 (1991) (describing large economic capacity of Katanga vis-à-vis the whole Congo).

[38] See, e.g., James Rupert, Yeltsin Cancels Trip to Ukraine for Treaty-Signing, WASHINGTON POST, April 3, 1996, at A15 (on continuing disagreements over Black Sea fleet).

[39] Cf. Vienna Convention on the Law of Treaties, May 23, 1969, art. 61, 1155 U.N.T.S. 331, 346 (withdrawal from treaty allowed due to "permanent disappearance or destruction of an object indispensable" for its execution); Ivo D. Duchacek, External and Internal Challenges to the Federal Bargain, PUBLIUS, Spring 1975, at 41, 43–44.

[40] See GRAND COUNCIL OF THE CREES, SOVEREIGN INJUSTICE: FORCIBLE INCLUSION OF THE JAMES BAY CREES AND CREE TERRITORY INTO A SOVEREIGN QUÉBEC 207–12 (1995); but see Thomas M. Franck et al., L'Intégrité Territoriale du Québec dans l'Hypothèse de l'Accession à la Souveraineté, in 1 LES ATTRIBUTS D'UN QUÉBEC SOUVERAINE 377, 402–5 (Commission d'Étude des Questions Afférentes à l'Accession du Québec à la Souveraineté ed., 1992).

III. Uti Possidetis As Anachronism

Whatever the illogic of uti possidetis in the abstract, it remains a historical fact that states applied the policy during the decolonization of Latin America and Africa. Why not, then, assume that it represents good law at the turn of the twenty-first century?

One response to the decolonization precedent turns on a critical factual distinction between earlier episodes and today. The boundaries between different parts of one colonial empire that were later transformed into international borders did not serve the same functions as those of typical internal boundaries today. The border between, for example, one French colony and another in French Africa was more of a dividing line than the border between one French department and another or between U.S. states. The governors-general, governors, and other authorities of each colonial territory typically enjoyed extensive authority and independence internally, far more than did officials in internal units in the metropole.[41] Indeed, neighboring colonies themselves often had different legal status vis-à-vis the metropole, suggesting again that the lines dividing them assumed what one might call semi-international status.[42] Uti possidetis, then, was less illogical in the past than it would be today because the borders to be transformed more closely resembled international borders than do the administrative borders of nation-states.

Beyond this historical distinction, the principal reason for different treatment of these situations lies in the profound transformation of the legal landscape regarding self-determination since the earlier eras—a sea change that renders such a policy far less defensible today. Before this change, roughly from the birth of the United Nations until the early 1960s, the international community focused upon one form of self-determination: decolonization. This decision made perfect sense at the time, for colonialism represented an easily identifiable violation of nearly anyone's notion of self-determination, one that meshed with both increasing American (and Soviet) power vis-à-vis Europe and the growing sense that Africans and Asians were entitled to determine their destiny free of imperial control. In that historical context, uti possidetis kept decolonization orderly and created the possibility for a national identity and some basis for nation building. By extinguishing claims from both neighbors with irredentist claims and minority groups with secessionist tendencies, it

[41] See, e.g., William B. Cohen, The French Governors, in AFRICAN PROCONSULS: EUROPEAN GOVERNORS IN AFRICA 19, 23–27 (L. H. Gann & Peter Duignan eds., 1978); JEAN SURET-CANALE, FRENCH COLONIALISM IN TROPICAL AFRICA 1900–1945, at 308–13 (Pica Press 1971) (1964); Anthony H. M. Kirk-Greene, On Governorship and Governors in British Africa, in AFRICAN PROCONSULS, supra, at 209, 230–32.

[42] See FRANÇOIS LUCHAIRE, DROIT D'OUTRE MER 100–105 (1959) (categories of French territories); KENNETH ROBERTS-WRAY, COMMONWEALTH AND COLONIAL LAW 19–62 (1966).

enabled new states to concentrate on economic and social development, thereby helping to prevent the perfect from being the enemy of the good.[43] As for those minorities within the new states who could not advance their interests through sufficient ballots (assuming their government even allowed elections), states showed less interest.

The 1960s, however, were marked by the emerging recognition that self-determination did not simply equate with decolonization. The International Covenant on Civil and Political Rights (ICCPR) included the right of self-determination, and one not explicitly limited to decolonization, at the beginning of a human rights instrument.[44] The 1970 Friendly Relations Declaration pushed the frontiers of self-determination with respect to the territorial aspect of a state. In elaborating upon the U.N. Charter's principle of equal rights and self-determination of peoples, the declaration suggested that the borders of a state may not be sacrosanct if the government does not represent "the whole people belonging to the territory without distinction as to race, creed, or colour."[45] The declaration signaled that a state's national unity is earned by its government; it is not a fait accompli.

In one sense, this shift may have no impact on uti possidetis as a principle to govern future breakups. By opening up the possibility of lawful breakups, the Friendly Relations Declaration might suggest that the new entities ought simply to correspond to the administrative units of the old. The need to avoid border disputes would thus matter as much as it had during the breakup of empires, justifying continued recourse to uti possidetis. But the declaration, along with the ICCPR, recognizes other important values. It thus could suggest that *new* states ought to be drawn in such a way that they are likely to be led by a government "representing the whole people." This is not a recipe for borders determined along ethnic lines alone, but it does open the door to borders fashioned so that groups will not simply be an unwelcome, oppressed minority in a new state.[46]

[43] See Jeffrey Herbst, *The Creation and Maintenance of National Boundaries in Africa*, 43 INT'L ORG. 673, 685–87 (1989).

[44] December 19, 1966, art. 1, 999 U.N.T.S. 171, 173.

[45] G.A. Res. 2625, Annex, U.N. GAOR, 25th Sess., Supp. No. 28, at 121, 124, U.N. Doc. A/8028: "Nothing in the foregoing paragraphs shall be construed as authorizing or encouraging any action which would dismember or impair, totally or in part, the territorial integrity or political unity of sovereign and independent States conducting themselves in compliance with the principle of equal rights and self-determination of peoples as described above and thus possessed of a government representing the whole people belonging to the territory without distinction as to race, creed, or colour." *See also* Robert Rosenstock, *The Declaration of Principles of International Law Concerning Friendly Relations: A Survey*, 65 AM. J. INT'L L. 713, 732 (1971); ANTONIO CASSESE, SELF-DETERMINATION OF PEOPLES: A LEGAL REAPPRAISAL 120 (1995).

[46] See Hurst Hannum, *Synthesis of Discussion*, in PEOPLES AND MINORITIES IN INTERNATIONAL LAW 335 (Catherine Brölmann et al. eds., 1993); *cf.* WILL KYMLICKA, MULTICULTURAL

For example, suppose a group representing the majority of a particular administrative unit of a state, but a minority within that state, intends to split off from the state because there is no possibility that that state will provide a "representative government" as required under the Friendly Relations Declaration. If that group plans to abuse minorities within their new state, then the areas controlled by those minorities might be better off within the remnants of the old state (especially if that minority was part of the majority in the old state) or even another state. The Serb-dominated parts of Croatia might be one example; parts of the former Soviet Union might be others.

The years since 1970 have been characterized by further landmarks elaborating the scope of internal self-determination. The 1975 Helsinki Final Act stated that "all peoples have the right, in full freedom, to determine, when and as they wish, their internal and external political status" and thereby contemplated a right of internal self-determination broader than that suggested in the Friendly Relations Declaration.[47] By the early 1990s, the end of the Soviet Empire had led to an even more profound shift as governments and international organizations began to embrace more explicitly the notion that liberal democracy represented the only legitimate form of government.[48]

This recognition of the primacy of political participation also exerts some pull on the sanctity of uti possidetis. If the overriding purpose of a state is to permit its populace to advance the values of the people through a democratic process, then the formation of a *new* state ought to take into account that goal. One method of promoting that policy is to ensure that the members of the new state truly seek membership in it and adjust frontiers in a manner to produce an acceptable degree of participation. The special nature of transitions to new statehood was admitted by the first League of Nations legal commission examining the Aaland Islands question, which recognized that the rights of unwilling participants cannot be discounted during the process of new state formation.[49] Of course,

---

CITIZENSHIP: A LIBERAL THEORY OF MINORITY RIGHTS 113 (1995) ("fair way to . . . draw boundaries . . . [involves] ensuring that all national groups have the opportunity to maintain themselves as a distinct culture, if they so choose").

[47] Helsinki Final Act, *supra* note 20, principle VIII, 14 I.L.M. at 1295. *See* Antonio Cassese, *The Helsinki Declaration and Self-Determination, in* HUMAN RIGHTS, INTERNATIONAL LAW AND THE HELSINKI ACCORD 83, 100–103 (Thomas Buergenthal ed., 1977).

[48] *See, e.g.,* Charter of Paris for a New Europe, November 21, 1990, 30 I.L.M. 190 (1991); Vienna Declaration and Programme of Action, June 25, 1993, para. 8, *in* WORLD CONFERENCE ON HUMAN RIGHTS: THE VIENNA DECLARATION AND PROGRAMME OF ACTION JUNE 1993, at 30–31, U.N. Doc. DPI/1394–39399–August 1993–20M (1993) (support for promotion of democracy).

[49] *See* Report of the International Commission of Jurists Entrusted by the Council of the League of Nations with the Task of Giving an Advisory Opinion upon the Legal Aspects of the Aaland Islands Question, League of Nations O.J. Spec. Supp. No. 3, October 1920, at 10 (noting that inclusion of islands within Finland when the latter formed part of Russia did not

if the administrative borders already serve to define a polity dedicated to democracy and with a populace behind it, then modifications would be unnecessary.[50] And the situation of new states differs from that of peoples long present in a state offering them full civil rights, who would seem to have a weak claim to border adjustments to put them in a neighboring state.[51]

This view is not without risks. To meet fully the needs of dissatisfied groups trapped within a new state could lead to a perpetuation of secessions, much like atomic fission, or a patchwork of enclaves of one state within another. Thus, democratic theory cannot be carried to this extreme, and other methods will always be required to provide those disaffected groups with political participation.[52] Nevertheless, under certain circumstances, such as those in the former Yugoslavia or parts of the former Soviet Union, an adjustment of the frontier may prove necessary for democracy building.

IV. IMAGINING THE ALTERNATIVES: TOWARD RATIONAL LINE DRAWING

Despite the functional and normative handicaps of uti possidetis, its defenders can fall back on two claims: (1) the location of borders is unimportant because liberal democratic states can function within any borders; and (2) any alternative to uti possidetis is not feasible and a recipe for ethnic violence. The first reflects our cosmopolitan ideal, reflected in Fernando R. Tesón's chapter, to build pluralist, democratic states within whatever borders states have upon their birth. But democracy alone, even where it has sprouted in new states, does not guarantee the rights of minorities nor address those groups that do not wish to be part of the polity.[53] Moreover, in the states in the former Yugoslavia and Soviet Union where democracy has not taken root, the assumption that post-independence borders must coincide with pre-independence lines has

---

mean that they were lawfully a part of an independent Finland if their people did not wish to be).

[50] See THOMAS M. FRANCK, FAIRNESS IN INTERNATIONAL LAW AND INSTITUTIONS 168 (1995) (uti possidetis stronger for democratic state protecting minorities than for a state persecuting them).

[51] See id.; but see Harry Beran, Self-Determination: A Philosophical Perspective, in SELF-DETERMINATION IN THE COMMONWEALTH 23, 27–31 (W. J. Allan Macartney ed., 1988) (continuing right to secession in existing states).

[52] See, e.g., Lani Guinier, No Two Seats: The Elusive Quest for Political Equality, 77 VA. L. REV. 1413, 1458–87 (1991) (proposing voting scheme based on "interest representation" to promote voice of minorities).

[53] See generally Renée de Nevers, Democratization and Ethnic Conflict, in ETHNIC CONFLICT AND INTERNATIONAL SECURITY 61 (Michael E. Brown ed., 1993).

meant only expulsions and refugee crises, ethnic cleansing within the state, or even, as discussed in Lori Fisler Damrosch's chapter, genocide.

Thus, as much as liberal internationalists should cherish the idea of diverse peoples living harmoniously together, we cannot, as John Chipman points out, "impose a cosmopolitan diktat."[54] Cosmopolitanism must remain the goal, not only because it strives for people identifying themselves not exclusively in terms of real or imagined blood lines but because many minorities will live within areas where border changes are not feasible. It may, however, in certain instances, have to take account of the need to avoid gross abuses of peoples left in states where they do not wish to be or that will not treat them with dignity.[55]

This strips the defense of uti possidetis to its negative core—the absence of any other solution. This argument won the day during the African decolonizations, in most instances with good reason. But the options are not so stark, and it remains possible to lay the basis for a principled alternative. Four elements would define this new policy.

First, uti possidetis should form only a starting point for disposition of territory—a provisional remedy along the original Roman model. It means that, during the creation of new states, if the new entities cannot agree upon an appropriate division of territory, they should respect the existing lines of control—likely to be designated by administrative lines—until an authoritative determination is reached upon new boundaries.[56] This policy may well have underlain the 1992 opinion of the European Community's Yugoslavia Arbitration Commission that endorsed uti possedetis for contemporary breakups, as it presumably sought to limit Serbia's infiltration into parts of Bosnia-Herzegovina and Croatia. In many situations, states will and should retain the borders. But at least they will consider the idea of improving the welfare of individuals and long-term stability by revising frontiers rather than assuming them to be permanent by default. Equally important, the possibility of border revisions may cause some secessionist groups to rethink their claims to statehood entirely and consider internal power-sharing arrangements such as those discussed in David Wippman's chapter.

The most immediate consequence of this starting point is a new, and admittedly heavy, burden on decision makers: to engage directly the issue of the location of international borders rather than retreat behind the

54 John Chipman, *Managing the Politics of Parochialism, in* ETHNIC CONFLICT AND INTERNATIONAL SECURITY, *supra* note 53, at 237, 261.

55 *Cf.* Avishai Margalit & Joseph Raz, *National Self-Determination,* 87 J. PHIL. 439, 459 (1990) (approving secessions only if they "respect the basic rights of . . . inhabitants").

56 *Cf.* Jan Klabbers & René Lefeber, *Africa: Lost between Self-Determination and Uti Possidetis, in* PEOPLES AND MINORITIES IN INTERNATIONAL LAW, *supra* note 46, at 37, 63 (arguing in the decolonization context that uti possidetis means only that attainment of independence is not per se a ground to invalidate existing boundaries).

simple but anachronistic decolonization form of uti possidetis. They must, when faced with the possibility or actuality of breakups, see if there is a *significantly better* line and draw the best line under the circumstances—significantly better because the displacement costs of adjusting borders cannot be ignored.

Who are these decision makers? They may be national diplomats negotiating the size of the new state. But a policy that moves away from the simplicity of uti possidetis may well necessitate the creation of some type of institutional mechanism to help resolve the matter in the event that negotiations bog down. This could take the form of a mandatory or optional regional arbitration or conciliation commission to which states would repair during secession crises.[57] States could also agree to withhold recognition of new entities until agreement is reached through one of these processes upon new borders (again with the hope for some resolution short of dissolution). And they will have to lend their full support for the negotiated, conciliated, or arbitrated outcome.

Second, border revisions must be implemented through peaceful means alone. For states that have already split up into new states, this means nothing more or less than adherence to Article 2(4) of the U.N. Charter. As for disputes within a state, as Ruth Wedgwood discusses in her chapter, international law does not yet forbid the use of force in these conflicts, although norms of necessity and proportionality, as well as aspects of the law of war, apply.[58] A blanket prohibition would work to the detriment of both legitimate governments fighting unjustified secessionist or other insurgent movements as well as democratic resistance forces attempting to overthrow tyranny. But where the elites within the state have all accepted a process leading to autonomy, secession, or dissolution, then they should abstain from the use of force to adjust boundaries with which they are not satisfied and begin negotiations toward that end. This, of course, is what the EC and the U.N. urged upon the Yugoslav parties in 1991, and the latter groups' scorn for it highlights the hazards of all remedies—including uti possidetis—in this field.

Third, diplomats, conciliators, or arbitrators should scrutinize existing administrative lines for their suitability as international boundaries. Several factors will merit consideration. The age of the line is significant due to an aversion to opening closed issues as well as the likelihood that the populations have developed a sufficient sense of community identity or

---

[57] *See, e.g.,* Convention on Conciliation and Arbitration within the CSCE, December 15, 1992, 32 I.L.M. 557 (1993).

[58] *See, e.g.,* Geneva Convention Relative to the Protection of Civilian Persons in Time of War, Aug. 12, 1949, art. 3, 6 U.S.T. 3516, 3518, 75 U.N.T.S. 287, 288–90; Protocol Additional to the Geneva Conventions of 12 August 1949, and Relating to the Protection of Victims of Non-International Armed Conflicts (Protocol II), Dec. 12, 1977, 1125 U.N.T.S. 609.

otherwise adjusted to the borders.[59] Also relevant is the process by which the border was derived (such as constitutionally authorized versus through the command of a dictator). If a boundary is forced upon an area by a powerful central authority or a powerful neighboring administrative unit, it would not reflect the minimal wishes of the inhabitants, and their inability to change those borders ought not be probative.[60] In order to address directly functional suitability, negotiators or arbitrators will have to take account of the viability of the new entities that emerge from secessions or breakups. Will the existing frontiers allow the states resulting from a breakup—including the remnant of the prior state—to govern themselves sufficiently and develop economically? If the borders contain irrational elements for the governance and economic development of separate states, then decision makers will have to consider alternatives. This question, too, is, of course, not without ambiguity.[61]

Finally, to ensure appropriate focus on the human rights of the affected inhabitants, decision makers will need to ensure that any lines to replace the administrative borders originate in a process in which the people of the particular territory have a voice in their future status. This suggests the need, perhaps already legally required, for some form of consultation with the populace of a disputed territory on its future (although perhaps not a binding vote).[62] In practical terms, this may well amount to a need to resurrect one of the successes of the Versailles Treaty, the internationally supervised plebiscite.[63] Plebiscites have their own difficulties, of course, namely determining the size of the plebiscite area, the voting unit within the plebiscite area, and the location of the line to be drawn as a result of the plebiscite. Each matter will likely prove the subject of intense political negotiations during self-determination disputes as each group seeks to define the terms of the plebiscite in a manner to secure it the maximal territory. But the issue is not beyond imaginative solutions and a bit of creative diplomacy.[64]

---

[59] See Kaiyan Homi Kaikobad, Some Observations on the Doctrine of Continuity and Finality of Boundaries, 54 BRIT. Y.B. INT'L L. 119, 130–34 (1983) (noting importance of traditional boundaries). Cf. Lea Brilmayer, Secession and Self-Determination: A Territorial Approach, 16 YALE J. INT'L L. 177, 199–200 (1991) (relying upon immediacy of historical grievance to justify secessions).

[60] Even lines "freely arrived at" may still be inappropriate for international borders based on an earlier criticism of uti possidetis—that is, their location might well have been premised on the continued unity of the state, and separation breaks that bargain.

[61] For example, a state need not be crippled if the existing lines render it landlocked or reliant upon energy from abroad. But some lines seem especially troublesome, such as those that deprive one state of access to other states and the sea. See MELLOR, supra note 31, at 70.

[62] See Western Sahara, 1975 ICJ 12, 33 (October 16) (consultation required during decolonization except if population not a "people" or "special circumstances" obtain); CASSESE, supra note 45, at 190; but see BROWNLIE, supra note 16, at 170 (binding plebiscite not required).

[63] See generally 1 SARAH WAMBAUGH, PLEBISCITES SINCE THE WORLD WAR 3–45 (1933).

[64] For examples of practical approaches, see, e.g., Ali Khan, The Kashmir Dispute: A Plan for

If an effective legal framework for responding to ethnic conflict entails some degree of predictability of outcome, an assault on extending the decolonization form of uti possidetis to the breakup of states would appear to undermine the cause. For that formulation is clearly the easiest short-run method for determining the borders of a new state. But law, of course, is about justice, legitimacy, and long-term stability as well. And self-determination, by its nature, is an enormously complex and rich process in international law. If its goal is to enable peoples to realize their human rights, then the complexity of the territorial element cannot be wished away through a simple formula. That solution both encourages breakups that might be avoided if the parties considered the inequities and inefficiencies resulting from a split along the lines of uti possidetis and perpetuates or exacerbates injustices in the case of states that do divide.

Any alternative will clearly be more difficult to implement than the status quo, and the lack of centralized institutions may lead many to conclude that, by necessity, uti possidetis should develop into a rule for these situations. Even under the approach suggested here, the scrutiny of existing borders may well lead to a determination that many should become the boundaries of new states, and perhaps the burden of proof should lie on those who seek to challenge them. But to adopt that position automatically perpetuates a subterfuge—a formalized self-determination whereby a new state forms along the administrative lines of the old unit, but which neglects the underlying territorial issues that prompted the dissatisfaction initially and perhaps lays the groundwork for a new round of interstate conflicts and attempted secessions. In attempting to limit territorial claims during breakups, uti possidetis can instead simply reward the leaders of secessionist movements by more readily granting them a new territory, while offering an uncertain benefit to the human rights and political participation of the inhabitants or the public order of the region. Only a direct engagement of the territorial question, with all its complexities, is likely to control the breakup of states in a manner consistent with human dignity.

Regional Cooperation, 31 COLUM. J. TRANSNAT'L L. 495, 532–35 (1994) (proposal for size of Kashmir plebiscite); 1 WAMBAUGH, *supra* note 63, at 504–5 (proposal for drawing final line to balance winners with losers in each territory).

5

Pushing the Limits of the Liberal Peace: Ethnic Conflict and the "Ideal Polity"

Anne-Marie Slaughter

Can international law help prevent ethnic conflict? Can international legal instruments or institutions help design or implement potential solutions to problems of ethnic conflict? Alternatively, does international law prohibit such solutions? The chapters in the first half of this volume offer a range of analytical lenses—historical, philosophical, doctrinal—with which to scrutinize the complex components of the phenomenon we identify broadly as ethnic conflict. Many of them locate affirmative responses to ethnic conflict in international law, but only by redefining our concept or understanding of ethnic conflict itself. The chapters in the second half of the volume offer more concrete institutional, doctrinal, or policy responses, efforts to survey existing international legal norms and arrangements that either are or could be addressed to problems of ethnic conflicts. They challenge scholars to count up successes, to analyze failures, and to analogize current conflicts to historical examples in both categories.

This chapter takes a slightly longer perspective. Instead of asking how international law responds to ethnic conflict, it examines the ways in which ethnic conflict is likely to shape international law. This approach treats ethnic conflict as an empirical fact, a historical phenomenon, a contemporary curse. On the assumption that international law is the skin of international society, a set of efforts to respond normatively and potentially coercively to a historically contingent set of problems, the fact of international conflict will be—is being—recorded in international legal norms. Indeed, Nathaniel Berman reminds us of the many ways in which existing norms were forged in previous eras in which ethnic conflict was the dominant or most dangerous form of conflict in the international system.

Part I of this chapter identifies two themes running through a number of the proposed responses—group rights and political settlement—and examines their larger implications for the international legal order. The impact of ethnic conflict on human rights law is easiest to discern. The apparent change is the addition of group rights to individual rights, with the concomitant focus on government treatment of minorities and the recognition of groups as well as individuals as subjects of international law. On closer inspection, however, it is not clear whether groups will be better protected, and hence the potential for inter-group violence reduced, by adding targeted group rights rather than relying on the traditional liberal rights of freedom of association and expression. Further, the entire debate over group rights in the context of international concerns over ethnic conflict could spur reflections about the definition of *groupness* in many societies without visible ethnic problems.

The second theme running through these chapters is the redrawing of the often fluid boundary between the legal and the political spheres. The rise of group rights may be understood as the further colonization of the political by the legal; on the other hand, the relative success of informal efforts at mediating simmering ethnic conflicts suggests the value of expanding the repertoire of political solutions rather than searching for new rights and remedies. Diplomats and lawyers may pursue these paths simultaneously, but as Berman's chapter suggests, legal efforts may once again founder on difficulties in reaching a consensus about generalization with respect to group identity.[1]

Part II takes a further step back and examines two additional dimensions of more fundamental change in the international legal order, dimensions that ethnic conflict may not cause so much as expose. First is the development of a permanent structural bridge between domestic and international institutions, exemplified in the links between the International Criminal Tribunal for the Former Yugoslavia (ICTFY) and domestic courts. These links portend a new and quite different architecture for the international legal system, disaggregating states into their component legislative, executive, judicial, and administrative institutions and forging vertical bridges to their supranational counterparts.

Second is the emergence of a stylized liberal state as a kind of "ideal polity," almost mystically endowed with an array of characteristics that are supposed to assure both domestic and international peace and prosperity. As a particular regional strategy, the political leverage exerted by Western European states on Central and Eastern European leaders seeking to join the Western club may be successful at resolving or forestalling

---

[1] Berman at 44. (Page citations in this chapter are to this volume unless otherwise indicated.)

conflicts currently on the political horizon. The larger assumption, however, that the existence of liberal institutions and legal guarantees will themselves provide a lasting framework for the political coexistence of ethnic groups is, to say the least, unproved. But to the extent that it foreshadows the imposition of a one-size-fits-all reconceptualization of the state as a basic unit of the international legal order, it heralds a post-Westphalian order.

I. Individuals versus Groups, Law versus Politics

Individuals versus groups, law versus politics: these are old and inevitably false dichotomies. Nevertheless, a number of the chapters in this volume initially appear to turn on these distinctions. Whether group rights should exist independently of the rights guaranteed to individual members of the group, whether and how to use the flexibility of political settlement in place of the apparent certainty and clarity of legal entitlements—these are questions that structure both theoretical and practical approaches to ethnic conflict. The answers to these questions will leave a lasting impact on the international legal order.

A. Which Groups Get What?

For one group of legal scholars, social theorists, and political philosophers, the emergence of ethnic conflict as the paradigm of war in the post–cold war era poses the theoretical challenge of identifying and accommodating group rights. For those who understand ethnic conflict as the recrudescence of longings for national self-determination long frozen during the cold war but irrepressibly bursting forth in its wake, group identity is a dimension of human flourishing that cannot be denied and probably should be protected. Some of these scholars affirmatively embrace group rights as a response to the anomie of atomistic liberalism; others reluctantly concede their necessity in the face of disturbing but seemingly irrefutable empirical evidence of nationalist striving around the world. But all agree with David Wippman's reluctant conclusion, in Chapter 8: "consociational practices [favoring collective over individual rights] . . . may . . . be the only means by which members of ethnic groups can maintain their identities and still participate meaningfully in the life of the larger society."[2]

Other scholars recoil at the oversimplification of a wide array of geographically and culturally diverse conflicts— each with its own peculiarly

---

[2] Wippman at 240.

combustible mix of historical grievance, ideological conviction, economic and social stratification, political opportunity, and individual leadership—under the generic name "ethnic conflict." To Berman, for instance, the label "ethnic conflict," as opposed to "nationalism," reflects the predispositions of the classifiers far more than any essential attributes of the classified.[3] In his view, the problem has been misdiagnosed. And the cure will prove much worse than the disease.

Lea Brilmayer and Fernando Tesón both seek to shift the understanding of ethnic conflict away from group conflict, or conflicts of ethnicity— however defined—to claims of injustice or violations of individual rights. Brilmayer identifies claims for corrective, retributive, or distributive justice in virtually all "nationalist" struggles. On her account, nationalism is not about aspirations for a nation based on some kind of cultural or ethnic or religious homogeneity, but rather about redressing a specific and identifiable set of historical wrongs. Once the issue is reframed this way, international law has an entire set of adjudicatory, prescriptive, and enforcement tools for resolving these problems. She is very pessimistic about the prospects for making these tools effective; nevertheless, they exist.

In a similar vein, Tesón strongly rejects the notion that ethnic conflict is a special kind of group conflict based on a concept of group rights as distinct from individual rights. He recategorizes these claims of group rights in terms of the rights of the individual members of the group. He argues further, privileging individual rights and the human rights law that instantiates those rights, that governments have no right to preserve cultures that are not themselves supported by affirmative individual choice. He also joins with Brilmayer in arguing that group identity, as such, cannot found a moral claim to a special entitlement any more than it can justify deprivation of a preexisting entitlement.

Diane Orentlicher, in Chapter 12, lends a more sympathetic ear to group rights claims, bringing alive the dilemmas arising from the Latvian government's proposals effectively to deny citizenship to most members of its Russian minority. Must a nation-state submit to the forcible dilution of its identity by a previous conqueror? Yet can it dispossess individuals who have lived virtually their entire lives as Latvians of membership in the only polity they know? Her story not only poses the civil rights of the individual against the national identity rights of the group, but also contrasts ethnic with civic conceptions of group identity. In the end, however, Orentlicher also turns to individual rights as offering the most promising solution— not only to specific rights of nationality guaranteed to individuals in instruments such as the Universal Declaration of Human Rights

[3] Berman at 27.

but also to the more familiar civil and political rights protecting individuals against discrimination on the basis of ethnicity, race, or religion.

Here's the rub. It is precisely these canonical protections against discrimination on the basis of membership in a particular group that lie at the core of the cherished liberal ideal of individual equality before the law that are likely to be violated by consociational practices. As Wippman recognizes, "[c]onsociational solutions to ethnic conflict rest explicitly on the differential provision of tangible and intangible goods to individuals on the basis of their ethnicity."[4] And as Antonia and Abram Chayes recount, this perception has belatedly fueled opposition to a framework convention to be added to the European Convention on Human Rights that codifies principles designed to protect minority rights. This Convention "embodies a vision of the multicultural nation-state," in sharp contrast to the French "ideal of republicanism" which seeks to "decouple the state and ethnic identity," and permits no formal distinctions between citizens.[5] The opposition to this new vision is being led by Vaclav Havel, who ultimately refused to preside over the dissolution of Czechoslovakia.

What will be the outcome of this debate? In the short term, it will simply continue. In the medium term, international human rights law will almost certainly expand to include additional provisions for group rights. These provisions will be developed and adopted not only due to concern over the prevention of future ethnic conflicts, but also because they will attract support from proponents of a more general backlash against the universalism of current human rights provisions championing the individual over the family, the community, the tribe, and the nation. In the longer term, the present opponents of group rights may yet have their day; provisions for group rights should ultimately lead to a renewed focus on the definition of groupness. This second debate is most likely to take place in societies that are not necessarily riven by ethnic conflict but that nevertheless possess "discrete and insular minorities" whose abilities to make their voices meaningfully heard in the political process are limited.

Why should group rights fare any better in the 1990s than the minority rights provisions did in the treaties of the interwar period?[6] The answer, I think, lies in the interim development of human rights law as a distinct and important body of law. On the one hand, the existence of this body of law means that provisions governing governments' treatment of their own citizens are now codified and accepted in international law. On the other hand, the very growth of this body of law, founded on fundamental

---

[4] Wippman at 213.

[5] Chayes & Chayes at 187.

[6] For a comprehensive discussion of the origins and implementation of these treaties, *see* Nathaniel Berman, *"But the Alternative Is Despair": European Nationalism and the Modernist Renewal of International Law*, 106 HARV. L. REV. 1792 (1993).

liberal premises about the worth and dignity of the individual and hence the need to ensure certain inalienable rights of the individual against the state, has led to fissures within the human rights community along both East/West and North/South lines.

Some of these fissures are false, manufactured by repressive governments seeking to deflect international criticism of their actions by charging the critics with cultural imperialism. Others manifest themselves in the tired garb of hopelessly abstract debates between universalism and cultural relativism, the latter often spiced with the chic decentering of postmodernism. Still others, however, flow from a more telling and durable critique charging that the Western—particularly the United States—conception of human rights elevates rights above responsibilities and assumes a wary if not outright antagonistic relationship between individuals and the state, precluding more communal visions of self-governance based on social solidarity.[7]

Even assuming, however, the incorporation of some rights specifically attaching to groups in existing international legal instruments, the question remains whether general support for legal acknowledgment of the importance of group membership to the development of individual identity will extend to provisions governing political power sharing. Power sharing bespeaks an emphasis on process that contrasts sharply with the static absolutism of rights, the process of negotiation and compromise, of winning some and losing some. The lessons learned from this process, it is argued, generate norms that reduce the likelihood of violent conflict. In a pluralistic democracy, these norms emerge from the experience of alternation in power by two or three broadly representative parties.[8] In an ethnically riven society, in which clearly defined minorities will never have the opportunity to alternate in power as long as they vote on the basis of

[7] See MARY ANN GLENDON, RIGHTS TALK: THE IMPOVERISHMENT OF POLITICAL DISCOURSE 76 (1991) ("Each day's newspapers, radio broadcasts, and television programs attest to our tendency to speak of whatever is most important to us in terms of rights. . . . Our habitual silence concerning responsibilities is more apt to remain unnoticed."); Makau wa Mutua, *The Banjul Charter and the African Cultural Fingerprint: An Evaluation of the Language of Duties*, 35 VA. J. INT'L L. 339, 344 (1995) ("In the West, the language of rights primarily developed along the trajectory of claims against the state; entitlements which imply the right to seek an individual remedy for a wrong. The African language of duty, however, offers a different meaning for individual/state-society relations: while people had rights, they also bore duties.").

[8] See BRUCE RUSSETT, GRASPING THE DEMOCRATIC PEACE 33 (1993) (arguing that the "norms of regulated political competition, compromise solutions to political conflicts, and peaceful transfer of power are externalized by democracies in their dealings with other national actors in world politics"); SAMUEL P. HUNTINGTON, THE THIRD WAVE: DEMOCRATIZATION IN THE LATER TWENTIETH CENTURY 6–7 (1991) (The "sustained failure of the major opposition political party to win office" indicates failure of democratic norms of unrestricted competition for power.); see also ALBERT O. HIRSCHMAN, A PROPENSITY FOR SELF-SUBVERSION (1995).

their minority status, the only option may be to replace the normal sequence of temporal power sharing with constitutional arrangements guaranteeing simultaneous power sharing.

This vision of power sharing, as Lani Guinier has eloquently articulated in the context of U.S. domestic politics, requires departing from the principle of one (hu)man, one vote.[9] But if members of some subdivision of a particular polity are entitled to more votes by virtue of the privileges accorded that subdivision in the constitutional or legislative power-sharing arrangements, the fundamental question inevitably reasserts itself: how to define the relevant group. Here, however, the question is reframed: which group(s) of individuals are entitled to political power disproportionate to their number as a percentage of the polity as a whole? Guinier's answer is to create a political system that favors the expression of preferences by any and all groups, defined according to the commonality of their expressed political goals. This solution appears to take a step in the direction of the ideal compromise: a system that would allow all individuals to define themselves as members of whatever group they pleased, while preventing them from ever being labeled and differentially treated as members of a group as defined by others.

B. The Limits of Law

Group rights, of some kind, may be international law's long-term response to ethnic conflict. Such a response fits the standard teleological account of twentieth-century international law that Berman seeks to challenge: the shift from individual to group rights reflects the continuing expansion of the legal into the political, the legal colonization of ever larger areas of political life. The imperialist metaphor is apt: law equates with civilization and politics with barbarism, law with domestic order and politics with international anarchy. This account is bolstered by the canonical narrative of human rights law after 1945, in which the march of progress rests on the slow but steady expansion of the international legal regulation of a government's treatment of its own citizens. The next step is from the regulation of a government's treatment of individuals to a government's treatment of groups.

Another set of responses to ethnic conflict, however, is more likely to acknowledge the limits of law. A number of the authors in this volume call for political rather than legal solutions, or at least seriously question the value of legal solutions. These choices of political over legal means are not the wholesale abdication of law in the face of the intractability of

[9] Lani Guinier, [E]racing Democracy: The Voting Rights Cases, 108 HARV. L. REV. 109, 131–32 (1994) (suggesting that collective group preferences "might be measured by using innovative electoral schemes like cumulative voting and proportional representation").

politics; as Berman reminds us, law and politics mutually construct and shape each other.[10] The embrace of more political approaches is motivated instead by pragmatic recognition of the relative merits of formal rule-oriented solutions versus brokered compromises designed to address particular problems in particular contexts.

Chayes and Chayes tackle the question of conflict prevention—stoppering the evil genie of ethnic hatred in the bottle. They survey the various measures that have been taken by a host of international and regional organizations in the name of conflict prevention, concluding that the informal mediation efforts made by individuals acting as neutral emissaries from regional organizations are far more effective than formal legal responses. Indeed, they find evidence in the efforts of the OSCE and its high commissioner for national minorities of the power of persuasion and of "managerial" modes of conflict prevention—the management of conflict rather than its forcible stifling.[11] What is needed now is "ad hoc interaction" among particular missions and NGOs to encourage "flexible, non-hierarchical processes."[12] Orentlicher also praises the practical mediation efforts of international and regional organizations, and notes their innovative and flexible invocations of international law in responding to the problems posed by the Baltic citizenship policies.[13] These authors describe a new domain of mixed law and politics, a pragmatic domain focused above all on solving the problem at hand.

Ruth Wedgwood proposes another division between the legal and the political, calling for legal regulation of means to achieve an unforeseeable variety of political ends. She argues for extending the prohibition on the use of force in Article 2(4) of the U.N. Charter to internal conflict. As part of this extension, she would impose a duty of exhaustion of remedies on all parties to an internal conflict, requiring them to seek arbitration, mediation, or even adjudication of their dispute from bodies ranging from the Permanent Court of Arbitration in the Hague to the OSCE Office for Democratic Institutions and Human Rights to national courts sitting *ex aequo et bono*. The point of such dispute resolution alternatives would be explicitly *not* to develop a general set of principles about the political rights of minorities, much less a right to self-determination or secession, but rather "political hand tailoring, bespoke suits that fit a particular political history, state of conflict, surviving strands of fellow feeling, and possible common advantage."[14] In sum, she advocates a legal emphasis on process combined with a political determination of substance.

---

[10] Berman at 27.
[11] Chayes & Chayes at 181–85.
[12] *Id.* at 208–9.
[13] Orentlicher at 298–99.
[14] Wedgwood at 251.

Overall, the 1990s will add another chapter to Berman's tale of the constantly shifting and contested boundary between legal and political responses to ethnic conflict. But the contributions to this volume suggest that learning has taken place: the authors here display little of the hubris of the interwar period. On the contrary, they are acutely aware of the limitations of their craft. David Wippman, for instance, advances consociationalism as a "least worst alternative."[15] Chayes and Chayes acknowledge that the efforts of regional organizations to address ethnic conflict in Eastern and Central Europe and the former Soviet Union have thus far been "disappointing and their potential elusive."[16] Such humility may be partly a result of critical reflections on the past. Above all, however, it bows before the enormity of present problems and reflects the chastened idealism that the simple experience of the twentieth century must compel.

II. Toward a New International Architecture

Even group rights cannot obviate the need for individual accountability. Lasting peace in countries and regions riven by ethnic conflict must be built on a measure of justice. Perhaps the most innovative response to ethnic conflict lies in the architecture of the ICTFY. It holds potential for creating a set of personal and permanent links between domestic courts and supranational tribunals, harbingers of new modes of organizing and governing global society. At a deeper level, these links are predicated on assumptions about the existence and functioning of specific domestic institutions—courts unswayed by political pressures and devoted to the rule of law. These assumptions dovetail with yet more detailed assumptions about the optimal organization of a state that are becomingly increasingly explicit in the European regional context. We are witnessing the emergence and perhaps the enshrining of an "ideal polity," cast in the image of Western liberal democracy. It may not be ideally suited to address the problems of ethnic conflict, but it is likely to take on a life of its own.

A. Judicial Agents

Berman argues persuasively that previous international legal efforts to address nationalism or ethnic conflict have involved a "dual expansion," a simultaneous move below the surface of the state to regulate the "primitive" forces within and above it to a sophisticated supranational authority.

---

[15] Wippman at 241.
[16] Chayes & Chayes at 180.

The dissolution of the line between the domestic and the international has thus again been inherent in the very idea that international law should regulate ethnic conflict. But what is striking and arguably novel about current efforts is that they are establishing links between domestic and international *institutions,* according each a distinct sphere of governance and linking them on the basis of common function. The ICTFY, for instance, establishes a direct link between national and supranational courts by placing primary responsibility for prosecuting individuals indicted for war crimes on national courts. If the ICTFY determines that a national court is not fulfilling its obligation, it is then entitled to ask to take over the case.[17]

Recognition of the duty of national courts to enforce international obligations is not new. Lori Fisher Damrosch points out, for instance, that the Genocide Convention envisions that national courts will handle all genocide prosecutions against individuals, while the International Court of Justice will hear genocide claims against states.[18] But these are twin and separate tracks based on the traditional assumption that national-level institutions govern individuals and international institutions govern states. The innovation of the new tribunal is that it establishes a dialogue between like institutions at the national and supranational level, institutions engaged in a common enterprise but with varying expertise.

The development of similar transjudicial communication has been most developed in the European Union, in which national courts are empowered by the Treaty of Rome to refer cases involving questions of European law up to the European Court of Justice (ECJ). The ECJ renders its opinion and effectively sends the case back to the referring national court for final decision.[19] The result is the creation and strengthening of

[17] U.N. Security Council Resolution 827 established the Yugoslav war crimes tribunal and contains the statute that sets forth the structure, procedures, and jurisdiction of the tribunal. Statute of the International Tribunal, *Report of the Secretary-General Pursuant to Paragraph 2 of the Security Council Resolution 808 (1993),* U.N. SCOR, 48th Sess., Annex at 36, U.N. Doc. S/25704 (1993), U.N. SCOR, 48th Sess., *revised by* U.N. Doc. S/25704/Corr. 1 (1993). Article 8 of the implementing statute gives the tribunal "concurrent" jurisdiction with the national judicial systems that have emerged from the collapse of the former Yugoslavia. The availability of concurrent jurisdiction means the national legal systems have the right to try a case or refer it to the tribunal as they see fit. However, Article 9 of the implementing statute gives the tribunal the power to declare a national judicial proceeding null and void and to institute an independent judicial proceeding on its own. This provision is based on a belief that international regimes have supremacy over national legal systems. It could subject war criminals to double jeopardy if they were tried and acquitted by national courts. The implementing statute, however, provides that the accused can be retried by the tribunal if the national judicial proceedings are deemed to be flawed. Under the terms of the statute, the tribunal has the unprecedented ability to render national judicial proceedings invalid. *See* Karl Arthur Hochkammer, *The Yugoslav War Crimes Tribunal: The Compatibility of Peace, Politics, and International Law,* 28 VAND. J. TRANSNAT'L L. 119 (1995).

[18] Damrosch at 272–73.

[19] For further discussion of this and other forms of transjudicial communication, *see* Anne-

an autonomous "community of law."[20] The prosecutor of the ICTFY, Richard Goldstone, and the Tribunal itself have already demonstrated their autonomy from the political branches of the United Nations. As Ruth Wedgwood points out, the Security Council resolution that created the tribunal deliberately did not identify the conflict as international or internal but simply gave the tribunal jurisdiction over all violations of the law of armed conflict.[21] The appeals chamber of the tribunal has subsequently ruled that atrocities committed in civil wars are international crimes, thereby significantly expanding international jurisdiction over activities once thought to be a matter exclusively between a state and its citizens.[22] Matched with equally independent national prosecutors and courts, a legal process could be set in motion quite independently of the political process, leading to a measure of the international justice (as opposed to international law) that Brilmayer is so pessimistic about ever achieving. Her pessimism may prove well founded within the traditional international legal system. But harnessing like institutions at the national and supranational level may produce very different results.

An additional strength of this approach concerns the possibility that it will allow the Bosnians themselves to participate in bringing the criminals among them to justice. Should political conditions permit, the emphasis in the design of the tribunal on national prosecutions in the first instance allows a reconstituted Bosnian polity, or even reconstituted Serb, Croatian, and Muslim polities within the former Bosnia, to cleanse their own houses. It remains possible that as political winds shift and formerly silenced voices begin to be heard, many Bosnian Serbs will be prepared to turn against their former leaders, calling for their prosecution as war criminals.[23] The supranational institution provides both the legal impetus for such an initiative, by indicting the accused, and marshals the legitimacy of the international community behind national action.

These links between domestic and international institutions could foreshadow a new international architecture in which the primary actors are the disaggregated domestic institutions of individual states—courts, legislatures, executive branches, administrative agencies—interacting quasi-autonomously with one another and with their supra- and subnational

---

Marie Slaughter, *A Typology of Transjudicial Communication*, 29 U. RICHMOND L. REV. 99 (1995).

[20] Walter Mattli and I used this term in explaining the remarkable success of the European Court of Justice in constructing a European Community legal system with direct impact on nationals of the member states. *See* Anne-Marie Burley & Walter Mattli, *Europe before the Court: A Political Theory of Legal Integration*, 47 INT'L ORG. 41 (1993).

[21] Wedgwood at 246.

[22] *Dusko Tadic*, Case No. IT-94-1-AR72, October 2, 1995, *reprinted in* 35 I.L.M. 32 (1996).

[23] Chris Hedges, *Top Leader of the Bosnian Serbs Now under Attack from Within*, N.Y. TIMES, January 4, 1996, at A1.

counterparts. What is equally noteworthy, however, is that the primary locus of action and accountability is national. The structure of the ICTFY assumes, indeed requires, that the vast majority of war criminals be brought to justice at the national level, with the supranational tribunal designed to spur, guide, supervise, and monitor national-level proceedings.

In one sense this is nothing new; international agreements have always been predicated on the assumption and obligation of domestic implementation. The difference here is that whereas states were the traditional subjects of international law and were thus bound to give effect to the obligations binding them or answer for their failings in this regard to other states before an international body, here international law purports to regulate individuals directly and to hold them directly accountable before an international tribunal. In this context, domestic courts function not as domestic actors invisible and unaccountable behind the opaque shield of the state, but rather as agents of a higher corporate body—a body comprised of all states acting collectively in their international lawmaking capacity. This posture can be understood as resting on certain assumptions about the way in which these courts will fulfill their tasks, assumptions that may in turn be transformed into obligations to meet certain standards.

The principal assumption embedded in a structure of supranational direction and national initiative and implementation is of a measure of judicial independence from the political branches of state governments: Not the independence of judicial review, but simply of presumed neutrality as between disputants and insulation from political pressures.[24] In other words, the independence inherent in a fidelity to the law as written or made through recognized judicial processes.[25] Only on such a foundation can a genuine community of law be constructed. This assumption

---

[24] The design of the tribunal does not assume that courts are completely independent of political branches; after all, member states of the United Nations must pass implementing legislation to permit domestic prosecutions for war crimes. Thus national courts must await political authorization. Once forthcoming, however, it must be general in terms, leaving lots of discretion to both prosecutors and courts. In many countries, once the legal processes are begun, political interference is difficult if not impossible.

[25] Cf. Thomas Buergenthal, *International Tribunals and National Courts: The Internationalization of Domestic Adjudication*, in RECHT ZWISCHEN UMBRUCH UND BEWAHRUNG: FESTSCHRIFT FÜR RUDOLF BERNHARDT 702 (Ulrich Beyerlin et al. eds., 1995). Buergenthal concludes that three elements are needed to facilitate the process of the internationalization of domestic courts: "first, the existence of international tribunals with jurisdiction to deal with complaints by States and individuals alleging violations of international legal obligations; second, the recognition by domestic courts—this will not always come easy or without some political pressure—that we live in a world in which the routine interaction between national and international tribunals is in the national interest because it promotes the rule of law; and third, the existence of domestic legal institutions that permit and facilitate this interaction." *Id.* at 16.

was easy to make within the context of the European Community in 1957 and quite possible to make within the context of the members of the Council of Europe today. But the jurisdiction of the ICTFY is universal.

On the other hand, perhaps the structure of the Bosnia tribunal assumes a collaborative effort between national and supranational courts in an effort to build a global community of law. Where national courts can take the lead, they should. Where they are disabled, overborne, or nonexistent, the supranational tribunal will step in. This image leads to the further prospect of the potential socialization and strengthening of national judges in the independent enforcement of international law through regular contact with the supranational tribunal.[26] Of course, unlike in the European Community, the ICTFY and its Rwandan counterpart are starved for funds even to adjudicate the cases brought. In addition, national courts must depend for the cases brought before them not on individual litigants with commercial interests at stake but on national prosecutors subject to a welter of conflicting legal and political considerations.

On balance, the institutionalization of links between domestic and national judicial institutions is only beginning. And it may not, in the end, have a measurable impact on bringing the perpetrators of atrocities in this round of ethnic conflict to justice. It is, however, a significant advance over Nuremberg. It conjures a world in which courts play a dual role as servants of both the domestic and the international legal system.[27]

B. The Limits of the Liberal Peace

The creation of international legal institutions premised on assumptions about the domestic structure of participating states has far-reaching implications. The innovation of human rights law was to hold states responsible for the treatment of their citizens and thus to accord individuals status as sometime subjects of international law. The incorporation of assumptions about the existence and nature of national courts in the creation of an international institution may signal an equally radical shift in the focus and concern of the international legal order: from how states treat their citizens to how states themselves are configured.[28] This shift is readily

[26] Eric Stein and Hjalte Rasmussen, among others, describe the way in which the European Court of Justice helped socialize national judges as agents of the European Community legal system, through means ranging from champagne receptions in Luxembourg to seminars in national judicial centers. Eric Stein, *Lawyers, Judges, and the Making of a Transnational Constitution*, 75 AM. J. INT'L L. 1 (1981); HJALTE RASMUSSEN, ON LAW AND POLICY IN THE EUROPEAN COURT OF JUSTICE (1986). *See also* G. Federico Mancini, *The Making of a Constitution for Europe*, 26 COMMON MARKET L. REV. 595 (1989).

[27] Friedrich Kratochwil, *Contract and Regimes: Do Issue Specificity and Variations of Formality Matter? in* REGIME THEORY AND INTERNATIONAL RELATIONS (Volker Rittberger ed., 1993).

[28] Thomas Franck's call for recognition of a right of democratic governance prefigures this shift, but he still frames his argument in terms of individual rights. *See* Thomas M. Franck, *The Emerging Right to Democratic Governance*, 86 AM. J. INT'L L. 46 (1992). Recognition of the

observable in the context of regional organizations such as the EU, the Council of Europe, and the OSCE, in which the template of an ideal polity is being used as leverage to try to quell ethnic conflict in would-be members.

Whether these criteria for membership will ripen into universal requirements for recognition for statehood is a large question beyond the scope of this chapter. Of more immediate relevance is whether these criteria, even if met by the states on which they are being imposed, will in fact dampen existing ethnic conflict and forestall future outbreaks. We may have reached the limits of the liberal peace.

Chayes and Chayes note that the tools that regional organizations can use to avert ethnic conflict include the intangible inducements of belonging to the community of democratic nations that is the imprimatur of membership in the Council of Europe.[29] Admission to the Council of Europe (COE) is conditioned on signature and ratification of COE human rights instruments and on demonstrable democratic practices. It has deliberately kept a number of states from Central and Eastern Europe and the former Soviet Union in a halfway house to full membership to maintain maximum leverage on them as they make the transition to full democracy and assured human rights protections.

Liberal democracy thus becomes the hallmark of a coveted, exclusive status. It can also become the caesura that marks a definitive transition, symbolizing what a country is not as much as what it is. Chayes and Chayes observe that one incentive for countries to join the COE is "to make explicit that the country has broken from past Soviet domination and is joining the circle of democracies."[30] In-country missions sponsored by the OSCE have also contributed to moderating ethnic conflict by such actions as providing support for delegations observing parliamentary elections, organizing seminars for officials to discuss the principles of a democratic constitution, and advising governments on human rights issues.[31]

Membership in the EU provides similar but even stronger incentives. The EU is the ultimate community of liberal states. Membership is "premised upon liberal democracy, respect for human rights, the rule of law and a market economy."[32] The EU also engages in more direct democratization efforts, including "support for democratic infrastructure and inter-

---

right of each individual to representation in his or her polity can still be encompassed within the framework of human rights law. The potential shift that I describe would alter the definition of statehood itself and alter fundamental assumptions about the identity of the principal actors in the international system.

[29] Chayes & Chayes at 187, 189–191. *See also* Jean L. Manas, *The Council of Europe's Democracy Ideal and the Challenge of Ethno-National Strife, in* PREVENTING CONFLICT IN THE POSTCOMMUNIST WORLD (Chayes & Chayes eds., 1996).

[30] Chayes & Chayes at 189.

[31] *Id.* at 186 describing the activities of the in-country OSCE mission in Moldova).

[32] *Id.* at 197.

parliamentary cooperation, demarches in favor of democracy, assistance in creating a free media and election monitoring."[33] On the economic side, the European Bank for Reconstruction and Development was explicitly charged with "applying the principles of multiparty democracy, pluralism, and market economics."[34] The same template can be found in the Badinter Commission's criteria for recognition of new states out of the former Yugoslavia: respect for minority rights, the rule of law, democratic rules, and civil liberties.[35] Finally, moving beyond Europe, the World Bank and the International Monetary Fund have adopted the mantra of "good governance" as an "enabling condition" for development, code for democracy and respect for human rights.[36]

Why should the emergence of this particular ideal polity be surprising? Realists, after all, will argue that once again the most powerful states in the international system are setting out to remake the world in their own image. Critical theorists might well concur. After all, Berman's emphasis on the social construction of groups through projection of a set of cultural conceptions would lead him to find the social construction of an ideal polity unremarkable.

It is also possible to see the particular ideal polity being enshrined as the entirely predictable, and indeed foreshadowed, continuation of the trends that Thomas Franck identified as giving rise to a "right of democratic governance."[37] If such a right is established at the individual level, the emergence of a democratic polity as the basic unit of the international system is the natural corollary at the systemic level. And attributes other than democracy itself, such as guarantees of civil and political rights, are already provided for in international human rights instruments. These instruments must further assume some version of the rule of law where they do not explicitly provide for it.

Of greater moment here, however, is the specific context in which the outlines of this particular ideal polity have emerged and the purposes that its attributes are supposed to serve. Chayes and Chayes spell out the logic behind the practices of the various European and global institutions that they canvass: The "assumption [is] that Western-style democracies operating under the rule of law and protecting fundamental human rights do not experience much violent internal conflict."[38] Liberal democracy is thus being advanced less as an individual or even a national entitlement

---

[33] *Id.* at 198.

[34] Article I, Charter of the European Bank for Reconstruction and Development.

[35] Wedgwood points out that these criteria assimilate very closely to the minimum criteria for membership in the European Union, "as if recognition and membership were the same." Wedgwood at 253.

[36] Chayes & Chayes at 193.

[37] *See* Franck, *supra* note 28.

[38] Chayes & Chayes at 187.

and more as a cure for ethnic conflict. As such, it is being offered as a
solution for a problem it has never demonstrably been able to solve.

Many of the proponents of the democratic entitlement, or, more generally, those such as myself who have advocated drawing distinctions
among states based on their domestic political regime, have drawn on
scholarship demonstrating that democratic states are significantly less
likely to go to war with other democratic states. In light of this phenomenon—frequently referred to as the "democratic peace"—inscribing the
features of liberal democracy as an ideal polity embedded in and promoted by international law can be said to promote international peace.

No systematic evidence exists, however, to demonstrate that liberal
democracy has an equally pacific effect on *internal* ethnic strife. In addition to prominent empirical examples—the festering problems of Northern Ireland, the Basque country, Catalonia, Corsica, Cyprus, and Quebec
—the leading explanations of the causal links between democracy and
peace do not readily translate into the context of domestic conflict among
ethnic groups. The structural explanation assumes that parliaments vote
on war, whereas ethnic conflict presumes divided parliaments or parliaments in which one of the potentially warring parties is a distinct minority. The normative explanation assumes the deep inculcation of norms of
peaceful change and positive-sum bargaining that flow from long experience of alternating parties in power.[39] Yet to the extent that ethnic conflict
results from the desire of persistent minorities to secure the rights and
privileges accompanying majority political power, they are by definition
unlikely ever to have had the experience of such alternation.

Indeed, David Wippman reminds us that Arend Lijphart's theories of
consociationalism were all premised on the assumption that pluralist democracy was unlikely to flourish in a deeply ethnically divided society.
Consociationalism is a form of democracy, but it is deeply in tension with
many of the most basic tenets of liberalism, as I have noted. The move
to add specific protections for minority rights to various international
legal instruments heretofore deemed to be sufficient to structure life in a
liberal democracy equally reflects a recognition that ethnic conflict poses
special problems. The vision and to a large extent the empirical experience
of the ideal polity largely assumes that these problems have already been
solved.

In sum, many of the responses to ethnic conflict on the part of regional
and international institutions seem to herald a deeper shift in the international legal order. A new template of the attributes of statehood—the

---

[39] These two explanations have been advanced by Bruce Russett based on his own research into the empirical phenomenon of the democratic peace and a comprehensive review
of the literature. *See* Russett, *supra* note 8.

prerequisite elements for participation in the international legal order—appears to be emerging. This template is offered as a prescription for peace in the face of the principal source of contemporary conflict, ethnic conflict. Unfortunately, however, while liberal democracy may be the best cure available for a host of ills, its efficacy in this case is unproved. Liberalism assumes a polity. It offers little guidance for creating one—or holding one together.

The nationalism of the nineteenth century has become the ethnic conflict of the twentieth century. We no longer think of ethnic groups as necessarily forming nations. We no longer think that nations are entitled to states or even that nation-states are uniquely appropriate units.

The twentieth-century response to bloodshed triggered by the perception and distortion of ethnic differences focuses more on the organization of existing states than on the creation of new ones. Individuals have the right to participate in their own governance, arguably bolstered by specific political guarantees so that their voices can be meaningfully heard. They are entitled to the legal protection of the rights they are given. These rights entail obligations on the part of specific state institutions—legislatures, courts, executives. Individual entitlement thus translates into state structure.

Ruth Wedgwood writes, "The state has lost its opacity."[40] States traditionally were conceived of as billiard balls and black boxes—organized in any fashion their rulers wished. Human rights law introduced standards for the way in which these rulers treated their subjects. The array of international legal responses to ethnic conflict reflects a further step toward the imposition of formal requirements concerning the way in which states are themselves constituted. In this world, titular rulers will be acknowledged as the reflection and instrument of a higher authority, as subject to the sovereignty of their subjects. Liberal democracy may not be a cure for ethnic conflict. But it may be the best that the international legal order has to offer.

[40] Wedgwood at 242.

PART II

Institutional and Policy Responses to Ethnic Conflict

6

U.N. Engagement in Ethnic Conflicts

David J. Scheffer

In the closing years of the twentieth century, the business of maintaining international peace and security has centered on how effectively the United Nations, regional organizations, and responsible governments can manage ethnic conflicts. The longevity of this particular phase of international peace management remains speculative. But unless a fair number of such conflicts are contained and then extinguished, the prospects for global security during the twenty-first century will be grim. The United Nations in particular faces unprecedented challenges in its capabilities to perform its Charter duties and to be a relevant peace builder during its second fifty years.

This chapter examines how the United Nations engages in ethnic conflicts. Conventional wisdom assumes that U.N. engagement is limited to often ineffective peacekeeping operations in strife-torn countries. In reality, however, peacekeeping is only one of a wide range of tools the United Nations employs to varying effect in its efforts to manage ethnic conflicts. The law and practice of the United Nations in this area have evolved at an accelerating pace during the 1990s and in ways that would have astonished the framers of the Charter in 1945. They would not have anticipated that ethnic conflicts of largely internal character would necessitate U.N. engagement on so many fronts. But population growth, refugee flows, trade in conventional arms, the collapse of cold war discipline imposed by the superpowers, and the pursuit of power by local warlords for personal,

The views and opinions expressed in this chapter are solely the author's and do not necessarily represent those of the U.S. Department of State.

nonideological gain have combined to create societies within which ethnic tensions—often already fueled by traditional interethnic bigotry—explode in ways that demand international attention.

I have chosen to focus broadly on how the United Nations *engages* in ethnic conflicts, beginning in part I with the goals of U.N. engagement. These goals include containment of ethnic conflicts, support for self-determination, promotion of democracy, and institution building. The legal basis for the pursuit of these goals, particularly by the Security Council, is examined in Part II. Central to this analysis is the legal authority for peaceful measures (primarily under Chapter VI of the U.N. Charter), the legal authority for coercive measures (under Chapter VII or VIII of the Charter), and the legal authority for norm elaboration and quasi-judicial pronouncements (such as by the General Assembly or Economic and Social Council). Such legal authority has itself evolved in recent years to reveal the U.N. Charter as a living document that can be applied effectively, at least in theory and sometimes in practice, to contemporary challenges.

Part III of this chapter examines the means by which the United Nations seeks to implement its policy goals. In particular, Part III discusses seven modes of engagement in ethnic conflicts: hortatory actions, diplomatic intervention, sanctions, military and humanitarian interventions, implementation of peace agreements, and international judicial intervention. In the conclusion, this chapter will discuss both the strengths and weaknesses of U.N. approaches to ethnic conflicts.

I. GOALS OF U.N. ENGAGEMENT

Ethnic conflicts pose both a challenge and an opportunity for the United Nations. The challenge arises from the need to contain and, if possible, to defuse such conflicts. The danger is that conflict will spread, confronting the United Nations, particularly the Security Council, with political pressures that dictate some kind of response aimed at managing the conflict so as to minimize its threat to international peace and security. The opportunity arises from the fact that ethnic conflicts may create the space for significant social and political changes and thus can be occasions to promote democracy, uphold the principle of self-determination, or undertake the building, or rebuilding, of a state. Political realities will determine which goals are pursued in different conflicts and with what resources and international support.

A. Conflict Containment

The eruption of an ethnic conflict, or the danger of one's erupting, can and often does pose a threat to international peace and security. Even an ethnic conflict that on the surface appears strictly internal in character can rapidly evolve into a crossborder refugee crisis, a regional political question, widespread economic dislocation, and a security threat to neighboring states. U.N. political, economic, or security organs frequently address such conflicts, particularly if national governments create a political vacuum through their own failed policies, acquiescence, or inaction, or if the conflict involves the commission of atrocities or the transgression of international boundaries. In such cases, pressure can build among governments and nongovernmental organizations to use the U.N. system in some fashion to try to contain and, if possible, help resolve the conflict.

Containing an ethnic conflict can serve a central purpose of the U.N. Charter, namely to maintain international peace and security.[1] If ethnic conflicts are left unchecked and untended (as, in fact, they often are), the risk only grows larger that the conflict will involve neighboring or other interested states. The consequences may well compel the Security Countil to act.

Every peacekeeping operation and U.N.-authorized enforcement action is an exercise in conflict containment. The immediate objective is to prevent the conflict from spreading by monitoring a cease-fire, patrolling a buffer zone, or, in the case of enforcement, stopping or rolling back an aggressor force. In some cases, the goal of containment may also be pursued through the other modes of implementation described in Part III of this chapter.

The importance of the U.N.'s response to ethnic conflicts may be self-evident in much of the U.N.'s work, but it is worth considering that the ethnic rivalry that drives so many modern conflicts was not foremost in the minds of the framers of the U.N. Charter. Their world of conflict was one where national armies, one being a clear aggressor, battled across international boundaries. Drafting Charter provisions to address such black and white arenas of conflict was difficult but achievable.[2] Today the same Charter provisions must be used to address the very different circumstances, often of great complexity and sometimes internal in character, that arise from ethnic discord. Although Chapter VII of the Charter is structured to defeat aggression, ethnicity cannot (and of itself should not) be defeated. In its violent manifestations, ethnicity can be contained or even creatively transformed as experienced in Bosnia following the Dayton accords of 1995 and in Cambodia and Mozambique in the early 1990s. Therefore, containment or some kind of transformation can become the goal whether or not member states realize it when they resort to the United Nations or seek U.N. approval. Ethnic conflicts that are only con-

---

[1] U.N. CHARTER art. 1, sec. 4.

[2] See generally HANS KELSEN, THE LAW OF THE UNITED NATIONS (4th prtg. 1964); D. W. BOWETT, UNITED NATIONS FORCES (1964); RUTH B. RUSSELL, A HISTORY OF THE UNITED NATIONS CHARTER (1958).

tained are likely to remain on the U.N.'s overall agenda.[3] They will fester, being neither fully resolved nor fully fought. But the goal of conflict containment is usually the best the United Nations can strive for in the absence of enough political influence or military clout to dictate control of ethnic aspirations or to transform a situation.

B. Self-Determination

Ethnic conflicts frequently center on competing self-determination claims, and thus become defined in the context of self-determination movements. As a collective body of sovereign states, the capacity of the United Nations to embrace principles of self-determination has always been limited. The U.N. Charter's recognition of the principle of self-determination of peoples,[4] its inclusion in the international covenants on human rights,[5] long-sustained efforts to promote the principle for the Palestinian people, and its utility as a tool to criticize certain regimes (such as South Africa under apartheid) have helped keep the issue of self-determination on the U.N.'s agenda. The U.N. General Assembly has long provided qualified support for self-determination movements associated with the demise of colonialism, including even the endorsement of the use of force by "national liberation movements" to overcome colonial control.[6] But the member states of the United Nations, particularly those liberated from colonial rule, are not enthusiasts of separatism fueled by self-determination movements and ethnic conflict. Thus, the General Assembly and the Security Council typically seek to maintain and restore international peace and security, and to end contemporary ethnic conflicts, but not to promote revolutionary political change within member states.

The character of self-determination movements has evolved considerably since World War II, as have their objectives.[7] But within the General

---

[3] For example, the ethnic conflicts in Kashmir and Cyprus have occupied the attention of the Security Council and other U.N. bodies for decades despite their relative lack of hostilities.

[4] See U.N. CHARTER, art. 1, sec. 2 and art. 55.

[5] International Covenant on Civil and Political Rights, art. 1, G.A. Res. 2200 (XXI), U.N. GAOR, Supp. (No. 16) 52, U.N. Doc. A/6316 (1967); International Covenant on Economic, Social, and Cultural Rights, art. 1, G.A. Res. 2200 (XXI), 21 U.N. GAOR, Supp. (No. 16) 49, U.N. Doc. A/6316 (1967).

[6] Resolution on the Definition of Aggression, art. 7, G.A. Res. 3314 (XXIX), 29 U.N. GAOR, Supp. (No. 31) 142, U.N. Doc. A/9631 (1975); Declaration on Principles of International Law Concerning Friendly Relations and Co-operation among States in Accordance with the Charter of the United Nations, art. 1, G.A. Res. 2625 (XXV), 25 U.N. GAOR, Supp. (No. 28) 121, U.N. Doc. A/8028 (1971); CHRISTOPHER O. QUAYE, LIBERATION STRUGGLES IN INTERNATIONAL LAW (1991).

[7] MORTON HALPERIN, DAVID J. SCHEFFER & PATRICIA SMALL, SELF-DETERMINATION IN THE

Assembly, the U.N.'s response mechanism remains stuck in the mid-twentieth century. The General Assembly focused on self-determination in the context of anticolonialism and foreign domination for decades and continues to frame its primary concerns in this increasingly dated context. In recent years the General Assembly has adopted resolutions that continue to approach the issue of self-determination in this vein. The resolutions have addressed such topics as the "universal realization of the right of self-determination,"[8] the right of the Palestinian people to self-determination,[9] the use of mercenaries to impede the exercise of the right of peoples to self-determination,[10] and the importance of the speedy granting of independence to colonial countries and peoples.[11]

The considerable interest in self-determination for the Palestinian people doubtless will continue until the peace process of the 1990s finally leads to stable interethnic and interreligious relations in the Middle East. The role of mercenaries may well evolve as new forms of peacekeeping and civil-military (CIVPOL) personnel are resorted to by international and regional organizations in conflict areas. But in their traditional role mercenaries are likely to continue to be viewed as agents of foreign domination of a sovereign nation and people. Whatever the merits of these views (the United States has voted against such resolutions each year), their narrow focus has hindered the broader application of a modern principle of self-determination. Partly as a result, the General Assembly has yet to recognize self-determination as a freestanding principle the implementation of which spans a range of options and is integral to the resolution of many ethnic conflicts.[12]

The UN50 Declaration of 1995 illustrates the General Assembly's narrow approach to self-determination.[13] Adopted by the General Assembly on the fiftieth anniversary of the United Nations, the declaration reaffirms the right of all peoples to self-determination and to take "legitimate action" to realize that right. But as with previous resolutions, the UN50 Declaration qualifies the right by insisting on the preservation of the territorial integrity and political unity of sovereign and independent states. The preamble reads in part: "Through the process of decolonization and the elimination of apartheid, hundreds of millions of human beings have been and are assured the exercise of the fundamental right of self-determination." Section 1 continues:

NEW WORLD ORDER (1992); HURST HANNUM, AUTONOMY, SOVEREIGNTY, AND SELF-DETERMINATION: THE ACCOMMODATION OF CONFLICTING RIGHTS (rev. 1996).

[8] G.A. Res. 50/139 (1995); G.A. Res. 49/148 (1994).
[9] G.A. Res. 50/140 (1995); G.A. Res. 49/149 (1994).
[10] G.A. Res. 50/138 (1995); G.A. Res. 49/150 (1994).
[11] G.A. Res. 50/39 (1995); G.A. Res. 49/89 (1994).
[12] See HALPERIN, SCHEFFER & SMALL, supra note 7, chapter 5.
[13] G.A. Res. 50/6 (1995).

We will continue to reaffirm the right of self-determination of all peoples, taking into account the particular situation of peoples under colonial or other forms of alien domination or foreign occupation, and recognize the right of peoples to take legitimate action, in accordance with the Charter of the United Nations, to realize their inalienable right of self-determination. This shall not be construed as authorizing or encouraging any action that would dismember or impair, totally or in part, the territorial integrity or political unity of sovereign and independent States conducting themselves in compliance with the principle of equal rights and self-determination of peoples and thus possessed of a Government representing the whole people belonging to the territory without distinction of any kind.[14]

In negotiations leading up to the UN50 Declaration, the United States asked whether the right to take "legitimate" action would raise questions as to where the legally accepted authority for that right exists. The U.N. Charter does not authorize it, nor is there a definition of what "legitimate" action is. The United States, though, agreed to its inclusion.

The United States also raised concerns about the reference to a "fundamental" right of self-determination in the preamble of the UN50 Declaration. Without a firm basis in international law (including the U.N. Charter and the Universal Declaration of Human Rights) to identify the "fundamental" characteristics of the right of self-determination, such terminology could burden the right with highly controversial interpretations and foster extreme demands for its implementation in the cause of violent separatism. A further difficulty with the word *fundamental* is that its use implies a hierarchy of rights for one principle over another. In practice, the United Nations has not been entirely consistent in using the term *fundamental*, and many rights have at one time or another been so designated. Nonetheless, the United States joined consensus to describe self-determination in this manner.

Some member states would not accept references to self-determination in the UN50 Declaration without balancing references to the territorial integrity of states. And other member states opposed references to colonialism or foreign occupation, although they ultimately conceded these points. One Middle East delegation's proposals to describe the "right of peoples to resist foreign occupation" and the alternative—the right to "the use of all legitimate means to achieve self-determination"—were rejected. On balance, the UN50 Declaration revealed the muddled state of practice and the lack of a real consensus on the contemporary meaning of self-determination. Some might regard the declaration as countenancing

[14] The UN50 Declaration draws in part from the 1993 Vienna Declaration on Human Rights, which also addresses the right of self-determination. U.N. Doc. A/CONF.157/24 (Part I) 20–46 (1993), *reprinted in* 32 I.L.M. 1661 (1993).

separatism arising from an ethnic conflict if the "sovereign and independent" state in question was *not* conducting itself "in compliance with the principle of equal rights and self-determination of peoples" and was *not* possessed of "a Government representing the whole people belonging to the territory without distinction of any kind." But applying such an argument in practice doubtless would invite challenge from the government in question and other governments concerned about any precedent that might be established.

Beyond such rhetorical exercises, however, the Western Sahara has been a key example of the U.N.'s continuing effort to preserve and enforce the right of self-determination and to avert a continuation of the fifteen-year conflict between the government of Morocco and the guerrilla forces of the Popular Front for the Liberation of Saguia el-Hamra and Rio de Oro (POLISARIO) that ended with a cease-fire in 1990. The U.N.'s objective is to hold "a free, fair and impartial referendum for self-determination of the people of Western Sahara."[15] The U.N. Mission on the Referendum in Western Sahara (MINURSO) has played a largely successful role in monitoring the cease-fire that went into effect in September 1991 but, more recently, a far more frustrating role in seeking the implementation of the settlement plan agreed to by the government of Morocco and the POLISARIO. The elements of the settlement plan remained unfulfilled as of early 1997. These included full implementation of the process to identify eligible voters and of a code of conduct, the release of all political prisoners, the confinement of POLISARIO troops, and arrangements for the reduction of Moroccan troops in the Western Sahara territory. But the U.N.'s effort to register eligible voters for a referendum on self-determination in Western Sahara has been a historic undertaking to resolve an ethnic conflict through the ballot box rather than on the battlefield. At a minimum, the United Nations has engaged in a self-determination project, with respect both to the deployment of an observer mission to monitor a cease-fire and implement a settlement plan as well as to the actual running of elections. Whether this ambitious endeavor will bear fruit remains an open question, subject in large part to the political agendas of the two sides.

C. Engineering Democracy

The United Nations has increasingly worked to encourage democracy as the preferred form of government for member states.[16] This has had a

---

[15] S.C. Res. 1017 (1995).

[16] For the early stages of this development, *see* Thomas M. Franck, *The Emerging Right to Democratic Governance*, 86 AM. J. INT'L L. 46 (1991); HALPERIN, SCHEFFER & SMALL, *supra* note 7, at 60–65. *See also* Enhancing the Effectiveness of the Principle of Periodic and Genuine Elections: Report of the Secretary-General, U.N. Doc. A/49/675 (1994).

profound effect on the U.N.'s approach to the management and prevention of ethnic conflicts. U.N. elections assistance has become an essential
preventive measure to diminish the risk of ethnic conflict and manage
peacefully what is at stake in many ethnic disputes. Other tools include
decolonization support, designing procedures to smooth and facilitate
transitions to democracy and to build democratic alternatives to conflict,
drafting constitutions, instituting administrative and financial reforms,
strengthening domestic human rights laws, enhancing judicial structures,
training human rights officials and monitors, and helping armed opposition movements transform themselves into democratically competitive
political parties. Such U.N. elections assistance has become important in
erecting new political societies in the aftermath of ethnic conflicts.

The General Assembly has adopted an evolving set of pro-democracy
resolutions that have established a solid foundation for U.N. initiatives.
Between the forty-eighth and forty-ninth General Assemblies, a sea
change occurred in the body's support for democracy. The forty-eighth
General Assembly adopted a schizophrenic set of resolutions on elections
assistance. On the one hand, a majority of member states approved a
resolution proclaiming "respect for the principles of national sovereignty
and non-interference in the internal affairs of states in their electoral processes."[17] There was no "universal need" for the United Nations to provide electoral assistance. This resolution was opposed by the United
States and most of the economically developed world. On the other hand,
a majority of member states approved a resolution commending the work
of the U.N. Electoral Assistance Division.[18]

In the fall of 1994, at the forty-ninth General Assembly session, a dramatic shift occurred. Sixty-two member states cosponsored a far-reaching
resolution initiated by the United States to enhance "the effectiveness of
periodic and genuine elections and the promotion of democratization."[19]
Only Iran opposed the resolution. As the U.S. permanent representative
to the United Nations, Madeleine K. Albright, observed, "[w]ith General
Assembly adoption of this resolution, the international community states
its strong support of the right of every individual to participate in his or
her own government through free and fair elections. This resolution will
enable the United Nations to continue and expand upon its assistance to
new and emerging democracies. The resolution is the most far-reaching
ever passed by the U.N. on democratization."[20] The resolution built upon
U.N.-assisted electoral successes in South Africa, Cambodia, Mozambique, Malawi, and Eritrea—all arenas of violent ethnic conflicts in recent

17 G.A. Res. 48/124 (1994).
18 G.A. Res. 48/131 (1994).
19 G.A. Res. 49/190 (1994).
20 USUN Press Release #233-(94), December 23, 1994.

decades. The Fiftieth General Assembly adopted, without any opposition, a nearly identical resolution.[21] It also adopted a resolution recognizing "that the Organization has an important role to play in providing timely, appropriate and coherent support to the efforts of Governments to achieve democratization within the context of their development efforts."[22] The Fiftieth General Assembly also encouraged "Member States to promote democratization and to make additional efforts to identify possible steps to support the efforts of Governments to promote and consolidate new or restored democracies."[23]

Such resolutions will be replicated and built upon in subsequent General Assembly sessions. Support for democratization has become a regular agenda item for the General Assembly and a growth industry for the organization as a whole. An increasing number of member states are requesting assistance for elections. Between 1989 and 1992, only seven governments lodged requests for electoral assistance; but from 1992 to 1995, eighty-two requests were submitted.

Peacekeeping missions in countries beset by ethnic conflict have relied upon U.N. electoral assistance to pave a road toward reconciliation.[24] Cambodia (UNTAC), Namibia (UNTAG), Mozambique (ONUMOZ), Angola (UNAVEM), and Haiti (UNMIH) are countries where U.N. peacekeeping missions ensured an environment in which the United Nations could assist with the preparation and conduct of free and fair elections. Each month the U.N. Electoral Assistance Division, which is part of the Department of Peacekeeping Operations, publishes a listing of its current operations. In April 1995, for example, the Electoral Assistance Division was active in Armenia, Bangladesh, Benin, Brazil, Chad, Côte d'Ivoire, Equatorial Guinea, Ethiopia, Gambia, Guinea, Haiti, Honduras, Mexico, Mozambique, Sierra Leone, Tanzania, and Western Sahara.[25] In short, the U.N. Elections Assistance Division has become a key engine for democracy worldwide.

The role of democratization has consequences for self-determination. By promoting democracy, and defending it, the international community through the United Nations effectively is defending the right of self-determination in societies recently torn asunder or at great risk from interethnic conflict. In fact, one could argue that electoral assistance and support for the right of democracy are eclipsing the old rhetoric of self-determination as the bedrock principle of U.N. practice toward ethnic

[21] G.A. Res. 50/185 (1995).

[22] G.A. Res. 50/133 (1995).

[23] Id.

[24] See Sally Morphet, UN Peacekeeping and Election-Monitoring, in UNITED NATIONS: DIVIDED WORLD 183–239 (Adam Roberts & Benedict Kingsbury eds., 2d ed. 1993).

[25] Electoral Assistance Activities of the United Nations System during April 1995, United Nations Electoral Assistance Division, Department of Peacekeeping Operations.

conflicts. Instead of sanctioning the use of force to defend an increasingly outdated notion of self-determination in the context of decolonization, the United Nations is more inclined to look to democratic alternatives as the more pragmatic vehicle for the realization of self-determination. In practice, the United Nations is fusing self-determination and democratization through organization, supervision, verification, coordination, or other support of elections.

D. Institution Building

Interestingly, a large part of the U.N. Charter was conceived to manage territories that are susceptible to ethnic conflict. Chapters XI, XII, and XIII focus on non-self-governing territories and on an international trusteeship system. The whole concept behind these chapters of the Charter was to ensure the safety of the inhabitants of such territories and to assist them on the road to self-government. The almost fifty-year history of the applicability of these provisions, which effectively ended with the independence of the U.S. trust territory of Palau in 1994, reveals a significant number of ethnic conflicts associated with these territories. The methods by which the United Nations reacted to these ethnic conflicts included U.N. peacekeeping operations, sanctions regimes, hortatory resolutions, actions before the International Court of Justice, and diplomacy. The fact that the trusteeship system has now expired only diminishes the potency, but not the historical relevance, of these chapters.[26] The implementation of Chapters XI, XII, and XIII preceded modern-day involvement by the United Nations in the development of multiethnic societies and in the promotion of self-government and democracy.

An important goal of the United Nations in managing ethnic conflict is *necessarily* to assist in limited ways with the building of the existing or new nation(s) that arise from the containment or resolution of an ethnic conflict. Diplomats may shun nation building in their lexicon; but the goal is clearly to assist in establishing or restoring coherent political, economic, and security institutions that will strive for stability, promote democracy, and achieve some tolerable level of economic development. "Institution building" or "peace implementation" are the preferred characterizations.

In 1993, the Security Council concluded that several measures were essential to revive and stabilize Somalia.[27] The United Nations pursued similar objectives in connection with other conflicts, some of which were ethnic in character. Examples include the societal challenges associated

---

[26] For an interesting discussion linking contemporary issues with the trusteeship system, see Ruth E. Gordon, *Some Legal Problems with Trusteeship*, 28 CORNELL INT'L L. J. 301 (1995).

[27] S.C. Res. 814 (1993).

with and following the peacekeeping operations in Mozambique, Bosnia, Cambodia, Angola, and Haiti in the 1990s.

Institution building can be an important and difficult aspect of U.N. efforts to prevent the resumption of an ethnic conflict where the institutions of statehood are dismantled or dangerously fragile. As a goal, these societal tasks often take precedence during or in the immediate aftermath of an ethnic conflict when it may be essential to fulfillment of the U.N.'s other goals— to contain the conflict, fulfill the principle of self-determination, or promote a democratic society. In many cases, the United Nations sees institution building or peace implementation as the preventive medicine needed to stop the cycle of violence between ethnic antagonists. At whatever stage the United Nations engages in an ethnic conflict, its final objective is more often than not the initiation of some kind of uniquely tailored exercise that seeks to establish a societal infrastructure conducive to ethnic harmony. The fact that the task is so difficult and idealistic speaks to its realism, not its futility.

II. Legal Authority for U.N. Engagement in Ethnic Conflicts

The U.N. Charter is a reservoir of legal authority for the engagement in ethnic conflicts by a number of U.N. entities. For example, the General Assembly, acting under Chapter IV of the Charter, can provide elections assistance, deploy human rights monitors and advisory services, and administer humanitarian assistance to the displaced. The Secretariat, acting within its authority under Chapter XV, can be instrumental in exposing the facts about an ethnic conflict and advising other U.N. bodies, notably the Security Council, on plans for direct U.N. engagement. However, my focus here will be on the Security Council because arguably the most controversial challenges to legal authority arise from council engagement in ethnic conflicts.

The Security Council's legal authority to address an ethnic conflict typically rests on one of three separate Charter provisions. First, Chapter VI of the Charter authorizes the Security Council to investigate, and recommend appropriate procedures or methods of adjustment for, any dispute or situation that is likely to endanger the maintenance of international peace and security. Second, Chapter VII authorizes the council to determine the existence of any threat to or breach of the peace, or act of aggression, and make recommendations or decisions on how to maintain or restore international peace and security. Finally, Chapter VIII encourages the United Nations to support the efforts of regional arrangements or organizations ("agencies" in Charter parlance) to seek the pacific settlement of disputes or to enforce the peace. The determination that an ethnic conflict falls within the authority of either Chapter VI, VII, or Chapter VIII of the Charter normally is a threshold requirement before the Security Council entertains consideration of it.

A. Legal Authority for Peaceful Measures (Chapter VI)

The power of the Security Council under Article 34 to *investigate* an ethnic conflict that "might lead to international friction or give rise to a dispute" exposes a wide range of ethnic conflicts to Security Council scrutiny. One could argue that many internal ethnic conflicts have within them the seeds of a broader conflict that might lead to international friction or that an internal ethnic conflict standing alone might lead to international friction because of the violence, human rights violations, economic dislocation, or political instability that could arise from it. Particularly in light of the growing sensitivity of both the General Assembly and the Security Council to violations of international humanitarian law in ethnic conflicts, and the often massive refugee flows into neighboring countries, the concept of what might constitute a threat to international peace and security has expanded since 1945.

Consequently, there is cause to review Article 2(7) of the U.N. Charter, which in the past provided a shield behind which ethnic conflicts of a strictly internal character traditionally have been able to escape international scrutiny. Article 2(7) prohibits the United Nations from intervening "in matters which are essentially within the domestic jurisdiction of any state" or requiring members "to submit such matters to settlement." This is the classic prohibition on interference in the internal affairs of a member state that continues to dominate the perspective of a large number of governments with respect to the U.N.'s legal authority to intervene in many ethnic conflicts. Nothing about Article 2(7) suggests that "matters which are essentially within the domestic jurisdiction of any state" are frozen as of 1945 or cannot evolve with changing circumstances. What may have been considered strictly domestic jurisdiction, or the internal affairs, of a state in 1945 will not necessarily apply at the end of the twentieth century. The development of international law since World War II, particularly international humanitarian law, human rights law, and environmental law, shows that many nominally internal matters are open to the expanding reach of international norms. Therefore, despite exhortations about respect for not interfering in the internal affairs of a state, those affairs are increasingly subject to rigorous scrutiny by the international community and particularly by the United Nations acting through its major organs—the General Assembly, the Economic and Social Council, the Security Council, and the International Court of Justice.

B. Legal Authority for Coercive Measures
(Chapters VII and VIII)

Claims of domestic jurisdiction do not preclude enforcement action. By its own terms, the noninterference principle of Article 2(7) "shall not prejudice the application of enforcement measures under Chapter VII." If the Security Council determines that an ethnic conflict threatens or is a breach of international peace and security, and follows that determination with enforcement measures under Chapter VII authority, then the Article 2(7) prohibition on U.N. intervention is extinguished.

Clearly, if an ethnic conflict spills across or threatens the integrity of an international border, the threat to international peace and security required for invocation of Chapter VII is presumptively established. Because this frequently occurs with ethnic conflicts, the activation of Chapter VII and the direct involvement of the Security Council has become common. Exceptions remain, of course, particularly where the ethnic conflict involves a permanent member of the council.

Chapter VIII of the Charter provides another means for action under the authority of the Security Council but directly by regional bodies. The premise of Chapter VIII is that "regional arrangements or agencies" take on the burden of pacific settlement and, when "appropriate," enforcement actions. In the immediate aftermath of the cold war, it quickly became apparent that regional organizations were not prepared for this hefty assignment. The Security Council shouldered the burden of peace enforcement under Chapter VII, either directly through U.N. peace operations or indirectly through authorization of multinational military operations. But the peacekeeping capabilities of regional entities are evolving. Moreover, the budgetary crisis at the United Nations, coupled with the constraining mandates under which U.N. peacekeeping operations must perform during hostilities, has compelled the secretary-general to propose that the council react to conflicts by authorizing self-paying multinational coalitions or by delegating authority to regional bodies to take military action.[28] Although this places the United Nations strictly in the authorizer but not implementer role, it is driven by the practical realities of waning financial and political support for the United Nations.

C. Legal Authority for Norm Elaboration
and Quasi-Judicial Pronouncements

The Charter pledges all member states to respect the principle of equal rights and self-determination of peoples and to promote respect for hu-

[28] Supplement to an Agenda for Peace, U.N. Doc. A/50/60, S/1995/1 (1995), at 18–19.

man rights and fundamental freedoms.[29] Like threats to or violations of international peace and security, human rights abuses and denial of self-determination have opened the door to U.N. engagement in various ethnic conflicts. Many ethnic conflicts, for example, can be described as disputes over conflicting visions of self-determination. When the United Nations, through a General Assembly resolution, a Security Council action, or an advisory opinion or judgment of the International Court of Justice, responds to the aspirations of self-determination by a people, the resulting U.N. engagement can influence the resolution of the conflict.

There is a lot of relevant treaty law outside of the U.N. Charter, such as treaties covering refugees and the protection of internally displaced persons, which this chapter does not attempt to address with respect to the engagement of a host of U.N. agencies in ethnic conflicts. Nor is there any discussion here of the decisions of the International Court of Justice or the international criminal tribunals for the former Yugoslavia and for Rwanda that help establish legal norms that can be of significant influence in managing an ethnic conflict and its aftermath. But brief mention should be make of key U.N. organs other than the Security Countil.

The Economic and Social Council addresses ethnic conflicts whenever recommendations are adopted by the council pertaining to human rights or freedoms relating to any such conflict pursuant to Article 62 of the Charter. Similarly, the resolutions adopted each year by the General Assembly pertaining to a wide range of ethnic conflicts set forth scores of recommendations for disputing parties to follow. The General Assembly can deploy human rights monitors into such conflicts or even act, with limited authority under the Uniting for Peace Resolution, in response to an ethnic conflict if the Security Council fails to address the issue or remains deadlocked on it.[30] But these examples only scratch the surface of initiatives by U.N. organs under a wide range of circumstances and under the authority of the Charter.

III. Modes of Implementation

The U.N.'s methodology of engagement in ethnic conflicts might be described as one of "flexible response." Depending on the circumstances of the particular ethnic conflict or dispute confronting the United Nations—and the views of the members of the Security Countil and of a majority of the General Assembly—the organization can respond flexibly with any one of at least seven mechanisms of engagement, ranging from

[29] U.N. Charter, art. 55.
[30] G.A. Res 377A(V), 5 U.N. GAOR, Supp. (No. 20) 10, U.N. Doc. A/1775 (1951).

hortatory resolutions of the General Assembly to military enforcement action by the Security Council. By setting forth these mechanisms of engagement as a coherent whole, I do not mean to imply that member states view their participation in any particular mechanism as part of such a holistic enterprise regarding ethnic conflicts. Governments join together to use any particular mechanism on its own merits and for political reasons that may have only scant association with any grander scheme for managing an ethnic conflict. Rather, this chapter strives to provide a conceptual framework within which to identify U.N. activities relating to ethnic conflicts.

A. Hortatory Actions

The power of the declared word should not be underestimated (or overestimated). Throughout each year a profusion of General Assembly and ECOSOC resolutions, Security Council resolutions and presidential statements, resolutions of the U.N. Commission on Human Rights, and reports by the secretary-general pronounce on ethnic conflicts and the means to manage or prevent them. These hortatory instruments also establish the framework within which other mechanisms of intervention can be launched.

For example, throughout the conflict in the former Yugoslavia, the General Assembly, the Security Council, and the U.N. Commission on Human Rights adopted resolutions condemning the carnage and urging strict compliance by all parties with international law and Security Council resolutions.[31] The General Assembly similarly addressed the genocide committed in Rwanda in 1994 and what needed to be done in its aftermath.[32] The General Assembly has supported steps to stem the tide of genocide in Burundi.[33]

It has become an almost daily function of the Security Council to address ethnic conflicts in its informal and formal deliberations and in the adoption of resolutions and presidential statements. A survey of any recent compilation of such documents reveals a wealth of condemnatory, advisory, obligatory, and operational provisions spanning the authority vested in the Security Council by the U.N. Charter. For example, on May 12, 1995, a typical day, the Security Council adopted Resolution 993, which extended the U.N. observer mission in Georgia.[34] In addition to that operative, and very important, action, the council reaffirmed the right

[31] *See, e.g.*, G.A. Res. 49/10 (1994); G.A. Res. 49/196 (1994); G.A. Res. 49/205 (1994); G.A. Res. 59/192 (1995); G.A. Res. 50/193 (1995).
[32] G.A. Res. 49/206 (1994); G.A. Res. 50/200 (1995).
[33] G.A. Res. 50/159 (1995).
[34] S.C. Res. 993 (1995).

of all refugees and displaced persons affected by the Abkhaz conflict to return to their homes in secure conditions in accordance with international law; deplored the continued obstruction of such return by the Abkhaz authorities; expressed its full support for the efforts of the U.N. secretary-general to achieve a comprehensive political settlement, including on the status of Abkhazia; and urged the parties to refrain from any unilateral actions.

The primary function of the U.N. Commission on Human Rights (UN-HRC) is to seize the attention of governments with hortatory, but frequently piercing, resolutions. Although the UNHRC focuses on the protection of individual human rights within a country, it necessarily addresses issues central to many ethnic conflicts. In its 1996 session, for example, the UNHRC blamed the Bosnian Serbs for the lion's share of human rights violations in Bosnia-Herzegovina.[35] In a special session, the UNHRC supported ongoing peace negotiations and preventive diplomacy efforts for Burundi.[36] In 1994, the UNHRC condemned the genocide in Rwanda[37] and again supported the U.N.'s efforts to promote self-determination in the Western Sahara.[38] In some cases, ethnic groups could gain or lose from the UNHRC's collective judgment on the conflict in which they had been or continued to be engaged, both in terms of the groups' international standing and their own self-perception.

These pronouncements by U.N. organs and agencies sometimes have the effect of framing the issues in an ethnic conflict for the international community as a whole. They can put a global focus on a conflict that can outlast momentary media coverage. In a few cases, the target states care enough about what is being said of them that they react—usually defensively—and therefore the process has some effect. But enforcement action is only a very remote possibility.

B. Diplomatic Intervention

The United Nations relies heavily on diplomacy to prevent, manage, or end ethnic conflicts. It is an obvious but underrated activity within the U.N. system. In New York and Geneva, the very functioning of U.N. organs confronted with the issue of ethnic conflict requires daily rounds of diplomatic activity ranging from formal sessions of the Security Council to telephone calls among the political counselors of diplomatic missions. Rarely exposed to public view, the thousands of diplomatic contacts that occur each day among the U.N. missions of member states and by

---

[35] U.N. Doc. E/CN.4/RES/1996/71.
[36] U.N. Doc. E/CN.4/1996/1.
[37] U.N. Doc. E/CN.4/RES/1996/76.
[38] U.N. Doc. E/CN.4/RES/1996/6.

them with U.N. officials constitute a process of diplomatic intervention that cannot be quantified or comprehensively described. But it is the most central element in how the United Nations and its member states react to ethnic conflicts.

In the past, most envoys deployed to negotiate the settlement of inter-state conflicts have been representatives of particular national govern-ments. But in recent years, the U.N. secretary-general—acting through the appointment of his own "special representative"—has often become a major diplomatic presence in ethnic conflicts. He has appointed special envoys or special representatives, usually on the recommendation of the Security Council or the General Assembly.

The special representative's mandate can cover one or more of a wide range of tasks: to observe and review the situation within a country (as James Jonah did in Burundi in late 1993), to help negotiate a cease-fire (as Jacques-Roger Booh-Booh sought to do as genocide swamped Rwanda in April 1994 and a succession of special representatives have done in Tajiki-stan), to oversee U.N. electoral monitoring and coordinate activities of other monitors (such as Lakhdar Brahimi did in South Africa in 1993–94), or to implement a peace agreement (as Aldo Ajello did in Mozambique in 1993). Special representatives have been appointed to pressure recal-citrant parties to participate in a peace process (as several special repre-sentatives and the secretary-general himself have done in Liberia), to revive a peace process (as Edouard Brunner was asked to do in May 1993 in Georgia), to oversee the transformation of a government and its mili-tary (as Alioune Blondin Beye has done in Angola), to negotiate a peaceful resolution of an ethnic conflict (as Cyrus Vance sought to do in Bosnia and Herzegovina in 1993), to broker a national reconciliation agreement (as Alvaro De Soto did in El Salvador in the early 1990s), to administer a U.N. peacekeeping operation (as Yasushi Akashi did with the U.N. Protection Force (UNPROFOR) in the former Yugoslavia and his successor, Kofi An-nan, did in 1995 with the United Nations Peace Force in the former Yugoslavia), to oversee peace implementation projects (as Ismat Kittani did in Bosnia in 1996), or to rule as a de facto governor-general of a territory in transition (as Jacques Klein did with UNTAES in Croatia in 1996 and 1997).

Sometimes the Security Council will agree to send its own special mis-sion of selected council members to investigate a situation and report back to the council. Recent examples include missions sent to Bosnia,[39] Burun-di,[40] Mozambique,[41] and the Western Sahara.[42] Of course, the deploy-

[39] S.C. Res. 819 (1993).
[40] U.N. Doc. S/PRST/1994/47 (1994).
[41] U.N. Doc. S/PRST/1994/51 (1994).
[42] S.C. Res. 995 (1995); U.N. Doc. S/1995/431; S.C. Res. 1002 (1995).

ment of the secretary-general's special representative or of a Security Council special mission can be used to avoid, at least for some tolerable period of time, the harder decisions about economic sanctions or military intervention that the Security Council arrives at reluctantly and often tardily. Usually, however, the secretary-general and the Security Council would not be able to function effectively without the presence of their representatives on the ground to assist with the preparation of reports by the secretary-general and the decisions that need to be made, particularly by the Security Council, in connection with an ethnic conflict. The council typically will not act without first receiving a report from the secretary-general that, in turn, is heavily influenced by the information and assessments received from the secretary-general's special representative. Nor, if there has been a council mission to the area, will the council act without first hearing a report from its representative(s) who participated in the mission.

The U.N. Commission on Human Rights has its own diplomatic weapon in the form of special procedures, namely working groups or special rapporteurs who investigate and ultimately bring to the attention of the General Assembly specific human rights abuses or the human rights situation in a particular country.[43] In the mid-1990s, for example, special rapporteurs (or representatives) presented reports on human rights violations in numerous countries where ethnic conflicts were under way, simmering, or on hold, including the former Yugoslavia[44] and Sudan.[45] This form of U.N. engagement carries some risk of undermining stability by challenging a government's record of protecting the human rights of an ethnic group. On the other hand, special rapporteurs serve the therapeutic function of exposing at least some information about the treatment of ethnic groups within a country and thereby better inform the Security Council and the General Assembly of situations that may require their attention. Probably one of the most effective UNHRC mechanisms was the Working Group on Disappearances, which issued some critical reports on Sri Lanka and encouraged the Sri Lankan government to get their security forces under control. Such practical engagement with those in power can sometimes do more good than condemnations or sanctions.

C. Sanctions

The first half of the 1990s witnessed an extraordinary application of the Security Council's sanctions power. In many cases this power was exer-

---

[43] See Tom J. Farer & Felice Gaer, *The UN and Human Rights: At the End of the Beginning, in* UNITED NATIONS, DIVIDED WORLD, *supra* note 24, at 240, 286–87.

[44] U.N. Docs. E/CN.4/1996/63 and E/CN.4/1995/57.

[45] U.N. Docs. E/CN.4/1996/62 and E/CN.4/1995/58.

cised in connection with ethnic conflicts or with the protection of a particular ethnic group following a major interstate armed conflict. The most
far-ranging sanctions regime has been that enforced against Iraq following its invasion of Kuwait in 1990.[46] Though it began as a response to
crossborder aggression, the sanctions regime assumed even broader importance in the spring of 1991, when Saddam Hussein turned his defeated
Revolutionary Guard against the Kurdish population of northern Iraq,
which had sought to resist his rule. Months later the Iraqi army moved
against the Shiite population in the marshes of southern Iraq. Two primary objectives of the U.N. sanctions regime against Iraq thus have been to
prevent the Iraqi government from acquiring the means to inflict further
injury on these ethnic populations and to deter Saddam Hussein from
taking aggressive action against them for fear of its impact on the resolve
of the Security Council to take military action against the Iraqi army.
Movement of Iraqi army contingents north into Kurdish areas or south
into the marshes where the Shiites live risks a military response by one or
more of the coalition partners of the Gulf War.[47]

Arms embargos have been a typical Security Council sanction in response to ethnic conflicts. Examples include Rwanda,[48] Liberia,[49] the former Yugoslavia,[50] Angola,[51] and South Africa.[52] It is relatively easy for
the members of the Security Council to agree on imposition of an arms
embargo, particularly at the onset of a violent ethnic conflict. Enforcement
of arms embargos is much more difficult but still more easily achieved
than enforcement of broader sanctions regimes. As a result, arms embargos are often the sanction of first resort.

Cutting off the flow of arms to all parties in an ethnic conflict can result
in lopsided advantages for one side or the other, as the conflict in the
former Yugoslavia clearly demonstrated. Arms embargos can also be difficult to lift. The prolonged ordeal over the lifting of the arms embargo on
Bosnia is the most prominent case in point.[53]

Diplomatic sanctions are also popular instruments for exerting leverage
on the parties to ethnic conflicts and other threats to international peace
and security. Articles 4, 5, and 6 of the Charter can be used as legal
authority for denying membership in the United Nations, for suspending

[46] S.C. Res. 661 (1990).
[47] S.C. Res. 949 (1994). During the Iraqi offensive into northern Iraq in August and September 1996, the United States responded with cruise missle attacks on select military targets in
Iraq.
[48] S.C. Res. 918 (1994); S.C. Res. 997 (1995).
[49] S.C. Res. 788 (1992).
[50] S.C. Res. 713 (1991); S.C. Res. 727 (1991).
[51] S.C. Res. 864 (1993).
[52] S.C. Res. 418 (1977).
[53] S.C. Res. 1021 (1995). Lifting an arms embargo also became a difficult action of protracted duration for the Security Council in the case of Rwanda. S.C. Res. 1011 (1995).

the rights and privileges of membership, and for expelling a member from the organization, respectively. Article 41 explicitly designates "the severance of diplomatic relations" as a measure short of using force to enforce Security Council decisions. Action by the Security Council to isolate a rogue government can result in similar actions against that government by other international agencies, depending on their treaty requirements.[54] The United Nations can also bestow a practically significant status on an ethnic group by granting it observer status. The Palestine Liberation Organization is one such example.[55]

Economic sanctions are the Security Council's sledgehammer, short of using military force. In addition to the application of economic sanctions on Iraq, the council has used such sanctions to some effect against Serbia and Montenegro and the Bosnian Serbs.[56] Sanctions imposition and relief were directly associated with the degree of cooperation by Serb leaders with their ethnic counterparts in the region. They have also been used to support the rule of law and establish individual accountability for crimes against the members of ethnic groups, in particular to urge cooperation by the Serbs with the International Criminal Tribunal for the former Yugoslavia.[57] (The threat of sanctions also was a useful pressure point on the government of Croatia to seek cooperation with the tribunal and to cease military action against Croatian Serbs.)

D. Military Intervention

The most visible form of U.N. intervention in ethnic conflicts is military intervention. Peace observation, peacekeeping, and peace enforcement operations are used under differing circumstances to manage ethnic conflicts. With very rare exceptions, the purpose is not to defeat or overwhelm one side in the conflict; rather, the Security Council authorizes a military operation in order to (1) stabilize the situation and separate warring factions through the implementation of a cease-fire or peace agreement, (2) prevent further atrocities and human suffering, (3) facilitate the delivery of humanitarian assistance, or (4) prevent an armed conflict and associated atrocities from occurring or reoccurring. Examples of U.N. peace operations associated with ethnic conflicts in recent years are well

[54] With respect to Security Council action against, for example, Libya, see S.C. Res. 748 (1992). See generally FREDERIC KIRGIS, INTERNATIONAL ORGANIZATIONS IN THEIR LEGAL SETTINGS 585–603 (2d ed. 1993).

[55] See G.A. Res. 3237 (1974), 29 GAOR Supp. 31 (A/9631), at 4 (1974).

[56] S.C. Res. 757 (1992); S.C. Res. 787 (1992); S.C. Res. 820 (1993); S.C. Res. 942 (1994); S.C. Res. 943 (1994); S.C. Res. 988 (1995); S.C. Res. 992 (1995); S.C. Res. 1003 (1995); S.C. Res. 1015 (1995); S.C. Res. 1022 (1995).

[57] S.C. Res. 1022 (1995).

known and widely examined in the literature: UNPROFOR in the former Yugoslavia, UNAMIR in Rwanda, UNOMIL in Liberia, UNIFIL in southern Lebanon, UNDOF in the Golan Heights, UNFICYP in Cyprus, UNOMIG in Georgia, and UNAVEM in Angola. Critics would argue that some of these operations are among the least successful of U.N. peace operations: some failed because too much was asked and too little given (UNPROFOR); some failed because the situation spun out of control (UNOMIL); and some failed because of the long-term international investment in a low-risk status quo (UNFICYP).

UNPROFOR no doubt will stand out as an operation that achieved some of its humanitarian objectives but could not meet the larger challenge of bringing the ethnic conflict among the three countries (Croatia, Bosnia and Herzegovina, and the Federal Republic of Yugoslavia) and among their ethnic populations under control and to an end. The Security Council authorization of a multinational Implementation Force (IFOR) in December 1995 to police the implementation of a peace agreement negotiated among the parties outside U.N. supervision signifies both the limits of the United Nations and ultimately its flexibility to defer to and legitimize a stronger and more effective military operation.

The Middle Eastern operations (UNIFIL, UNDOF, and UNTSO) are strictly holding patterns designed to serve as buffers between Israel and Lebanon or Syria until negotiated peace agreements can establish permanent arrangements for security. UNFICYP on Cyprus is another example of a U.N. military force that preserves stability, although it may also have delayed the ultimate resolution of the conflict between the Greek and Turkish populations. The longevity of these operations attests both to their durability and to their inability to instill enough confidence in the competing ethnic groups for them to resolve their seemingly intractable disputes.

Recent experience with U.N. military operations suggests a number of key questions that should be posed in connection with the Security Council's consideration of military intervention in future ethnic conflicts, whether for peacekeeping under the Charter or enforcement action under Chapter VII. They include the following:

(1) Under what Charter authority should the Security Council act?

(2) At what stage of an ethnic conflict should a U.N. military operation be introduced?

(3) Is the U.N. operation intended to prevent the eruption, continuation, or resumption of an ethnic conflict?

(4) Is the purpose of the U.N. operation simply to stop the fighting and stabilize the situation?

(5) Is the purpose of the U.N. operation to help develop a multiethnic society?

(6) Will the U.N. operation, in fact, further ethnic cleansing by creating and patrolling separation lines?

(7) Will the U.N. operation engage in nation-building activities?

(8) Should the Security Council turn to a multinational military force rather than a U.N.-commanded peace operation?

The Clinton administration's review of multilateral peace operations, culminating in the issuance of Presidential Decision Directive 25 (PDD-25) in May 1994, addressed some of these questions and established factors that the U.S. government takes into account in determining its support for and participation in multilateral peace operations, particularly those initiated by the U.N. Security Council.[58] Some elements of the PDD-25 exercise were introduced at the United Nations and influenced creation of factors that facilitate decision making within the Security Council and the U.N. Department of Peacekeeping Operations. Because ethnic conflicts are a predominant feature of peacekeeping operations in recent years, any U.N. military intervention will be deeply influenced by how member states such as the United States evaluate the risks, costs, and opportunities of such interventions. That has become as much an exercise in national capitals as it has in New York at the United Nations.

The planning for some kind of on-call force will play an important role in structuring a timely and effective U.N. military role in ethnic conflicts.[59] The nonimplementation of Article 43 of the U.N. Charter after World War II left a vacuum in U.N. enforcement capabilities that has been filled in recent decades, first with peacekeeping operations created under the authority of, though nowhere explicitly described within, the Charter and second with enforcement operations authorized under Chapter VII that typically have drawn on ad hoc multinational coalitions. But this evolution in U.N. practice has not addressed the urgent need for both preventive and reactive military capabilities to manage explosive ethnic conflicts. Unless the Security Council can act quickly, many ethnic disputes will spin out of control.

The starting point for such rapid response has been the creation of a data base of the standby capabilities of member states. U.N. officials described the U.N. Standby Arrangements System in 1995 in the following terms:

[T]he Standby Arrangements System is an efficiency enhancement process based on conditional offers by Member States of specified resources which

[58] See United States: Administration Policy on Reforming Multilateral Peace Operations, 33 I.L.M. 795 (1994).

[59] See David J. Scheffer, United Nations Peace Operations and Prospects for a Standby Force, 28 CORNELL INT'L L. J. 649 (1995).

could be made available within agreed response times for UN peacekeeping operations. These resources can be military individuals or units, civilian police, specialized personnel (civilian and military), services as well as material and equipment. The agreed-upon resources remain on "standby" which implies that they remain in their home country, where requisite training is conducted to prepare them to fulfill specific tasks or functions in accordance with UN training guidelines. Standby resources are to be used exclusively for peacekeeping operations mandated by the Security Council and should not be confused with peace-enforcement units, which are described in the Agenda for Peace as forces meant to respond to "outright aggression, imminent or actual." Institutionalization of the process calls for the Member State[s] to provide the Secretariat with detailed information and data related to probable contributions from their States.[60]

The Standby Arrangements System is not what was envisaged by the drafters of Article 43 of the Charter, but it is a beginning. To date, it is more the norm than the exception that governments that have identified logistical and troop capabilities do not follow through when the situation warrants. Nonetheless, the Standby Arrangements System proved useful in mid-1996 as the United Nations was examining how to react to ethnic violence in Burundi. The system helped provide the kind of data that informed U.N. planners of what could be requested in the event an international force were formed either to stand by outside Burundi or to enter Burundi to prevent or stop genocide.

The critical questions for the future center on the realistic functions and capabilities of U.N. military operations. First, there must be an effective military response mechanism. That will require several building blocks over a number of years, the initial step being the Standby Arrangements System I have discussed. Second, the Security Council needs to improve its ability to intervene militarily early enough to prevent hostilities from commencing or spinning out of control. Third, peace and security should not be the only goal in a U.N. military operation. The underlying ethnic dispute must be addressed and military intervention must be tailored to open up opportunities for the parties and the international community to implement a peace.

E. Humanitarian Intervention

Humanitarian intervention—either nonforcible or forcible—is perhaps the most significant action the United Nations can undertake in connec-

---

[60] United Nations Standby Arrangements Systems, Briefing by U.N. Officials to Member State Representatives, in New York City (June 16, 1995).

tion with ethnic conflicts, which invariably have devastating consequences on civilian populations. Few can argue against the moral imperative of humanitarian intervention, but the methodology invites a debate
over legal authority and practical means to bring relief to civilians. Because the combatants in ethnic conflicts often target civilian populations
and defy the rules of conventional armed conflict, the justification for
some kind of humanitarian intervention by the United Nations or some
other entity (nongovernmental organization, regional organization, multinational coalition, or national government[s]) assumes much greater importance. With the end of the cold war and the seeming proliferation of
humanitarian catastrophes and atrocities in the wake of ethnic and other
internal conflicts, the international community has been confronted with
the enormous challenge of using a more complex and controversial set of
options for resolving armed conflicts. It will be many years before the dust
settles on the debate over the limits of justifiable humanitarian intervention.

The cascade of literature on humanitarian intervention in the 1990s will
offer any scholar or practitioner a wealth of views and examples.[61] I have
written elsewhere of the need for a modern doctrine of humanitarian
intervention and for criteria that will better guide the international community in responding to the humanitarian calamity that often arises from
ethnic conflicts.[62] There is a clear need to reach beyond traditional definitions of humanitarian intervention and to explore the range of nonforcible
and forcible interventions that are both justifiable and essential to address
modern humanitarian challenges. A major question is whether the international community will gradually accept humanitarian intervention as
an independent legal right and political necessity without, for example,
being tied to "self-defense," or under a growing range of situations, requiring the consent of the target government.

From a legalistic point of view, four critical questions should be posed
in connection with humanitarian intervention. (1) Must there be a threat
to international peace and security for the United Nations to consider
either nonforcible or forcible humanitarian intervention? (2) What circum-

---

[61] A brief contemporary sampling includes Y. K. Tyagi, *The Concept of Humanitarian Intervention Revisited*, 16 MICH. J. INT'L. L. 883 (1995); Richard Falk, *The Complexities of Human-
itarian Intervention: A New World Order Challenge*, 17 MICH. J. INT'L. L. 491 (1995); SEAN
MURPHY, HUMANITARIAN INTERVENTION: THE UNITED NATIONS IN AN EVOLVING WORLD
ORDER (1996); FERNANDO R. TESÓN, HUMANITARIAN INTERVENTION: AN INQUIRY INTO LAW
AND MORALITY (1996); Rein Mullerson & David J. Scheffer, *Legal Regulation of the Use of Force*,
in BEYOND CONFRONTATION: INTERNATIONAL LAW FOR THE POST–COLD WAR ERA 93, 117–24
(Lori Damrosch, Gemady Danilenko, & Rein Mullerson eds., 1995).

[62] David J. Scheffer, *Toward a Modern Doctrine of Humanitarian Intervention*, 23 U. TOL. L.
REV. 253 (1992).

stances should give rise to a right of nonforcible humanitarian intervention? (3) What circumstances should give rise to a right of forcible humanitarian intervention? (4) Is collective authorization required to legitimize
forcible humanitarian intervention? A final question might well be, what
is the cost of not intervening, nonforcibly or forcibly, in an ethnic conflict?[63] From a pragmatic point of view, skeptical governments would ask:
(1) How do you prevent abuse? How do you keep Great Powers or regional powers from using the humanitarian objective as a guise to intervene for political reasons? (2) What are the limits? Is the intervention
simply to protect civilians, or does the military force challenge the perpetrators of human misery, whether of official or rebel character? (3) What
happens next?

Invocation of the doctrine of humanitarian intervention is a means for
the United Nations to engage in an ethnic conflict without necessarily
taking sides. The engagement is often inescapable. At the outset, it may be
very limited in scope, beginning with nonforcible delivery of humanitarian aid. Some U.N. peacekeeping operations have recently been deployed for the express purpose of facilitating the delivery of humanitarian
assistance in an ethnic conflict. UNPROFOR in the former Yugoslavia served
this purpose, as did UNOSOM in Somalia and UNAMIR in Rwanda. But the
introduction of the United Nations or other international or nongovernmental organizations to deliver humanitarian aid establishes a beachhead
in an ethnic conflict from which the United Nations ultimately may need
to take more forcible initiatives. The experiences in Somalia and Bosnia in
the early 1990s reflect this evolution in the U.N.'s role. In Liberia, U.N.
efforts to facilitate the delivery of humanitarian assistance have presented
the Security Council and member state governments with the issue of
whether to go beyond the regional peacekeeping and U.N. observer missions already deployed within that country and to use force in order to
deliver humanitarian assistance.

The Security Council and individual governments can exert considerable pressure upon warring parties not to obstruct or prevent the delivery
of humanitarian assistance—such as warning that severe sanctions or
military intervention will result in the event of noncooperation. There is
emerging a practice of nonforcible humanitarian intervention whereby
the pressure of an international organization, and the threats it and member state governments can make, may encourage acquiescence—perhaps
grudging and fraught with danger—from the national government or
warring party.

---

[63] This question frames one of the factors in PDD-25. *See* United States: Administration
Policy on Reforming Multilateral Peace Operations, *supra* note 58, at 803.

F. Peace Implementation

Ethnic conflicts have become the target of peace implementation, a postconflict process that seeks to ensure a smooth transition from deployment of a foreign military presence to implementation of a peace agreement so that an ethnic conflict is resolved. The emerging pattern is the negotiation of a peace agreement among warring factions, followed by the introduction of a U.N.-authorized or established military operation to stabilize the peace and simultaneously the introduction of a civilian implementation process that focuses on economic reconstruction, infrastructure repair, elections, human rights observance, and sometimes judicial accountability for war crimes.

The most prominent example is the Dayton General Framework Agreement and its annexed agreements, agreed to in November 1995 by the Bosnian, Croat, and Serb parties in the Bosnian conflict.[64] The U.N. intervention in Bosnia and Croatia failed to resolve the conflict and, many would argue, exacerbated it by failing to use sufficient force under the authority granted by the Security Council. With Security Council authorization, NATO finally took decisive steps in the summer of 1995 following the Srebrenica massacres to force the parties to the table for peace talks. The culmination of that process at Dayton, Ohio, in the fall of 1995 established a military and peace implementation process in which the United Nations continues to play an important role.

The Security Council authorized NATO to deploy IFOR into Bosnia to separate and to some extent disarm the warring military forces and to create a balance among them.[65] The Security Council also suspended the application of economic sanctions against the Bosnian Serbs and the Federal Republic of Yugoslavia but empowered two key officials in the military and peace implementation process to reimpose sanctions fully if either party fails to comply with the Dayton agreement.[66]

As part of the peace implementation process, the UNHCR played the critical role in facilitating the return of refugees to their homes in Bosnia. The Security Council established an International Police Task Force (IPTF) pursuant to the Dayton agreement for the purpose of monitoring the performance of local police, who will bear the long-term responsibility for ensuring the success of the Dayton agreement.[67] The experience of the IPTF in Bosnia, as well as the police component of the U.N. peacekeeping operation in Haiti in 1994–96, revealed how critical this component of peace implementation will be in coming years. In the future, the United

---

[64] See 35 I.L.M. 75 (1996).
[65] S.C. Res. 1031 (1995).
[66] S.C. Res. 1022 (1995).
[67] S.C. Res. 1035 (1995).

Nations will need to upgrade significantly its capabilities in training and monitoring local police forces in order to provide the kind of local security that ethnic populations demand in order to move freely, resettle, and live peacefully with their ethnic counterparts in their neighborhoods or regions. Other organizations, such as the Organization for Cooperation and Security in Europe, can provide vital assistance in these efforts. Already, such organizations have assumed major roles in activities such as the holding of elections throughout Bosnia. Of necessity, peace implementation arrangements will grow as a major feature of U.N. practice in assisting ethnic groups and their governments to emerge from armed conflicts.

G. International Judicial Intervention

In the aftermath of the cold war a frequent question is, who is the enemy? Often the question has an unorthodox answer. Increasingly, member states rely on the United Nations to identify the enemy as a violator of international humanitarian law. Particularly in the case of ethnic conflicts, which breed atrocities against civilians, the enemy can be individual leaders and their rogue lieutenants who commit international crimes against civilian populations. On its face, there is little new about the existence of such war criminals, but their prominence in the absence of superpower rivals and surrogate warring states has generated a new system of international judicial intervention.[68]

It has become a growing practice in the Security Council to condemn, hold accountable, and occasionally initiate judicial or quasi-judicial procedures against violators of international humanitarian law in ethnic and other conflicts. Any survey of Security Council resolutions since 1990 will disclose that on a regular, indeed predictable, basis the Council approaches ethnic and other violent conflicts falling within its jurisdiction with one eye on security and another on the law. The latter may not dominate the attention of the council, but compliance with and often enforcement of international humanitarian law plays a leading role in council business in the 1990s.

The Security Council's actions in the Gulf War—including those related to criminal matters, such as the Baghdad regime's war crimes, and to civil matters leading to the creation of the U.N. Claims Commission—evolved with the emergence of the Yugoslav conflict. For the former Yugoslavia, the council employed a succession of instruments, including condemnations, warnings, the establishment of an International Commission of Investigation,[69] and, in early 1993, the formation of the International

[68] *See* David J. Scheffer, *International Judicial Intervention,* 102 FOREIGN POLICY 34 (1996).
[69] S.C. Res. 780 (1992).

Criminal Tribunal for the former Yugoslavia.[70] The council took similar steps to deal with the genocide in Rwanda in 1994, again moving from condemnations, to warnings, to the establishment of a "commission of experts,"[71] followed by the creation of the International Criminal Tribunal for Rwanda.[72] With respect to Burundi, the Council created an International Commission of Inquiry in 1995 with the mandate of investigating the 1993 coup attempt and the subsequent massacres within Burundi between Hutus and Tutsis.[73] The failure to establish any accountability for those atrocities was believed to have fueled continuing atrocities in Burundi through 1996.

The Yugoslav, Rwandan, and Burundian conflicts led to the council's creation of judicial or quasi-judicial institutions. Though the war in El Salvador was not of an ethnic character, the establishment of the Truth Commission in El Salvador and its final report in 1993 also was a pathbreaking step designed to address massive human rights violations that occurred during an internal armed conflict.[74] Other conflicts—some of ethnic origins—in which the Security Council has addressed the issue of individual accountability for violations of international humanitarian law include Somalia, Liberia, Haiti, Mozambique, Angola, the Sudan, the Middle East, and Cyprus.

International judicial intervention in ethnic conflicts helps manage such conflicts in several ways. First, it establishes individual accountability and diffuses group liability that can fuel further tension and conflict between ethnic groups. Second, judicial intervention can be a less risky and less costly means of addressing the underlying issues in an ethnic conflict than resort to economic sanctions or military intervention may be. Although they will rarely serve as the sole or even the major basis for resolution of conflicts, judicial or quasi-judicial measures can channel anger and tension into peaceful channels that can facilitate overall settlements. Third, such measures can serve a critical preventive function not only for the ethnic conflict at hand but also for other potential flashpoints. Though it will probably take decades to establish potent enough threats of judicial intervention to deter determined war criminals, a strong beginning has been made in the work of the international criminal tribunals for the former Yugoslavia and Rwanda. The precedents they establish will resonate for a long time to come. They already have had an enormous influence on the U.N.'s recent examination of the International Law Com-

[70] S.C. Res. 814 and S.C. Res. 827 (1993).
[71] S.C. Res. 935 (1994).
[72] S.C. Res. 955 (1994).
[73] S.C. Res. 1012 (1995).
[74] See Thomas Buergenthal, The United Nations Truth Commission for El Salvador, 27 VAND. J. TRANSNAT'L L. 497 (1994).

mission's proposal to establish a permanent international criminal court.[75] If established, the court should serve as both a deterrent and as a readily available enforcer of international humanitarian law against the individuals who, in the final analysis, are the source of the atrocities that characterize ethnic conflicts in our times.

There are significant reasons explaining why U.N. engagement in ethnic conflicts is growing. Action by the United Nations signifies international engagement and approval in confronting ethnic discord within and between nations. For political and often military and economic reasons, a multilateral approach through the United Nations—if only, for example, to authorize intervention by a multinational force—is more readily justified under international law to skeptical governments and often can garner more resources than unilateral or strictly coalition efforts can. The United Nations and its various organs have the capacity to elaborate norms that not only legitimize U.N. action but also establish principles for future conduct by nations and ethnic groups. In the context of ethnic conflicts, this is particularly important because ethnic claims often challenge established legal frameworks of governance. When the United Nations pronounces and acts upon principles of self-determination, democratization, humanitarian intervention, and international humanitarian law, ethnic groups can be profoundly influenced as they seek to establish the legality of their claims and the legitimacy of their actions. The United Nations also has the capacity to lock in the outcome of an ethnic conflict by confirming the legitimacy of territorial and political gains (or losses) or, short of that, by policing a cease-fire that freezes such gains until a peace settlement can be negotiated and implemented. U.N. peacekeeping operations can serve this latter purpose, but so, too, can a multilateral operation authorized by the U.N. Security Council (such as IFOR in Bosnia following the Dayton accords of late 1995). A ruling on genocide, for example, by a U.N. judicial body such as the International Court of Justice or one of the international criminal tribunals can influence the conduct of dueling political authorities or isolate through indictment individual rulers who are responsible for stimulating ethnic conflict through the commission of atrocities.

Of course, the strengths of U.N. engagement in ethnic conflicts are counterbalanced by considerable shortcomings and weaknesses. U.N. action typically requires long lead times to implement. This is particularly true for U.N. peace operations and for judicial proceedings before the International Court of Justice and the international criminal tribunals.

---

[75] *See* U.N. Doc. A/49/355 (1994), at 32–42. Subsequent work on the draft statute is reflected in U.N. Doc. A/50/22 (1995), U.N. Doc. A/AC.249/1 (1996), and U.N. Doc. A/51/22 (1996).

Volatile ethnic conflicts simply do not conform to the U.N.'s time schedule. Often unilateral or regional or coalition efforts will be far more effective in part because they are more timely.

The challenge to sovereignty arising from many U.N. actions can fuel resistance from national governments struggling against ethnic challenges. Opposition within the United Nations to such interference can dilute the U.N.'s powers and its ability to respond in a timely and meaningful way. The seeming erosion of sovereignty is further complicated by the fact that the United Nations, through its engagement in ethnic conflicts, can help establish new sovereign entities that will challenge long-established ones.

Another fundamental characteristic of U.N. practice is the requirement for unanimity among the permanent members of the Security Council before peacekeeping or enforcement action or ad hoc criminal tribunals can be initiated. Where such unanimity is lacking, other avenues of action outside of the United Nations (or perhaps in other, less powerful U.N. organs) will be more attractive. For example, the Organization for Security and Cooperation in Europe monitored and sought to mediate the ethnic separatist conflict in Chechnya without any involvement by the Security Council.

Finally, the budgetary crisis at the United Nations and the lack of political will to address some ethnic conflicts limits the U.N.'s ability to engage in them.[76] The lack of funding for current operations, much less for ambitious undertakings that would prevent ethnic conflicts from erupting into full-scale war and atrocities or launch humanitarian interventions quickly upon the outbreak of hostilities to stop widespread slaughter, has proven to be a severe constraint on effective U.N. intervention. Contingency funds have become practically nonexistent at the United Nations, with the result that any planned intervention will take much time to organize and to finance adequately. Unilateral or regional initiatives often will have more options for financing and thus a greater likelihood of being implemented.

In this chapter I have sought to explain the wide scope of U.N. engagements in ethnic conflicts. Overall, there is no question that the options for U.N. engagement are numerous and that U.N. involvement can often be instrumental in managing or resolving an ethnic conflict. But in the final analysis, the political will of national governments remains the central element of all U.N. action and of more effective measures that often must

[76] See Proposed Programme Budget for the Biennium 1996–97, Report of the Secretary-General, March 28, 1996, 50th Session, Agenda Item 116, U.N. General Assembly, U.N. Doc. A/C.5/50/57 and U.N. Doc. A/C.5/50/SR. See also U.S. government statements in USUN Press Release 71 (May 21, 1996); USUN Press Release 67 (May 15, 1996); USUN Press Release 29 (May 11, 1996).

be pursued outside of the U.N. system. Deliberations within the United Nations consist of daily decisions by governments that view the United Nations as an instrument of their own respective policies. Sometimes the United Nations serves those policies. It continues to show promise—as the premier international institution—in translating the will of governments and their citizens into international action. But it would be fallacious to assume that there is a monolithic United Nations that can act independently to wrestle ethnic animosities and violence. The answer every day remains in the foreign and defense ministries of member states, in the actions of ethnic groups, and in the collective will of each nation's citizenry.

7

Mobilizing International and Regional Organizations for Managing Ethnic Conflict

Antonia Handler Chayes and Abram Chayes

[A]s we look ahead, the onus will clearly shift to the civilian agenda. There the signs are more troubling. The formal structures of civilian implementation—committees, commissions, and human rights chambers—are being set up according to Dayton. But we must look at the larger—and more disquieting—picture. By itself, the military can do little more than silence the guns and partition the country.

Thus wrote Carl Bildt, former prime minister of Sweden and the high representative of the international community charged with the civilian task of social and economic reconstruction of Bosnia-Herzegovina, little more than three months after signature of the Dayton peace accords.[1] In fact, not much tangible peace building was started in the first ninety days. One official, working with the OSCE on elections, returned from Sarajevo discouraged by the fact that, although there were many international, regional, and nongovernmental organizations in evidence in Sarajevo, the only hammers and nails were supplied by the citizens themselves.[2] Responsibilities have been assigned to many organizations. Nevertheless, although one-quarter of the critical year of NATO's commitment had passed, there was considerable creative improvisation but little planning, cooperation, and flow of needed funds on the civilian side. The performance is depressingly familiar to those who have followed the efforts of

The authors thank Chris Cervenak for her help in drafting this paper.
1 Carl Bildt, *Keeping Bosnia in One Peace,* WASH. POST, March 31, 1996, at C2.
2 Confidential interview, March 1996.

international and regional organizations to deal with internal conflicts in the post–cold war world.

Although ethnic and tribal wars have raged throughout history, the efforts of international and regional organizations to deal with such conflicts are relatively recent. Historically, the U.N., and before it the League of Nations (as well as regional political organizations such as the OSCE), focused on conflict between states, the traditional domain of international law and politics. Both states and individuals instinctively turned to international organizations in responding to the internal conflicts that have dominated the post–cold war security agenda, but the question remains: what can international and regional organizations really do to manage ethnic conflict, and where have they succeeded or fallen short, individually and collectively?

Most of the analysis and criticism attempting to answer this question has focused on the United Nations, which has the primary responsibility for the maintenance of international peace and security. But regional and other international organizations have been engaged in the enterprise to a greater or lesser extent. Nowhere is the concentration of such organizations richer or more sophisticated than in Europe. We focus on their experience in attempting to deal with ethnic conflict in the transitional and often volatile states of Eastern and Central Europe (ECE) and the former Soviet Union (FSU).

By "managing ethnic conflict" we mean to include more than preventive diplomacy in traditional terms—that is, activity that takes place before the outbreak of violent conflict. We include efforts in the course of violent confrontation to prevent escalation and to provide the parties with breathing space to compose their differences.

We include efforts to prevent the recurrence of conflict after a settlement is reached. These phases cannot be kept entirely separate. A situation can move from one to another and back again. Often the same forces operate in each, and the same instruments must be used, although the different phases may call for different approaches or emphases.

International and regional organizations are the formal vehicles through which consensus for action to deal with conflict is established by the relevant international community. They should be able to bring greater resources, power, legitimacy, and expertise to bear on complex international problems than any one state or ad hoc grouping. Yet international organizations are composed of states, and concerted action even within a single organization requires building consensus. Typically, the process of reaching the necessary level of consensus is slow and cumbersome. A single state or group of states can often bring enormous pressure—positive or negative—on the organizations' decision-making process. Thus, intervention is often too little, too late, or too tentative. Complicating the situation further, international organizations, like individual states, have multiple agendas; and as became clear in the EU recognition policy in the former Yugoslavia, these disparate agendas may play out in unexpected ways.[3]

Thus far the effectiveness of these organizations in coping with internal conflict in the ECE and FSU has been disappointing and their potential elusive. Not only is each organization struggling with internal impediments to action, but also a fully concerted strategy to mobilize the resources of this rich organizational structure is not yet available. Each organization has its own charter and its own mandate, priorities, bureaucracy, and budget. Memberships, though overlapping, are not identical. Within a single nation, organizational "stovepipes" lead to different domestic political actors. Although it is common and true to cite limitations of resources to explain deficiencies, it is also true that more than $3 billion annually has been expended in the former Yugoslavia alone, with a deployment even before the Dayton agreement of some 6,000 civilian personnel and 40,000 soldiers and police officers.[4]

Careful analysis of the record to date and the juxtaposition of the performance of relevant organizations suggest some ways in which their contribution could be improved over that of the first half-decade since the cold war. For purposes of discussion, we divide the organizations into three groups, excluding the U.N., which is discussed in Chapter 6. The first includes those that have an explicit focus on conflict prevention but dispose of very limited resources. In this group are the trans-European regional organizations—the Organization for Security and Cooperation in Europe (OSCE) and the Council of Europe (COE)—which pursue the lowest-key and least coercive form of conflict prevention. The second group comprises organizations with political and economic resources but with little or no focus on managing ethnic conflict. Here we find the international financial organizations—the International Monetary Fund (IMF), the World Bank, and the European Bank for Reconstruction and Development (EBRD). They have power and influence to mount a conflict prevention and management strategy but have hardly begun to do so.

---

[3] EU recognition policy in the former Yugoslavia changed dramatically. Before the conflict erupted in mid-1991, the E.C. commission's goal was to maintain a unified Yugoslav state. As the crisis progressed, countries backed away from this aim, with Germany in particular taking an inflexible position in support of recognition of separate states of Slovenia and Croatia and doing so in December 1991. For a discussion of recognition policy and its consequences, see Mario Zucconi, *The European Union in the Former Yugoslavia: A Case Study*, in PREVENTING CONFLICT IN THE POST-COMMUNIST WORLD: MOBILIZING INTERNATIONAL AND REGIONAL ORGANIZATIONS 237 (Antonia Handler Chayes & Abram Chayes eds., 1996) (hereinafter "PREVENTING CONFLICT").

[4] Jarat Chopra & Thomas G. Weiss, *The United Nations and the Former Second World: Coping with Conflict*, in PREVENTING CONFLICT, *supra* note 3, at 522. UNPROFOR's annual budget approaches $2 billion, UNHCR's is about $500,000, and another billion dollars are spent annually by other governmental, intergovernmental, and nongovernmental organizations.

Here, too, is the European Union and its offering of conflict inhibitors—the effect of its example and the aspiration for membership. In the third group are organizations with military power but that, as products of the cold war, have yet to address systematically the problem of ethnic conflict. These are the regional security organizations—the North Atlantic Treaty Organization (NATO) and the Western European Union (WEU).

I. Trans-European Political Organizations

Membership in the OSCE and COE is confined to European countries (and, by extension, to the United States and Canada in the case of the OSCE) and is open to all of them, including the countries of Eastern Europe and the successor states of the Soviet Union.[5] The OSCE and COE are thus arguably the organizations best suited for dealing with internal conflict in these states because they are the best informed and most closely concerned. Both organizations undertake low-key intervention in nascent conflict, employing various forms of mediation, confidence building, or norm development. Budgetary restrictions prevent more than very limited efforts at technical assistance or other kinds of material aid.

The OSCE's typical operation brings all stakeholders into dialogue in an attempt to prevent conflict from erupting. It requires detailed knowledge of the conditions in the area and more or less continuous mediatory activity. The work of the high commissioner on national minorities and various in-country missions illustrate this model. The COE develops human rights norms and standards of democratic governance, which it then imposes as conditions of membership for new applicants. In doing so, it places pressure on them to improve their performance in these areas.

A. The Organization for Security and Cooperation in Europe

The most novel and potentially effective methods of preventing ethnic conflict have been developed by the OSCE.[6] The traditional settlement and enforcement model for international intervention in conflict begins with fact finding, the results of which are discussed by the organization's political decision-making body. This body then typically directs the parties to undertake certain actions (such as, cease hostilities) and to accept high-level intermediation. Coercive economic or military measures may

[5] The OSCE was formerly the Conference on Security and Cooperation in Europe. The name was changed at Budapest in 1994.

[6] This discussion is based on the chapter by Diana Chigas with Elizabeth McClintock and Christophe Kamp, *Preventive Diplomacy and the OSCE: Creating Incentives for Dialogue and Cooperation, in* PREVENTING CONFLICT, *supra* note 3, at 25 (hereinafter "Chigas"). The primary author, Diana Chigas, is the director of the Conflict Management Group's Project on Preventive Diplomacy in the OSCE.

also be prescribed to help ensure the parties' cooperation. Whatever success this settlement and enforcement model has had in dealing with full-blown international conflicts—and the record is at best doubtful—it is wholly unsuited to the earlier stages of ethnic conflicts:

> Traditional methods . . . [using] confrontation, pressure and advocacy will frequently only exacerbate conflict, while traditional strategies of mediation of conflict, with their emphasis on "carrots" and "sticks" to induce settlements, are inadequate to deal with long term psychological, social, economic and political problems at the root of ethno-national conflict. . . . They implicate the most fundamental of human aspirations and needs (such as identity, recognition, security, meaningful participation in political processes) and cannot be "solved" through negotiation of legally binding and enforceable agreements.[7]

In the early stages of a conflict, neither the parties nor the issues are likely to be crystallized. The problem, then, is to help set up processes that will get at underlying strivings and discontents before they harden into intractable and violent conflict.

The OSCE attempts to do this by shifting its conflict prevention focus from settlement of the underlying dispute to initiation of cooperative management and dialogue. As Diana Chigas puts it, "[the OSCE's] strategy has been to build on its existing structures for multilateral discussion, and especially its inability to undertake any enforcement action. . . . It has proceeded by dialogue and 'jawboning' at early stages of conflict where large scale intervention would be inappropriate."[8] Successful OSCE interventions are therefore quiet and low key.

This approach to intervention fits the roles and structures of the OSCE. The organization is essentially a forum for multilateral discussion; it operates on the basis of consensus, and seeks to promote security through dialogue, not coercion.[9] Given the OSCE's inability to enforce commitments of participants, it has depended on and developed methods of persuasion to gain adherence to its principles. Ironically, the requirement for consensus among the fifty-two nations that form the OSCE, so often cited as an impediment to action, may be its greatest strength. This requirement does limit the OSCE's ability to sanction violators of OSCE norms, but it has also prompted the organization to adopt creative approaches to conflict prevention.

---

[7] *Id.* at 28–29.

[8] *Id.* at 42.

[9] *Consensus* is defined as the absence of any objection that would be an obstacle to the decision under consideration. *Id.* at 33.

The consensus requirement also enhances the legitimacy of OSCE norms, thereby generating pressure on governments to respect them. It is hard for a state to reject a normative command adopted by consensus after a serious and lengthy debate within the organization in which all take part. Thus, the OSCE has been able to play a pioneering role in the effort to develop and promote international recognition of minority and group rights. In 1990, at its Copenhagen meeting, it adopted a path-breaking document containing an unprecedented enumeration of minor-ity rights. This document served as the starting point for the Council of Europe's work in this field, discussed later in this chapter.

The primary instruments for OSCE intervention in ethnic conflict are "the missions of short and long duration" and the high commissioner on national minorities (HCNM).[10] The missions often cover a broader subject matter and are less localized geographically within a country than the activities of the HCNM, but they share the same goals. Both serve as early warning mechanisms for the OSCE. They provide transparency within and outside the affected country and work with governments and the parties in conflict to prevent escalation. The basis for successes achieved is not power but persuasive influence and the ability to offer alternatives to escalation.

1. The High Commissioner on National Minorities

The HCNM has been described as "perhaps the most important and innovative of the OSCE's new preventive diplomacy instruments, and the core of the OSCE's preventive diplomacy approach. It was created explic-itly as an 'instrument of conflict prevention at the earliest possible stage,' to provide early warning and early action on tensions involving national minorities that could escalate into conflict endangering peace and securi-ty. It is the first and only OSCE institution with authority to initiate pre-ventive diplomacy activities on its own judgment and without a prior mandate."[11]

The formal mandate of the HCNM is a reflection of traditional conflict prevention practice. It provides for an information-gathering stage, fol-lowed by an "early warning" to political bodies of an impending dispute, then for authorization of "early action" in the form of mediation, and, finally, the implementation of an "action plan."[12] This procedure proved

[10] In addition, there are other OSCE institutions involved in conflict prevention more generally. For example, there is the Conflict Prevention Centre in Vienna, which works primarily in the military realm, helping to implement confidence and security-building mea-sures and to coordinate exchange of military information.

[11] Chigas, supra note 6, at 38, citing Helsinki Document, The Challenges of Change, Summit Decisions, chap. I (15) (1992).

[12] Helsinki Decisions, chap. II (1 to 37) (1992).

unworkable in practice and has never been employed. In fact, the first HCNM, former Dutch foreign minister Max van der Stoel, said he would feel that his mission had failed if he had to issue a formal early warning.

Instead, the HCNM acts relatively independently of the OSCE bureaucracy. He has the authority to initiate country visits on his own responsibility, although he consults informally with the chairman in office (CIO) and interested OSCE states to assure political support.[13] The HCNM also enjoys independence from both the governments and the minority populations involved. As the HCNM explained his role, "[i]f the OSCE commitments such as contained in the Copenhagen Document are violated, the High Commissioner has, of course, to ask a government concerned to change its line, reminding it that stability and harmony are as a rule served best by ensuring full rights to persons belonging to a minority. However, he also has to remind the members of a minority that they have duties as well as rights."[14]

This independence allows the HCNM to act as a mediator working to prevent conflict by promoting dialogue and cooperation among the parties. In contrast to the classical conception of the mediator, however, the HCNM acts as an "insider third party."[15] "Insider" does not imply less neutrality but more continuous involvement closer to the ground than a typical international mediator might achieve. The HCNM operates within the state structure, putting pressures upon the government while attempting to win its confidence and that of the other parties. The objective is not a one-shot attempt at conflict resolution but rather to start processes going, whether in politics, in the legislative forum, or through intense round-table dialogues in which the contending parties can begin to know and trust each other, thus creating the time and space for managing conflict.

The HCNM is working on issues relating to the minorities—Russian-speaking, Hungarian, Slovakian, Macedonian, Greek, or Albanian—in about ten countries. His activities have generally encompassed a process of visits and regular telephone communication for purposes of familiarizing himself with the situation, developing relationships with the parties, communicating recommendations to the governments concerned, and fol-

[13] For discussion of this point, see Chigas, *supra* note 6, at 88 n. 66.

[14] Max van der Stoel, *The Role of the CSCE High Commissioner on National Minorities in CSCE Preventive Diplomacy, in* THE CHALLENGE OF PREVENTIVE DIPLOMACY 44 (S. Carlsson ed., 1994). An example of HCNM interventions in which he exercised this independence is in Estonia in mid-July 1993. At that time, he intervened to facilitate resolution of a dispute sparked by the call for referenda on "national-territorial autonomy" by two Russophone-dominated city councils and by the Estonian parliament's passage of a controversial law on aliens. Similar interventions were also undertaken in Macedonia, Ukraine, and Albania. Chigas, *supra* note 6, at 55.

[15] *See* Chigas, *supra* note 6, at 49–50.

lowing up to address issues or tensions that arise during the course of his involvement or during the implementation phase of his recommendations.[16]

2. In-Country Missions

Unlike the HCNM's office, OSCE in-country missions, otherwise known as "missions of long-duration," are not mentioned in any of the OSCE constitutive documents. Rather, they were developed to respond to specific situations. There are now seven local missions, four of which are preventive diplomacy missions (Estonia, Latvia, Macedonia, and Ukraine); the remaining three are crisis management missions (Georgia, Moldova, and Tajikistan).

Like the HCNM, the preventive diplomacy missions are aimed at de-escalation and management of tensions in order to permit longer-term conflict resolution. The missions' structure and functions, however, are somewhat different from those of the HCNM. The missions are resident in the country for at least six months and are visible and operational throughout the country. Their activities typically involve traveling from town to town to talk with officials, citizens, and NGOs and receiving individual complaints of mistreatment. The missions' mandates are often broader than that of the HCNM, including military, economic, social, and political issues as well as minority policies. In practice, the missions have also become involved in areas not originally envisioned.

In contrast to the relative independence of the HCNM, the missions may be described as instruments of the political process of the OSCE. They have no independent authority: the Senior or Permanent Council creates them, defines their mandate, and informally supervises them. The missions are also dependent on the continuing consent of the host country. While the Permanent Council exerts pressure on the host governments not to withhold consent for the missions' activities, "the missions are forced to work cooperatively with the government and refrain from too much criticism of it, so as not to jeopardize their continued existence."[17]

As with the HCNM, the most effective missions have managed these pressures along with the need to gain the confidence of the minority populations by becoming third-party insiders to the conflict. They involve themselves with all the relevant parties, gaining knowledge and their confidence and thereby building an effective third-party role. Successful preventive diplomacy missions, as in Estonia, Latvia, Macedonia, and

[16] *Id.* at 53.
[17] *Id.* at 57.

even Serbia, also enjoy significant political support from nations such as the Scandinavian countries and the United States, which exert bilateral influence on the host governments. Such support is lacking for the crisis management missions, however, presumably because at the crisis management stage it would require a greater investment of resources and political capital than the influential countries are prepared to make.[18] Without such backing and potential coercion, the crisis management missions have not succeeded in compelling parties to negotiate.Nevertheless, they have sometimes played an important pre-negotiation/mediation role, helping parties to set the groundwork that may lead to conflict resolution.

The in-country missions have enjoyed a number of successes in conflict prevention. For example, in Macedonia, the OSCE mission facilitated an agreement between the government and the Albanian leadership to defuse a November 1992 riot. The OSCE mission in Latvia was instrumental in the negotiation and implementation of the agreement on the Russian withdrawal from the Skrunda military installation. The mission to Moldova helped to negotiate a release of hostages, engaged the breakaway Trans-Dniester Republic in dialogue, provided support for delegations observing the parliamentary elections in 1994, organized a seminar for officials to discuss the principles of a democratic constitution, and advised the government on human rights issues. In Estonia, the mission is on the commission in charge of implementing a Russian-Estonian agreement on Russian military pensioners.

The OSCE processes are not necessarily an ideal or universal solution. They seem to have most success in relatively low-intensity situations. But homeopathic medicine does not cure pneumonia, and the CSCE (as the organization was known at the time) was ineffective in dealing with the raging conflict in the former Yugoslavia. In addition, the OSCE is pitifully underfunded, with a total budget of $27 million. Moreover, the processes established by in-country missions may not take permanent root by the time the missions leave. Already there is some backlash. The Baltic states, for example, have expressed concern that they are being singled out and have pushed for the HCNM and missions to leave. Finally, although a framework agreement for U.N.-OSCE cooperation exists, and although the OSCE consults regularly with the U.N. and the U.N. participates at OSCE meetings as an observer, much more is needed to ensure that they work together effectively in the field. All in all, however, the focus on conflict prevention, the willingness to become deeply involved as a quasi insider, the modest goals, and the absence of bureaucratic sclerosis make the OSCE a very important model.

18 *Id.* at 61.

B. The Council of Europe

The focus of Council of Europe activities is only indirectly conflict prevention. Its mandate is to establish and to some degree enforce norms of civilized and democratic national behavior. The COE proceeds on the basic assumption that Western-style democracies operating under the rule of law and protecting fundamental human rights do not experience much violent internal conflict. Focusing on human rights issues in the context of its more general democracy mission, the COE works on elaborating norms of state conduct and increasing states' agreement to and compliance with them. Its potential conflict prevention role flows from its powers to grant or withhold the imprimatur of COE membership on the basis of the applicant's compliance with norms of individual and minority rights.[19] The combination of recognized norms on these matters and more stringent application of admission requirements may have long-term effects on the way the transitional states of the ECE and FSU address ethnonational conflict.

1. Norm Development and Promotion

In recent years, the council has focused on completing a framework convention to the European Convention on Human Rights specifying the principles for the protection of national minorities.[20] In earlier times the council had embraced the ideal of republicanism, notably championed by France, which maintains that the state must strictly adhere to a policy of formal nondiscrimination among citizens based on ethnic identity or other ascriptive characteristics. This conception sought to decouple the state and ethnic identity. But gradually this traditional emphasis on individual human rights has been seen as inadequate for societies racked by sharp ethnic division. A policy of formal nondiscrimination among individuals, it was argued, does not assure governmental neutrality or equality of status among groups. The shift to a minority rights emphasis, although resisted by some, was driven by the search for answers to secessionist impulses in the post–cold war setting. The concept of minority rights concedes that ethno-nationalism and public life cannot be delinked and thus embodies a vision of the multicultural nation-state. It requires that the state establish official mechanisms for the recognition and protection of minority ethno-national identities.

The COE has followed a convoluted path in developing norms of mi-

[19] Our discussion of this role draws upon many of the insights contained in Jean E. Manas, *The Council of Europe's Democracy Ideal and the Challenge of Ethno-National Strife, in* PREVENTING CONFLICT, *supra* note 3, at 99.

[20] *See* text at note 22 *infra.*

nority rights. As early as 1990, the Venice Commission, a COE organ, collaborated informally with the OSCE on the preparation of the path-breaking Copenhagen Document enumerating an array of minority rights. In 1991, the Venice Commission presented a Draft European Convention for the Protection of Minorities, generally similar to the Copenhagen Document, but including provisions for enforcement through the European Court of Human Rights. Although this draft was not adopted, the COE created yet another commission of experts to draft a definitive instrument by 1993. But at the COE's Vienna summit in October 1993, the push for legal recognition of minority rights was aggressively challenged by defenders of the traditional view, including Vaclav Havel, in the wake of the dissolution of Czechoslovakia. Institutionalizing interethnic differences, it was argued, would impede efforts to forge a nation around other commonalities. The Vienna summit contented itself with directing the preparation of an additional protocol to the European Convention on Human rights "in the cultural field" containing "provisions guaranteeing individual rights, in particular for persons belonging to national minorities."[21] In addition, the secretariat was instructed to draft a more general framework convention specifying the principles that governments must respect to ensure the protection of national minorities living within their territory. The COE completed its work on its Convention on the Protection of National Minorities, which was signed by twenty-one states, in early 1995.[22]

The Vienna summit also charged the secretariat with following a minority-conscious policy in helping member states and candidates for membership to consolidate their systems of democratic governance. Council outreach, however, is confined to modest confidence-building projects, workshops, and technical assistance designed to reinforce relevant norms. Its activities include providing legal advice to Eastern European states on the impact of legislation on minorities (for example, of language and citizenship laws), support for bilingual radio stations in Croatia (Italian / Croat) and Estonia (Estonian / Russian), and conducting minorities / nationalities seminars. Like the OSCE, COE activities are low key and cost little because resources are extremely limited. They depend upon the

---

[21] Manas, *supra* note 19, at 130–31, quoting Declaration of Vienna Summit, 1993. It is expected that this additional protocol would have an enforcement mechanism: violation by a signatory state would trigger the full European Convention on Human Rights system, including jurisdiction where applicable of the European Court on Human Rights. The new convention, however, is not expected to provide for an enforcement mechanism that is as strict as the European Convention on Human Rights system.

[22] Twelve states must ratify this convention for it to enter into force; as of early 1996, only four states had done so. This problem also affects the European Charter for Regional or Minority Languages, which needs five ratifications for entry into force and has only three to date. British Broadcasting Corp., January 24, 1996.

power of persuasion, prestige, and the pressures of members to induce conformity with council norms.[23]

2. The Allure of Membership

Norm elaboration and enforcement are inextricably linked to membership, and the attraction of COE membership has been used by the council to gain compliance with its norms. Membership is formally conditioned on a minimum respect for human rights, and the COE has tried, with varying degrees of success, to use the admissions process to pressure candidate states to improve their human rights record. Generally, admission is coupled with the signature and ratification of COE human rights instruments, including the European Convention on Human Rights, and, for most, acceptance of the jurisdiction of the European Court of Human Rights.

Since the end of the cold war, the COE has had an onslaught of applications for membership from Eastern Europe. The motivations for seeking COE membership are varied: to show that the new governments are committed to human rights and democratic principles; for the accompanying boost that membership gives to a government's legitimacy; to silence internal and external critics by arguing that the state's human rights record meets COE standards; and to make explicit that the country has broken from past Soviet domination and is joining the circle of democracies. On this score, COE membership is an alternative to the NATO or EU clubs, where entry is more difficult.

Membership in the COE has not been granted as readily as in the OSCE. Approximately half of the applicants are not yet full members. The COE has tried expressly to use the application process as a tool to bring about change in or test the extent of democratic reforms.[24] During the admissions process, the COE reviews the applicant's human rights record, makes recommendations, and may hold up admission until the occurrence of some critical event, such as elections. Yet countries with mediocre human rights records, such as Romania, have been admitted, providing that they commit to certain reforms soon after admission and appear to be making substantial progress toward democracy. In respect of minority rights norms, admission of new states will be conditioned on compliance

[23] For example, the Demosthenes program, aimed at transmitting democratization expertise from Western officials to Central and Eastern Europe, had a budget of about U.S. $10 million in 1994. Much of the money is spent on tranportation and lodging of government officials who attend.

[24] Unlike the CSCE, the COE did not immediately admit all applicants. See Manas, supra note 19, at 140 n. 22, for discussion of the status of applicants since 1989.

with the new Convention, and member states may be condemned if they violate it.[25]

In order to maximize its leverage over nonmembers, the Parliamentary Assembly created special guest status for pending COE applicants. To be a special guest, a country must ratify the U.N. Covenants on Civil and Political Rights and on Economic, Social, and Cultural Rights and accept the Helsinki Final Act and other CSCE declarations. Guest status establishes a framework for the COE to exert formal and informal pressures on the state through extended and intensive public discussion of the state's performance.

The need to be a member in good standing of the organized international community is a powerful motivator of state behavior, especially in countries emerging from long periods of totalitarian rule. Membership means access to economic resources, political status, and legitimacy. But it would be a mistake to conceive the effect of norms of state conduct solely in terms of the "carrot" of membership or the "stick" of rejection or suspension (whether in the COE or the other European organizations, all of which require adherence to democratic and human rights goals). A state accepting these norms also accepts an obligation to justify its conduct in the light of them, both within the bodies of the organization and in the larger community, and to submit to scrutiny when challenged. Grievances of minority groups are couched in terms of the norms, and negotiations and mediation are framed by them. The seemingly endless discussions of the meaning and application of the legal norms and standards in these forums not only strengthens their authority but often elicits more detailed understanding of their content and commitments as to performance. For example, what starts out as the affirmation of a broad and generally accepted standard on the rights of minorities to use their own language may wind up as a detailed negotiation over street signs or the language in which official proceedings are to be conducted in a particular region. Agreements that emerge are likely to be complied with because they are tailored to the particular case and because the state has participated in the process and explicitly committed to the outcome.[26] This leads to something of a dilemma in the council's (and other organizations) use of leverage based on admission to membership:

[25] See Order No. 484 (instructions to the Committee on Legal Affairs to examine applicant's respect for protocol rights). It should be noted that admission has not been denied for failure to comply with the additional protocol, although Romania and the Slovak Republic were admitted with the understanding that their legislation would be brought into compliance. Manas, *supra* note 19, at 134.

[26] For further discussion of the role of international organizations in generating compliance with norms, see ABRAM CHAYES & ANTONIA HANDLER CHAYES, THE NEW SOVEREIGNTY: COMPLIANCE WITH INTERNATIONAL REGULATORY AGREEMENTS (1995) (hereinafter "THE NEW SOVEREIGNTY").

[H]ow strict ought the Council be in interpreting and applying the requirements of democracy and respect for human rights as a prerequisite for
admission? On the one hand the Council could take a relatively loose approach to these requirements, which would lead to the immediate admission of East European states. This, in turn, would consolidate these states'
break from authoritarianism. With these states incorporated into the Council's human rights regime, the Council could more effectively influence the
conduct of those states. The loose approach has, however, a significant
downside: since membership is the biggest incentive the Council has to
offer, easy admission deprives the Council of its most important tool to
effectuate changes in applicant countries.

On the other hand, the Council could take a stricter approach to the
admission requirements. This stricter approach would ensure that the prize
of membership would be granted only to the truly deserving. . . . Although
this approach constitutes a good use of the membership tool, it risks depriv-
ing the Council of leverage over borderline states where the leadership is
open to democratization and human rights, but is unwilling to move too
rapidly in that direction.[27]

II. TRADE AND DEVELOPMENT INSTITUTIONS

The second group for discussion encompasses organizations with political and economic resources but with at best a limited focus on conflict
management. These international organizations represent an important
pool of economic resources, far exceeding those available in bilateral assistance programs, that could be deployed to help resolve questions that
might lead to conflict or to mitigate conflict once begun. Yet for a variety
of reasons rooted in the traditions of these institutions and, to some extent, in their constitutive documents, they have been hesitant to apply
these powers in any coherent or systematic way to the problems of internal conflict, even in cases that seem to threaten the overall goals of the
institutions.

A. International and Regional Financial Organizations

Unlike the organizations discussed in Part I, the IFIs—the International
Bank for Reconstruction and Development (World Bank) and the International Monetary Fund (IMF)—and the European Bank for Reconstruction
and Development (EBRD) have substantial funds to offer ECE and FSU
nations. All three institutions are deeply involved in the economic trans-

[27] Manas, *supra* note 19, at 112.

formation of these countries. Thus far, however, they have not focused on the impact of their lending operations on ethnic conflict. Indeed, Susan Woodward argues that IMF policies in regard to the former Yugoslavia, which in the late 1980s was the sixth-largest user of the Fund's resources, helped to dismantle the federal political structure and played into the hands of secessionist groups and nationalist leaders.[28]

1. The IFIs

Traditionally, the World Bank and the IMF were supposed to be guided in their lending operations by purely economic considerations—in the case of the Bank, the ability of the project to repay the loan; in the case of the Fund, the ability of the country to cure its balance of payments problems within a reasonable period.[29] Political matters, particularly the internal social and governmental arrangements of the borrowing country, were supposed to be disregarded. It is apparent, however, that business considerations alone dictate closer attention to the effect of ethnic conflict and conflict prevention on their investments. The IFIs are already deeply involved in economic transformation and are likely to be asked to pay the cost of reconstruction in the aftermath of conflict. Despite their reputation for institutional rigidity, the IFIs have begun to broaden their agenda to take account of the economic impact of such problems as environmental pollution, resource depletion, and population growth. But, it will require a considerable change in organizational culture and, in some cases, perhaps, changes in mandate and charter to bring the IFIs to contemplate a conflict prevention and management strategy.

The World Bank was established in the aftermath of World War II to help rebuild the war-torn countries of Europe as well as to "develop the resources and productive capacity of the world, with special reference to the less developed countries."[30] After the successful postwar recovery of Europe, the primary focus of the Bank's activities shifted to the developing countries. With the end of the cold war, the ECE and the FSU became new areas of concentration. The Bank has traditionally insisted that under Article IV of its charter it can only consider the economic soundness of projects it funds and cannot be diverted by political or social considerations. Indeed, it took the position that it could not respond to U.N. General Assembly resolutions calling for an embargo on economic relations with South Africa and Portugal because of their racial policies.

[28] Susan Woodward, Balkan Tragedy (1995).

[29] This portion of the chapter draws on the work of Wolfgang H. Reinicke, *Preventing Ethno-National Conflict: What Role for International Financial Institutions, in* Preventing Conflict, *supra* note 3, at 281.

[30] World Bank Info. Briefs, #A.02.4–94, quoting Lord Keynes.

This purist perspective has already changed. Over the past decade, as the Bank has entered the field of structural adjustment lending, it has begun to pay attention to enabling conditions without which sound economic development is impossible. These conditions address matters such as environmental degradation, governance, poverty reduction, and income distribution. The Bank has also begun to raise the issue of undue military expenditures. The introduction of these heretofore extraneous criteria has led the World Bank into a far greater participatory process involving publics and NGOs.

The IMF advances resources not for projects but to protect the currencies of its members in times of balance-of-payments difficulties. In order to ensure repayment of these advances, however, it conditions them on economic reform in the borrowing country. In general, these conditions have consisted of standard monetarist prescriptions with little attention paid to the social and political impacts of the policies. In recent years, however, along with the World Bank, the IMF has acknowledged the importance of these other aspects of the problem of successful structural adjustment. Thus, the issues of poverty, good governance and levels of military spending, though construed more narrowly than by the Bank, have become part of the Fund's policy-based criteria.

In the wake of the recent changes in the ECE/FSU region, the IMF began to provide assistance there through the Systemic Transformation Facility (STF), founded in April 1993.[31] By January 1994, eleven countries, including Russia, had drawn on the STF for a total of SDR 1.5 billion. In order to access the funds of this facility, countries must adopt certain types of monetary policies and institutions. The IMF has set four reform goals for the ECE: first, replacing centralized planning and management with a market-oriented system; second, establishing a financial system with market-based interest rates; third, taking actions such as privatization to liberalize the operations of firms and markets; and finally, creating a viable social safety net, with resources for unemployment insurance and job retraining.[32] While these four goals are primarily associated with economic system transformation, the IMF also has begun to include enabling conditions.

These enabling conditions and reform goals are justified as contributing to economic development and stability and thus to the security of the organizations' advances and objectives. But if the conditions we have enumerated are relevant to the soundness of World Bank and IMF funding, it is hard to see why the issues of ethnic relations themselves should not be added to the list. Given that the IFIs are deeply involved in system

---

[31] Reinicke, *supra* note 29, at 296, *citing Bretton Woods Commission,* 1994, at C-266.
[32] IMF Annual Report 1991.

transformation in multiethnic states, they cannot ignore the possibility that ethnic groups will compete, even violently, to redefine divisions of the economic, political, and cultural pie. Thus far, however, the IFIs have failed to employ seemingly obvious measures such as requiring non-discrimination among ethnic groups in Bank projects or ensuring that the resources they provide do not go exclusively to the ruling majority or to the regions where it is concentrated.

The IFIs also have a major role to play in providing economic backing for political/military solutions to ongoing ethnic conflicts. There was some such involvement in South Africa, where the Bank announced a major lending program to take effect immediately after successful elections. In the Middle East, a Bank study established overall assistance goals for the autonomous area. In Haiti, the Bank conducted studies of the requirements for economic rehabilitation. The reconstruction elements of the Bosnian peace settlements are also based on a major World Bank study. But the IFIs need to go further. As Wolfgang Reinicke explained:

> The resources of the IFIs, especially the Bank's, could help to make a financially and economically unattractive but otherwise acceptable settlement—including the division of a country—more attractive. For example, IFIs could promise the prospective new states not just membership in their organizations but a continuation of their support of system transformation. In fact, there are indications that the Washington Accords of April 1994 which led to the creation of the Muslim-Croat federation were backed by IFI commitments. Within a few months of the accord, the World Bank approved a $128 million loan to Croatia. A $250 million IMF loan is currently pending.[33]

In the future, financial support for conflict management should be coordinated not only among IFIs but also with other relevant international organizations.

2. The European Bank for Reconstruction and Development

The EBRD was organized, in the euphoria after the fall of the Berlin wall, to be the premier financial instrument through which European resources would be channeled into ECE and the transforming but still united Soviet Union.[34] In contrast to the charters of the traditional IFIs, the EBRD charter (the Agreement Establishing the EBRD) is not neutral with

[33] Reinicke, *supra* note 29, at 317 (footnotes omitted).
[34] We draw on the work of Melanie H. Stein, EBRD counsel, in her chapter *Conflict Prevention in Transition Economies: A Role for the EBRD? in* PREVENTING CONFLICT, *supra* note 3, at 339.

regard to the political and economic systems of borrowers. Article I enjoins the Bank "to foster the transition towards open market-oriented economies and to promote private and entrepreneurial initiative in Central and Eastern European countries committed to and applying the principles of multiparty democracy, pluralism and market economics."

The EBRD is also different from other international financial institutions in that it focuses its funding on the private sector.[35] In fact, the EBRD finances infrastructure reconstruction or development only to the extent it is necessary for private-sector development and transition to a market economy.Unlike the World Bank, the EBRD need not obtain a sovereign guarantee in respect of its private- and public-sector activities.

The first president of the Bank, Jacques Attali, took the EBRD's political orientation seriously and implemented it aggressively. He established a political unit to monitor recipient states' compliance with Article I requirements. The EBRD became involved in the organization and sponsorship of activities in support of parliamentary processes, constitution drafting, and human rights protection. For example, the EBRD and the Council of Europe organized a closed conference on Baltic minorities and citizenship in October 1991.

Ethno-national conflict was high on Attali's agenda, and he made a number of strong moves, not only in connection with the EBRD's investment activities but also as an independent political spokesman. For example, he protested, by letter, Estonia's threatened enactment of legislation that effectively prevented ethnic Russians from taking on Estonian citizenship. But Attali's commitment to Article I requirements as well as his flamboyant methods offended some of his European shareholders. The issue came to a head as Yugoslavia was disintegrating. Attali urged increased attention to minority rights issues; pushed preparation of regional projects that would facilitate the economic integration of the countries in the region; and suggested that the board, to demonstrate solidarity with those working for peace in the Balkans, convene its meeting scheduled for July 13, 1992, in Sarajevo or, if this was impossible due to security considerations, in Split or some other location in the former Yugoslavia. Although the move for increased attention to multicountry projects was approved, the EBRD board of directors rejected the proposal to convene the July meeting in Sarajevo, arguing that it would improperly politicize the role of the Bank.[36]

After little more than two years in office, Attali departed in quasi disgrace. His replacement was Jacques de Larosière, a former managing director of the IMF and an impeccably conservative IFI bureaucrat. The

---

[35] As of the end of 1994, about 62 percent of EBRD funds were for private-sector projects and 38 percent for state-sector projects. *Id.* at 345.

[36] *Id.* at 350–51.

new president disbanded the political unit and otherwise abandoned the political mandate; EBRD activities aimed at promoting democracy, human rights, and the rule of law in ECE were ended. Since then, the EBRD's financing activities have gone forward with only the minimum legally required attention to the criteria specified in Article I. In February 1994, the board of directors adopted *Operation Policies: Guidelines for the Medium Term,* which states that the political aspects of the Bank's mandate should not be "a separate, 'proactive' task" for the EBRD, and so blessed Larosière's approach.[37]

Under the broad rubric of Article I, however, there certainly is room for the EBRD to be sensitive to considerations of democracy building and conflict prevention without overt intervention in political affairs. As with the IFIs, the EBRD has a range of tools to assist in conflict prevention, from nonconfrontational confidential communiqués to suspension of loans. Indeed, existing EBRD projects are working in this direction by fostering interdependence (and so increasing the cost of conflict) in the ECE/FSU region. Examples include loans in April 1994 for Brest-Minsk-Russian border highway improvements and projects for promoting Czech-Slovak trade.

This discussion of the IFIs and the EBRD suggests that the enormous power of financial institutions can be harnessed to conflict prevention, even though that is not their primary purpose. It is not spurious to argue that portfolio protection alone should prompt these organizations to concern themselves with internal conflict. Their prewar investment in the former Yugoslavia has been substantially lost.[38] If consciousness of their impact on potential conflict informed IFI and EBRD strategies more self-consciously, the leverage for conflict prevention might be increased significantly, especially in combination with the magnet of membership in the EU. Coordination with other international organizations would also increase the effectiveness of any IFI/EBRD conflict management strategies.

B. The European Union

The European Union's potential for dealing with ethnic conflict rests mainly on the attraction of membership but also includes its own external economic and political policies toward states that are not members.[39]

---

[37] *Operational Policies* was based on the findings of the task force on Operational Priorities established by Larosière in October 1993. The final report of the task force recommends that the bank's political activities not be prominent and be confined to monitoring political conditions to the extent necessary for operational purposes.

[38] Stein notes that, to date, the EBRD has not sustained losses due to ethno-national conflict. Stein, *supra* note 34, at 354.

[39] This discussion draws heavily on the work of three Europeans with close knowledge of the European Union: John Pinder, *Community against Conflict: The EC's Contribution to Ethno-*

Given the EU's extraordinary economic power, history, and values, some have argued that the aspiration to enter this community by itself will serve as leverage to prevent conflict in many of the former ECE nations and perhaps in those areas of western FSU where membership may be within reach. As John Pinder observes, "the combination of prosperity, peace and freedom that Central and East Europeans saw embodied in the Community was attractive, and it encouraged them to throw off the Soviet system."[40] In fact, almost all ECE countries and many in the Commonwealth of Independent States (CIS) have expressed their desire to join the EU, with Poland and Hungary making the first formal applications in 1994. Brussels has not yet decided who will be accepted and when.

It is widely accepted that EU membership itself will be a powerful guarantor of democracy and a market economy. Membership is premised upon liberal democracy, respect for human rights, the rule of law, and a market economy. Candidate countries must meet specified democratic and economic requirements as well as accept the goals of political union.[41] Although EU states are not always models on the issue of ethno-national conflict—witness Greece and Turkey in Cyprus, Spain in the Basque region, France in Corsica, and Great Britain and Ireland in Ulster—the assumption is, as with the COE, that membership will go a long way toward creating the climate in which internal peace can be maintained or restored.

But the very attraction of membership explains why admission may not happen soon. Agricultural and other forms of protectionism will not die easily. The effort to achieve democracy in transitional states will take some time, and membership deferred may make the transition harder. Nevertheless, the idea of early admission with the hope that membership criteria can be met once inside has not been viewed favorably. Each additional member complicates the EU's internal problems—its capacity to make decisions, take action, and develop its institutions.

1. Trade and Economic Assistance

The EU's budget is relatively small, its political powers are embryonic, and a common currency remains a receding ideal; but the EU has substantial plenary power over internal and external trade. By far the most im-

---

National Peace in Europe, in PREVENTING CONFLICT, *supra* note 3, at 147; Reinhardt Rummel, *The European Union's Politico-Diplomatic Contribution to the Prevention of Ethno-National Conflict, in* PREVENTING CONFLICT, *supra* note 3, at 197; and Zucconi, *supra* note 3, at 237.

[40] Pinder, *supra* note 39, at 148.

[41] The Maastricht Treaty provides that members' "systems of government are founded on the principles of democracy." Brussels is asking new applicants to meet the Copenhagen criteria—democratic requirements as well as preconditions for market economies and economic competition. For further discussion, see *id.* at 185–90.

portant assistance given to the ECE and FSU is in the form of trade.[42] Both exports and imports have grown rapidly, especially between the EU and the Visegrad countries, where economic reform was faster paced than elsewhere in ECE.[43] A network of trade agreements has been concluded, the most important of which are the Europe agreements, which are conceived as a critical first step toward ultimate membership.[44] These agreements contain provisions for regular political dialogue, thus introducing the other parties to the institutions and procedures of the community. Nonetheless, protectionism in the EU remains serious, particularly in agriculture, steel, and other products of interest to ECE countries. It has embittered relations and hampered growth and transition to market economies.

There are a number of programs for direct assistance to democratization and marketization. The EU provided much of the impetus and funding for the EBRD. The Poland-Hungary Reconstruction Assistance program (PHARE) and Technical Assistance to the CIS (TACIS) contribute about ECU 1.5 billion a year each to the institution of market democracies and the building of infrastructure.[45] These EU democratization efforts include support for democratic infrastructure and interparliamentary cooperation, demarches in favor of democracy, and assistance in creating free media and election monitoring. The proposed trans-European networks for transportation and communications infrastructure hold out particular promise for bringing the ECE countries into close and constructive relationships with the EU and with each other. All these programs have enjoyed varying degrees of success and have been criticized as being insufficiently aggressive in the face of countercurrents.

The EU took a major political/economic initiative in committing $1.5 billion in support of the reconstruction aspects of the Dayton agreements for peace in Bosnia. Of this about $150 million was earmarked for urgently needed assistance. But three months after the signature of the accords,

[42] For example, for Bulgaria, the Czech Republic, Hungary, Poland, Romania, and Slovakia—the six countries with Europe agreements—total exports to the community of transport equipment were 58 percent higher in January–August 1993 than they were a year earlier. *Id.* at 174. For more figures on trade, see *id.* at 174–75.

[43] The state parties to the Visegrad Agreement are the Czech Republic, Hungary, Poland, and Slovakia. They managed an export growth of at least 54 percent from 1990–92. *Id.* at 174.

[44] The Europe agreements provide for establishing industrial free trade between the community and partner states over a certain time. The community has five years, while the partner has up to ten years, to remove all tariffs and quotas. For further discussion, see *id.* at 175–78.

[45] The PHARE program was launched by the EC and OECD to help economic reform and structural adjustment, with subsidiary goals such as the support of democratic institutions and the protection of minorities. TACIS is financed solely from the community budget. Its purpose is similar to PHARE's, and the mechanism is to pay for experts to CIS countries.

there was little evidence of a prompt start for concrete activity on the ground in Bosnia.

2. Political Action

The draw of membership and the value of trade and assistance has been supplemented by the EU's political initiatives to manage conflict in ECE and FSU. The EU is in the midst of its own transition from a mainly economic power to a political power, an actor and mediator on the global stage with the capacity to further regional peace and stability. The Treaty on European Union (Maastricht Treaty), in force since 1993, created the Common Foreign and Security Policy (CFSP) as a framework to coordinate and ultimately unify EU foreign policy. "Theoretically, CFSP can draw on economic sticks and carrots of the Union, and on military support from WEU and NATO. . . . [In practical terms] this is the exception rather than the rule."[46] Thus far, it has resulted more in coordination than in unity, more in declarations than action. Nevertheless, a structure is in place for more ambitious concerted foreign and security policy undertakings in the future.

The first major venture in this domain, the EU policy toward recognition of the former Yugoslav republics, was launched while the ink was drying on the Maastricht Treaty. Far from generating a well-designed and deliberated common policy, the CFSP permitted Germany to hijack the EU and secure instant recognition of the breakaway republics. The Conference on Yugoslavia, in large part an EU instrument, laid down criteria that were to be met before the former Yugoslav and FSU republics would be granted recognition, including in particular, provisions for the protection of the rights of minorities. It also established an Arbitration Commission made up of the chief justices of the highest courts of five European countries to determine whether applications for recognition met these criteria. Before the commission had even considered the issues, however, the EU, at Germany's insistence, announced on December 15, 1991, its intention to recognize Croatia and Slovenia a month later. On the appointed date, although the commission advised that neither Croatia nor Bosnia fully complied with the criteria, the EU states went ahead with recognition on schedule. (At the same time, responding to a Greek veto, they refused to recognize Macedonia, although the commission had ruled favorably on its compliance with the criteria.) Bosnia was recognized in April after it declared its independence. Almost all observers of the Balkan crisis agree that recognition at this point was an egregious blunder. It

[46] Rummel, *supra* note 39, at 211–12.

made Bosnia's declaration of independence a certainty and, by transmuting republican boundaries into international borders, reduced the room to negotiate that might have truncated if not averted the war. The CFSP, said the Italian foreign minister, was more important than Bosnia.[47]

Two notable though lesser instances of CFSP action were the intermediation that helped lower tensions over the Gabcikovo-Nagymoros dam between Hungary and Slovakia and the assumption of responsibility for the administration of the town of Mostar in Croatia to stabilize an uneasy peace. In the first, it successfully mediated an agreement providing for eventual submission of the dispute to the International Court of Justice. In Mostar, the EU agreed to take over the administration of the city in order to end the fighting between Bosnian Croats and Muslims. The ultimate objective was to turn over the administration to a freely elected municipal parliament. After an initial period of moderate success, the operation ran into trouble when, in the wake of the conclusion of the Dayton accords, negotiations over the integrated police force broke down. The outcome of the effort remains in doubt.

On a broader scale, the Stability Pact for Europe initiated by French Prime Minister Balladur was a mechanism to get ECE and FSU countries to work on neighborly relations and address their own border and minorities problems in preparation for membership in the union.[48] Although at first it was regarded as paternalistic, the initiative has been seriously engaged. Fifty nations attended the opening conference in May 1994. Two regional round tables, one for the Baltic and one for the Visegrad countries, held five meetings at which boundary problems and transborder issues were discussed. Settlements and agreements on these issues were consolidated in another stability pact, signed at the final meeting of the initiative in Paris in 1995. Further monitoring of the agreements was handed off to the OSCE.

Because of the EU's power and its draw for ECE and FSU nations, it should have a leading role in orchestrating the efforts and strategies of other European organizations.[49] This potential has yet to be realized. As we have noted, there are difficulties in achieving consensus even within

---

[47] See Zucconi, *supra* note 3, at 247–48.

[48] The goals and procedures of the plan were presented in a report annexed to the communiqué of the December 1993 European Council meeting in Brussels. The communiqué and the Annex I (Stability Pact: Summary Report) are reprinted in Agence Europe, No. 6127, December 12, 1993, at 1–12.

[49] The CFSP tries to draw on other institutions or coordinate their work. The EU has interacted closely with the U.N. in conflict prevention in the former Yugoslavia. It has given major support to OSCE preventive dipomacy activities and has participated in OSCE activities, such as fact-finding missions on human rights compliance. Relations between the COE and EU have expanded recently. Finally, EU has worked with the WEU and NATO in developing dialogue with ECE/FSU countries and managing conflict together. *See* Rummel, *supra* note 39, at 223–27, for further discussion of EU relations with these organizations.

the EU for CFSP action. It has not even begun to address the institutional rivalries between separate organizations with overlapping but not congruent membership and the difficulties of aligning complex international bureaucracies that wish to pursue their own policies in conflict prevention and otherwise.

III. SECURITY ORGANIZATIONS

Before the Dayton accords, traditional European security organizations had not played a significant part in the effort to manage ethno-national conflict, although NATO was charged with some limited tasks in relation to the peacekeeping operations in Bosnia. These organizations are largely the products of the bipolar cold war system and are shaped by that history. They are now seeking to adapt to the new realities of the post–cold war world, and a major test of their ability to do so looms in the deployment of a force in Bosnia to implement the peace agreement reached in Dayton. In this section, we look at the role and work of NATO and the WEU in this area, primarily for the period before the Bosnian peace agreements.[50]

A. The North Atlantic Treaty Organization

NATO efforts at policy reorientation in the post–cold war era show the organization's understanding of the critical importance to security of managing internal conflicts. In its final communiqué of June 10, 1993, NATO's North Atlantic Council (NAC)—its highest decision-making body—declared: "Conflict prevention, crisis management, and peacekeeping will be crucial to ensuring stability and security in the Euro-Atlantic area in the years ahead. . . . While reaffirming that the primary goal of Alliance military forces is to guarantee the security and territorial integrity of member states, we will contribute actively to these new tasks in order to enhance our security and European stability."

The contributions that NATO can make to conflict prevention and mitigation are varied. On one end of the spectrum has been the NATO role in large-scale peace operations. This role began with active yet discrete participation in peace enforcement activities, such as NATO's enforcement of the no-fly zone over Bosnia-Herzegovina and safe areas in the former Yugoslavia and of the embargo in the Adriatic Sea. It grew to the actual

---

[50] Two chapters in PREVENTING CONFLICT, *supra* note 3, are the basis of this section: first, Antonia Handler Chayes & Richard Weitz, *The Military Perspective on Conflict Prevention: NATO*, at 381; second, David S. Huntington, *A Peacekeeping Role for the Western European Union*, at 429.

command of peace operations, through IFOR (and subsesquently SFOR), the NATO-led multinational force in Bosnia in support of the Dayton agreements.

In the future, NATO may continue to carry out small military tasks of considerable, even crucial, importance. Military forces may often serve as a form of muscular diplomacy in which military force is in the background and used in conjunction with diplomatic efforts and in coordination with a wide variety of civilian tasks. In a pre-conflict situation, security organizations may contribute a military presence that can play a part in coordination, communications, and logistics. Such assistance may prove particularly effective at the very early stages of a conflict when the parties' positions have not hardened and compromise and resolution may be possible. Even the show or shadow of military force can buy time and space for nurturing voluntary settlement options, as in the preemptive deployment of U.N. troops in Macedonia.[51]

Once hostilities have broken out, peace operations may require more military support. The establishment and operation of headquarters for coordination and communication in a conflict zone, such as the one established by NATO in Zagreb for the United Nations Protection Force (UN-PROFOR), requires considerable military skill and experience, particularly when the force is multinational in character. Other military activities at this stage may include not only interposition of forces but also a demonstration of force to ensure that innocent civilians are protected, that a full range of humanitarian missions can be accomplished, and that agreements will be respected.

NATO has for some time been preparing for this wide spectrum of potential conflict management activities. To be sure, some of these activities may be performed by ad hoc U.N. forces with appropriate training and equipment. Nevertheless, there are clear advantages favoring NATO if the operation requires military sophistication and expertise. The alliance currently possesses Europe's most effective multinational command, control, communications, intelligence, and logistical structures.

In terms of NATO's mandate and legal ability to engage in such activities in the post–cold war era, it should be noted that NATO retains its Article V core function—deterrence against direct threats to its members. The new question is, "On what basis does NATO perform any peace operation beyond the scope of its collective defense charter in the area of

---

[51] For a description of the composition and mission of this Macedonian requested deployment, which since January 1993 has involved about 1,200 military observers, infantry battalions, and civilian police from Canada, the United States, and various Nordic countries, see Julie Kim & Carol Migdalovitz, *Macedonia: Former Yugoslav Republic of Macedonia Situation Update* (Washington: Congressional Research Service, February 18, 1994), at 9–10.

its member states—i.e., 'out of area'?"[52] Although NATO lawyers have not formally addressed the question of how NATO's legal mandate enables it to conduct peace support operations in ECE and FSU, it appears that such activities may be covered by Article II of the North Atlantic Treaty, which calls for cooperation "towards the further development of peaceful and friendly international relations by . . . promoting conditions of stability and well-being." The 1994 Brussels summit, without express reference to any authority in the treaty, decided to support, on a case-by-case basis, peacekeeping and other operations under the authority of the U.N. Security Council or the responsibility of the OSCE.

NATO's pre-Dayton participation as a partner of the U.N. in peace operations in the former Yugoslavia, which came early in its post–cold war mission review, gave some sense of its capability in supporting peace operations. Although these early missions barely tested the coordinated military potential of NATO, the establishment of a headquarters unit in Zagreb and the participation in the Adriatic embargo suggests what it can contribute at this stage. The experience in enforcing the no-fly zones and safe havens in the former Yugoslavia illustrates both the potential and the inherent difficulties of a U.N.-NATO partnership. These operations were conducted satisfactorily from a technical point of view; but they were not exacting operationally, and there were inherent limits to their practical effectiveness. Tensions arose from time to time over the objectives and implementation of policies announced by the U.N. Security Council.[53] Yet the limitations both of the U.N. Charter and the North Atlantic Treaty require that NATO perform its peace operations in ECE or FSU on the authority of the U.N. or OSCE, rather than on its own initiative, unless there is a direct threat to NATO territory.

With the establishment of IFOR to implement the military aspects of the Bosnian peace agreements, NATO finally had a peace operation that was commensurate with its resources and capabilities. The command and control problems that had plagued the earlier efforts at cooperation with UNPROFOR were obviated when the Security Council, in a very broad resolution, approved an arrangement whereby the force will be directly under NATO command and political guidance without interposition by the U.N. The deployment of almost 60,000 troops, including contin-

---

[52] For extensive discussion of this issue, see Chayes & Weitz, *supra* note 50, at 395–98.

[53] For example, the dual-key procedure, whereby NATO could propose military action but U.N. approval was required, was frustrating to NATO. Response time eventually improved but not without problems. For example, three hours elapsed before senior U.N. officials approved the request of the U.N. commander in Bosnia for NATO air strikes to defend French peacekeepers under attack by Serbs near Bihac. By the time NATO received the request, the Serb units had withdrawn. *See* Michael R. Gordon, *Serbian Gunners Slip Away As US Planes Await UN Approval*, N.Y. Times, March 14, 1994, at A8.

gents from Russia and elsewhere in Eastern Europe, in the middle of winter over exacting terrain in a war-destroyed country was again carried out with admirable technical proficiency. The action underscored that NATO—and particularly U.S.—logistical, transport, and communications capability is indispensable for any large-scale deployment at a distance from home bases. Further, the initial military tasks of establishing a cease-fire line of almost 1,000 kilometers in length and supervising the withdrawal of the contending forces to a distance of two miles went off without serious incident.

Yet the fate of the total post-Dayton operation remains questionable. All the nonmilitary aspects, from return of refugees, to reconstruction, to war crimes, have been remitted to various independent civil entities under the loose umbrella of the high representative, Carl Bildt. Many of the organizations we have discussed above have been assigned roles: the EU, the World Bank, and the EBRD to fund and implement reconstruction; the OSCE to conduct elections; UNHCR to ensure the return and resettlement of refugees; the International War Crimes Tribunal to investigate war crimes and take offenders into custody. Resources in hand are limited. Coordination among these entities at the headquarters level is embryonic, although many are represented in a series of functional working groups that the Office of the High Representative has established in Sarajevo, dealing with subjects such as water supply, transport, communications, electricity, and so on. Coordination with IFOR remained difficult after the first three months of 1996 because from the beginning, IFOR commanders tried to confine their mission narrowly to the military elements we have noted. In the first weeks, this effort at bifurcation came under pressure when IFOR refused to accept responsibility for arresting war criminals and protecting mass grave sites and other evidence of war crimes. Although by mid-March there seemed to be growing awareness among some NATO officials that the success of the operation would depend importantly on the nonmilitary components, there was little in the way of practical action to deal with the diffusion of authority and responsibility. Most important, the whole mission operated in the shadow of the U.S. commitment to withdraw its forces—about one-third of the total—at the end of a year. Almost nobody thought that either the military or civilian aspects of the Dayton accords could be completed by that time. There has been some relaxation of IFOR rigidity as NATO leaders realize that certain tasks can be performed without the dreaded "mission creep" and without needless jeopardy of life. Thus, Joint Civilian Commission (JCC) working groups dealing with issues such as water and wastewater, electricity and telecommunications are being staffed by Civilian-Military Committee (CIMIC) liaison, mid-level officers from the U.S. Army Reserves in their standard form of organization; and the American military sector has been paying local civilians to make necessary repairs. Constructive independent civil action is also taking place. OSCE has plunged into its tasks of mounting elections in the autumn of 1996 and of preparing verification machinery for arms control. UNHCR continues its work with refugees. But the concerted effort needed to achieve a peaceful society while IFOR is on the scene has not begun.

The largest political dilemma facing NATO has been the issue of the enlargement of its membership. Like accession to the EU, membership in NATO is an important inducement for maintaining a democratic and market orientation in Eastern Europe. NATO created a number of devices to begin to include ECE and FSU nations, starting with the North Atlantic Cooperation Council (NACC) in November 1992, which served as a useful first step toward the integration of the former Communist bloc into NATO. Under the rubric of the Partnership for Peace (PfP), which was established in early 1994 and is open to any OSCE member, there is the possibility of more individualized contacts, including joint training and exercises between the forces of NATO members and ECE and FSU states.[54] A number of the partners are participating in IFOR.

Nevertheless, the prospect of extending NATO eastward to the borders of Russia stirred opposition, especially from nationalist forces in Russia, contributing to the fragility of the present government. President Yeltsin's outburst at the December 1994 Budapest CSCE summit and later at the U.N. and Russia's extended refusal to join PfP were manifestations of the problem. The United States persisted, however, and on May 27, 1997, the sixteen NATO members and Russia signed a Founding Act that provided for institutionalized consultation on all NATO decisions. This Russian acquiescence paved the way for the admission of Poland, Hungary, and the Czech Republic. Whether any other ECE countries will follow remains in doubt, as does the relevance of NATO and its ability to participate in the actual conflicts of ECE and FSU.

B. The Western European Union

The nine-nation WEU has been denominated the European pillar of the North Atlantic Alliance, but the basic question is whether it will ever

---

[54] The PfP Framework Document is reprinted in 3 RFE/RL RESEARCH REPORT 22–23 (March 25, 1994). Each participant agrees to a standard framework and to an individual partnership program specifying its military and political commitments and its level of anticipated collaboration with NATO. PfP participants must also agree to ensure the democratic control of their armed forces; promote the transparency of their defense planning; respect international law principles, the U.N. Charter, and the OSCE; and be prepared to participate in certain operations under their auspices.

develop into an effective security force for Europe or if it will continue to be a shadow conception of the French, who seek an alternative to the U.S.-dominated NATO.[55] WEU member states have expanded its legal mandate to permit military operations outside of Western Europe and have pledged to undertake "the effective implementation of conflict-prevention and crisis management measures, including peacekeeping activities."[56] The WEU has played a small part, largely symbolic, in some military activities in relation to the Balkan conflict, such as naval operations in the Adriatic Sea and on the Danube River to enforce U.N. sanctions against the former Yugoslavia; and it has engaged in some peacekeeping activities under its own banner—mine sweeping during the Iran-Iraq war and naval operations during the Gulf War. Yet although the WEU would be free to act in some circumstances when NATO may not, either because of legal restrictions or choice (presumably pressure from the United States), it has neither forces, command structure, nor capabilities of its own. It must rely entirely on contributions of its members—who are also the members of NATO and the EU—or of NATO itself.

The WEU in theory could provide a halfway house for ECE and FSU nations through its associate partner status or some other device, earlier than the current pace of integration in NATO or the EU will allow.[57] But because the WEU has no military forces, it cannot now offer the security guarantees that these nations are seeking. Thus, such expedients are likely to be seen by the intended beneficiaries as yet another way of delaying entry into both the EU and NATO.

The root of the WEU's present ineffectiveness is the unwillingness of its members to commit the resources necessary to make it into an actual military force. Even if they were to do so, a significant part of the assets needed for any large operation, such as airlift and command, control, communications, and intelligence, are U.S. forces, whether under U.S. or NATO command. So, as the French have ruefully come to recognize, a WEU operation of any size would probably have to have NAC approval. The key relationship to watch is that of the WEU and the EU as the latter

---

[55] The WEU was formally linked to the Maastricht Treaty on European Union: under Article J4, the WEU is "an integral part of the development of the Union" and is to "elaborate and implement decisions and actions which have defence implications." This language represents a compromise between the French position that the WEU should be incorporated into the EU and the British position, reluctant to refer to the WEU at all in Maastricht and resisting the concept of European defense integration.

[56] Western European Union Council of Ministers, *Petersberg Declaration on WEU and European Security*, Bonn, June 19, 1992.

[57] Associate partner status was offered first in May 1994 in response to NATO's PfP. This status, open to all of the Forum for Consultation countries, permits new associate partners to participate in WEU council and working group meetings, establish links with the WEU planning cell, and join in certain operations carried out under WEU auspices. The status does not provide any security guarantees or decision-making powers.

develops its CFSP. The gradual French rapprochement to NATO suggests that the umbrella may be NATO itself, but the idea of a European pillar is still very much alive.

Thus, it remains unclear whether there is a capable and willing military force in Europe ready to shoulder the burdens of peacekeeping should the situation require it. Recent developments show that the U.N. is now open to subcontracting peacekeeping functions to individual states or to other organizations, such as NATO. Under a subcontract, the U.N. authorizes a single nation or group of states to implement U.N. decisions.[58] For example, the Security Council authorized Russia to deploy more troops in Georgia to end the three-year-old conflict there and by similar action approved the U.S. operation in Haiti. The latest example of this device—and its major test—is the NATO-led IFOR in Bosnia.

IV. The Way Ahead: Are Effective Joint Strategies Available?

This chapter has described the strengths and weaknesses, activities and potential of a number of organizational players in preventing and managing ethnic conflict. Despite the rich array of regional organizations available in Europe, as well as the immense potential of the U.N., the traditional pleas for coordination and interlock have achieved little in the way of concerted efforts. There has been some cooperation (and much tension) among the U.N., EU and NATO in the former Yugoslavia. But some highly relevant actors, such as the IFIs and even the EU, are only beginning to recognize the importance of the contribution they might make to conflict prevention and mitigation and how important their capabilities could be if they were to exercise their potential leverage. As yet these players do not avail themselves of potential synergies and possibilities for reinforcing action, nor do they find it easy to engage at the ground level, where internal conflicts tend to have their origins and early growth.

A more multifaceted, concerted approach would necessarily include many of these organizations. But it will not be easy to achieve effective joint action on a sustained basis. The organizations that focus directly on preventing conflict (the OSCE and COE) need more resources. The organizations with economic resources and political clout need to turn their attention more directly to conflict management. The security organizations need to adapt to the new challenges of widespread ethnic conflict, including the challenge of working effectively with the other types of

---

[58] Jarat Chopra & Thomas G. Weiss, *The United Nations and the Former Second World, in* Preventing Conflict, *supra* note 3, at 507, 525.

organizations. If all the organizations worked together more effectively, the chances of successful intervention would be greater. For example, the modest successes of the OSCE in the Baltics might have been enhanced by greater availability of funds to develop language, job, and education programs and by closer synchronization with the process of integration of the European Union.

It will not be easy to achieve effective and sustained joint action, for both legal and institutional reasons. The organizations are highly centralized and slow-moving bureaucracies. They are all institutions in transition, trying to adapt to a radically changed environment. Many international organizations have yet to overcome the stricture against intervention in matters within the domestic jurisdiction of states, which was a fundamental norm of the state system after World War II in which the organizations were born and have lived. Even though there is overlapping membership, the separate legal identities and bureaucratic hierarchies of the organizations operate to defeat effective and integrated deployment of available international resources. The states that form them have not provided clear direction, and it is problem enough for each organization to reach a consensus among its own members without trying also to reach agreement with other international organizations. The operational arms, with some exceptions such as UNHCR, find it difficult to deal with the unorganized and irregular groups of shifting composition and legitimacy that characterize internal conflict.

Joint action is not achievable with the existing ways of doing business. The usual prescription of consultants and study commissions is "better coordination." But there is no superordinate body to coordinate the activities of these organizations. In any case, coordination at the level of organizational headquarters will not produce a coherent basis for mobilizing the diverse resources of international organizations, both governmental and nongovernmental, to attack discrete and constantly shifting problem situations, each of which is to a considerable degree unique and thus inaccessible to bureaucratic routines.

If concerted strategy and effective joint action cannot be achieved by the methods of interagency coordination or interlock, what are the alternatives? The experience of the past few years, while generally disappointing, holds some clues to a different approach. It seems relevant that such successes as we have been able to report, such as the OSCE high commissioner on national minorities, are the result of flexible, nonhierarchical processes working close to the ground in direct contact with the parties involved in the conflict. This more hopeful performance, we think, reflects a difference in strategy and organizational arrangements between the OSCE and traditional international organizations. The OSCE's lack of bureaucratic resources and its consensus decision process are sources of strength, or at least efficacy, rather than weakness.

This suggests that strategic mobilization and coordination may be more likely to emerge from ad hoc interaction among missions of international organizations and NGOs working in particular situations. The model would be a nonhierarchical, team-based approach bringing together the capabilities and resources of the wide range of international organizations and NGOs in a particular conflict area. Although it is too early to specify the characteristics of such a model, it should be possible to conceptualize a way of catalyzing the early development of such a concerted strategy, tailored to the needs of particular situations, perhaps using different coalitions and lead agencies in different situations. Such a conception would have to address four main elements:

First, there must be a method for activating problem-solving groups that bypasses the elephantine decision-making processes of the standard bureaucratic organizations. It would be necessary to be able to form such groups quickly and in the early stages of a conflict. One of the main problems is that the political will for intervention does not emerge until the conflict has reached a relatively high level of intensity and violence, by which time the available resources may be inadequate to the task. The OSCE experience is important evidence that such an expedited decision process for early intervention is possible and can be combined with the necessary political accountability.

Second, it is important to find a formula for delegating broad operational control to the group in the field, as is the common doctrine of military organizations, reserving only broad policy guidance for headquarters. The U.N. experience has been that, although the initial mandate passed by the Security Council is vague and general (due to the necessities of achieving political consensus), there are often subsequent efforts to micromanage both by the council and the secretariat. The initial mandate should concentrate on defining the overall mission and strategy of the operation in general terms and leave the task group with wide leeway for carrying it out.

Third, there must be a more realistic conception of the goals of intervention. Short of all-out enforcement action, as in Kuwait, it cannot be to defeat one of the parties and impose a solution on the situation. The objective must be to initiate a process by which the parties themselves can manage their continuing conflicts and disputes, a process that generates innovative possible solutions and broadly supported outcomes. This is the approach taken by the HCNM in creating ethnic round tables and other ongoing conciliation processes, and it might be equally effective even after the conflict intensifies.

Fourth, there must be a method for ensuring overall political accountability. Although operational control and responsibility should be lodged firmly in the field-level, problem-solving group, it cannot be permitted to proceed completely on its own without review and guidance from the ultimate political authorities of the parent organizations. The OSCE experience again shows that accountability can be achieved by informal consultative processes with key officials of the organization and its interested members or by informal supervisory groups.

As this sketchy account suggests, much remains to be done in conceptualizing an effective mechanism for bringing organizations engaging in peace operations into an effective and synergistic relationship. A concerted effort of imagination to discover how to achieve joint action among the participants is now the top agenda item in efforts to mobilize international organizations for preventing ethno-national conflict.

8

Practical and Legal Constraints on Internal Power Sharing

David Wippman

"Federalism will preserve Yugoslavia." That was the headline of a 1991 op-ed piece written by a leading expert on federal systems and their use as a device to manage ethnic conflict.[1] In retrospect, looking to federalism for Yugoslavia's salvation may sound absurd. Not only did federalism fail to preserve the union in Yugoslavia, it may have contributed significantly to that country's violent disintegration.[2] Moreover, the apparent failure of federalism is not confined to Yugoslavia. Even though almost all of the countries to emerge from Socialist rule in the former Soviet Union and Eastern Europe contain significant ethnic minorities, the only three states to break apart have been the three republics organized along federal lines: the Soviet Union itself, Czechoslovakia, and Yugoslavia.[3]

Why, then, do federalism and, more generally, ethnic power sharing seem to be the remedy of choice in recent attempts to broker political settlements to ethnic conflicts? At the outset of the crisis in Yugoslavia, both the United States and the European Union urged interethnic accommodation within a federal Yugoslavia. When the federation dissolved, the U.N. and the EU proposed a loose federal system centered on ethnic power sharing and local autonomy as the basis for a political settlement of

The author thanks John Barceló III, Kevin Clermont, Cynthia Farina, and the participants in Anne-Marie Slaughter and Andrew Moravcsik's seminar on international law and international relations for helpful comments on an earlier draft of this chapter.

[1] *See* Daniel J. Elazar, *Federalism Will Preserve Yugoslavia*, Jerusalem Post, July 18, 1991.

[2] *See, e.g.*, Ellen Comisso, *Federalism and Nationalism in Post-Socialist Eastern Europe*, 1 New Eur. L. Rev. 489, 491 (1993); Valerie Bunce, Nationalism, Secession, and Federalism: The End of Yugoslavia, The Soviet Union, and Czechoslovakia (forthcoming).

[3] *See* sources cited in note 2 *supra*.

the conflict in Bosnia.[4] The U.N. has proposed similar measures for the resolution of ethnic conflicts in Georgia,[5] Nagorno-Karabakh,[6] and Cyprus.[7]

The argument in favor of such solutions is deceptively simple. In societies with deep ethnic cleavages, competition for political power often results in the domination of one ethnic group by another. Groups that fear political marginalization, and the erosion of ethnic identity that often accompanies it, may mobilize politically in ways that threaten other ethnic groups. To avoid this scenario for ethnic conflict, some countries have sought to balance power among ethnic groups and to afford each group some measure of political autonomy. In countries with geographically concentrated ethnic minorities, federalism often appears to be a natural way to establish a system in which ethnic groups can share power at the center and still exercise substantial local autonomy over issues of particular interest to each group. The claim that federalism would preserve Yugoslavia thus has to be understood as part of a broader claim that techniques of political engineering designed to establish government by ethnic group consensus can do much to hold multiethnic countries together.

In at least some cases, in countries as diverse as Switzerland and Nigeria, this consociational approach to ethnic conflict seems to have succeeded in establishing a substantial measure of intergroup harmony. Indeed, advocates of consociationalism go so far as to claim that in deeply plural societies government by ethnic group consensus is the only way to achieve intergroup harmony within the confines of a democratic political system.[8]

But current efforts to resolve ethnic conflict through consociational political settlements carry their own problems and dangers. In general, such settlements are extremely difficult to achieve. They depend on interelite communication and cooperation, commodities that are in short supply when ethnic tensions are sharp enough to produce large-scale interethnic political violence. Even when consociational settlements can be put into place, they often prove inefficient, unstable, and short-lived. Moreover,

---

[4] *See* Report of the Secretary-General on the International Conference on the Former Yugoslavia, U.N. Doc. S/24795 & Annex VII (1992), 31 I.L.M. 1549 (1992) (describing negotiations among the contending factions and reprinting the Vance-Owen proposed constitutional structure for Bosnia).

[5] Report of the Secretary-General Concerning the Situation in Abkhazia, Georgia, S/1994/80, para. 23 (January 25, 1994).

[6] *See* S.C. Res. 822 (1993); Press Release, SC/5604, 3,205th meeting (April 30, 1995).

[7] *See* Set of Ideas on an Overall Framework Agreement on Cyprus, Annex to the Report of the Secretary-General on His Mission of Good Offices in Cyprus, S/24472 (August 21, 1992) (outlining a bicommunal, bizonal structure for Cyprus); S.C. Res. 750 (1992) (endorsing the concept of a bicommunal, bizonal federation).

[8] *See, e.g.,* Arend Lijphart, *Majority Rule Versus Democracy in Deeply Divided Societies,* 4 POLITIKON 113, 114 (1977).

consociationalism's emphasis on ethnic group identity and autonomy may impede the formation of a larger national identity and even foster the creation of destructive rival nationalisms.

At a minimum, ethnic power sharing may interfere with the ability of the population of the state as a whole to determine its form of government and political affiliations. By design, ethnic power sharing is intended to limit the majority's political freedom of action. In its most commonly proposed format, it authorizes ethnic minorities to veto important decisions concerning the political future of the state. Insofar as self-determination is viewed as a right of the population of the state as a whole, this aspect of power sharing may be deemed politically and legally problematic.

Finally, consociational structures, at least in certain applications, may conflict with the liberal individualist paradigm that underpins contemporary international human rights norms. Consociational solutions to ethnic conflict rest explicitly on the differential provision of tangible and intangible goods to individuals on the basis of their ethnicity. Accordingly, consociational solutions to ethnic conflict may conflict with human rights principles mandating equal rights of political participation for all and barring discrimination on the basis of race, religion, or ethnicity.

This chapter explores these issues in the following order. Part I discusses consociationalism and related forms of political engineering, and their potential application to ethnic conflict, with particular attention to their relevance for proposed solutions to contemporary conflicts. Part II considers the relationship between consociational solutions to ethnic conflict and principles of public international law pertaining to territorial integrity and self-determination. Part III explores the extent to which consociational systems may be considered compatible with international human rights norms.

I. Consociational Theory and Its Application to Ethnic Conflict

The upsurge in ethnic conflict in recent years has generated renewed interest in the efforts of political theorists to identify governmental structures and practices conducive to the limitation of ethnic strife. In the relatively recent past, ethnic diversity was commonly seen "as an automatic recipe for social conflict."[9] During the era of decolonization, many political scientists argued that "a homogeneous or integrated political

[9] Kenneth D. McCrae, *Theories of Power-Sharing and Conflict Management* 93, 94, in CONFLICT AND PEACEMAKING IN MULTIETHNIC SOCIETIES (Joseph Montville ed., 1991).

culture" was necessary to government stability and efficiency.[10] Accordingly, they urged newly decolonized states to engage in "massive nation-building efforts to overcome 'primordial' loyalties and to create a more homogeneous political culture."[11] Political leaders in many emerging states took this admonition seriously and sought to suppress local ethnic affiliations in favor of a larger national identity. The process was often brutal and generally unsuccessful.[12]

The enthusiasm for nation building was complemented by an evolving faith in liberal individualism and majoritarian democracy. After World War II, the interest in national self-determination and minority rights that characterized the interwar period yielded to an emphasis on political liberalism and individual rights.[13] In the post-war political paradigm, civic nationalism was favored over ethnic nationalism, and individual rights were favored over collective rights. As individuals, minorities were entitled to participate without discrimination in the political and social life of the state, but they were not entitled to collective political autonomy. Ostensibly, the state was to treat ethnicity with "benign neutrality," but in practice ethnic minorities were expected to assimilate into the dominant political culture.[14] Within the limits imposed by individual human rights norms, democratically elected political majorities were free to govern as they saw fit.

A. Characteristics of Consociationalism

Beginning in the 1970s, a number of political scientists, notably Arend Lijphart, challenged some of the fundamental assumptions underlying the postwar response to ethnic diversity. Lijphart argued that in plural societies—that is, societies with deep ethnic cleavages—majority rule is both ineffective in managing ethnic tensions and incompatible with democracy.[15] In a straight majority rule system, some portion of the electorate is invariably excluded from political decision making. This exclusion is tolerable so long as the current minority party can reasonably anticipate that, by modifying its policies, it can prevail in subsequent elections. Indeed, the very fact that the party now in the minority may soon become

[10] *Id.* at 93.

[11] *Id.* at 94.

[12] *See, e.g.,* Alemante G. Selassie, *Ethnic Identity and Constitutional Design for Africa,* 29 STAN. J. INT'L L. 1, 18–19 (1992).

[13] *See, e.g.,* PATRICK THORNBERRY, INTERNATIONAL LAW AND THE RIGHTS OF MINORITIES 6 (1991); Adeno Addis, *Individualism, Communitarianism, and the Rights of Ethnic Minorities,* 66 NOTRE DAME L. REV. 1219, 1239–44 (1991).

[14] *See* Selassie, *supra* note 12, at 17.

[15] *See* AREND LIJPHART, DEMOCRACY IN PLURAL SOCIETIES: A COMPARATIVE EXPLORATION (1977); Lijphart, *supra* note 8, at 113.

the majority may induce the existing majority party to moderate its policies in anticipation of its possible later defeat.[16]

But majority rule becomes a "principle of exclusion" when ethnic cleavages are sharp and "correspond closely to political preferences."[17] In such cases, voting becomes much like taking a census. Ethnic minorities are excluded from power for extended periods, majority rule becomes the tyranny of the majority, and interethnic relations deteriorate.

To solve this problem, Lijphart and others have advocated adoption of a consociational model of democratic government, derived in large part from an analysis of historical successes in managing ethnic diversity in countries such as Belgium and Switzerland. Briefly summarized, consociationalism seeks to resolve intergroup differences through "techniques of consensus rather than majority rule."[18] Lijphart identified four characteristics of any consociational democracy: grand coalition, mutual veto, proportionality, and segmental autonomy. Each is designed to ensure that the political interests of ethnic minorities are protected within a larger plural society. The grand coalition principle requires that each of the principal ethnic groups within a state shares in the governance of the state as a whole. In Lijphart's words, "majority rule is replaced by joint consensual rule."[19] The mutual veto affords each ethnic group the right to block legislation it deems inimical to its vital interests. Proportionality replaces the winner-take-all principle as the "basic standard of political representation, civil service appointments, and allocation of public funds."[20] Finally, segmental autonomy mandates that each ethnic group exercise "as much decision-making authority as possible" on areas of "exclusive concern" to it.[21]

As Lijphart himself acknowledges, pure consociational democracy exists in very few countries. But many incorporate at least some consociational elements into their political systems. Others adopt a large variety of other political practices, both formal and informal, to achieve some of the same effects as consociational democracy. Such practices include devolution of authority to regional or local elected bodies, administrative decen-

---

[16] *See* DONALD HOROWITZ, ETHNIC GROUPS IN CONFLICT 84 (1985) (noting that permanent majorities have few incentives to be moderate toward politically marginalized ethnic minorities).

[17] Lijphart, *supra* note 8, at 115.

[18] McCrae, *supra* note 9, at 93.

[19] Lijphart, *supra* note 8, at 118.

[20] *Id.* at 119. When ethnic groups differ greatly in size, proportional representation may yield to over representation of the smaller group to ensure that its influence is not marginalized.

[21] *Id.* For this purpose, Lijphart notes that federalism may constitute "[a] form of segmental autonomy that is especially suitable for plural societies." *Id.; see also* Arend Lijphart, *Non-Majoritarian Democracy: A Comparison of Federal and Consociational Theories,* 15 PUBLIUS 3, 5, 10 (1985).

tralization, reserved seats and offices, and various electoral techniques designed to foster interethnic vote pooling and coalitions.[22] All of these practices recognize the salience of ethnicity in political life and seek to accommodate it in ways that diverge from simple majority rule.

B. Proposals for Settlement of Contemporary Conflicts

In promoting settlements for contemporary ethnic conflicts, the international community has strongly urged adoption of various consociational or quasi-consociational practices. In Bosnia, the U.N. has promoted a series of plans designed to share power among the warring ethnic groups and provide each with a substantial measure of local autonomy. The 1992 Vance-Owen plan, for example, called for constitutional recognition of the three principal ethnic groups and for a "decentralized State with significant functions carried [on] by 7 to 10 autonomous provinces."[23] Although geographical, historical, economic, and other factors influenced the designation of provincial boundaries, the primary consideration was ethnic balance. The plan also mandated ethnic power sharing in all governmental bodies. In the legislature, the lower house was to be elected on the basis of proportional representation, but representatives in the upper house were to be named by the ethnically dominated provinces. Although the prime minister was to be elected by the lower house, other ministers were to be chosen "with due account for group balance."[24] Group balance was also required for the judiciary. Overall, the plan's provisions for provincial autonomy, provincial representation in the central government, and group balance in the civil service and judiciary rendered it strongly consociational.

The group of experts appointed to mediate between the Georgian government and Abkhazian separatists have similarly worked to achieve a consociational "division of competencies between the Georgian authorities and the Abkhaz authorities" in a new federal arrangement for Georgia.[25] A preliminary declaration accepted by both parties in the conflict implicitly confers substantial autonomy on Abkhazia, including the right to its own constitution, legislation, and state symbols, and directs that the

[22] For a comprehensive listing of "constitutional devices and legal arrangements" for plural societies, see Claire Palley, *Constitutional Law and Minorities*, Minority Rights Group Report No. 36 at 6–19 (1978) (on file with author).

[23] *See* Report of the Secretary-General on the International Conference on the Former Yugoslavia, *supra* note 4, 31 I.L.M. at 1584; *see also* Paul C. Szasz, *The Fragmentation of Yugoslavia*, in Proc. Amer. Soc'y Int'l L. 33, 34, 36 (1994).

[24] Report of the Secretary-General, *supra* note 4, sec. IV A(2)(d), 31 I.L.M. at 1588.

[25] Declaration on Measures for a Political Settlement of the Georgian/Abkhaz Conflict, Annex to Report of the Secretary-General Concerning the Situation in Abkhazia, Georgia, S/1994/253 (March 3, 1994).

parties will exercise "powers for joint action" in the areas of foreign policy, border guards, customs, energy, transport, communications, and the protection of the rights of national minorities.[26]

The U.N.'s most detailed, and most overtly consociational, settlement proposal is the set of ideas put forward by the secretary-general for resolution of the continuing ethnic conflict in Cyprus.[27] The set of ideas envisions establishment of a "bizonal and bi-communal federal republic" composed of two separate but "politically equal" federated states, one controlled by Turkish Cypriots, the other by Greek Cypriots.[28] Each state would have "identical powers and functions," including responsibility for "security, law and order and the administration of justice in its territory."[29] Within their federated state, Turkish Cypriots would have the authority to legislate for themselves on all matters that might affect their cultural identity, including education, social welfare, and economic development. In addition, Turkish Cypriots are guaranteed "effective participation . . . in all organs and decisions of the federal government."[30] Although they constitute less than 20 percent of the population, Turkish Cypriots would be entitled to elect half of the members of the upper house of the legislature and would possess veto power over all central government legislation. They would also be guaranteed disproportionate representation in the executive branch, civil service, and judiciary. In short, Turkish Cypriots would be full partners with the Greek Cypriot majority.[31]

Each of the proposals I have described seeks to replace simple majority rule with various techniques of achieving political consensus among ethnic groups, at least on issues of vital importance to those groups that would otherwise feel threatened by straight majority rule. In addition, each proposal confers some measure of self-rule on those ethnic minorities that wish it. In theory, these proposals carry important potential benefits. They represent a format within which competing ethnic groups can live together peacefully, retain their collective identity, and cooperate on issues of common concern, without any one group dominating any other.

C. Obstacles to Successful Settlements

Unfortunately, the obstacles to achieving and maintaining settlements along the lines proposed by the U.N. are legion, and the U.N.'s attempts to broker such settlements have yet to yield any fruit. To succeed in such

[26] *Id.* para. 9.
[27] *See* Set of Ideas on an Overall Framework Agreement on Cyprus, *supra* note 7, para. 2.
[28] *Id.* para. 9.
[29] *Id.* at 11.
[30] *Id.* para. 5.
[31] For a more detailed analysis of the proposals for settling the conflict on Cyprus, see David Wippman, *International Law and Ethnic Conflict on Cyprus,* 31 Tex. Int'l L.J. 141 (1996).

attempts, the U.N. must do two things. First, it must persuade the parties and their external supporters that a balanced political settlement is in their interest. Second, it must assist the parties in devising a plan that will work once it is put into operation. It is hard to say which is the more difficult task.

1. Forging an Agreement

There are many possible reasons why ethnic groups within a given state may choose to adopt techniques of consensus government. An external threat may lead to an internal compromise on a theory of "united we stand, divided we fall." Similarly, the groups involved may consider themselves economically stronger if they can achieve some measure of internal harmony. Conversely, they may fear the bloodshed that often occurs when ethnic groups fight for control of the state or when one group fights the government in an attempt to secede. In close cases, lingering ties based on shared historical experience may tip the balance in favor of working out political arrangements acceptable to all concerned.[32] In addition, external pressures, which may include economic and military sanctions or positive inducements such as trade, aid, recognition, and membership in international organizations, may persuade internal actors to pursue settlements they would not otherwise accept.

For such settlements to succeed, the political elites within each group must appreciate the dangers of social fragmentation and be prepared to compromise to avoid those dangers.[33] To that end, they must be prepared to accept plural regulation of ethnic group interests and to abandon homogenization as a short- or long-term goal.[34] Unfortunately, political leaders may often conclude that they have more to gain by pursuing conflict than by seeking to abate it.[35] Mobilizing ethnic differences may prove a convenient vehicle for unscrupulous leaders such as Slobodan Milosevic or Franjo Tudjman to gain and hold power during periods of sharp political transitions.[36] Moreover, politicians seeking compromise solutions may find themselves vulnerable to the phenomenon of "ethnic outbidding," as more militant proponents of the cause accuse them of selling out the interests of the nation.[37]

[32] See Comisso, supra note 2, at 490.

[33] McCrae, supra note 9, at 95, 102.

[34] Ivo Duchacek, Antagonistic Cooperation: Territorial and Ethnic Communities, 7 PUBLIUS 3, 13 (1977).

[35] Donald Horowitz, Making Moderation Pay, in CONFLICT AND PEACEMAKING IN MULTI-ETHNIC SOCIETIES 452 (Joseph Montville ed., 1991).

[36] See V. P. Gagnon, Jr., Ethnic Nationalism and International Conflict: The Case of Serbia, 19 INT'L SECURITY 130, 131 (1994/95).

[37] See MILTON J. ESMAN, ETHNIC POLITICS 43 (1994).

Once ethnic conflict turns violent, the intensity of the passions aroused makes it difficult for the parties to engage in meaningful negotiations.[38] At that point, even if ethnic group leaders are prepared to pursue compromise solutions, they may be frustrated by a more militant rank and file. In Sri Lanka, for example, popular opposition scuttled apparently moderate compromises worked out between the leaders of the contending ethnic communities.[39]

Structural and historical factors may also impede efforts to negotiate a balanced settlement. For example, nearby kin states with irredentist ambitions may exacerbate conflict for their own ends. In addition, gross inequalities in group size or socioeconomic status may make negotiations difficult because the larger or more powerful group seldom sees any compelling reason to make concessions.[40] A prior history of interethnic conflict will also make it more difficult to achieve the minimum levels of trust necessary to any negotiated settlement. Finally, the decision-making calculus of both internal and external actors will shift continually in response to changes in the political and military fortunes of the internal contestants as well as in response to changes in external conditions. Accordingly, the opportunities for negotiating and implementing a balanced political settlement will vary widely not only from one conflict to another but also at different points in time during any particular conflict.

2. Implementing an Agreement

Even if warring ethnic groups do manage to agree on consociational terms for their continued association, the resulting agreement is likely to prove both difficult to implement and difficult to maintain. This is particularly true when the local autonomy that is an essential part of such agreements is accomplished through federalism.

a. Problems with Consociational Settlements. Consociational political systems depend on creating and maintaining consensus among ethnic groups. As a result, they are inherently cumbersome and inefficient. By design, elections do not yield a majority with a mandate to govern in particular ways. Instead, elections produce multiple majorities who must then agree on the adoption of particular policies. This process is often lengthy and complex, and the policies that result are notable more for their compromise nature than for their efficacy.[41]

---

[38] *See* McCrae, *supra* note 9, at 97.

[39] *See* HURST HANNUM, AUTONOMY, SOVEREIGNTY AND SELF-DETERMINATION 302–3 (1990).

[40] *See* Tedd Gurr, *Settling Ethnopolitical Conflicts, in* MINORITIES AT RISK 290, 311 (Tedd Gurr ed., 1993).

[41] *See, e.g.,* Lijphart, *Majority Rule, supra* note 8, at 123; Stephen Ellmann, *The New South*

In some cases, consociational structures may produce political gridlock. This is particularly likely if ethnic minorities acquire the power to block legislation essential to the continued operation of the government.[42] The history of Cyprus provides a case in point. In 1960, Cyprus adopted a strongly consociational constitution, which gave Turkish Cypriots broad-ranging veto authority over legislation that might be inimical to their interests. The system collapsed in less than three years.[43] Greek Cypriots resisted efforts to establish autonomous Turkish Cypriot municipalities and stalled full implementation of constitutional provisions requiring disproportionate Turkish Cypriot representation in the civil service. In response, Turkish Cypriots vetoed budget and tax legislation necessary to the continued financing of the government's operations.[44] Interethnic fighting erupted shortly thereafter, leading ultimately to a Turkish military invasion and the de facto partition of the island.[45]

Even consociational systems that avoid gridlock tend to give way to other forms of government within one or two generations, if not earlier. As time passes, shifts occur in the size, power, and interests of the various ethnic groups. Settlements that may have seemed reasonable at the time they were reached may soon appear unduly onerous to one or more parties.[46] In particular, members of a majority ethnic group may come to resent what they view as unfair privileges conferred on members of other ethnic groups. As political leaders committed to the original consociational bargain pass from the scene, new political entrepreneurs may arise and seize on shifting ethnic group sentiments to further their own careers.

Notwithstanding these difficulties, the failure of consociational systems is generally cause for dismay. In some countries, as in Malaysia and Fiji, consociational structures are replaced relatively peacefully but by systems designed to ensure the political supremacy of the dominant ethnic group. In other countries, such as Lebanon and Cyprus, the failure of consociational governments brings civil war and foreign military intervention.

African Constitution and Ethnic Division, 26 COLUM. HUM. RTS. L. REV. 5, 5 (1994) (noting "the reduction of any single group's ability to work its will through the political process").

[42] *See, e.g.*, Robert Howse & Karen Knop, *Federalism, Secession and the Limits of Ethnic Accommodation: A Canadian Perspective*, 1 NEW EUROPE L. REV. 269, 286 (1993) (noting potential for "deadlock and paralysis" inherent in minority veto); Ivo D. Duchacek, *Consociational Cradle of Federalism*, 15 PUBLIUS 35, 40 (1985) (same).

[43] *See generally* Thomas Ehrlich, *Cyprus, the "Warlike Isle": Origins and Elements of the Current Crisis*, 18 STAN. L. REV. 1021, 1033 (1966); Wippman, *supra* note 31, at 146.

[44] *See, e.g.*, Marios L. Evriviades, *The Legal Dimension of the Cyprus Conflict*, 10 TEX. INT'L L. J. 227, 243 (1975); Ehrlich, *supra* note 43, at 1041.

[45] The fighting that began in 1963 was quickly quelled by the dispatch of international peacekeeping forces, but the rupture between the Greek and Turkish Cypriot communities was not healed, and consociational government was not restored. A coup by extremist Greek Cypriots in 1974 provoked a Turkish invasion and the effective partition of the island. *See* Ehrlich, *supra* note 43, at 1040–62; Wippman, *supra* note 31, at 146–47.

[46] *See* HOROWITZ, *supra* note 16, at 584.

Only rarely do countries outgrow the need for consociational practices by developing a coherent national identity that permits political disputes to be handled through majority rule governance.

b. The Perils of Ethno-Territorial Federalism. Consociations structured as ethno-territorial federations seem particularly vulnerable to catastrophic collapse. This may appear surprising because, on its face, federalism may seem the ideal structuring device for achieving unity at the national level while allowing local diversity and control over issues of particular concern to minorities, such as language, education, and provision of social welfare services. Consociational federalism has worked reasonably well in countries as diverse as Switzerland, Canada, Belgium, and Lebanon.[47]

But many of the potential problems associated with consociational practices can be magnified in an ethnically based federal system. While consociationalism in any form can heighten ethnic group affiliation and hinder the creation of a larger national identity, ethno-territorial federalism seems particularly conducive to the creation of rival, internal "nations."[48] For ethnic nationalists, autonomy in a federated state can never be anything other than a second best alternative, a way station on the road to secession. Ethno-territorial federalism may assist them in pursuing full independence by equipping ethnic groups with the territory and political infrastructure necessary to form their own independent state.[49] It is therefore not surprising that when the Soviet Union, Yugoslavia, and Czechoslovakia broke apart, each split along the borders of its former federal republics.

The reaction of the international community to the breakup of Yugoslavia may have inadvertently encouraged the view that ethno-territorial federalism can be used as a halfway house to full independence. The European Union's premature recognition of the former federal republics' independence, coupled with the Badinter Commission's decision to apply the principle of uti possidetis to freeze the boundaries of the new states along their former federal borders,[50] might be taken as a sign that the international community will more readily accept attempts at secession by groups inhabiting federal substates than it will similar attempts by other groups.[51]

[47] Lebanon first adopted a set of consociational practices in 1943 as part of the Lebanese National Pact. Although that pact did not formally establish a federal system, it did treat the ethnic communities in Lebanon "almost as the units of a federal state." HOROWITZ, *supra* note 16, at 583, quoting GEORGE E. KIRK, CONTEMPORARY ARAB POLITICS 117 (1961).

[48] *See, e.g.*, Duchacek, *supra* note 34, at 19; *see also* Bunce, *supra* note 2 (arguing that ethno-territorial federalism in Yugoslavia created "proto-nations," and, eventually, "proto-states," at the republic level).

[49] Howse & Knop, *supra* note 42, at 274.

[50] International Conference on the Former Yugoslavia Arbitration Commission, Opinion No. 3, 31 I.L.M. 1499, 1500 (1992).

[51] *See* Hurst Hannum, *Self-Determination, Yugoslavia and Europe: Old Wine in New Bottles?* 3 TRANSNAT'L L. & CONTEMP. PROBS. 57, 65 (1993); *see also* Marc Weller, *The International*

Even in the absence of external encouragement, advocates of independence can easily put federal authorities into a difficult dilemma. As Robert Howse and Karen Knop have argued, if the central government is strong and vigorously pursues statewide policies in areas within its jurisdiction, it will be accused of being domineering; if the central government is weak and leaves policymaking largely to the substates or provinces, it will be labeled superfluous.[52] Similarly, if the federal government pursues economic or other policies that are in the common national interest but that in the short term disadvantage the substate controlled by a particular ethnic group, the government may be open to charges of exploitation.[53]

Not surprisingly, then, it is easy to point to cases in which ethnic federalism has failed spectacularly. But in evaluating proposed solutions to contemporary conflicts, we must be careful not to overgeneralize from the failure of consociational practices, including ethnic federalism, to avert ethnic conflict in specific cases. In particular, we must take care to determine whether the failure at issue was inherent in consociationalism as an approach to the management of ethnic conflict or whether it can be otherwise explained. If the problem can be traced in part to the consociational or federal character of the state involved, then we must ask whether modifications to the governmental structures and electoral policies in place might have generated a more successful result.

Nigeria's experience with quasi-consociational federalism provides a good example. As Donald Horowitz observes, "the Nigerian evidence shows that federalism can either exacerbate or mitigate ethnic conflict."[54] In the first Nigerian Republic, which lasted from 1960 to 1966, the country was divided into three main regions, each dominated by a particular ethnic group and an associated political party. This arrangement unduly magnified the power of the three principal ethnic groups and encouraged them to struggle for power at the center, thus heightening existing conflict tendencies.[55] Following the Biafran civil war in 1967, the three regions were divided into twelve states, in part to break up the dominance of the northern region. Eventually, the country was further subdivided into

---

Response to the Dissolution of the Socialist Federal Republic of Yugoslavia, 86 Am. J. Int'l L. 569, 570–74 (1992). A later opinion of the Badinter Commission implicitly limits the circumstances in which substate federal units may dissolve a federal state, by finding that "the existence of a federal state, which is made up of a number of separate entities, is seriously compromised *when a majority of these entities, embracing a greater part of the territory and population,* constitute themselves as sovereign states with the result that federal authority may no longer be exercised." International Conference on the Former Yugoslavia Arbitration Commission, Opinion No. 8, 31 I.L.M. 1521, 1522 (1992).

[52] *See* Howse & Knop, *supra* note 42, at 275.

[53] *Id.* at 276.

[54] Horowitz, *supra* note 16, at 603.

[55] *Id.*

nineteen, and then thirty, states.[56] The proliferation of new states allowed previously submerged intraethnic divisions among the three principal ethnic groups to surface, particularly in the north.[57] In addition, "[t]he new arrangements transferred a good deal of conflict from the all-Nigeria level to the state level."[58] On at least some issues, the fulcrum of competition shifted from ethnic identity to state interests, leading to interethnic cooperation instead of conflict.[59] The net effect of the changes, coupled with electoral requirements that forced Nigerian presidential candidates to appeal to ethnic groups other than their own for support, was to create a more complex, and less divisive, politics at the center.[60] In short, the design of particular ethnic federations, and of their electoral policies, has a great deal to do with their success or failure as mechanisms for the management of ethnic conflict.

Many of the problems commonly associated with ethnic federalism might be lessened or avoided by changes in constitutional design. For example, federation need not lead to secession, even when state lines are designed to create ethnically homogeneous substates. In some cases, the creation of such substates may facilitate the emergence of subethnic cleavages that will militate against any unified position on independence, as was the case in Nigeria. In other cases, the adoption of economic development or other policies favorable to a particular subunit may induce its members to prefer continued federation over an impoverished independence.[61] In addition, states may adopt policies designed to provide employment to a significant percentage of an ethnic group's members outside the substate in which that ethnic group constitutes the majority.[62] These and other policies can limit secessionist sentiment while still preserving the benefits of autonomy for groups that might feel threatened in a unitary state.

c. Pushing for Consociational Settlements. The more difficult question is whether complex constitutional bargains can be negotiated and implemented after ethnic conflict has turned violent, as the U.N. tried to do in Bosnia and is still trying to do in Cyprus, Georgia, Tajikistan, Burundi, and elsewhere. In the past, most successful ethnic federations, including states often cited as models of successful ethnic federalism, such as Switzerland, Belgium, and Canada, evolved slowly, voluntarily, and in re-

---

[56] ESMAN, *supra* note 37, at 44.

[57] HOROWITZ, *supra* note 16, at 606–7; Selassie, *supra* note 12, at 45.

[58] HOROWITZ, *supra* note 16, at 604.

[59] *Id.* at 612.

[60] *Id.* at 613.

[61] *See generally* HOROWITZ, *supra* note 16, at 626–27 (describing structural and distributive policies designed to create disincentives to secession).

[62] *Id.*

sponse to particular historical conditions. Moreover, in countries such as Switzerland and Belgium, ethnic differences tend to be "less ascriptive in character, less severe in intensity, less exclusive in command of the loyalty of participants, and less preemptive of other forms of conflict" than is the case in many other deeply divided societies, particularly those in which ethnic conflict has already turned violent.[63] Accordingly, one might be tempted to conclude that a state "founded on ethnic federalism in a context where separatist inclinations are high and unifying institutions are weak is unlikely to survive as a unified nation."[64] If that assessment is correct, it follows that the U.N. has been pursuing the wrong approach to settling a number of important contemporary conflicts.

But as I noted earlier, we must be careful not to overgeneralize from the failure of consociationalism in particular cases. Moreover, it is also possible to identify at least some instances in which consociational federalism or the devolution of power to substate regions has brought an end, if only temporarily, to violent ethnic conflict. In the Sudan, for example, an agreement on southern autonomy in 1972 ended nine years of brutal civil war.[65] The agreement functioned reasonably well for ten years until revived Islamic sentiment in the north prompted government officials to reject southern autonomy, thus reigniting a civil war that still continues. In that case, there was nothing inherent in the system itself that prompted its demise, and it is extremely doubtful that any other system of government would have worked more successfully.[66] Similarly, a quasi-federal power sharing system adopted in Lebanon at the time of its independence in 1943 worked reasonably well for more than thirty years before it, too, fell victim to renewed civil war.[67] These cases suggest that even after armed conflict has begun it is still possible "to apply the Nigerian pound of cure."[68]

But in the Sudan, such an agreement became possible only after the parties fought long enough to recognize "the destructiveness of the civil

[63] *Id.* at 572. As Horowitz notes, there is a cause-and-effect problem in looking at countries such as Switzerland and Belgium as models of consociational conflict management. It is unclear whether consociationalism in such countries is successful because ethnic divisions have been less significant from the start or whether ethnic divisions are less significant because consociational practices have been successful. *Id.* Moreover, even states with a long history of peaceful consociational governance may still divide along ethnic lines. In both Belgium and Canada, for example, centrifugal forces remain strong.

[64] Selassie, *supra* note 12, at 44–45.

[65] *See* HANNUM, *supra* note 39, at 312; HOROWITZ, *supra* note 16, at 615–16.

[66] As Hannum notes, the autonomy agreement "offer[ed] a framework for political development within the Sudan" that failed not because of its inherent flaws but "primarily because [President] Numeiri increasingly refused to accept its basic premise, that is, meaningful southern autonomy beyond the manipulation of the central government." HANNUM, *supra* note 39, at 326–27.

[67] HOROWITZ, *supra* note 16, at 583–84.

[68] *Id.* at 474.

war" and to conclude that "there would be no peace without some degree of autonomy for the south."[69] A similarly destructive conflict preceded the 1989 Ta'if Accord, which reinstituted a form of interconfessional power sharing in Lebanon, this time under Syria's supervision.[70] It would be a Pyrrhic victory at best if consociational settlements could only be installed after the parties fight to exhaustion.[71]

The principal unanswered question here is whether the international community, acting through the United Nations or regional organizations such as the OSCE, can exert sufficient pressure on contending ethnic communities to induce them to adopt a balanced settlement either before ethnic conflict breaks out or, if that is not possible, in time to limit the ensuing damage. The evidence to date is not encouraging. Although the United Nations has taken some promising steps to enhance its capacity to engage in preventive diplomacy, it is extremely difficult for the U.N. to propose dramatic changes to a country's constitutional system unless the country is already on the verge of political collapse. Otherwise, the U.N. is likely to be accused of infringing on the domestic jurisdiction of the affected state, and its efforts are likely to be rejected by whichever party anticipates that it will be disadvantaged by whatever arrangements the U.N. wishes to propose.

Once conflict begins in earnest, the parties' positions harden, and political elites may be locked into uncompromising postures. Under such conditions, half-hearted measures such as arms embargoes and political condemnations of forcible boundary changes and human rights violations are unlikely to have much effect. So long as one or more parties perceives a potential advantage in continuing the conflict, proposals similar to the Vance-Owen plan are likely to be ignored or, even worse, may stimulate renewed fighting as parties seek to position themselves to take advantage of and shape proposed territorial divisions. In this context, external actors may consider delicate constitutional bargains involving complicated internal boundary drawing to be too uncertain and complex to be accomplished through external pressure. Such proposals may then be rejected in favor of simpler and geographically "cleaner" settlements.

In Bosnia, for example, the Vance-Owen plan, with its balanced power-sharing provisions and carefully delineated ethnic provinces, initially attracted considerable international support. But neither the U.N. nor any of the other international organizations promoting the plan could agree on sanctions or inducements strong enough to persuade the Bosnian Serbs

[69] HANNUM, *supra* note 39, at 323.

[70] *See* Michael C. Hudson, *The Domestic Context and Perspectives in Lebanon, in* INTERNATIONAL ORGANIZATIONS AND ETHNIC CONFLICT 126, 144–46 (Milton Esman & Shibley Telhami eds., 1995).

[71] HOROWITZ, *supra* note 16, at 473–74.

that they would come closer to accomplishing their aims by accepting the plan than they would by further military action. Over time, the Vance-Owen plan gave way to a series of plans, with each successive plan coming closer to accepting the outright partition of Bosnia into two or three separate states.[72] Ultimately, the international community succeeded in forcing the warring parties to sign the Dayton accords. But those accords, though nominally consociational, appear in reality to pave the way for the eventual partition of Bosnia.

Thus, there are ample grounds for pessimism concerning the willingness and the ability of international organizations to impose a Vance-Owen–style plan on an ongoing ethnic conflict. In some countries, such as Angola and Cambodia, the U.N. has had considerable success in pressuring warring parties to accept a settlement package premised on the conduct of internationally supervised elections. In such cases, sanctions such as arms embargoes and aid cutoffs can be targeted against whichever party resists the conduct of elections or refuses to respect their outcome. But the complexity of consociational or quasi-consociational solutions makes it much harder for the U.N. to devise appropriate sanctions or incentives. Parties must be induced not simply to accept elections but to relinquish control over territory and to accept either substantially more, or substantially less, central government control over the state than they might desire. Plans of this sort are open to constant revision to produce a fairer settlement or at least a settlement that is more attractive to one party or another. As a result, it is hard for external actors to insist on acceptance of any particular plan on a principled basis, and it is easy for internal parties to conclude that they ought to hold out for a more favorable version of whatever plan is under consideration. Even if all parties accept such a plan, and even if outside states are prepared to commit troops to oversee the plan's implementation, it is hard to know how those troops should proceed if one party or another reneges on its obligations under the plan. As the Turkish invasion of Cyprus demonstrated, it is far easier to separate ethnic communities by force than it is to ensure the continuance of a consociational constitutional system that depends on the parties' voluntary cooperation.

Still, it does not follow that the U.N. and other international organizations have no business pursuing consociational settlements in ongoing ethnic conflicts. As difficult and complex as such settlements may be, the alternatives may be even less attractive. In Bosnia, as in Cyprus before it, partition became a viable option only through a process of ethnic cleansing. From this one might conclude that the international community

---

[72] For a description of the various peace plans proposed in Bosnia, see Paul C. Szasz, *Peacekeeping in Operation: A Conflict Study of Bosnia*, 28 CORNELL INT'L L. J. 685 (1995).

should be more tolerant of proposals for compulsory population exchanges as an alternative to genocide and ethnic cleansing on the road to the physical separation of geographically interspersed ethnic combatants. But even "voluntary" population exchanges of the sort the U.N. has conducted in the past are morally and legally objectionable, and the U.N. and the International Conference on Yugoslavia both expressly rejected such transfers as the basis for a solution in Bosnia.[73] Moreover, population exchanges alone will not solve territorial disputes or protect ethnic minorities that remain trapped within territory controlled by another ethnic community.

In at least some cases, then, pursuit of Vance-Owen–style plans may be the best available option. And although the U.N. has not as yet successfully pressured parties to accept such a plan, it might be able to do so if it intervened early and indicated a readiness to use force against any party that did not lay down its arms pending adoption of a comprehensive settlement. In Bosnia, for example, many observers think that, in 1990 and 1991, a combination of economic incentives and creative diplomacy, coupled with a genuine readiness to oppose militarily the use of force by any faction, could have resulted in a peaceful and balanced settlement.[74] Similarly, an early and forceful intervention by the guarantors of the 1960 Cyprus constitution might have prevented its untimely collapse in 1963.[75]

In the end, it may be that no amount of constitutional engineering or external pressure will suffice to avert war among peoples who are determined to live apart. But in some cases, constitutional engineering and external pressure might change the way the parties look at the possibility of living together.

II. Self-Determination and Consociationalism

Of course, even if we conclude that consociational settlements are both politically desirable and operationally feasible, we should not assume that they are necessarily compatible with international law or the policies that underlie it. Under the prevailing view of contemporary international law,

[73] See G.A. Res. 46/242, preamble and para. 6 (1992); S.C. Res. 771 (1992); S.C. Res. 779 (1992); Report of the Secretary-General on the International Conference on the Former Yugoslavia, 31 I.L.M. 1552, 1560 (1992). Notwithstanding its recent condemnation of population exchanges, the U.N. has supervised large-scale exchanges on several occasions in the past, as the lesser of two evils in a given case. See, e.g., U.N. Doc. S/11789 & Add. 1 (August 5, 1975) (agreement on Greek and Turkish Cypriot population exchange).

[74] See, e.g., Steven L. Burg, The International Community and the Yugoslav Crisis, in INTERNATIONAL ORGANIZATIONS AND ETHNIC CONFLICT 235, 249 (Milton Esman & Shibley Telhami eds., 1995).

[75] Ehrlich, supra note 43, at 1046.

self-determination has been transformed in large part into a democratic entitlement—that is, a right to representative government shared by all of the people residing within a given state.[76] In this formulation, self-determination is typically seen as a right to be exercised principally through majoritarian democratic political processes. As I have noted, however, consociationalism is explicitly anti-majoritarian. Indeed, the goal of consociationalism is to restrain majority groups and to substitute consensus politics for the more adversarial system of majority rule. Thus, self-determination and consociationalism might seem to conflict.

But equating self-determination with majoritarian democracy oversimplifies a complex right. As Gregory Fox observes, internal self-determination implies the creation of "inclusive political processes"; majoritarian elections are only part of these processes and must be accompanied by and balanced with protection for minority rights and, in appropriate cases, with "the construction of autonomy regimes within states."[77] In Fox's view, self-determination is best understood as an "organizing principle" that serves to refocus "autonomy claims from the expectation of independence brought on by the success of decolonization to modes of participation in the domestic political arena."[78]

This understanding of self-determination goes a long way toward accommodating the current trend in international law toward heightened recognition of collective minority rights and, in particular, of the right of minorities to "effective political participation" in the governance of the states in which they reside. This right of effective participation has been expressly delineated in a number of recent international treaties, declarations, and resolutions.[79] Typical of these recent legal instruments is the U.N. General Assembly's 1992 Declaration on the Rights of Persons Belonging to National or Ethnic, Religious, or Linguistic Minorities.[80] The

---

[76] See Thomas M. Franck, *The Emerging Right to Democratic Governance*, 86 AM. J. INT'L L. 46 (1992). For a brief discussion of the historical evolution of self-determination, see Chapter 1 of this volume at 8–13.

[77] Gregory H. Fox, *Self Determination in the Post–Cold War Era: A New Internal Focus?* 16 MICH. J. INT'L L. 733, 752–55 (1995).

[78] *Id.* at 755.

[79] *See, e.g.,* Document of the Copenhagen Meeting of the Conference on the Human Dimension of the CSCE, art. 35 (1990), 29 I.L.M. 1305, 1319 (1990) ("The participating States will respect the right of persons belonging to national minorities to effective participation in public affairs."); European Commission for Democracy through Law, Proposal for a European Convention for the Protection of Minorities, art. 14 (1991), *reprinted in* 12 HUM. RTS. L.J. 270 (1991) ("States shall favor the effective participation of minorities in public affairs."); Report of the CSCE Meeting of Experts on National Minorities, part III, July 19, 1991, 31 I.L.M. 1692, 1696–97 (1992) (recognizing "the right of persons belonging to national minorities to effective participation in public affairs"); Framework Convention for the Protection of National Minorities, art. 15, February 1, 1995, 34 I.L.M. 351, 354 (1995) ("The Parties shall create the conditions necessary for the effective participation of persons belonging to national minorities in cultural, social, and economic life and in public affairs, in particular those affecting them.").

[80] G.A. Res. 47/135, U.N. Doc. A/RES/47/135 (1992), 32 I.L.M. 911, 915 (1993).

declaration urges states to respect the cultural identity of ethnic minorities, and to ensure that members of such minorities "have the right to
participate effectively in cultural, religious, social, economic, and public
life."[81] In addition, the declaration states that members of minority groups
"have the right to participate effectively in decisions . . . concerning the
minority to which they belong or the regions in which they live."[82] Although the precise content of this emerging right to effective political
participation has not been defined with any clarity,[83] it implicitly accords
minority group members participatory rights going beyond the majoritarian formula of one person, one vote.[84] At a minimum, effective political participation is incompatible with a majoritarian political system that
operates to exclude ethnic minorities from any meaningful participation
in the political life of their state.

Fox's characterization of the right of self-determination is also consistent with the fact that, notwithstanding the contemporary tendency to
equate the "self" in self-determination with "the entire territorial state,"[85]
the right as articulated in numerous international covenants expressly
applies to "peoples" rather than to states. Although many commentators
have circumvented this inconvenient phraseology by simply redefining
peoples to mean all the people within a given state,[86] it is clear that *peoples*
originally meant something quite different than states and that self-determination was not a principle of popular sovereignty but a right to oppose
alien (that is, colonial) subjugation.[87]

Understanding self-determination to encompass different modes of political participation under different circumstances helps to bridge the gap
between the anticolonial and popular sovereignty aspects of the principle.
At one extreme along a continuum of political participation—colonial
subjugation—self-determination may operate principally as a right to
independent statehood. At the other extreme of the continuum—a mono-
ethnic state or a multiethnic state in which ethnicity has not been politically mobilized—self-determination may operate principally as right to

---

[81] *Id.* art. 2(2).

[82] *Id.* art. 2(5).

[83] The declaration itself contains several built-in limitations on the application of the right
to effective political participation. In particular, paragraph 3 of Article 2 qualifies the right of
minorities to participate in decisions concerning their group or region with the requirement
that the right be exercised "in a manner not incompatible with national legislation." Read
literally, this qualification could swallow the rule; but read in the context of the declaration as
a whole, it presumably refers to national legislation that is designed to regulate the form of
minority participation rather than legislation that effectively blocks such participation altogether.

[84] *See* HANNUM, *supra* note 39, at 471.

[85] Fox, *supra* note 77, at 752.

[86] *See* THORNBERRY, *supra* note 13, at 18.

[87] *See, e.g.,* Thomas M. Franck, *Postmodern Tribalism and the Right to Secession, in* PEOPLES
AND MINORITIES IN INTERNATIONAL LAW 3, 10 (Catherine Brölmann, René Lefeber & Marjoleine Zieck eds., 1993).

majoritarian democracy. In between, in ethnically politicized multiethnic states, self-determination may operate as a principle that requires "that each people should be given the opportunity to participate in the decision-making process of the state."[88] Otherwise, self-determination for the majority of the state's population may effectively preclude self-determination for a significant minority.[89]

The need for countermajoritarian protections is most obvious when the central government consistently discriminates against a particular ethnic group.[90] At that point, in the words of the Friendly Relations Declaration, the government cannot be deemed to be "representing the whole people belonging to the territory without distinction of race, creed, or colour."[91] But even when the government does not openly discriminate against particular groups, consociational practices may still be required to enable minority ethnic groups to participate meaningfully in the political life of the state.[92] Thus, in deeply divided societies, consociationalism is not only compatible with self-determination but may be the only way to give effect to self-determination that is consistent with the rights of minorities to effective political participation.[93]

III. Human Rights Issues

From an individual rights standpoint, consociational solutions to ethnic conflict are inherently problematic.[94] Arguably, they violate at least three

[88] Jan Klabbers & René Lefeber, *Africa: Lost between Self-Determination and Uti Possidetis, in* Peoples and Minorities in International Law 37, 43 (Catherine Brölmann, René Lefeber & Marjoleine Zieck eds., 1993).

[89] *Cf., e.g.,* Asbjorn Eide, *In Search of Constructive Alternatives to Secession, in* Modern Law of Self-Determination 139, 147 (Christian Tomuschat ed., 1993) (noting that self-determination applies to all of the people within the territory concerned, not just the majority); European Community Statement, October 6, 1991, quoted in Burg, *supra* note 74, at 245 ("the right to self-determination of all peoples of Yugoslavia cannot be exercised in isolation from the interests and rights of ethnic minorities within the individual republics"); Alain Pellet, *The Opinions of the Badinter Arbitration Committee: A Second Breath for the Self-Determination of Peoples,* 3 Eur. J. Int'l L. 178, 179 (1992) (arguing that "the notion of 'people' is no longer homogeneous and should not be seen as encompassing the whole population of the state" and should include recognition of the "identity" of ethnic communities within states).

[90] *See* Otto Kimminich, *A "Federal" Right of Self-Determination?* in Modern Law of Self-Determination 83, 92 (Christian Tomuschat ed., 1993).

[91] Declaration on Principles of International Law Concerning Friendly Relations and Co-operation among States in Accordance with the Charter of the United Nations, G.A. Res. 2625 (XXXV 1970).

[92] *See* Klabbers & Lefeber, *supra* note 88, at 44 (noting that "an autonomy arrangement or a biased federal state structure" may be necessary to protect ethnic minorities).

[93] *Cf.* Henry J. Steiner, *Ideals and Counter-Ideals in the Struggle over Autonomy Regimes for Minorities,* 66 Notre Dame L. Rev. 1539, 1545–46 (1991) (arguing that norms of collective self-determination and political participation may support the creation of autonomy regimes for ethnic minorities).

[94] The U.S. legal system has struggled for many years to balance concerns over the exclu-

specific human rights norms. First, they explicitly differentiate among the members of groups on the basis of characteristics such as race, religion, and language rather than on neutral merit-based criteria.[95] Second, ethnic power-sharing practices may dilute the political power of individuals who are not members of a protected ethnic group and thereby violate their participatory rights. Finally, at least some of the autonomy schemes now under consideration as part of proposed consociational settlements would place restrictions on efforts by members of some ethnic groups to settle in areas controlled by members of another ethnic group, arguably in violation of the right to freedom of movement and residence.

A. Prohibited Discrimination?

In varying ways and to different degrees, consociational systems confer a disproportionately large share of political power, state resources, and government positions on members of minority communities. Arguably, such policies violate both general norms of nondiscrimination, of the sort set out in the International Covenant on Civil and Political Rights,[96] and specific norms of nondiscrimination, of the sort set out in the International Convention on the Elimination of All Forms of Racial Discrimination.

On its face, the latter convention might seem to prohibit outright the distribution of government benefits and political power on the basis of ethnicity by forbidding "any distinction, exclusion, restriction or prefer-ence based on race, colour, descent, or national or ethnic origin which has

---

sion of minorities from meaningful political participation with "[t]he dream of a Nation of equal citizens in a society where race is irrelevant to personal opportunity." *City of Richmond v. J. A. Croson Co.*, 488 U.S. 469, 505 (1989) (O'Connor, J.). To a large degree, U.S. courts have tried to address problems of exclusion through general principles of nondiscrimination. In the voting rights area, courts have sometimes struck down districting plans found to violate the Fourteenth Amendment's equal protection clause or the Fifteenth Amendment's guaran-tee that the right to vote shall not be denied or abridged on account of race. *See* Orentlicher, *supra* note 51, at 69 n. 312 (citing cases). On occasion, courts have upheld the creation of majority nonwhite districts as a means to remedy the past exclusion of minorities from political power. *See, e.g., White v. Regester*, 412 U.S. 755 (1973). In other cases, however, the courts have held that the deliberate creation of such districts amounts to unconstitutional discrimination. *See, e.g., Miller v. Johnson*, 115 S. Ct. 2475 (1995).

[95] *See* Steiner, *supra* note 93, at 1551.

[96] Article 2 of the International Covenant on Civil and Political Rights requires that each state party "ensure to all individuals within its territory . . . the rights recognized in the present Covenant, without distinction of any kind, such as race, colour, sex, language, reli-gion, political or other opinion, national or social origin, property, birth or social status." According to the U.N. Human Rights Committee, reasonable positive measures "aimed at correcting conditions which prevent or impair the enjoyment of rights under article 27" may "constitute a legitimate differentiation under the Covenant." U.N. Human Rights Committee, General Comment No. 23(50) on Article 27 of the International Covenant on Civil and Political Rights, Doc. CCPR/C/21/ Rev. I/Add. 5 (April 6, 1994). But the wide-ranging benefits and authority conferred on minority groups under some consociational settlements appear to go well beyond the limited corrective measures apparently envisioned by the Human Rights Committee under Article 27.

the purpose or effect of nullifying or impairing the recognition, enjoyment or exercise, on an equal footing, of human rights and fundamental freedoms in the political, economic, social, cultural or any other field of public life."[97] In theory, the purpose of consociational settlements is to protect the rights of ethnic minorities, not to nullify or impair the rights of the rest of the population. Still, consociational practices inevitably have the effect of favoring one set of individuals over another on the basis of their membership in an ethnic group or, at least, on the basis of their residence in an ethnically defined subnational political unit.

It is hard to justify this result within the literal terms of the convention itself. The convention acknowledges that "special measures" may be taken for the advancement of particular racial or ethnic groups in order to ensure that those groups have equal rights and opportunities. But such measures may be taken only if they do not "lead to the maintenance of separate rights for different racial groups. . . ."[98] Almost by definition, consociational settlements are designed to lead to the maintenance of, if not different rights, then differentially effective rights. Moreover, the convention requires that special measures be discontinued "after the objectives for which they were taken have been achieved."[99] Consociational constitutions generally contain no provisions for their eventual demise; and insofar as they afford ethnic minorities veto authority over national initiatives, they should probably be seen as intended to be permanent.

Nonetheless, we should not jump to the conclusion that consociational systems necessarily violate international law norms barring racial or ethnic discrimination. Despite their ethnically based countermajoritarian provisions, consociational settlements of the sort proposed in Cyprus and Bosnia have been widely endorsed by a broad range of states; it is, after all, the United Nations that has helped to draft these proposals and pressed for their acceptance. Moreover, a survey conducted by the European Commission for Democracy through Law demonstrates that "positive discrimination" in favor of ethnic and other minorities is now fairly common in Europe, in keeping with a general shift from "a strictly individual conception of the protection of minorities to a more collective conception. . . ."[100] Among the positive measures employed by various European states to protect minorities are the devolution of power to ethnic federal and regional subunits, electoral adjustments, and other consociational and quasi-consociational mechanisms.[101]

[97] 660 U.N.T.S. 195, 5 I.L.M. 352 (1966).

[98] Id. art. 1(1).

[99] Id.

[100] See Report on the Replies to the Questionnaire on the Rights of Minorities, in EUROPEAN COMMISSION FOR DEMOCRACY THROUGH LAW, THE PROTECTION OF MINORITIES 58 (Council of Europe Press, 1994).

[101] See generally id. at 56–75.

Acceptance of consociational practices in these and other countries rests on an understanding that the differential distribution of political power and related goods is permissible so long as it is necessary to protect the rights of ethnic minorities and does not unduly infringe on the rights of the majority. In the language employed by various human rights bodies and tribunals, measures taken to enhance the status of ethnic and other minorities do not constitute prohibited discrimination within the meaning of the pertinent international human rights covenants if those measures are based on criteria that are "reasonable and objective," if their aim "is to achieve a purpose which is legitimate" under the applicable covenant, and if the measures employed are "proportionate" to the ends sought.[102]

Although this standard is vague and may be difficult to apply in close cases, it reflects the unfortunate reality that, in societies with sharp ethnic cleavages, the only way to achieve an effective balance of the rights of different ethnic groups may be to accept practices that would not be permissible in a less divided society. Within limits, then, consociational practices should be viewed not as creating separate or discriminatory rights for ethnic minorities but as enabling ethnic minorities to exercise their rights on a level as close to parity with the dominant groups in society as is feasible in an imperfect social system. This seems to be the spirit animating the 1991 Proposal for a European Convention for the Protection of Minorities, which was drafted by the European Commission for Democracy through Law.[103] That proposal clearly acknowledges the collective dimension of the rights of ethnic groups[104] and the importance of positive state action to protect those rights.[105] Moreover, the proposed convention expressly recognizes the importance of equality between groups in society as well as equality between individuals and treats measures designed to promote both forms of equality as inherently non-discriminatory: "The adoption of special measures in favour of minorities or of individuals belonging to minorities and aimed at promoting equality between them and the rest of the population or at taking due account of

[102] General Comment 18, Non-Discrimination, Compilation of General Comments and General Recommendations Adopted by Human Rights Treaty Bodies, U.N. Doc. HRI\GEN\1\Rev. 1 at 26 (1994); see also, e.g., Mathiue-Mohin & Clerfayt v. Belgium, 10 Eur. Ct. H. R. (Series A) (1988) at 1 (upholding Belgian law regulating membership in the Flemish Council).

[103] The proposal is reprinted in 12 Hum. Rts. L. J. 270 (1991).

[104] Various articles of the proposed convention mandate the protection of "ethnic minorities, as well as the rights of individuals belonging to those minorities." See, e.g., id. arts. 1(1), 3, 4(2), 14.

[105] See Explanatory Report on the Proposal for a European Convention for the Protection of Minorities, in THE PROTECTION OF MINORITIES, supra note 100, at 24, 26 ("Solutions to the problems of minorities lie in, on the one hand, the respect for the principles of non-discrimination and, on the other, positive action such as proclaiming individual and collective rights.").

their specific conditions shall not be considered as an act of discrimination."[106]

Admittedly, the proposed convention was not adopted; a more individual rights–oriented convention, the Framework Convention for the Protection of National Minorities, was adopted instead. But that convention
also provides that measures undertaken "to promote . . . full and effective
equality between persons belonging to a national minority and those
belonging to the majority" shall not "be considered to be an act of discrimination."[107]

It does not follow, of course, that the mere existence of significant ethnic
cleavages justifies any practice that can be described as consociational. In
some cases, states may adopt practices that go beyond what is necessary
to maintain a balance among ethnic groups and expressly place one group
in a position of dominance over another. In Fiji, for example, the constitution adopted in 1990 guarantees indigenous Fijians a working majority in
the legislature and primacy in selecting the president and prime minister.[108] As a result, Fijians of Indian descent, who constitute a slight majority of the total population, are permanently, and impermissibly, reduced
to a secondary political status.[109]

B. Conflicts with Participation Rights

The power-sharing aspects of consociationalism might also be deemed
to violate specific norms mandating equal rights of political participation
for all. These rights include the right "to take part in the conduct of public
affairs," the right "to vote and to be elected at genuine periodic elections,"
and the right "to have access, on general terms of equality, to public
service in his country."[110] For members of the majority, the right to take
part in the governance of the state is undeniably diluted by constitutional
arrangements that afford minority ethnic groups political power disproportionate to their numbers, whether that is accomplished through reserved seats and offices, minority veto rights, or similar devices. Similarly,
for members of the majority, both the right to vote and the right to hold
elective office are rendered less effective by countermajoritarian electoral
arrangements. Under the set of ideas proposed for Cyprus, for example,
Turkish Cypriots would have the right to elect a disproportionately large

[106] *Id.* art. 4(2).

[107] Framework Convention, *supra* note 79, art. 4(2) and 4(3). Similar language can be found
in the Report of the CSCE Meeting of Experts on National Minorities, *supra* note 79, part IV.

[108] Ved P. Nanda, *Ethnic Conflict in Fiji and International Human Rights Law*, 25 CORNELL
INT'L L. J. 565, 570–71 (1992).

[109] *Id.* at 575.

[110] International Covenant on Civil and Political Rights, art. 25. Similar language may be
found in Article 21 of the Universal Declaration of Human Rights.

number of officials, who, in turn, could block virtually any important legislation advocated by the Greek Cypriot majority. From this perspective, a Turkish Cypriot's vote is worth more than a Greek Cypriot's vote. Finally, the right to have access to public service on equal terms may be infringed on by requirements that positions in the civil service and the military be filled with minority group members at a rate disproportionate to their numbers, as often occurs in consociational political settlements. Under the Cyprus set of ideas, for example, Turkish Cypriots would be entitled to 30 percent of positions in the civil service, even though they constitute only 18 percent of the total population.

In practice, however, states have interpreted international instruments mandating respect for individuals' rights of political participation with sufficient flexibility to encompass most, if not all, of the provisions found in contemporary consociational settlement plans. The take-part clause of Article 25 of the International Covenant was drafted in terms "sufficiently abstract and porous . . . to permit democratic and nondemocratic states to assert that they satisfied the norms' demands."[111] Although the evolution of the right to political participation now makes it hard for nondemocratic states to make such claims, the right is still highly abstract and does not purport to mandate the adoption of any particular kind of democratic system. Read literally, the take-part clause is at least minimally satisfied by any political system that allows all citizens of the state to exercise some reasonable measure of influence on the conduct of public affairs, whether or not that system permits members of a particular ethnic group to exercise even greater influence on public policy in relation to their numbers. Otherwise, the take-part clause would effectively mandate straight majority rule, which it was not intended to do. Such a majoritarian reading of the clause would greatly impair, if not extinguish, any ability of substate ethnic minorities to influence the conduct of public affairs in states with sharp ethnic cleavages and, in the process, would conflict with the evolving right of effective political participation for minorities, as I have discussed.

Of course, the take-part clause, like all the rights specified in Article 25 and in the covenant as a whole, is supposed to be applied in a non-discriminatory fashion. But as I have argued, insofar as consociational systems are designed to create and maintain a political balance among ethnic groups rather than to establish the dominance of one group over others, the nondiscrimination aspect of the take-part clause should also be deemed satisfied.

Similarly, the elections clause in Article 25 should not be read to mandate adoption of any particular electoral system. As Henry Steiner points

---

[111] Henry J. Steiner, *Political Participation As Human Right*, 1 HUMAN RTS. Y.B. 77, 86 (1988).

out, during the drafting of the International Covenant, "[b]road agreement developed that the International Covenant could not impose upon its parties one or another of the different electoral systems current among liberal democracies."[112] The French delegate specifically argued against adoption of any principle mandating "that all votes ha[ve] the same weight," on the ground that such a principle "would condemn territorial constituencies and point toward proportional representation."[113] This view prevailed, leading to a provision worded broadly enough to encompass a wide variety of electoral systems, even though those systems may "exert markedly different influences on the distribution of political power" and may in some cases either "blot out" or "heighten" the political power of the minority.[114] In keeping with this understanding of Article 25, many states, in Europe and elsewhere, employ a variety of electoral practices to enhance the political influence of ethnic minorities.[115] Again, a contrary interpretation of Article 25, one that insisted on reading the right to political participation as a one person, one vote rule, would in some cases effectively exclude ethnic minorities from any meaningful representation in government.

In its draft General Comment on Article 25, a working group of the Human Rights Committee notes that ordinarily "the vote of one citizen should, within the framework of each state's electoral system, be equal to the vote of another," and that district boundaries should not be skewed "in a way which discriminates against any group of voters."[116] The committee goes on to note, however, that "[a]ffirmative measures may be justified to ensure representation of minorities . . . in the conduct of public affairs," provided such measures are "compatible with article 25 and the principle of equal suffrage." At a minimum, then, electoral systems designed to create a reasonable political balance among ethnic groups should not be deemed incompatible with Article 25 or similar provisions in other human rights instruments.

As the European Court of Human Rights has held, states have a "wide margin of appreciation" in organizing their electoral systems; "all votes" need not "have equal weight as regards the outcome of [an] election," and states may legitimately pursue policies "designed to achieve an equilibrium" among "various regions and cultural communities" so long as such policies are reasonable and proportionate to the ends sought.[117] Accord-

---

[112] *Id.* at 90.

[113] Quoted in *id.*

[114] *Id.* at 107–8.

[115] *See* Report on the Replies to the Questionnaire on the Rights of Minorities, *supra* note 100, at 72–75; HOROWITZ, supra note 16, at 629–51.

[116] Draft General Comment on Article 25 of the Covenant, Recommendation by the Working Group, CCPR/C/CRP.1, March 21, 1995.

[117] *Mathiue-Mohin & Clerfayt v. Belgium, supra* note 102, para. 54, 57 (applying Protocol No. 1, art. 3 of the European Convention on Human Rights).

ingly, consociational practices, including voting schemes designed to heighten the political influence of minority groups, should be deemed compatible with the right to vote and to hold office so long as the practices at issue provide some reasonable mechanism for ascertaining the will of the "people," understood to mean all of the people within the state, not just the majority.

Perhaps the most difficult practice to reconcile with the language of Article 25 is that of affording ethnic minorities disproportionate representation in civil service and other government posts. Article 25 mandates access to such positions on "general terms of equality." If that language is understood to mean that individuals are entitled to government positions based solely on neutral criteria of merit,[118] then there would seem to be little room for preferential treatment of ethnic minorities except insofar as such treatment is required to alleviate the effects of prior or existing discrimination.[119] Inclusion of such provisions in consociational settlements, however, typically represents not so much an effort to alleviate the effects of discrimination in the past as an effort to balance power between or among ethnic groups in the future and to ensure that each ethnic group feels adequately represented in the institutions of government. It might be possible to interpret "general terms of equality" broadly enough to encompass political systems that focus on the equality of groups rather than of individuals, in keeping with present trends toward recognition of collective rights, but such an interpretation seems inconsistent with the predominantly individual rights focus of the covenant itself.

On the other hand, like the other terms of Article 25, the language about general terms of equality was designed to be sufficiently broad and vague to encompass the wide variety of practices already in place among the parties that participated in the covenant's drafting. Moreover, the draft General Comment to Article 25 specifically provides that "affirmative measures should be taken to ensure that citizens belonging to underrepresented parts of the population have an equal opportunity to have access to public service."[120] In this context, the numerically disproportionate distribution of government service opportunities to members of minority groups, so long as the intent is to protect rather than to discriminate against such groups, probably passes muster. Certainly, many states, then and now, have put such requirements into place without attracting much

[118] In its draft general comment on Article 25, *supra* note 116, a working committee of the Human Rights Committee notes that public service should be based on "merit and equal opportunity" and that, "[t]o ensure access on general terms of equality, the criteria for appointment and the processes for appointment, promotion, and dismissal must be reasonable, objective and non-discriminatory."

[119] The Human Rights Committee has noted that, as long as preferential treatment "is needed to correct discrimination in fact, it is a case of legitimate differentiation under the Covenant." General Comment No. 23 (50), *supra* note 96.

[120] *Id.*

criticism on human rights grounds. The validity of such practices undoubtedly depends in large measure on the extent to which they deviate from the norm of equal individual access, the breadth and importance of the positions covered, the duration of the practices, and the political circumstances that induced their adoption. At a minimum, it seems too broad a conclusion to hold that ethnic group preferences in government employment can never be justified except as a remedy for prior discrimination.

C. Infringements on Freedom of Movement and Residence

Territorially based autonomy regimes for a particular ethnic group may require some ability to exclude members of other ethnic groups from taking up residence in the area designated as the autonomous region of the first group in order to prevent population movements from undermining that group's control of the region.[121] On their face, such provisions may seem to violate international norms guaranteeing citizens the right to move freely within their country and to reside wherever they choose (as well as general nondiscrimination norms).[122] At the extreme, ethnically based local autonomy may even resemble the South African homelands system established by the white-dominated minority government. Indeed, at least one commentator has sharply criticized power-sharing proposals in Bosnia on the ground that they establish a form of apartheid in violation of the International Convention on the Punishment and Suppression of the Crime of Apartheid.[123]

Again, however, state practice accepts, and even encourages, the adoption of autonomy schemes designed to protect and preserve minority ethnic groups and their cultures. For example, the OSCE, at its 1990 Copenhagen meeting, expressly declared that the creation of "local or autonomous administrations corresponding to the specific historical and territorial circumstances" of particular minorities may be "one of the possible means" for states to fulfill their obligation to protect and promote the

---

[121] Under the set of ideas for Cyprus, for example, Greek Cypriots may be barred from settling in the Turkish Cypriot federated state if necessary to preserve its ethnic character. Set of Ideas, *supra* note 7.

[122] *See* International Covenant on Civil and Political Rights, *supra* note 96, art. 12(1) ("Everyone lawfully within the territory of a State shall, within that territory, have the right to liberty of movement and freedom to choose his residence."); Universal Declaration of Human Rights, art. 13, G.A. Res. 217 A(III), U.N. Doc. A/810, at 71 (1948) ("Everyone has the right to freedom of movement and residence within the borders of each state."); [European] Convention for the Protection of Human Rights and Fundamental Freedoms, Protocol No. 4, art. 2(1) ("Everyone lawfully within the territory of a State shall, within that territory, have the right to liberty of movement and freedom to choose his residence.").

[123] *See* Francis Boyle, Memorandum to the Parliament of the Republic of Bosnia and Herzegovina, March 24, 1994 (on file with author).

"ethnic identity" of particular "national minorities."[124] Similarly, the 1991 Report of the CSCE Meeting of Experts on National Minorities lists territorial autonomy as one of the approaches used by European states to achieve "positive results" for the protection of national minorities "in a democratic manner."[125] Many states have adopted autonomy regimes for minorities with few objections from other states.[126] In general, such schemes are considered to be compatible with human rights norms, and, in some cases, they may be essential to the protection of minorities and minority cultures.

Although autonomy regimes may sometimes necessitate restrictions on individuals' freedom to choose their place of residence, such restrictions must be considered acceptable so long as they are narrowly tailored to protect the ethnic identity of a particular group. The European Framework Convention for the Protection of National Minorities recognizes that states should "refrain from measures which alter the proportions of the population in areas inhabited by persons belonging to national minorities" if such measures are designed to impair the rights of the affected minorities.[127] From this starting point, it is not much of a jump to conclude that states may also adopt measures designed to avoid such changes in population proportions if they are necessary to protect the identity and rights of particular national groups.

It is true that autonomy regimes for ethnic groups within states may foster group concentration and segregation. But autonomy regimes intended to protect ethnic minorities should not be confused with apartheid schemes designed to suppress subordinate populations. Autonomy regimes are designed to permit ethnic groups to participate in the cultural and political life of the state on terms of equality with other groups. Apartheid schemes such as the now defunct homeland system in South Africa are designed to facilitate and perpetuate the privileged status of the politically dominant social group. Both kinds of regimes may result in the territorial concentration of particular groups, but they differ radically in

---

[124] Document of the Copenhagen Meeting of the Conference on the Human Dimension of the CSCE, para. 35 (June 1990), 29 I.L.M. 1305 (1990).

[125] Report of the CSCE Meeting of Experts on National Minorities, Geneva, *supra* note 79, part IV.

[126] For discussion of various kinds of autonomy regimes, see generally HANNUM, *supra* note 39; *The Protection of Minorities in Federal and Regional States*, in THE PROTECTION OF MINORITIES, *supra* note 100.

[127] Framework Convention for the Protection of National Minorities, *supra* note 79, art. 16. Some states objected to a similar provision in the proposal that led to the convention because they "thought such a principle could threaten the sovereignty of the State and that citizens of the majority group were entitled to settle anywhere." *See* Explanatory Report on the Proposal for a European Convention for the Protection of Minorities, in THE PROTECTION OF MINORITIES, *supra* note 100, at 33. The drafters of the proposal, however, deemed such a provision essential to protect minorities from assimilation. *Id.*

purpose and effect. The forced segregation of apartheid schemes is never justified, but the voluntary separation produced by some autonomy regimes may be a necessary price to pay for the protection of ethnic minorities in deeply divided societies.

For the reasons I have considered, consociational political settlements are not inherently incompatible with the rights guaranteed by the principal international human rights covenants; in some cases, they may be the only way to enable ethnic minorities to participate meaningfully in the political life of their state. On the other hand, consociational settlements clearly do not fit comfortably within the dominant individual rights paradigm of contemporary international law. In general, consociational settlements tend to favor collective over individual rights. As a result, many of the practices associated with consociationalism appear discriminatory when viewed from a liberal individualist perspective.[128]

Even more fundamentally, consociational systems may seem inherently regressive and atavistic in their emphasis on the importance of ethnicity. From the standpoint of liberal theory, political systems should be designed to maximize individual freedom and equality. The fact of an individual's birth into a particular group should carry no weight, and opportunities for everyone should be determined solely by individual merit rather than by possession of any of the ascriptive characteristics associated with ethnicity. By emphasizing ethnicity as the basis for distributing political power and associated benefits, consociational practices threaten to undermine important values widely shared in most western states.

For reasons I have noted, however, consociational practices may nonetheless be essential to achieving a peaceful and democratic coexistence among politically mobilized ethnic groups. Even if consociational practices are not necessary to avoid interethnic political violence, they may still be the only means by which members of ethnic groups can maintain their identities and still participate meaningfully in the life of the larger society. From the perspective of ethnic minorities, an exclusive focus on individual rights too often fosters either an unwanted assimilation into the dominant society or political marginalization and alienation. These outcomes also have significant costs, even from a liberal individualist perspective. Accordingly, one need not share the communitarian view of liberalism as excessively individualist to conclude that on balance consociational practices are beneficial in societies riven by sharp ethnic cleavages.

---

[128] As Henry Steiner has argued, power-sharing practices both build on and undermine important human rights ideals. Steiner, *supra* note 93, at 1545–46.

From a purely pragmatic standpoint, consociational solutions to ethnic conflict are best evaluated in relation to the available alternatives. When ethnic conflict turns violent, the options are likely to be few and grim. Partition is often suggested; but when ethnic minorities are geographically interspersed, partition can only be accomplished through population exchanges that even in the best of circumstances are likely to be coercive and to violate individual rights. Even more frequently, it is suggested that democracy coupled with respect for human rights will obviate the need for formal power-sharing arrangements. But experience teaches that such solutions are often ineffective or impossible to implement. Most often, ethnic conflict is resolved through the temporary triumph of one group over another, followed by efforts at homogenizing the society either through techniques of assimilation or outright expulsion of undesired ethnic groups. Compared to these alternatives, consociational solutions are likely to represent the least worst alternative in at least some cases. They may compromise some human rights ideals, but they may also help avoid the even greater injustices associated with other possible solutions.[129]

[129] *Id.* at 1547–48.

9

Limiting the Use of Force in Civil Disputes

Ruth Wedgwood

The state has lost its opacity. We look inside the state for a host of purposes. As international realists, we ask how politics and bureaucratic competition may influence national decisions to go to war. We ask under what conditions domestic groups may try to use international institutions as an alternative route to gain an advantage in domestic political debates. As spiritual doctors, we examine how the nation-state treats its own citizens, measuring domestic actions against the human rights standards of treaty instruments and customary international law and the granite face of jus cogens. Domestic legislators must fit their measures on environment, economy, and crime within the many international regimes newly governing domestic subjects. Monism—the integration of the domestic and international—is not the point of view of most Anglo-American judges but here, lay understanding is in advance of the courts.

This penetration of the state—looking beyond a point physics of Westphalia to the underlying structure of national government—is normative and remedial. Voice has been given in international forums to individuals as well as governments. Nongovernmental organizations supply an international civil society as Tocqueville intermediaries between individuals and official authority. Through duties *erge omnes*, individuals gain the intermediation of third-party governments.

But there is a black hole in this normative universe. International law has avoided discourse on the internal processes leading to formation of new states—through secession, partition, or reconfiguration. We linger at a safe positivist distance, observing that states are formed upon the breakup of empires, or struggles for national unification, or wars of decolonization. We are historically specific, admitting the facts on the ground, re-treating from the suggestion of standards, perhaps because in Titanic times law will have little to say and in ordinary times the status quo is abided. Versailles' brute force gave limited play to the ideal of self-deter-mination, reburied by Fascist armies and our acquiescence in Yalta. Afri-can and Asian colonial possessions won independence after the world war by permission of their parent states—a process described by Erik Eriksen through the formation of Gandhi's mature ego but as well the ego of the developing world. For holdout colonial masters, wars of national liberation pressed the point and gained a disputed foothold in interna-tional law—for example, in the attempt to assimilate wars of liberation to international conflict for *jus in bello*,[1] and in the General Assembly's ex-emption of wars of liberation from the definition of aggression.[2] But the historical process was complete before any consensus developed on the law. The civil wars that later burned in Africa and Latin America were insulated from legal discourse by *raison d'état* in the cold war's bipolar strategic conflict.

The war in Yugoslavia has changed this. Fifty years' effort to assure peace in Europe is revealed as anachronistic, addressing the wrong war. The work of Adenauer and Monnet was profoundly important, to be sure. It built a common European identity, stabilizing French-German relations in a deepening economic and political structure. The Euroskepticism of England and Scandinavia—hesitating to join an integrated heartland union—helped to mark the world-historic abandonment of rivalries on the continent. A U.S. security guarantee substituted for traditional bal-ance-of-power politics in Europe, and the cost was borne by the American public because of the dangers of strategic conflict and the need to contain Russia on the east bank of the Elbe.

With the success of the Fifty Years' Peace in Europe, the norm against the instrumental use of war in international relations finally took hold. The ban was not simply precatory but descriptive. Though exceptions had to be made for the *cordon sanitaire* and sphere of influence of each superpower, where intervention to police the affiliative ideology of re-gimes was common, the acceptance of interstate violence was trans-formed. Local wars in Asia and the Middle East were the exception and over relatively quickly. The rhetoric of self-defense demanded by the U.N. Charter had a solid workout but was indeed the tribute paid by vice

---

[1] *See* Protocol Additional to the Geneva Convention of 12 August 1949, and Relating to the Protection of Victims of International Armed Conflicts (Protocol I), art. 1(4), 16 I.L.M. 1391 (1977) (adopted June 8, 1977; entered into force December 7, 1978). *See also* Protocol Addition-al to the Geneva Convention of 12 August 1949, and Relating to the Protection of Victims of Non-International Armed Conflicts (Protocol II), 16 I.L.M. 1442 (1977) (adopted June 8, 1977; entered into force December 7, 1978).

[2] G.A. Res. 3314 (XXIX) (1974).

to virtue. Clausewitzian logic was retired. Interstate war was no longer celebrated as an admissible instrument of international policy. Aberrations are fitted within justifications of self-defense or humanitarian intervention, or, like Iraq's attack on Kuwait, brand the actor as an outlaw state. The use of force between nations must satisfy a vocabulary of self-defense or the advancement of common goods such as democracy or human rights. Countries no longer admit to the use of war for treasure or ambition.

This architecture was a magnificent achievement. The U.N. Charter has not been an insurance policy, to be sure. The Security Council has discretion whether to act on a particular violation of the norms that guarantee territorial integrity and political independence. The Great Powers still are needed for an effective international response. Resources and will are inadequate to assure complete police. The Charter's fluidity may have strengthened the norm; had the duty to respond been absolute, passivity would have seemed corrosive to the rule. Like the pulled punches of John Marshall, the U.N. Charter's incomplete promise of collective response allowed consistency: the norm is absolute, even if the response to violators rests in the judgment of victim, sympathizers, allies, regional organizations, and the United Nations.

The outbreak of civil war in Yugoslavia revealed the incompleteness of this architecture. It is important that a wider war was avoided. The traditional allies of Croatia and Serbia were schooled against conventional fighting over the last fifty years, and each had bigger fish to fry in the early 1990s—Germany in the consummation of Maastricht, Russia in the attempt to stabilize power within the Russian Federation and the CIS. Bosnia is a mountainous cul-de-sac, with no inherent attraction, quite unlike the regional crossroads of Macedonia. The five-nation contact group maintained confidence among the interested powers to prevent the ricochet reaction that caused World War I. Work in the Security Council encouraged patterns of consultation and avoided inadvertent provocation. Consultative practice was well oiled from the Persian Gulf War.

But the incompleteness of the U.N.'s security architecture was apparent in the fears that accompanied the conflict. Would Russia intervene if Serbia came under pressure? Would regional Islamic states overbear the secularism of the Bosnian Muslims? Would Belgrade's ambitions extend to the south and provoke fighting in Kosovo that might draw in Albania? Would Serbia send refugees over the southern border and elicit a reaction by Macedonian militia? The United States's initial disengagement, insisting that the Yugoslav war was primarily a European affair, stemmed in part from the fear that involvement could bring unwanted confrontation with Russia; protegés can engage superpowers. Without the calming example of the Czech and Slovak consensual divorce, the fighting in

Yugoslavia might also have demoralized governance structures else-where in Central Europe.

Civil war and international war enjoy no clear separation. Intervention in civil war precipitates international conflict. The supply of arms to civil combatants may be taken as *casus belli*. Displaced persons and refugees, wandering to avoid battle and ethnic retaliation, overwhelm map bound-aries just as the modern economy's capital flows also cross borders at will and erode local regulation.

The humanitarian problems of civil conflicts have been accepted as an international responsibility. U.N. development work, the structure of human rights law, CNN's expansion of the affective community, and the stubborn faithfulness of Red Cross reporting have made the human security of civilians a matter of wide concern in crisis situations as well as in ordinary circumstances. The agenda of the Security Council, focused on threats to international peace and security, has included the human-itarian challenges of civil conflicts as much as prevention or remedy of interstate war.

The gaping hole in our security architecture consists in the treatment of symptoms only. Dangers of regional destabilization and transborder refu-gee flows, plus urgent necessity, have sufficed to quiet the lawyers and to persuade the Security Council to use its full powers for humanitarian mitigation in cases of civil conflict. Threats to international peace and security under Chapter VII of the U.N. Charter are now read to include civil wars that present gross humanitarian violations, and textbook scru-ple is mustered only to the extent of preferring that the Charter be amended to conform to new practice. Though there is a new scruple about the political consequences of humanitarian aid, no serious voice has pro-posed that the U.N. should withdraw altogether from the business of coordinating and supplying humanitarian aid to areas of severe armed conflict, except to the extent that private groups might be able to perform more effectively because they are less averse to casualties and not identi-fied with security operations. Subsidiarity—the virtue of handling prob-lems at a local level—has not presented much alternative because regional organizations are generally underdeveloped. Private actors still require coordination and diplomatic aid, leaving the U.N. to play the role of representative.

In war crimes, too, the distinction between international and internal armed conflict has eroded. Careful differences between these varieties of conflict were proffered in 1977 to win adherence to the Additional Proto-cols of Geneva. Prisoner-of-war guarantees were held inapplicable to civil war, and universal jurisdiction for prosecution of grave breaches was also limited to international war. The humanitarian guarantees of common Article 3 of the 1949 Geneva Conventions were repeated in Protocol II, applicable to civil war, but enforcement was left to each signatory's self-restraint and initiative.

In the one-two punch of Yugoslavia and Rwanda, this difference has collapsed. The Security Council resolution creating the Yugoslav ad hoc war crimes tribunal deferred finding whether the conflict was international or internal but placed all serious violations of the law of armed conflict within the jurisdiction of the international court, theory to follow.[3] The ethnic cleansing of the war in Bosnia was asymptotic to genocide, cementing the propriety of international scrutiny. In creating a second war crimes tribunal for the Rwanda crisis, the Security Council abandoned any pretense that jus in bello violations in civil war lay outside international scrutiny.[4]

Is it sufficient to internationalize the symptoms of internecine war without worrying about root causes? Confining our focus to individual acts of brutality may, in a troubling sense, be diversionary. The acts of ethnic cleansing and forced migration took place within the studied enterprise of configuring an ethnic state by force. In the attempt to forcibly segregate populations for this purpose, ethnic cleansing no longer appears an individual aberration. Many of the other hardships on civilians result predictably from the fact of war itself—the sieges that attempt to force capitulation, the lapses from decent conduct that occur among embittered combatants whom moral sense abandons. Is it enough to hope that intermittent prosecution of individual violations will improve the standard of future civil conflicts? The question we are bound to ask is whether international law should continue to be agnostic about the use of systematic force in state formation and secession. Why shouldn't the legal presumption against the use of large-scale armed force to settle political and material questions, recognized in U.N. Charter Article 2(4) in interstate settings, be extended as well to intrastate conflicts?

This shift of imaginative paradigm—taking a ban readily accepted in the international setting and applying it domestically—is not simple. The essence of the state, after all, is thought to be the right to use force to make the law effective; so every positivist teaches. There are no natural markers within the state that resemble territorial boundaries to tell which use of force is legitimate police against opportunistic misbehavior and which is questionable. One can judge the legality of the use of force by the standard of domestic law in its ordinary and constitutional forms, but the very enterprise in a civil war is to change the state and the basic law.

---

[3] S.C. Res. 827 (1993). The October 1995 decision of the Hague tribunal reiterated the traditional limits of "grave breaches" jurisdiction under the 1949 Geneva Conventions but concluded that all serious humanitarian breaches could be punished as violations of the law and customs of war.

[4] S.C. Res. 955 (1994).

A standard limiting the use of force in resolving civil conflicts would have to apply, one also assumes, against rebels as well as governments. If the generating principle is concern about the side effects of war on innocent civilians, it does not much matter who initiates the anarchy of violence. If the generating principle is consent as the only acceptable basis for government, it does not matter who exercises the coercion of violence. Yet without the threat of resistance, actors in authority may be tempted to abuse their power; delegitimating the first visible use of force can pave the way for other types of destructive conduct. So, too, one can fairly ask whether we should judge all civil wars by the same standard. Basing political membership on ethnicity may be the culprit as much as the use of force. Certainly there would be less incentive for ethnic cleansing if the end state desired was a polity organized on principles of civic nationalism rather than ethnic nationalism, though in the real world of European constitutional theory and jus sanguinis we are often aware that even universalist political theory can serve as a polite mask for the social expectation of relative ethnic homogeneity.

Nonetheless, one returns to the facts on the ground. Most forms of civil war involve extraordinary violence to noncombatants. The disproportion in resources between insurgents and government often leads weakly endowed rebels to use guerrilla warfare—a method of fighting that systematically endangers innocent civilians by blurring the visible distinctions between combatants and noncombatants. Guerrilla forces often lack the resources to purchase the "smarter" weapons that can function more discriminately between civilians and combatants and often claim to lack the resources to take steps necessary to minimize injuries, such as mapping and marking the location of land mines. Nor should any romanticization of revolution lead one to forget that insurgents often seek to redirect allegiances by showing civilians—in the most direct, cynical, and brutal way—that the government can no longer protect them. So, too, the desire to assert control of territory, when the opponent can't be directly engaged, often leads government forces to scourge the contested area and to forcibly remove the inhabitants who might otherwise supply the guerrillas or be vulnerable to their foraging.

The moral intuition remains. With civil wars now fought by means that are as massively destructive as international conflicts, any humanitarian rationale for limiting the use of interstate force now overflows into intrastate settings. The ferocity of sustained warfare in Bosnia and Chechnya, the proliferation of civil war conflicts, and the clear concentration of modern war's harm on civilians provides adequate reason for the inquiry. In addition, our idealization of democracy—of consent as the foundation of government—entails the question of how to form as well as govern within a polity. The principles of justice and human dignity that lead us to demand consensual government have some application to state formation as well.

International stability is our third motive. Demonstration effects can be powerful. The success of civil violence in consolidating power may encourage potential combatants in a neighboring society to take up arms. Ethnic conflicts can spread; for example, the conflict between Hutus and Tutsis in Rwanda soon migrated across the border to Zaire. The energies of the international community can be sapped by civil war so thoroughly that there is little left to meet interstate conflicts.

Without the resolving power of war, how would decisions be reached on issues of secession, autonomy, and changes in constitutional structure? There is little developed law or sharp-edged determinate "right" answers on questions of state dissolution or constitutional structure. Public international law has recognized a right to democratic governance and free franchise, but has proffered no standards for entitlement to secession or autonomy.[5] Even in political thought we share no general theory of when a nationality or region is entitled to break away. The dangers and costs of secession to the parent government are evident. Geographic or security coherence may be at stake. Structural assistance and investment in infrastructure may have assumed long-term stability. And as the tragedy of Yugoslavia has reminded, the modus vivendi of cultures and nationalities within the larger society may be delicate, and sudden changes in majority-minority status may have a domino effect, at least where institutional guarantees of fair treatment are not assured.[6] Geographic contiguity gives no assurance of an easy break. The traditional residence of a national or cultural group in one geographic area can mask more complicated conditions—a political usufruct, in which other members of the polity have not disputed immediate settlement and use but claim a right to equal access and control. This was, indeed, the claim made by some Serbs and Croats about the administrative configuration of Bosnia and Herzegovina.

From the secessionist's point of view, there are equally compelling problems. A constitutional structure guaranteeing minority rights—in education, access to media, support of cultural organizations, local self-governance and subsidiarity, and some proportioned access to national

[5] Lately, in an autocratic cri de coeur, some nondemocratic governments of Asia and Africa have disputed that the right to participate in government—recognized in the Universal Declaration of Human Rights and the International Covenant on Civil and Political Rights—reflects customary law, jus cogens, or authoritative interpretation of the U.N. Charter. But the widespread adherence to the covenant, the development of additional regional norms such as the OAS Santiago Declaration and OSCE Copenhagen Document, and the institutional commitment of multilateral organizations to election monitoring, show the likely trend.

[6] Slovenia's and Croatia's declarations of independence led the Bosnian republic to hurtle down the same course, despite ample warnings that Bosnian Serbs would not be content to remain as an ethnic minority within Bosnia and would demand affiliation with Serbia.

political power—may seem enough to any outside observer. But it may not allay the distrust created by history and past violence. The political stability that forms the background thinking of a North American of the twentieth century does not come easily to a Central European or other witnesses to upheaval, and the relevant test in a cataclysmic logic is the worst case, not the idealized polity. National and cultural minorities may sense a historical opening—the considered judgment that political structure is amenable to change only in rare moments, when, for example, regional hegemons are preoccupied or international architecture is in flux. In Yugoslavia, the Soviet Union's fall and the new flexing of Germany in the European Community surely had something to do with the self-confidence felt by Slovenia and Croatia in defying the centralism of Belgrade.

We must live with the fact that international law has set no legal standard for when secession should be allowed or what form of constitution a parent government must allow a resistant minority. Indeed, champions of international organization are often as reluctant as parent governments to contemplate the fracturing of existing states. Decision mechanisms strained by expanding from, say, fifteen to twenty-seven voices, as in the likely expansion of the European Union in the next two decades, would be wrecked by a proliferation of microstates. Consensus would not survive as a standard. And the same tempers that give rise to secession can create justified fears of short-sighted decision making more generally. The imperial state that includes many different cultural communities within its boundaries is not considered an anachronism but an admirable attempt at civic coexistence.

With no easily identifiable juridical standards to apply in resolving internal disputes over political power and autonomy, doesn't violence have an attractive decisiveness? Wars end, and parties win. Though war, too, can be irresolute and protracted, can a party be asked to defer to a decision process that is legally indeterminate?

One answer is to set our sights lower, looking for process while remaining agnostic on substance. The duty of parties otherwise inclined to press their suit by arms may be no more than a duty of international exhaustion of remedies. As in any other arena, a duty to bargain in good faith doesn't guarantee agreement. But the very process of negotiation can create confidence, educate both sides on the concerns and latitude of opponents, and buy time. (The joke about the French general "awaiting events" is not so anti-Gallic as some suppose.) It is wise for any cautious traveler to be inoculated against the enthusiastic claims of alternative dispute resolution. Nonetheless, professional mediators are right to point out that it is often not necessary to look for applicable norms outside the arena of the dispute. With a duty to accept mediation, the parties may find standards mutually acceptable, even if one could not have deduced them exogenously. The premise of peacekeeping and preventive deployment is that delay may allow for reconciliation or change of circumstance. The interim accord between Greece and the former Yugoslav Republic of Macedonia is one successful example of the virtues of delay and mediation. Even solutions that might have seemed unattractive can be sweetened by the ability of the mediators to add to the pot, as the United States offered full diplomatic relations to Macedonia as an incentive to continue plugging on in the negotiations with Greece.

The institutional mechanisms for an obligation to exhaust peaceful means of mediation could be several. The OSCE commissioner on national minorities, the OSCE Office for Democratic Institutions and Human Rights, and Robert Badinter's new OSCE mechanism for reconciliation, suitably adapted, could fill the role. Special representatives appointed by the U.N. secretary-general and by regional organizations have functioned remarkably well in recent civil conflicts in Mozambique, Sierra Leone, and El Salvador.[7]

One could conceive of a second more radical step—a duty to resort to arbitration. If there are no established standards for resolution of questions of federal structure, autonomy, or even independence, neither are there any established standards for error. Whether or not there are justiciable rules, in a classical adjudicatory sense, there may be principles of reasonableness, a range of admissible solutions, and a duty to abide by any reasonable decision of the international community rather than resort to an adjudication by force. This is satisficing, not maximizing; but there is no reason to believe that violence gives a better approximation of a theory of justice. In a particular case of persistent violation of an established constitution and gross violation of human rights by a dominant ethnic majority, for example, a geographically compact minority's claim for substantial autonomy or independence could be persuasive. It could be made subject to conditions that respect the reliance interests of the former parent, including rights of passage, repayment of existing investments, long-term supply contracts from essential industries, and security guarantees. Again, the institutional vehicles are several. The Permanent Court of Arbitration in the Hague has issued new rules for disputes between state and nonstate entities. One could use specially appointed arbitration commissions, including arbiters appointed by the Security Council under Article 29 of the U.N. Charter. International courts can sit *ex aequo et bono*, using the power of analogy and test of experience, even where there is no single right answer.

For if there is no right answer, many answers aren't wrong. The desire

---

[7] *See* Cameron R. Hume, *The Secretary-General's Representatives*, SAIS REV. 75–90 (Summer–Fall 1995).

of a political or ethnic minority is, as often as not, to assure that there is some engagement and commitment by the international community; indeed, that is often the purpose of violence in the first place, not the belief that violence will decisively settle a dispute. To that extent, a duty of exhaustion runs in both directions. It assumes the willingness of the international community to provide a forum and the political attention to support mediatory and arbitral processes in seriously riven countries. It extends the domain of international attention from the analytically simpler tasks of human rights to the profession of political hand tailoring, bespoke suits that fit a particular political history, state of conflict, surviving strands of fellow feeling, and possible common advantage. It would require that statesmen apprised of serious civil disputes not reply that the matter is solely an internal affair, as the U.N. did initially in regard to Slovenian independence and the United States did when first pressed on attitudes toward Russian repression in Chechnya.

A duty of exhaustion is, if you like, the complement of preventive diplomacy. In a time of depleted foreign aid and donor fatigue, there has been great skepticism that preventive diplomacy will cure any political disease. There are too many conflicts, development strategies are too uncertain, and, in any event, political unrest may be fed by rising expectations. But a strong normative duty, embraced by the South as much as the North, to submit to scrutiny and mediation, even arbitration by suitable institutions, is one way of testing whether there is any strength in the brew.

One could abandon the model of a general legal duty to exhaust peaceful remedies and instead address the use of force in civil wars though the discretionary decisions of the Security Council. This would allow one to dodge some of the analytic problems of distinguishing ordinary police from civil war and to accommodate Whiggish worries of preserving a suitable right to resist. Simply, where fighting has become excessively destructive or destabilizing, the Security Council would have the authority to require a cease-fire by the parties, without their consent, and even to impose a peace plan. In the real political world, one wishes to avoid hollow pronouncements and hortatory statements. The Security Council would wisely reserve its action to cases where international resolve, available resources, and the ripeness of the dispute will support effective intervention. But the test case may again be Bosnia. If the fighting had continued indefinitely without agreement on a peace plan or map, could not the Security Council at some point have imposed a cease-fire even without party consent? The Dayton peace plan quietly embodies this model, in the alternative. Though the map establishing the Republika Srpska and the Muslim-Croat Federation within the new Bosnian state was drawn with the consent of the parties and embodied in a treaty instrument, the Security Council has directly authorized the use of force under Chapter VII to police violations of these *internal* borders, even if the parties withdraw their consent to the treaty.

Agnosticism toward intrastate violence is ripe for a change. An inductivist might argue the change has already occurred: we are waiting for eyes to open, for the other shoe to drop. The birth of a new norm delegitimating intrastate violence helps to give coherence to the international community's decision to recognize the breakaway Yugoslav republics, impose sanctions against Serbia, and impose an arms embargo on unequally armed former Yugoslav republics.

As has been widely observed, Germany's goading of the European Community to recognize the breakaway republics of Yugoslavia in late 1991 was a startling event. Europe has intervened in civil war disputes before: there was early recognition of Greece in its revolution against Turkey, and the London Conference recognized Belgium in 1831, long before fighting in the revolution against the Netherlands had ceased. Nonetheless, in classical international law, premature recognition of a secessionist entity is considered a belligerent act, and recognition is improperly premature so long as fighting has not yet ceased. Germany announced in midsummer 1991 that it intended to recognize Croatia and Slovenia as breakaway republics and half-nelsoned other European Community members on the evening of December 16, 1991, reversing an initial vote of three to twelve against recognition into a vote of fifteen to zero for recognition, spurning the urgent letters of Cyrus Vance and Javier Perez de Cuellar warning that a delay in recognition was needed to preserve some incentive for the republics to continue negotiating a confederal structure in the Hague Conference. Germany's action has been dismissed by some as a revival of German lebensraum, carving out a role for Germany as docent to Central Europe. Others more kindly explain it as the result of coincidence because the Soviet Union and Tito's federation were in extremis together and because a newly unified Germany completing its national bildungsroman felt it could not deny cultural arrival to any other nation. But the explanation that any member of the German foreign ministry will proffer, ardently, is that the recognition was supposed to stop the fighting. The internationalization of the borders, and invocation of the ban on interstate force, was, in German eyes, desirable as a way to deter Serbia's use of force to preserve the Yugoslav federation.

This act of recognition was radical by classical standards. The new conditions for recognition set out by the European Community[8]—that a

---

[8] Declaration on Yugoslavia, Extraordinary European Political Cooperation Ministerial Meeting, December 16, 1991, 31 I.L.M. 1485 (1992), *incorporating by reference* Declaration on the Guidelines on the Recognition of New States in Eastern Europe and the Soviet Union, December 16, 1991, 31 I.L.M. 1486 (1992).

republic respect minority rights, the rule of law, democracy, and civil liberties—are welcome additions to the traditional minima of the Montevideo Convention,[9] suitable to the Europe of the Paris Charter and Copenhagen Document. Recognition was assimilated rather closely to the political minima of the European Community, as if recognition and membership were the same. But the E.C. ministers took the extraordinary step of dispensing with the minimum Montevideo condition of effective control of territory, allowing recognition even where fighting had not ceased. This is all the more challenging because wartime stresses any effective rule of law. The E.C. decision may be glossed as quietly assuming that the attempt to preserve a polity by use of massive force is illegitimate and deserves little deference. Recognition of the breakaway republics internationalized their boundaries and outlawed Yugoslavia's centripetal violence. The Security Council's economic embargo imposed on the Federal Republic of Yugoslavia in 1992 to force the withdrawal of Yugoslav army forces from Bosnia and Herzegovina may be read in the same light—denying the legitimacy of using force to maintain the existence of the federation.[10]

The U.N. arms embargo imposed on all Yugoslav republics—originally at the request of Serbian President Slobodan Milosevic but maintained after recognition of the secessionist republics—can also be understood as the implicit statement that civil conflicts are not conducted as of right.[11] In an ordinary defensive war, the choice of weapons is left to the combatant; the international community assumes at most the right to rule out especially inhumane or indiscriminate weapons. But here, the Security Council asserted the right to limit how a civil war was fought, even at the cost of effective independence on the part of the Bosnian Muslims. If one takes the recognition decisions literally, the arms embargo makes no sense. The Security Council was surely not asserting the power to legislate the extinction of a recognized state (the Republic of Bosnia and Herzegovina) in the interests of regional stability. The inherent right of self-defense, recognized in Article 51, has never before shrunk to such a desiccated state. But the arms embargo can be given coherence as the statement that there is at best a limited right to use arms to wage a civil conflict.

A norm disallowing force is ambitious. The international community will not choose to become involved in every dispute and often will not act to suppress fighting. But some rule compliance comes voluntarily; nations value the opinion of other states, wish to be eligible for membership in voluntary associations and to gain esteem in the capital markets. Most of

[9] Convention on the Rights and Duties of States, 49 Stat. 3097, T.S. 881, 165 L.N.T.S. 19 (Montevideo, December 26, 1933).
[10] S.C. Res. 757 (1992).
[11] S.C. Res. 713 (1991).

the enforcement of the U.N. Charter comes through self-limitation. In some matters where one might fear a North-South split, the South has become a strong pillar for world opinion, as in the disdain for nuclear proliferation that has isolated rogue states.

A norm disallowing force could have very practical consequences, even after it is violated. In particular, in the Bosnian conflict, the willingness of the parties to agree on a map could have been affected, one may suppose, by the Security Council's assertion of unilateral authority to impose a map. NATO's reluctance to apply air power to respond to the shelling of Dubrovnik, Vukovar, and Sarajevo or to enforce a general cease-fire occurred for many reasons, but one was a perceived want of authority. The United Nations did not claim the right to call a halt to the conflict. Air power was eventually used to enforce the last safe zones and to provide close support to peacekeepers on the ground, and American policymakers cheerfully noted that this might soften the Bosnian Serb position on an overall settlement. But before Dayton, the NATO alliance was unable and unwilling to say that it had the prerogative to apply air power to any side that renewed an offensive because the basic inadmissibility of the use of force in civil war settings had not yet been announced.

Where parties linger and decline to reach a settlement, this new norm could be exquisitely important. In the constitutional separation of powers, the competing theories of the legitimate powers of each branch induce each to seek cooperation. So, too, the assertion of a right by the Security Council to draw and enforce a map is a likely way to concentrate parties' minds. A general duty to refrain from the use of force in civil disputes, or a discretionary right of the council to impose such a duty, would have allowed NATO to suppress new attacks early in the war and end the peekaboo of coy combatants who would not agree to anything accepted by their opponents.

Problems of defining the scope of allowable self-defense will still remain, of course. Where one side attacks in violation of a norm against use of force to resolve internal disputes, it makes no sense to require the other to flee or cringe before the assault. It would too easily invite violation of the norm. Article 51 of the U.N. Charter, with its controversial applications, has at times seemed a casuist's constraint, only requiring that jurists distend the word *self-defense* rather than describing how countries actually behave. But the native right of self-preservation cannot be easily set aside. At the same time, the right of self-defense is often taken to the limit, permitting the innocent party to seek the unconditional defeat of the erring party. In the case of domestic antagonists who must live together at close quarters, perhaps a more tailored doctrine of self-defense will be necessary. Should we see George Bush's halt shy of Baghdad as an amendment even of the interstate rule? Rolf Ekeus's special commission on Iraq, dismantling weapons systems and production facilities, has substituted for the blunter destruction formerly worked by raw power in the course of a full-court defense.

The use of force in situations of ethnic rivalry is especially troublesome if we feel any scruple about racial animus. Jus sanguinis as a test of citizenship, gathering in the flock based on blood rather than place of birth, has a link more easily seen by Americans than Europeans to the instrument of ethnic cleansing. Bloody Kansas was the natural concomitant of Stephen Douglas's popular sovereignty: where crucial decisions on territorial slavery were to be taken by the population actually present, the ground was fought over. So ethnic cleansing is the natural concomitant of ethnic civil war. Terror creates facts on the ground, the association of land and people, that tends to shape the eventual partition. In a sense all wars are genocidal in spirit; to muster fighting spirit, each government tends to harness the crudest racial sentiment, designating the enemy by names one hesitates to repeat on paper. But in a situation of intimate neighborhood, where the parties will continue living side by side, even if under separate sovereigns, the devil's special brew mixing violence and racialism is all the more dangerous to future stability. Whatever one's view on civil conflicts in general, an international norm against use of force in questions of ethnic secession makes good sense.

10

Genocide and Ethnic Conflict

Lori Fisler Damrosch

The fiftieth anniversary of the United Nations General Assembly declaration against genocide calls for sober reflection on our collective failure to prevent and punish genocide as a crime under international law.[1] Within two years the high aims of that declaration had been translated into the Convention on the Prevention and Punishment of the Crime of Genocide, yet that legally binding instrument has served neither to prevent nor to punish genocide.[2] Indeed, in the 1990s alone the staggering toll of human beings killed by reason of their group membership gives the lie to virtually all of the provisions of the Genocide Convention, except for the preambular recital that "at all periods of history genocide has inflicted great losses on humanity."[3]

Many of the defects in the Genocide Convention were evident from its inception and have attracted ample attention in the literature.[4] Among the best-known are (1) the decision taken in 1948 to confine the substantive

[1] Resolution on the Crime of Genocide, G.A. Res. 96(1) (December 11, 1946).

[2] Convention on the Prevention and Punishment of the Crime of Genocide, *opened for signature* December 9, 1948, 78 U.N.T.S. 277 [hereinafter Genocide Convention].

[3] *Id.* 2d preambular paragraph.

[4] Two important studies aimed at overcoming such defects were prepared under the auspices of the Sub-Commission on Prevention of Discrimination and Protection of Minorities of the Economic and Social Council of the United Nations. *See Study of the Question of the Prevention and Punishment of the Crime of Genocide* (N. Ruhashyankiko, Special Rapporteur), U.N. Doc. E/CN.4/Sub.2/416, July 4, 1978 [hereinafter Ruhashyankiko Report], and *Revised and Updated Report on the Question of the Prevention and Punishment of the Crime of Genocide* (B. Whitaker, Special Rapporteur), U.N. Doc. E/CN.4/Sub.2/1985/6, July 2, 1985 [hereinafter Whitaker Report]. For scholarly treatments, *see, e.g.,* GENOCIDE: CONCEPTUAL AND HISTORICAL DIMENSIONS (George J. Andreopoulos ed., 1994); ISRAEL W. CHARNY, GENOCIDE: A CRITICAL BIBLIOGRAPHY, vols. 1 & 2 (1988 and 1991).

scope of the convention to the protection of "national, ethnical, racial and religious" groups, while omitting comparable protection for political, economic, social, or other groups,[5] and (2) the reliance for criminal enforcement on tribunals "of the State in the territory of which the act was committed,"[6] notwithstanding the likelihood in most circumstances that such tribunals would remain under the sway of the very rulers who either directed or condoned the genocidal acts in the first place. These two defects—the first of conception, the second of implementation—are only the most blatant of the debilitating compromises that had to be made between 1946 and 1948 in order to produce a legal instrument with any hope of widespread acceptance.

Yet even this watered-down outcome commanded neither universal nor unqualified adherence. Among the early ratifiers, the Soviet Union and its satellites refused to be bound by the article providing for dispute settlement through the International Court of Justice; that court in due course gave its approval to such unilateral limitations of obligation, in the interests of facilitating acceptance of the substantive core of the convention by states that would not have ratified on an all-or-nothing basis.[7] Even worse, the United States did not become bound by the convention until 1989 and then only with conditions addressed not just to procedural aspects but also to the substantive core.[8]

This chapter will consider the legal definition of genocide in situations of ethnic conflict as well as questions of implementation through the legal institutions available to address such conflicts. My focus will be on integrating the substantive premises of the Genocide Convention—that genocide is a crime that *individual* human beings can and do commit against certain kinds of human groups and for which *states* can also be responsible—with effective implementation through workable institutions. Accordingly, Part I will consider conceptual problems in the definition of genocide in situations of ethnic conflicts, including problems having to do with the scope of protection afforded to ethnical (along with national, racial, and religious) groups as well as the difficulties arising when an ethnic group becomes embroiled in an armed conflict. Part II will turn to an examination of the shortcomings of the principal enforcement forums

[5] Genocide Convention, *supra* note 2, art. II.

[6] *Id.* art. VI.

[7] Reservations to the Convention on Genocide, 1951 ICJ Reports 15 (Advisory Opinion).

[8] The U.S. Senate gave advice and consent to ratification in 1986, but deposit of the U.S. instrument of ratification was delayed until November 25, 1988, following the enactment of implementing legislation. The convention entered into force for the United States on February 23, 1989. *See* MULTILATERAL TREATIES DEPOSITED WITH THE SECRETARY-GENERAL: STATUS AS OF 31 DECEMBER 1995, U.N. Doc. ST/LEG/SER.E/14 at 87, 90; DEPARTMENT OF STATE, TREATIES IN FORCE AS OF JAN. 1, 1995, at 358. The U.S. instrument of ratification contains two reservations and five understandings, some of which have important substantive implications (for discussion see text at notes 39, 52, 58).

specified by the Genocide Convention—domestic courts for cases against individuals and the International Court of Justice for claims of state responsibility—and will conclude by addressing the potential for overcoming those shortcomings through newly created and prospective international criminal tribunals.

My reflections about the Genocide Convention grow out of my involvement with the efforts of Human Rights Watch, a New York–based nongovernmental organization, to document and seek accountability for genocide committed against the Kurds of Iraq. Human Rights Watch has obtained, analyzed, and published overwhelming proof that in the waning days of the Iran-Iraq War, specifically in 1987–88, Iraq successfully waged a brutal war of extermination against its own Kurdish population. As many as 100,000 Kurds were killed through chemical weapons and firing squads in one of the clearest cases of genocide since World War II.[9] The obstacles to obtaining an authoritative juridical ruling on the legal consequences of these facts illustrate the importance of correlating a conceptually satisfactory definition of the crime of genocide with effective mechanisms for enforcement. Ambiguities in the convention's definition of genocide should be resolved through interpretations that would advance rather than thwart the convention's object and purpose: to prevent *and* punish genocide.[10]

I. CONCEPTUAL AND DEFINITIONAL QUESTIONS

An unavoidable tension complicates every effort to articulate and give effect to a legal definition of genocide. On the one hand, we have the sense that genocide is perhaps *the* ultimate crime and a consequent reluctance to trivialize the term by applying it uncritically to lesser forms of human brutality.[11] Yet on the other hand, we are concerned that, if the definitional threshold is set too high, only a consummated evil rivaling the Holocaust could qualify as genocide. The former tendency pushes toward a

---

[9] *See* HUMAN RIGHTS WATCH, IRAQ'S CRIME OF GENOCIDE (1995); HUMAN RIGHTS WATCH, GENOCIDE IN IRAQ: THE ANFAL CAMPAIGN AGAINST THE KURDS (1993). For even higher estimates (200,000 in 1988 alone), see DAVID MCDOWALL, A MODERN HISTORY OF THE KURDS (1996).

[10] *See* Vienna Convention on the Law of Treaties, art. 31, U.N. Doc. A/CONF 39/27 (1969) (a treaty is to be interpreted in light of its object and purpose).

[11] Genocide and aggression would be the two leading contenders for this place of dishonor. The Nuremberg Tribunal said that the initiation of a war of aggression "is not only an international crime; it is the supreme international crime differing only from other war crimes in that it contains within itself the accumulated evil of the whole." Judgment of the International Military Tribunal, Nuremberg, September 30, 1946, *reprinted in* 41 AM. J. INT'L L. 172, 186 (1946). For the view that genocide is "the ultimate crime," *see, e.g.*, Whitaker Report, *supra* note 4, at 5.

strict definition of genocide,[12] the latter toward a more flexible, pragmatic approach.[13]

For reasons to be discussed in Part II, juridical bodies have not yet given an authoritative interpretation of the Genocide Convention. Political leaders can pass judgment with fewer inhibitions; thus, it has become routine to condemn the mass slaughters in the former Yugoslavia, Rwanda, and elsewhere as genocide (or "genocidal," which may connote a broader set of circumstances, just as "murderous" has a more elastic meaning than "murder"). Even so, the political organs of the international community have been cautious in their application of the concept. The U.N. Security Council, for example, has condemned ethnic cleansing in the former Yugoslavia as "unlawful," "unacceptable," and "abhorrent"[14] but has deferred to other U.N. bodies for a substantive judgment as to whether ethnic cleansing in the Yugoslav conflict constitutes genocide.[15]

Two different kinds of judicial bodies are now being asked to apply the legal definition of genocide in concrete circumstances: (1) the International Court of Justice, which is seized with a claim concerning the responsibility of the Federal Republic of Yugoslavia (Serbia and Montenegro)

[12] In this vein, see, e.g., Alain Destekhe, The Third Genocide, 97 FOREIGN POL'Y 3, 4–5 (Winter 1994–95) ("Genocide is a singular and exclusive category of crime rarely seen this century. . . . [R]egardless of the scale of the crimes committed by Stalin, Mao, or Pol Pot, they were not genocide."). Destekhe would restrict the list of twentieth-century genocides to three—the Armenians by the Turks in 1915–16; the Nazi slaughter of Jews, Gypsies, and other minorities; and the massacre of Tutsis by Hutu militias in Rwanda in 1994. It should be evident from the discussion to follow that I believe his restrictive approach improperly detracts from the legitimate use of the Genocide Convention to prevent and punish such ethnically targeted crimes as those directed at the Kurds of Iraq or the Muslims of Bosnia. The Cambodian nightmare falls somewhat outside the scope of this volume (because its ethnic dimension— the "mini-genocides." of Vietnamese and other minorities—was minimal in comparison to the slaughter of Khmers by Khmers for non-ethnic reasons). For an able legal analysis of the Cambodian situation, see JASON S. ABRAMS & STEVEN R. RATNER, ACCOUNTABILITY FOR HUMAN RIGHTS ATROCITIES IN INTERNATIONAL LAW: BEYOND THE NUREMBERG LEGACY (1997).

[13] The Whitaker Report enumerates the following as nonexclusive examples of twentieth-century genocides, in addition to the Holocaust: "the German massacre of Hereros in 1904, the Ottoman massacre of Armenians in 1915–1916, the Ukrainian pogrom of Jews in 1919, the Tutsi massacre of Hutu in Burundi in 1965 and 1972, the Paraguayan massacre of Ache Indians prior to 1974, the Khmer Rouge massacre in Kampuchea between 1975 and 1978, and the contemporary Iranian killings of Baha'is." Whitaker Report, supra note 4, at 9–10 (citations omitted).

[14] S.C. Res. 819 (April 16, 1993).

[15] The legal question is pending before the International Court of Justice. See Case Concerning Application of the Convention on the Prevention and Punishment of the Crime of Genocide (Bosnia and Herzegovina v. Yugoslavia [Serbia and Montenegro]), 1993 I.C.J. Reports 3, 325 (Orders of April 8 and September 13, 1993, on Requests for Provisional Measures). In the resolution cited in the preceding note, the Security Council took note of the ICJ's order calling on Yugoslavia (Serbia-Montenegro) to do everything in its power to prevent the commission of genocide in Bosnia. For political condemnation of genocide in Bosnia by the U.N. General Assembly, see G.A. Res. 47/121 (1993); G.A. Res. 48/143 (1993); G.A. Res. 48/153 (1993).

under the Genocide Convention for actions committed in Bosnia-Her-zegovina, and (2) the International Criminal Tribunals for the former Yugoslavia and Rwanda, which have been created by the Security Council to adjudicate the criminal liability of individuals. Though these bodies have different forms of jurisdiction (the first involving responsibility on the state-to-state level, the second involving the prosecution of individuals), they will be applying the same legal definition of genocide, found in Article II of the Genocide Convention, which reads:

In the present convention, genocide means any of the following acts committed with intent to destroy, in whole or in part, a national, ethnical, racial or religious group, as such:

(a) Killing members of the group;

(b) Causing serious bodily or mental harm to members of the group;

(c) Deliberately inflicting on the group conditions of life calculated to bring about its physical destruction in whole or in part;

(d) Imposing measures intended to prevent births within the group;

(e) Forcibly transferring children of the group to another group.

I will now look at certain issues concerning the protection of ethnic groups under this definition and then will turn to issues arising when an ethnic group suffers in the course of an armed conflict.

A. "National, Ethnical, Racial, or Religious Group, As Such"

The effort in the Genocide Convention to codify a definition of the crime of genocide raises fundamental questions intimately linked to major themes of this volume. In common with several of the chapters, including those by Brilmayer and Tesón, we need to reflect here on the philosophical underpinnings of rule structures conferring legal protections on certain human groups when such protections would be unavailable to other kinds of groups or even to large numbers of individuals outside the framework of a protected group. But in contrast to Brilmayer and Tesón, whose concern is ethnic or national groups as aspirants to a privileged status (such as separate statehood or autonomy), my concern here is the protection of groups against physical extermination. Those (in this volume and elsewhere) who have denied that ethnicity or nationality should form a legitimate basis for group demands for special privileges might look with greater sympathy on the decision to create a legal regime for protecting such groups from physical destruction.

Such, at least, was the thinking in the aftermath of the Nuremberg trials as the draft of the Genocide Convention took shape. Following the insight of Raphael Lemkin, who coined the term *genocide*, the idea was that the destruction of groups qua groups is an especially heinous crime, not only because of the mass scale of group-directed violence but also because of the qualitative value attached to preservation of human communities from mortal attacks.[16]

On the one hand, the convention shields group members from life-threatening persecution on the basis of certain involuntary, immutable, or ascriptive characteristics, such as the ethnic community into which one is born. But on the other hand, to the extent that the convention endorses a vision of group-based community life, it does so only with respect to the specific kinds of groups enumerated in Article II's definition and only with respect to particularly vicious kinds of physical attacks. As a result, if three schemes of equal brutality were carried out—one on the basis of random terror, another targeted against political opponents or economic or social classes, and the third against a "national, ethnical, racial or religious group"—only the last would constitute genocide under the convention.

Nonetheless, it would be misleading to view the Genocide Convention as addressed solely to violence against groups defined exclusively on the basis of immutable characteristics such as the color of one's skin. Admittedly, an undertone of this philosophy runs through certain aspects of the *travaux préparatoires*. For example, at least some delegates explained the decision not to accord comparable protection to political groups on the basis that political affiliation is much more a matter of personal choice than the way one looks or the community into which one is born.[17] But the protections of the Genocide Convention are not restricted only to groups that are determined by some objective condition or accident of birth. Indeed, the convention protects ethnical groups even though (and perhaps because) ethnicity is to some extent a matter of choices and perceptions rather than immutable features. These choices and perceptions can emanate from individuals and groups, or they can be imposed on individuals and groups by outsiders such as the state.

In liberal societies, of course, both the degree of ethnic cohesiveness and

---

[16] RAPHAEL LEMKIN, AXIS RULE IN OCCUPIED EUROPE (1944); *see also* Lemkin, *Genocide As a Crime under International Law*, 41 AM. J. INT'L L. 146 (1947).

[17] *See, e.g.*, the remarks of Mr. Abdoh of Iran: "If it were recognized that there was a distinction between those groups, membership of which was inevitable, such as racial, religious or national groups, whose distinctive features were permanent; and those, membership of which was voluntary, such as political groups, whose distinctive features were not permanent, it must be admitted that the destruction of the first type appeared most heinous in the light of the conscience of humanity, since it was directed against human beings whom chance alone had grouped together. Those persons should therefore be given a larger measure of protection. Although it was true that people could change their nationality or their religion, such changes did not in fact happen very often; national and religious groups therefore belonged to the category of groups, membership of which was inevitable." U.N. GAOR, 6th comm., 3d sess., 1st part, 74th meeting at 99 (1948) [hereinafter 6th comm., 74th meeting].

the ability of individuals to choose or ignore an ethnic identity are highly fluid. In repressive societies, however, and especially in those that we might label pre-genocidal, the state influences and coerces such choices to a dangerous degree. In such societies, ethnicity has historically been a matter not only of an individual's subjective decision to align with a group but also of governmentally manipulated pressures attaching consequences to that decision. Such manipulations may tend either toward coerced denial of group life and disaffiliation from the group's heritage (as in the case of the Kurds of contemporary Turkey, where even speaking the Kurdish language has been penalized) or, what can be even worse, coerced identification of group members as a factual predicate for governmentally directed actions against the group, as in the case of the Kurds of Iraq in 1987–88.

As Human Rights Watch has explained, the Iraqi regime's treatment of the Kurds followed Raul Hilberg's classic paradigm of genocide, in which the group is first defined and thereafter channeled into concentrated locations to facilitate annihilation.[18] In the census immediately preceding the Anfal campaign of 1987–88, all Iraqis were required to register as either "Arab" or "Kurd." About the same time, the government identified areas consisting solely of Kurdish villages and demarcated them as "prohibited zones"; no Arab villages were located in these zones.[19] Through the census, Kurds living in the zones were offered the possibility of "return to the national ranks," which meant that they could accept the government's offer of resettlement outside their ancestral lands.[20] Kurds who failed to register in the census were treated as having forfeited Iraqi citizenship;[21] those who remained within the prohibited zones instead of returning to the national ranks were targets for physical extermination under government orders calling for the destruction of all animal and human life within

[18] Hilberg wrote that the only way in which a scattered group can be effectively destroyed is through the three steps of definition, concentration (or seizure), and annihilation: "This is the invariant structure of the basic process, for no group can be killed without a concentration or seizure of the victims, and no victims can be segregated *before the perpetrator knows who belongs to the group*." RAUL HILBERG, DESTRUCTION OF THE EUROPEAN JEWS 267 (1985), *quoted in* IRAQ'S CRIME OF GENOCIDE, *supra* note 9, at 4–5 (emphasis added in order to stress the point that the perpetrator may compel identifications different from those the group members might themselves choose or may attach draconian consequences to self-identifications).

[19] Smaller minorities inhabiting the same region, such as Chaldean Christians, Assyrians, and Yazidis, had fateful consequences to their choice of ethnic identification: if they registered as Arabs in the census, their villages were excluded from the prohibited zones, but if they were identified as Kurds, they were vulnerable to the Kurds' fate.

[20] This is not to say that all Kurds could have escaped physical destruction through a mere switch of loyalties or change of residence. Indeed, Anfal victims included those Kurds, known derisorily as the Jahsh ("donkey foals"), who had opted to serve as tools of the regime. But the offer of return to the national ranks was the last clear opportunity to avoid the extermination campaign that began with a vengeance (double meaning intended) shortly after the census.

[21] IRAQ'S CRIME OF GENOCIDE, *supra* note 9, at 6–7, 300–301.

the prohibited zones.[22] By the combination of compelling an ethnic identification, defining the prohibited zones so that only Kurds were included within them, and prohibiting all human life within the zones, the Iraqi regime laid the groundwork for genocide.

As this illustration suggests, a governmental decision to require individuals to declare their ethnicity can be fraught with consequences directly linked to the government's plans for destruction of the group. In such circumstances, it is hardly relevant to think in terms of subjective individual decisions to affiliate or disaffiliate with particular groups. Of course, the same can also be true of governmental pressures to choose or renounce a religion or to accept or reject a particular racial or national classification. To this extent, the four protected categories—national, ethnical, racial, and religious groups—have much in common.

We now can turn our attention to the question of what constitutes an ethnical group under the Genocide Convention and related legal instruments. The convention itself does not provide a definition of the term *ethnical* (nor, indeed, of any of the other potentially contested terms in Article II or elsewhere).[23]

The travaux préparatoires do shed some light on how the drafters conceived of a distinction between ethnical and other groups. The term was added to the list of protected groups by the U.N. General Assembly's Sixth (Legal) Committee on an amendment offered by the Swedish delegate. He explained that if the term *national group* implied a relationship to a nation-state, "then the convention would not extend protection to such groups if the State ceased to exist or if it were only in the process of formation."[24] Moreover, factors other than race or religion should be taken into consideration:

> In Switzerland, for instance, the whole of the traditions of a group, with its cultural and historical heritage, had to be taken into account. In other cases, the constituent factor of a group would be its language. . . . If a linguistic group were unconnected with an existing State, it would not be protected as a national group, but it could be protected as an ethnical group.
>
> The concept of a racial group was often ill-defined. Its race was not always the dominating characteristic of a group, which might rather be defined by the whole of its traditions and its cultural heritage.

[22] *Id.* at 5, 11–13.

[23] In adopting implementing legislation for the convention, the U.S. Congress did supply a definition of *ethnic group,* as "a set of individuals whose identity as such is distinctive in terms of common cultural traditions or heritage." 18 U.S.C. 1093 (2). This legislative definition has not yet come before a court for interpretation or application because no prosecutions have been brought in U.S. courts under the Genocide Convention.

[24] U.N. GAOR, 6th comm., 3d sess., 1st part, 73d–75th meetings, at 97, 115 (1948).

Addition of the ethnical group would make it possible both to clarify those ideas, and to extend protection to doubtful cases.[25]

That the Swedish proposal was adopted by eighteen votes to seventeen with eleven abstentions indicates that this was hardly an uncontroversial drafting change.[26]

Following the addition of ethnical to the list of protected groups, the drafting process reached one of its best-known decisions: to delete "political groups" from the draft convention.[27] Several objections had been expressed to protection of political groups within the ambit of the convention: one such objection, having to do with the relative mutability of political beliefs and associations as compared to other forms of group identification, has already been mentioned. In addition, some delegates argued that a U.N. convention should not intrude into the manner in which governments might deal with insurrections or other manifestations of political opposition, and they predicted that protection of political groups would make it impossible for a large number of states to ratify the convention.[28]

The decision not to protect political groups has had deleterious consequences not only for the application of the convention to situations in which unprotected political groups have themselves been targeted for extermination but also for situations in which explicitly protected groups—national, ethnical, racial, or religious—have been targeted for allegedly political reasons, either instead of or in addition to reasons having to do with group identity "as such." If an ethnic group serves as one locus of political opposition to an incumbent regime, for example, then a "defense" to the charge of genocide might be that the measures in question were intended to eliminate political opponents and not to destroy an ethnic group as such. I put the term *defense* in quotation marks because I believe that under a proper interpretation of the Genocide Convention, such an argument should fail.

A vivid illustration of this problem comes from the tragic situation in Rwanda, in which (according to most accounts) hundreds of thousands of

25 *Id.*

26 *Id.* at 115. Most objections raised during the discussion leading up to the vote had to do with perceptions of overlap with the concept of national group on the one hand and racial group on the other. The controversial question of protection of "political" groups had not yet been resolved and overshadowed the discussion of the Swedish amendment.

27 The draft had been prepared by an ad hoc committee of the Economic and Social Council and then went to the General Assembly's Sixth (Legal) Committee. The Sixth Committee initially retained protection of political groups by a vote of twenty-nine to thirteen with nine abstentions (*see* 6th comm., 74th meeting, *supra* note 17, at 115), but this decision was later reversed. *See* U.N. Docs. A/C.6/245 (October 23, 1948), A/760 and A/760/Corr. 2 (December 3 & 6, 1948).

28 *See, e.g.,* Statement of Mr. Abdoh of Iran, 6th comm., 74th meeting, *supra* note 17, at 99.

ethnic Tutsis and smaller but still substantial numbers of politically moderate Hutus were massacred in the first days of the crisis beginning in April 1994.[29] If the decimation of the Tutsi community would otherwise have met the definitional element of "intent to destroy, in whole or in part, a national, ethnical, racial or religious group, as such," then is that genocide rendered any less genocidal by virtue of the fact that political opponents were slaughtered as well? The rhetorical question suggests its own answer: but the difficulty remains that, because "intent" usually has to be inferred from observable phenomena rather than from direct windows into the psyche, the fact that moderate Hutus were killed along with ethnic Tutsis could complicate the process of proving to the satisfaction of the trier of fact the requisite intent to destroy the Tutsi ethnic group "as such."[30]

The correct interpretation of the Genocide Convention as a matter of law is that, although merely political groups are not protected, the explicit protection given to ethnic groups cannot be defeated by a contention that a particular ethnic group was really a political group, nor can a political motive for destruction of an ethnic group defeat that group's protection. Ethnic groups do not lose protection under the convention even if they include (or even consist almost entirely of) political opponents. The protracted consideration in the preparatory work of the distinction between *intent* and *motive* supports this interpretation. The drafters rejected alternative formulations that would have attached legal significance to the motive for the acts committed; instead, they adopted the "intent . . . as such" formulation. The reason for the clarification was succinctly articulated by the delegate of the United Kingdom to the Sixth Committee, Mr. Fitzmaurice: "Once the intent to destroy a group existed, that was genocide, whatever reasons the perpetrators of the crime might allege. [A phrase enumerating motives][31] was not merely useless; it was dangerous, for its limitative nature would enable those who committed a crime of genocide to claim that they had not committed that crime on grounds of one of the motives listed in the article."[32]

---

[29] See, e.g., HUMAN RIGHTS WATCH, GENOCIDE IN RWANDA (1994); AFRICAN RIGHTS, RWANDA: DEATH, DESPAIR AND DEFIANCE (revised ed. 1995); GERARD PRUNIER, THE RWANDA CRISIS: HISTORY OF A GENOCIDE (1995); Mariann Meier Wang, The International Tribunal for Rwanda: Opportunities for Clarification, Opportunities for Impact, 27 COLUM. HUM. RTS. L. REV. 177 (1995).

[30] In a recent ruling, a trial chamber of the International Criminal Tribunal for the former Yugoslavia has pointed out that "the constitutive intent of the crime of genocide may be inferred from the very gravity" of discriminatory acts. See Case No. IT-94-2-R61, Prosecutor v. Nikolic, Review of Indictment Pursuant to Rule 61, October 20, 1995. The trial chamber invited the prosecutor to consider indicting the defendant for genocide even though the original indictment consisted of twenty-four counts on charges brought under other articles of the tribunal's statute.

[31] The phrase under discussion would have read: "by reason of [or on account of]" group membership.

[32] U.N. GAOR, 6th comm., 3d sess., 1st part, 74th meeting at 118 (1948).

The Panamanian delegate supported the U.K. on this point: "[A] statement of motives would result in an inadequate definition, as it would allow the guilty parties to claim that they had not acted under the impulses of one of the motives held to be necessary to prove genocide."[33]

The Venezuelan delegate offered the "as such" language as the solution to this problem, explaining that proposal as follows: "[A]n enumeration of motives was useless and even dangerous, as such a restrictive enumeration would be a powerful weapon in the hands of the guilty parties and would help them to avoid being charged with genocide. Their defenders would maintain that the crimes had been committed for other reasons than those listed in article II."[34] The Venezuelan amendment was then adopted and the "motives" notion abandoned, thereby confirming that the requisite intent to destroy an ethnic group "as such" can be established even if the perpetrator alleges other motives (such as political) for the actions against the protected group.[35]

Before leaving the issues involved in interpreting the convention's grant of protection to ethnical groups, we should note a few related points. One issue concerns the extent of the protection, if any, to be given to preservation of a given culture, including its physical symbols such as synagogues or mosques as well as more intangible factors such as the language and traditions of the group. The Genocide Convention deals with the problem of cultural genocide through a determination that the essence of the crime of genocide is not the destruction of culturally significant buildings or interference with cultural practices but the particularly heinous acts against human members of the group that are enumerated in Article II (killing, causing serious bodily or mental harm, inflicting conditions calculated to bring about physical destruction, preventing births, and forcibly transferring children).[36] The convention thus does not require affirmative measures to perpetuate ethnic identity, nor does it prohibit actions that may have an adverse effect on ethnic cohesiveness but that differ qualitatively from the enumerated prohibitions on attacks against group members. Actions such as a ban on speaking the language of the group or teaching its history may well raise questions concerning fulfillment of the minority rights provisions of other international instruments and may well be precursors to the genocidal acts enumerated in Article II; but the legal definition of genocide entails a kind of attack on the physical integrity of group members that is quite different in character from mere restrictions on ethnic practices.

---

[33] *Id.* at 124.
[34] *Id.*
[35] *Id.* at 133.
[36] Concerning cultural genocide, see *id.*

Where such attacks on physical integrity have occurred, however, it is quite proper to refer to limitations on ethnically oriented activities as part of the evidence from which to infer an intent to destroy the group as such. Similarly, while mere destruction of structures or even of traditional means of livelihood would not by itself constitute genocide, such activities, when combined with acts that are prohibited by Article II, can supply evidence from which genocidal intent could be inferred. In the Kurdish case, the eradication not just of villages in the structural sense but of the human lives, on a mass scale, of those who had inhabited them constitutes not "cultural" genocide but genocide as defined in Article II. In response to an argument that a particular pattern of killings had no anti-group intent but was an unavoidable side effect of other conduct, proof that the killings were accompanied by deliberate destruction of symbols of group identity (for example, schools or libraries serving as repositories of the group's culture) would help establish the intent to destroy the group as such. For example, the fact that mosques in affected areas of Bosnia have been demolished without regard to military necessity should be probative of genocidal intent.[37]

B. Genocide and Armed Conflict

The Genocide Convention criminalizes genocide "whether committed in time of peace or in time of war."[38] Wartime exigencies are therefore no defense against a charge of genocide, whether committed by the initiator of aggression or by a party acting in self-defense. It bears recalling that the Nuremberg defendants proffered a "military necessity" defense, which the Nuremberg tribunal properly rejected.

Upon ratifying the Genocide Convention, the United States expressed an understanding of the obligations thereunder as follows: "That acts in the course of armed conflicts committed without the specific intent required by Article II are not sufficient to constitute genocide as defined by this Convention."[39] The gist of the concern reflected in this understanding is that a party should not be charged with genocide if, for example, a bombing campaign against a wartime adversary was not intended to

[37] I believe that the patterns of ethnic cleansing in the former Yugoslavia do constitute genocide in the legal sense or, perhaps more accurately, several genocides against different protected groups. For purposes of this chapter, I will treat the Yugoslav conflict as an ethnic one and the genocides as directed at ethnical groups. Muslims, of course, would presumably also fall under the Genocide Convention's protection of religious groups; but I consider that the Bosnian Muslims also constitute an ethnic group in view of the overall history of the former Yugoslavia's complex divisions.

[38] Genocide Convention, *supra* note 2, art. I.

[39] International Convention on the Prevention and Punishment of the Crime of Genocide, Cong. Rec. S1355–01 (daily ed. February 19, 1986), understanding (4).

destroy an ethnical group as such but resulted in group destruction regardless of intent.[40] In its most benign reading the understanding is superfluous, because no act could constitute genocide unless committed with the requisite intent as specified in Article II. Unfortunately, however, the U.S. understanding could give aid and comfort to parties charged with wartime genocide who might attempt to argue that their own intent was merely to win a war or suppress an armed insurgency and not to destroy a protected group.

Iraq's Anfal campaign against the Kurds again illustrates the problem. The operations directed at Kurds within Iraq's northern region took place near the end of the Iran-Iraq War and in proximity to the Iran-Iraq border, thus giving Iraq an opening for the legal contention that its measures were aimed not at the Kurds as such, but at those individuals who had supported the enemy and had refused to comply with decisions taken in the name of military necessity to secure the border region from Iranian incursions. A number of responses can be made to this argument, some of which are quite fact-specific (for example, that the pattern of killings includes attacks on large numbers of noncombatant women and children and even on Kurds who formed part of the pro-Iraqi militia, or that the measures taken were excessive in relation to any arguable military necessity in 1987–88, when negotiations for an end to the war with Iran were already far advanced). Other points in response to the same contention may hold more general interest in relation to the legal theory of genocide in time of armed conflict, in the context of both international wars (such as the Iran-Iraq War) and internal conflicts (such as Iraq's Anfal campaign).

History and political reality suggest that a link between genocide and aggression would hardly be coincidental: a state so contemptuous of international law as to initiate an armed attack on its neighbor would have even fewer compunctions about turning the instruments of violence against one of its own ethnic groups.[41] Thus, Iraq, which attacked Iran in 1980 and Kuwait in 1990, evidently had few inhibitions about violating international law's most fundamental norms. Concerning Iraq's putative defense that extreme measures against the Iraqi Kurds were required because of wartime conditions, we should remember that those conditions followed from Iraq's initial attack against Iran, which constituted a prima facie case of unlawful aggression.[42] Under general principles of

[40] For commentary on arguments equating the use of weapons of mass destruction in wartime with genocide, see Helen Fein, *Genocide, Terror, Life Integrity, and War Crimes: The Case for Discrimination, in* GENOCIDE: CONCEPTUAL AND HISTORICAL DIMENSIONS 95, 104–5 (George J. Andreopoulos ed., 1994) (urging that the concepts should be kept separate).

[41] On connections between genocide and war, see Ruhashyankiko Report, *supra* note 4, at 1–2.

[42] *See, e.g.,* U.N. CHARTER, art. 2(4), Definition of Aggression Resolution, G.A. Res. 3314 (1974). This is my personal conviction. My colleagues at Human Rights Watch remind me

"clean hands" applied in international jurisprudence as in all domestic legal systems, Iraq could not avoid responsibility for genocide on the ground that it had itself started a war that it then had to try not to lose.[43]

The case of the Iraqi Kurds also raises other questions concerning the armed conflicts issue, growing out of the protracted struggle between the Kurds and state authorities, which long antedated the Iran-Iraq War. From the point of view of Baghdad, the Kurds had been engaged for generations in an armed insurgency against Baghdad's rule, which Baghdad should be entitled to suppress. From the point of view of the Kurds—who perceive themselves as the largest territorially concentrated group on the planet that still lacks its own national home—their armed rebellion is entirely justifiable as an effort to vindicate their inalienable right to self-determination.[44] By analogy, advocates of Kurdish self-determination could cite various U.N. General Assembly resolutions in support of the proposition that Iraq could not legitimately suppress a self-determination movement by means of armed force, while the Kurds (under this argument) would be entitled to resort to forcible means and to seek assistance from others in order to vindicate the self-determination right.[45]

It is not necessary to take a position on the underlying self-determination issue in order to resolve the question of whether the extermination campaign can be justified as a permissible counterinsurgency measure. Clearly it cannot. One may acknowledge that Baghdad had legitimate interests in preserving Iraq's territorial integrity and in establishing the

---

that the organization takes no position on who is to blame for the Iran-Iraq War; all parties to any such conflict must abide by the laws of war and humanitarian norms regardless of who started the war.

[43] ICJ Statute, art. 38(1)(c) (court shall apply "the general principles of law recognized by civilized nations"). For ICJ jurisprudence on "clean hands" and similar doctrines, see, e.g., Diversion of Water from the Meuse (Neth. v. Belg.), P.C.I.J. (ser. A/B) No. 70, at 76–78 (1937).

[44] Compare Nathaniel Berman's discussion in this volume of the multiple claims and statuses of the Sudeten Germans with the stasis surrounding the Kurdish situation. In the aftermath of the Versailles Conference, the Kurds believed that they had been promised self-determination on the same basis as other peoples formerly under Ottoman rule, but this aspiration never became reality. See Lori Fisler Damrosch, Nationalism and Internationalism: The Wilsonian Legacy, 26 N.Y.U. J. INT'L L. & POL. 493, 504–7 (1994). Berman points out that group members construct their own identities at least partly in light of their understanding of the available legal categories. For the point of view that the Kurds have been less able than other groups to fashion a coherent national identity, see Marvin Zonis, The Dispossessed, N.Y. TIMES BOOK REVIEW, March 10, 1996 (reviewing McDowall, supra note 9).

[45] The relevant language from the General Assembly Declaration on Principles of International Law Concerning Friendly Relations and Cooperation among States in Accordance with the Charter of the United Nations, G.A. Res. 2625, 25 U.N. GAOR Supp. No. 28, at 121, reprinted in 9 I.L.M. 1292, and reiterated in other resolutions, is as follows: "Every State has the duty to refrain from any forcible action which deprives peoples . . . of their right to self-determination. . . . In their actions against and resistance to such forcible action in pursuit of the exercise of self-determination, such peoples are entitled to seek and to receive support in accordance with the purposes and principles of the Charter of the United Nations."

government's control over that territory, but it does not follow that those ends could be pursued by means of a program intended to destroy one of Iraq's ethnic groups in whole or in part. No matter how valid the ends, genocidal means are unjustifiable.

Because of the Kurds' transboundary location, their long-running struggle for self-determination has inevitably embroiled them in crossborder conflict, including the Iran-Iraq War. The Kurds saw themselves as betrayed by both Baghdad and Teheran and as chronically at the mercy of those in both capitals who would make and break alliances of convenience at will. Not surprisingly, many Iraqi Kurds saw the Iran-Iraq War as an opportunity for advancing their own agenda. If some Iraqi Kurds thought that their best hope for achieving their own state (or at least a more satisfactory form of autonomy) was to weaken Baghdad by siding with Teheran, their attitude was the natural consequence of generations of repression at the hands of successive rulers in Baghdad. It would be entirely appropriate in such circumstances to examine the entire dossier of the regime's treatment of the ethnic group in question, going back long before the wartime conditions erupted and before the acts of one of the warring parties crossed the threshold of physical attacks against an ethnic group within its own territory, in order to understand how the ethnic group came to be involved in violent conflict in the first place. Although mere repression of ethnic aspirations for self-determination is not by itself genocide, the severity and duration of that repression may shed light on the "intent" element of the offense of genocide and tend to refute a defense that brutal measures of extermination were required by military necessity or by alleged subversion or sabotage on the part of the group.

Some have suggested that the definition of genocide should be recast in order to afford protection to "nonviolent collectivities"—instances in which "victims were defenseless or were killed regardless of whether they surrendered or resisted."[46] While such a proposal is commendable to the extent that it could expand the convention's protections beyond the four categories of groups enumerated under Article II, it could also be problematic because it would seemingly condition protection on a group's willingness to remain passive. The Kurdish example shows that some ethnic groups may have good reason to fear that decades of intensifying brutality could culminate in genocidal violence against them. It would be a cruel irony if the victims' own resort to armed measures of self-protection had the consequence of defeating their legal protection under the Genocide Convention.

---

[46]   *Cf.* Fein, *supra* note 40, at 4, 95, 97.

C. Linking Concept with Consequences

Before turning to Part II, on implementation, some remarks on the connection between the conceptualization of genocide and the implementation of the Genocide Convention are in order. In relation to the questions posed elsewhere in this volume, especially in the Brilmayer and Tesón chapters, one might ask whether a finding that genocide has been committed could legitimize certain tangible steps aimed at correcting the wrong or preventing its recurrence. Hypothetically, for example, would the Kurds in the aftermath of a genocide campaign have a stronger argument for creation of a state of their own, on a theory of correction of gross injustice, than if they were to ground such a claim merely on an ethnical-national theory of self-determination?[47] On the plane of moral justification, the demand for creation of a new state to preserve and reconstruct communities decimated by genocide could present the same compelling cogency as the creation of the state of Israel following the Holocaust. Yet it is difficult to fashion the legal arguments for such a claim using traditional legal materials such as the Genocide Convention and the jurisprudence of the International Court of Justice. Because of the sacrosanct view of the territorial integrity of existing states in the corpus of international law, as that tribunal could be expected to apply it, it is highly implausible that the ICJ would believe itself competent to create a new state as a remedy for genocide. For similar reasons, the justifications for zones of protection (such as the no-fly zone enforced by the U.S.-led coalition with respect to part of Iraqi Kurdistan since 1991) have been articulated in political rather than legal terms.[48]

No doubt, the Security Council does have authority to adopt measures of military protection of endangered populations, under both Chapter VII of the U.N. Charter and Article VIII of the Genocide Convention.[49] More controversially, states acting unilaterally or together with other states could implement protective measures on the basis of implicit authority, as the United States and like-minded states did when the Iraqi response to the Kurdish uprising of 1991 (in the wake of the Kuwait War) threatened a repetition of the genocide of 1988.

Another question concerns whether the legal characterization of a course of conduct as genocide entails consequences of significance under

[47] On the question of secession to correct injustice, see the chapters in this volume by Brilmayer at 82–83, and Tesón at 110–11.

[48] For discussion, see Lori F. Damrosch, *Concluding Reflections, in* ENFORCING RESTRAINT: COLLECTIVE INTERVENTION IN INTERNAL CONFLICTS 348, 356–58 (Lori F. Damrosch ed., 1993).

[49] Article VIII provides: "Any Contracting Party may call upon the competent organs of the United Nations to take such action under the Charter of the United Nations as they consider appropriate for the prevention and suppression of acts of genocide [or related acts]." Genocide Convention, *supra* note 2.

the relevant system of criminal law. If the deliberate killing of, say, 100,000 members of an ethnic group constitutes genocide but a killing of similar magnitude directed against a political faction is something other than genocide (a crime against humanity, for example), what legal consequences turn on this distinction? Several kinds of response to this question are possible using analogies to domestic prosecutions, but other responses are unique to the nature of the international legal system.

As with domestic criminal law, the classification of an offense can have critical consequences both for the jurisdiction of potential tribunals and for the penalties that could be imposed. Simple murder is, to be sure, a serious offense; but certain kinds of murder will implicate federal rather than lower levels of jurisdiction, and some kinds of murder will entail heavier penalties than the basic offense (such as availability of the death penalty for murder of a law enforcement officer in some jurisdictions). Similar considerations apply in the case of genocide, which is typically ranked as a crime entailing the most serious penalties under national law.

Yet the domestic analogy is not completely apt. In a domestic system, if a crime is not a perfect fit with the most seriously ranked offense, a lesser included offense or other alternative is typically at hand; and if one level of jurisdiction is unavailable, another authority would usually have competence over the situation. In the international system, however, the patchwork nature of existing competences may mean an inadequate framework for response to even exceptionally serious crimes. In the case of genocide, certain forms of redress *may* be available that otherwise would be lacking even for such heinous acts as "crimes against humanity" or "grave breaches of humanitarian law." The underscoring is meant as a reminder that the category of genocide is legally defined in terms bearing only so much room for expansion and that in any event the supposed forums for holding the perpetrators of genocide to account may be more hypothetical than real.

II. Implementation through Legal Institutions

At the state-to-state level, the Genocide Convention contemplates implementation through the International Court of Justice for disputes between states parties "relating to the interpretation, application or fulfilment of the present Convention, *including those relating to the responsibility of a State for genocide.*"[50] The only other forums specifically mentioned in the convention are "a competent tribunal of the State in the territory of which the act was committed" or "such international penal tribunal as

---

[50] *Id.* art. IX.

may have jurisdiction with respect to those Contracting Parties which shall have accepted its jurisdiction."[51] The following section will deal with implementation against states through the ICJ; then we will consider criminal enforcement against individuals through national tribunals and the newly established and prospective international criminal tribunals.

A. The International Court of Justice

With more than one hundred states as parties to the Genocide Convention, one might expect at least some activity under Article IX's jurisdictional clause; but until Bosnia-Herzegovina brought its case against Serbia-Montenegro in 1993, that heading of jurisdiction had not been invoked. As I have noted, the Soviet Union and its satellites, along with some other states, had ratified the convention with reservations excluding ICJ jurisdiction. In early 1989 the Soviet Union removed its reservation, at just about the same time that the United States was finally completing its ratification *with* such a reservation.[52] After the Soviet Union's removal of its reservation and, perhaps more pertinently, after the disintegration of the Soviet bloc and related political changes, many ex-Soviet and East European states filed new instruments with the convention's depositary,[53] either removing old reservations or becoming a party through succession or accession without comparable reservations.[54] Only a few holdouts continue to reserve against the jurisdictional undertaking, with the United States being by far the most notorious.[55]

---

[51] *Id.* art. VI. Additionally, any party "may call upon the competent organs of the United Nations to take such action under the Charter of the United Nations as they consider appropriate" to prevent and suppress genocide. *Id.* art. VIII.

[52] The removal of the reservations for the former USSR and the Ukrainian and Byelorussian SSRs is noted in MULTILATERAL TREATIES, *supra* note 8, at 105 n. 10. The relevant document removing the Soviet reservation is reprinted in 83 AM. J. INT'L L. 457 (1989). The U.S. reservation reads: "(1) That with reference to article IX of the Convention, before any dispute to which the United States is a party may be submitted to the jurisdiction of the International Court of Justice under this article, the specific consent of the United States is required in each case." MULTILATERAL TREATIES, *supra* note 8, at 100.

[53] The former Socialist Federal Republic of Yugoslavia had been a party without reservation since 1950; three of its former republics (Bosnia-Herzegovina, Croatia, and Slovenia) filed declarations of succession in 1992. The issue of continuity of applicability of the convention in the case of *Bosnia-Herzegovina v. Serbia-Montenegro* is currently pending before the ICJ. At the provisional measures phase, the ICJ found a prima facie basis for the conclusion that both parties continued to be bound by the convention and its jurisdictional clause. 1993 ICJ at 11–16.

[54] As of 1995, the following states from the former Soviet bloc had removed their previous reservations to ICJ jurisdiction: Russia, Ukraine, and Belarus (March and April 1989); Hungary (December 1989); Mongolia (July 1990); Czech Republic and Slovakia (April 1991); and Bulgaria (June 1992). Estonia became a party without reservation on October 21, 1991, Latvia on April 14, 1992, and Moldova on January 26, 1993. MULTILATERAL TREATIES, at *supra* note 8, 87–94.

[55] Others include Argentina, Venezuela, Rwanda, and Spain. *Id.* at 88–90.

Nonetheless, Bosnia's suit against Yugoslavia (Serbia-Montenegro) remains the only case brought under Article IX, even though prominent instances of mass killings in a number of countries plausibly fall within the convention's scope. Candidates for Article IX actions include Cambodia, a party to the convention without reservation since 1950, and Iraq, a party without reservation since 1959.[56]

What accounts for states' reluctance to invoke the jurisdiction that is at least formally available to them? A small but probably not determinative factor may have to do with technical qualms about whether the known atrocities amount to genocide in the precise legal sense of Article II's focus on four kinds of protected groups: such legal doubts may have accounted for some reluctance in the Cambodian situation, where intense efforts by nongovernmental organizations over several years found no state that was willing to take up the case.[57] Another factor, which is legally beside the point but politically relevant, has to do with the absence of a tangible interest in bringing an ICJ claim.[58] In the legal sense, all state parties to the Genocide Convention have standing to raise a claim under Article IX; moreover, the duty to prevent and punish genocide is viewed as an obligation *erga omnes*, which all states have a legal interest in enforcing.[59] Politically, however, states seem unwilling to undertake the burdens of a protracted litigation unless they perceive something tangible to be gained by doing so. Accordingly, Bosnia has vigorously pressed its own claims

[56] Concerning others mentioned in the Whitaker Report (*supra* note 4)—for example, Iran's persecution of the Baha'i religious group—Iran has been a party since 1956, without reservation.

[57] In brief, the legal questions would concern whether the Khmer Rouge's mass killings of other Khmers constituted destruction of a "national, ethnical, racial, or religious group, as such," as opposed to destruction of unprotected political or economic groups. In support of the effort to bring an ICJ case involving Cambodia, nongovernmental proponents argued plausibly that the Cambodian national group had been attacked as such by means of a concerted effort to eliminate its leaders, its intellectuals, and others through whom Cambodian national identity was maintained. The various arguments are explained and evaluated in ABRAMS & RATNER, *supra* note 12.

[58] The Senate Foreign Relations Committee offered the following interpretation of Article IX's phrase "relating to the responsibility of a State for genocide": "This is understood in the traditional sense of responsibility to another state for injuries sustained by nationals of the complaining state in violation of principles of international law." S. EXEC. REP. No. 2, 99th Cong., 1st sess. at 12 (1985). The concern goes back to the Truman administration's representatives in the U.N. drafting process in 1948 and in the ratification controversy that began shortly thereafter and continued for forty years.

[59] *Cf.* RESTATEMENT OF THE FOREIGN RELATIONS LAW OF THE UNITED STATES, §§ 703(1)-(2) and 902, cmt. a ("When a state has violated an obligation owed to the international community as a whole, any state may bring a claim . . . without showing that it suffered any particular injury."). In the Barcelona Traction case, the ICJ identified certain obligations, including those respecting genocide, as owed "towards the international community as a whole. . . . By their very nature [these] are the concern of all States. In view of the importance of the rights involved, all States can be held to have a legal interest in their protection; they are obligations *erga omnes*" 1970 ICJ at 32.

for injunctive, declaratory, and monetary relief on behalf of the Bosnian state and its Muslim population; but no other country has yet perceived sufficient self-interest in undertaking such an effort on behalf of more remote victims.

Concerning the Kurds of Iraq, Human Rights Watch has initiated active discussions with more than a score of governments, all with admirable human rights records and all professedly sympathetic to the underlying claims. But we are still in suspended animation as far bringing an actual case to the ICJ. The governments haven't said no, but they haven't said yes either. It's hard to persuade states to stick their necks out for an altruistic cause: some don't want to prejudice their usefulness as honest brokers in negotiations on Middle Eastern matters; some are worried about their own ties with Iraq or about the possibility that Iraq could foment terrorism against them; some would be willing to carry the banner but lack the resources in terms of money or staff to commit to a major litigation; and for some, plain old bureaucratic inertia stands in the way of an affirmative decision.

The difficulties of finding a willing applicant even when the facts are clear, the law is clear, and the court's jurisdiction is indisputable create considerable pessimism about the prognosis for relying on the strictly state-to-state mechanism of the ICJ. Thus, we must look to other judicial bodies, whose jurisdiction would extend to the prosecution of crimes committed by individuals.

B. Criminal Enforcement against Individuals

Article VI of the Genocide Convention reads: "Persons charged with genocide . . . shall be tried by a competent tribunal of the State in the territory of which the act was committed, or by such international penal tribunal as may have jurisdiction with respect to those Contracting Parties which shall have accepted its jurisdiction." This provision needs to be read in conjunction with other provisions of the convention that establish duties on the part of states to prosecute and to assist in the prosecution of the crime of genocide. Under Article I, state parties "undertake to prevent and to punish" the crime of genocide. Article IV provides that persons committing genocide "shall be punished, whether they are constitutionally responsible rulers, public officials or private individuals." Article VI requires states to enact legislation to give effect to the convention and, in particular, "to provide effective penalties for persons guilty of genocide." Article VII provides that genocide shall not be considered a political crime for the purpose of extradition and commits the parties to grant extradition in accordance with their laws and treaties in force. In their ensemble, these provisions express a definite purpose on the part of the contracting parties to ensure effective enforcement of the convention through criminal trials.

An obvious flaw in this plan is that, when the apparatus of a state is either implicated in genocide or willing to turn a blind eye, all these fine promises are meaningless. This is exactly the situation of Iraq and the Kurds, where tens of thousands of people have disappeared into execution pits and mass graves and not a single criminal action has been initiated. Different but no less troubling problems arise when a new regime displaces the genocidal one—as in Cambodia or Rwanda—under conditions that are hardly ripe for the rendering of dispassionate justice.[60] Thus, in most cases of genocide, territorial tribunals are probably the least rather than the most satisfactory bodies for criminal prosecutions, except for the cathartic function that can be served by in-country trials of the perpetrators of genocide.

In theory, courts of third countries ought to be available as alternatives to territorial courts. This theoretical possibility is undercut, however, by several considerations, including the practical one that offenders are most likely to remain sheltered in the territory where the genocide has occurred. Even assuming that a third-country tribunal could establish in personam jurisdiction over the accused, legal challenges to the subject-matter jurisdiction of the tribunal might nonetheless thwart the possibility of criminal enforcement in national courts outside the territory where the acts were committed. One subset of those questions concerns objections to subject-matter jurisdiction under domestic law: to what extent does the relevant domestic legislation confer jurisdiction over extraterritorial crimes? The U.S. Congress, for example, has implemented the convention only on a limited extraterritorial basis, with legislation providing for jurisdiction in U.S. courts when the accused is a U.S. national as well as when the acts took place in the United States (thus supplementing the convention's provision for jurisdiction on a territorial basis with a nationality basis).[61] Significantly, however, the United States did *not* choose to implement the convention on a universality theory of jurisdiction, which would have enabled prosecutions to proceed against offenders in U.S. custody regardless of the place of the crime or the defendant's nationality. Thus, the United States opted not to exercise the maximum jurisdictional power available to it under international law, even though the weight of scholarly authority and the implementing legislation of a number of other countries support the availability of universal jurisdiction.[62]

---

[60] For a wide-ranging discussion of these and many other cases involving trade-offs between accountability and reconciliation in societies riven by trauma, see TRANSITIONAL JUSTICE: HOW EMERGING DEMOCRACIES RECKON WITH FORMER REGIMES (Neil J. Kritz ed., 1995).

[61] 18 U.S.C. § 1091(d).

[62] *See, e.g.,* RESTATEMENT OF FOREIGN RELATIONS LAW, 404; Kenneth Randall, *Universal Jurisdiction under International Law,* 66 TEX. L. REV. 785, 788–90 (1988).

If a genocide prosecution should go forward in a state party to the Genocide Convention that is not the state in which the act was committed, the defendant would doubtless attempt to argue that Article VI, in light of its negotiating history, gives "the State in the territory of which the act was committed" exclusive jurisdiction. But this argument should fail. It is true that the convention's drafters considered and rejected alternative formulations under which jurisdiction over genocide would have been established on the *aut dedere aut judicare* (either extradite or prosecute) basis that is now standard for other serious international crimes. Thus, the convention lacks the explicit confirmation found in subsequent treaties on other subjects that prosecution on extraterritorial bases of jurisdiction is proper. As they did with other compromises that were politically necessary in 1948, the states participating in the drafting process simply were not ready to treat genocide with the level of commitment to international cooperation that has since become almost routine for crimes (such as hijacking) that are much less serious than genocide but serious enough to warrant intensified international efforts at suppression. But this compromise merely means that the participating states did not *require* third countries to prosecute genocide; it does not bar them from undertaking such prosecution. The correct legal position is that, although the drafters of the Genocide Convention declined to impose a requirement of aut dedere aut judicare, the convention does not preclude states from prosecuting any offender over whom they may have custody, using any available theory of jurisdiction, including universality.

Article VI also holds out at least the theoretical prospect of prosecution "by such international penal tribunal as may have jurisdiction with respect to those Contracting Parties which shall have accepted its jurisdiction." The importance attached to consensual acceptance of jurisdiction was stressed repeatedly in 1948 when this provision took shape and also more recently as states have indicated their conditions for ratification. The United States, for example, appended the following understanding to its ratification: "(5) That with regard to the reference to an international penal tribunal in article VI of the Convention, the United States declares that it reserves the right to effect its participation in any such tribunal only by a treaty entered into specifically for that purpose with the advice and consent of the Senate."

Nonetheless, two new tribunals have been established on a basis that is compulsory rather than consensual. Acting under Chapter VII of the United Nations Charter, the Security Council has established an International Criminal Tribunal for the former Yugoslavia and an International Criminal Tribunal for Rwanda, both of which have jurisdiction to prosecute individuals for the crime of genocide without regard to consent on the part of the state in which the acts occurred or the state of nationality of the accused. As a concrete illustration of the controversial grounding of these tribunals' jurisdiction, it may be noted that Rwanda, which fortu-itously occupied a nonpermanent seat on the Security Council at the time of the vote on the resolution establishing the Rwanda tribunal, cast the only negative vote.[63] Motions challenging the subject-matter jurisdiction of the Yugoslavia tribunal have already been considered, and similar motions will surely follow in the Rwanda tribunal.[64] Although the argu-ments on these jurisdictional questions fall outside the scope of this vol-ume, I believe the tribunal was correct in finding that the Security Council had the competence under Chapter VII of the Charter to determine the existence of threats to the peace and to deal with those threats through creation of new criminal tribunals.[65]

These developments have contributed to momentum for completing the project anticipated in 1948—the establishment of an international pe-nal tribunal with standing jurisdiction over the crime of genocide. Over the last several years, the International Law Commission (ILC) has drafted a statute for such a body. The draft is now receiving high-level attention. Still to be resolved are questions having to do with the manner in which a standing international criminal court would be established and the means by which states could opt into or opt out of its eventual head-ings of jurisdiction.

Significantly, the ILC draft would place the crime of genocide in a privileged position with respect to the modalities of consensual submis-sion to jurisdiction. Once a state had agreed to become party to the court's statute, a separate consent would not be necessary to perfect the court's subject-matter jurisdiction over the crime of genocide, in contrast to all other crimes for which a specific indication of consent would be needed.[66] The ILC explained its position on this point:

---

[63] S.C. Res. 955, U.N. SCOR, 49th sess., 3,453d meeting, U.N. Doc. S/PV.3453, at 3, 14–16 (November 8, 1994). The new Rwandan government had called upon the United Nations to establish an international tribunal as a means of "eradicating the culture of impunity" that had characterized Rwandan society; but that government was not fully satisfied with the statute that the Security Council ultimately adopted and thus cast a negative vote to register its disagreement with aspects such as the exclusion of the death penalty. See Wang, *supra* note 29, at 177, 190, 195, 201–3; *see also* RWANDA: ACCOUNTABILITY FOR WAR CRIMES AND GENOCIDE (United States Institute of Peace, Special Report, January 1995).

[64] The Rwanda tribunal indicted eight Rwandans on genocide charges in December 1995; defense challenges to the indictment are expected. *See Exhumation Begins at Site of Killings in Rwanda*, N.Y. TIMES, January 21, 1996, at A5; *see also Judge Urges World to Heed Rwanda Crisis: Suspects in Genocide Are Said to Escape*, N.Y. TIMES, December 31, 1995, p. A4.

[65] *See Dusko Tadic*, Case No. IT-94-1-AR 72, October 2, 1995, 35 I.L.M. 32 (1996).

[66] This proposal for "inherent jurisdiction" has not escaped controversy. *See, e.g.*, Com-ments by Jamaica on the ILC Draft, in U.N. Doc. A/C.6/49/SR.22, *cited in* Jose E. Alvarez, *Legal Issues, in* A GLOBAL AGENDA: ISSUES BEFORE THE FIFTIETH GENERAL ASSEMBLY 243 (John Tessitore & Susan Woolfson eds., 1995).

In the Commission's view, the prohibition of genocide is of such fundamental significance, and the occasions for legitimate doubt or dispute over whether a given situation amounts to genocide are so limited, that the Court ought, exceptionally, to have inherent jurisdiction over it by virtue solely of the States participating in the draft Statute, without any further requirement of consent or acceptance by any particular State. . . . The case for considering such "inherent jurisdiction" is powerfully reinforced by the Genocide Convention itself, which . . . expressly contemplates its conferral on an international criminal court to be created (art. VI). The draft Statute can thus be seen as completing in this respect the scheme for the prevention and punishment of genocide begun in 1948—and at a time when effective measures against those who commit genocide are called for.

Much work remains to be done, and much political commitment to be mustered, before the proposed international criminal court can be brought into being and set about its vital work. Even under the best of the likely circumstances, innumerable hurdles would remain before persons such as those who ordered or committed the crimes against the Kurds of Iraq could be brought to justice. But in the absence of such a tribunal, not only those criminals but many others will escape justice indefinitely.

Just as crimes are committed by persons and not by abstract entities, the victims of the crime of genocide are the individuals—children, women, and men—who suffer personally when their group becomes a target for destruction.[67] The Genocide Convention has not yet become an effective instrument for their protection. It is up to all of us to make its promise a reality.

[67] Cf. Nuremberg trials, *supra* note 11, at 223.

11

Temporary Protection of
A Persecuted People

Michael Platzer

The specter of tens of thousands of persons fleeing ethnic cleansing in Bosnia and Rwanda has been dramatically presented on our television screens. What are the obligations of neighboring countries to admit these refugees? Or if there has been a massive influx of frightened refugees, can the receiving country summarily expel them?

During wars, or in their aftermath, there have always been large movements of people. In the past, members of an ethnic group fleeing to their homeland or other larger population groups fleeing persecution have often been admitted to countries en groupe on the basis of a political or humanitarian decision in line with traditional refugee law. In fact, the early international refugee agreements in the first half of the twentieth century protected specific groups of people such as Russians who no longer enjoyed the protection of the USSR, Armenians who were no longer subjects of the Ottoman Empire,[1] German refugees from the Saar, Czechs who had fled the Sudetenland, and Jews who had resided in Germany and Austria but were forced to flee Nazi persecution and had become stateless.[2]

The concern was, of course, to provide these millions of people with travel documents because they had become stateless and it was unlikely that they would ever return to countries of origin that had clearly articulated that they did not wish these subversive people to come back. At the end of World War II there were 1.5 million persons who refused to return

---

[1] *See* Arrangement of May 12, 1926, 89 U.N.T.S. 47.
[2] Constitution of the International Refugee Organization, December 15, 1946, 18 U.N.T.S. 3.

to their countries of origin. The London Agreement of October 15, 1945 authorized the issuance of travel documents to refugees from Germany, Austria, and Spain and to some smaller groups of persecuted people. The United Nations Relief and Reconstruction Agency provided some assistance to these people and helped with their resettlement. Their legal situation, however, was not clear, nor was it the responsibility of the states in which they resided.

In 1948, the U.N. Economic and Social Council, on the basis of a Human Rights Commission Resolution, requested the secretary-general to undertake a study on the protection of stateless persons. This led eventually to a conference of plenipotentiaries in 1951 to consider an international agreement to provide protection to refugees. But by 1951 the iron curtain had gone up, and the motivations for regulating the messy situation of millions of stateless people wandering around Europe ("refugees in orbit") had changed.

In 1951, the international community wished to establish common standards for granting asylum to those fleeing persecution from Communist or dictatorial regimes.[3] The haunting images of Jews being denied access by all countries during World War II (the "voyage of the damned") also helped lay the basis for an international treaty to provide a common framework to accept such persecuted people. The 1951 Geneva Convention on Refugees, however, was not designed to deal with large-scale crossborder migration but only with the individual cases of those seeking asylum based on an individualized fear of persecution. Moreover, the convention originally applied only to European refugees and those who were refugees "as a result of events" predating 1951 (that is, World War II and the imposition of Communist rule in Eastern Europe). This was changed by the 1967 protocol, which removed the 1951 deadline and encouraged parties to opt to apply the treaty to both European and non-European refugees.[4] In 1956, however, despite the convention's focus on individual cases, Hungarians fleeing Soviet tanks were admitted "en groupe" by Austria, which expected and received assistance with their resettlement to third countries. This was done again for the Czechoslovaks in 1968.

Strictly, the convention protects only those persons who are already on the territory of that state. Persons who are at the border (and not yet admitted) should, however, be treated in the spirit of the convention (that is, admitted). Article 33 of the Geneva Convention prohibits a state from *refoulement* (returning) of such a refugee to territories where his or her life

---

[3] Atle Grahl Madsen, *Refugees and Refugee Law in a World in Transition*, Mich. Y.B. Int'l Legal Stud. 291 (1982).

[4] *See* 1967 Protocol Relating to the Status of Refugees, January 31, 1967, 19 U.S.T. 6223, 606 U.N.T.S. 267.

or freedom would be threatened on account of race, religion, nationality, membership in a particular group, or political opinion. The principle of non-refoulement has been strengthened by Article 3 of the United Nations Convention against Torture and Article 3 of the European Convention for Human Rights, which proscribe expulsion or extradition to a country where a person may be exposed to torture or inhumane or degrading treatment. The 1967 U.N. Declaration on Territorial Asylum contains a similar provision, which prescribes that no person invoking the right of asylum under the Universal Declaration of Human Rights "shall be subjected to measures such as rejection at the frontier or, if he has already entered the territory in which he seeks asylum, expulsion or compulsory return to any State where he may be subjected to persecution."[5] Similar language is contained in the 1967 Resolution of the Committee of Ministers of the Council of Europe on Asylum to Persons in Danger of Persecution.[6]

The Organization of African Unity (OAU) Refugee Convention and the Cartagena Declaration go beyond the 1951 Geneva Convention and cite external aggression, occupation, foreign domination, circumstances that have seriously disturbed public order, general violence, internal conflicts, and massive violations of human rights as reasons for granting protection to refugees.[7] Under these instruments, there is no need to establish that a particular individual has a well founded fear of persecution or to make an individualized determination of the danger to that individual's life. Only the Latin American Convention requires a state to grant asylum or admission, but in practice the African states have opened their borders regularly to war refugees.[8] Africa, in fact, hosts more refugees and internally displaced persons than any other continent in the world. The OAU Convention and the Cartagena Declaration may, in part, explain the greater generosity of African and Latin American governments in accepting victims of war and persecution; or viewed more cynically, they may simply reflect the incapacity of these countries to seal their borders. Ethnic groups, especially in Africa, frequently straddle the artificially drawn international borders, a fact that partially explains the frequency of and response to transborder refugee flows in certain areas. In addition, host countries facing a large-scale influx of refugees or massive internal displacement commonly receive substantial amounts of international assistance.

[5] G.A. Res. 2312 (XXII) (1967).

[6] UNHCR, COLLECTION OF INTERNATIONAL INSTRUMENTS GOVERNING REFUGEES 305 (1988).

[7] Deborah Perluss & Joan F. Hartman, Temporary Refugee: Emergence of a Customary Norm, 26 VA. J. INT'L L. 551, 590–93 (1986).

[8] M. R. Rwelamira, Two Decades of the 1969 OAU Convention Governing the Specific Aspects of the Refugee Problems in Africa, INT'L J. REFUGEE L. (1989).

The United Nations high commissioner for refugees (UNHCR) and many refugee lawyers maintain that there are still two bodies of law to regulate the admission of traditional war and asylum refugees. (In fact, in most states' national legislation there are separate administrative provisions for admitting "refugees" and for admitting "asylum seekers.") Other observers feel that the Latin American and African conventions have undermined the Geneva Convention, which can be interpreted to cover anyone fearing for his or her life. These regional treaties have clearly established two types of refugees: the nonconvention (OAU / Cartagena) refugee fleeing generalized violence or war and the real convention refugee, who has an individualized fear for his or her life. Because the Geneva Convention did not provide for the traditional refugee who is fleeing generalized violence, some states have argued that the admission of nonconvention refugees is wholly subject to national law and that, if admitted, they can be returned as soon as the war has ended. Accordingly, under this view, there is no obligation in codified international law to admit refugees into a country's territory or to assist refugees, particularly in cases of a mass influx that might result in an impoverishment of the national population. In fact, even the Geneva Convention provides that certain articles may be suspended in times of national emergency.

In the 1950s, 1960s, and 1970s, when the number of refugees from Eastern Europe and the southern hemisphere remained limited, thanks respectively to the iron curtain and to the distance and expense of travel, the United States could be generous. U.S. policy changed, however, after its unhappy experience in 1980, when the United States admitted all of the Cuban refugees fleeing Cuba from Mariel Bay. In that exodus, Castro allowed hardened criminals to escape along with the other refugees, and they subsequently unleashed an uncontrollable crime wave in the United States.

At the same time, many Salvadorans—an estimated 750,000—had made their way to the United States fleeing the violence in their home country. Because the Reagan and Bush administrations supported the El Salvador government, the United States denied 97 percent of the asylum requests made from 1983 to 1989 by Salvadorans who said they faced persecution by their government.[9] At the same time, comparable political asylum claims involving aliens from Iran or Cuba were upheld, demonstrating discriminatory treatment dependent upon whether the refugee was from a country that had a friendly or a hostile relationship with the United States.

---

[9] Robert Rubin, *Ten Years After: Vindication for Salvadorans and New Promises of Safe Haven and Refugee Protection*, 68 INTERPRETER RELEASES 97 (1991); Derek Smith, *A Refugee by Any Other Name: An Examination of the Board of Immigration Appeals' Action in Asylum Cases*, 75 VA. L. REV. 681 (1989); Deborah Anker, *Discretionary Asylum: A Protection Remedy for Refugees under the Refugee Act of 1980*, 28 VA. J. INT'L L. 1, 43 (1987).

"Trophy refugees" (living symbols of the failure of rival ideologies) who managed to escape communism were given refugee status almost automatically, even though the majority would not have qualified according to a strict interpretation of the Geneva Convention. With the end of the cold war, however (there were never many refugees escaping the iron curtain), new waves of refugees fleeing other forms of totalitarianism and civil wars were reaching the United States. In 1994, the nation had 420,000 unadjudicated asylum claims. In order to get rid of this backlog and the presumption that it included many fraudulent claims, asylum procedures were streamlined, placing greater burdens on refugees to show that they had legitimate fears for their lives.[10]

In fact, the U.S. Supreme Court has upheld the higher standard established by Congress that a refugee must establish by objective evidence that his or her life would be threatened if returned to his or her home country and not just rely on a well-founded fear as stipulated in the Geneva Convention.[11] A respected scholar of refugee law, David Martin, notes that only the United States has made this sort of distinction in cases triggering the non-refoulement obligation.[12] Another maintains that the United States is not conforming to its international obligations because Article 33(1) of the convention extends to all refugees who have a well-founded fear.[13]

The United States has recognised that its refugee laws do little to protect individuals who are fleeing generalized violence in their countries. To deal with this problem, the country now offers temporary protected status to aliens from countries experiencing civil strife.[14] The Immigration Act of 1990 codified an existing safe-haven practice known as extended voluntary departure (EVD). Under EVD, the secretary of state identifies certain countries to which the return of aliens should be suspended. Since 1960, EVD has been granted to nationals from a dozen countries: Ethiopia, Uganda, Iran, Nicaragua, Afghanistan, Cuba, Laos, Vietnam, Cambodia, Czechoslovakia, Poland, and Rumania. After 1980, grants of official EVD became less frequent, and the Reagan and Bush administrations simply suspended the enforced deportation of Chinese students following the Tiananmen Square massacre. The successor device to EVD, temporary protected status (TPS), although it applies to predesignated groups of

[10] Joan Fitzpatrick, *Flight from Asylum: Trends Toward Temporary "Refugee" and Local Responses to Forced Migrations*, 35 VA. J. INT'L L. 13, 28, 30–32 (1994).

[11] Simon M. S. Kagugube, *Cardoza-Fonseca and the Well-Founded Fear of Persecution Standard*, 12 ILSA J. INT'L L. 85 (1988).

[12] David A. Martin, *Reforming Asylum Adjudication*, 138 U. PA. L. REV. 1247, 1264 (1990).

[13] Kagugube, *supra* note 11.

[14] Suzanne Seltzer, Note, *Temporary Protected Status: A Good Foundation for Building*, 6 GEO. IMMIGR. L. J. 773 (1992); Ari Weitzhandler, *Temporary Protected Status: The Congressional Response to the Plight of Salvadoran Aliens*, 64 U. COLO. L. REV. 249 (1993).

people, can only be given to persons who are already in the United States (or have continuously resided there) and who register with the Immigration and Naturalization Service.[15]

The desirability of registering alien nationals so that deportation proceedings could be expedited when the protected period lapsed was underlined by legislators who favored the new law. In fact, a special procedure was established for Salvadorans whereby they were to be automatically scheduled for deportation hearings at the conclusion of their period of protected status, and work authorizations for Salvadorans were to be renewed semiannually rather than annually.

After resolving the status of the persecuted Salvadorans, the United States was confronted with another mass influx of refugees, this time from Haiti after the military coup in 1990.[16] President Bush decided to send out the Coast Guard to interdict the refugee boats and forcibly repatriate the Haitians. In response to claims that the United States was violating the Geneva Convention principle of non-refoulement as the first country of asylum, the Bush administration countered that the 1967 protocol was not self-executing (its provisions need to be enacted into domestic law by Congress) and that Article 33(1) of the convention applied only to refugees "within the territory of a contracting state." Nonetheless, the United Nations high commissioner for refugees called on the United States to allow all Haitians on board U.S. Coast Guard vessels to be disembarked in the United States and screened for determination of their refugee status. Instead, the United States took the refugees to Honduras, Venezuela, Belize, and Guantanamo Bay, Cuba, and then arranged for their voluntary repatriation under an agreement signed with Haiti's dictator "Baby Doc" Duvalier. For domestic political reasons, President Clinton continued the practice of returning those who fled Haiti in small boats. This policy was effective in temporarily stopping the outflow of refugees, for what refugee, no matter how desperate, would risk putting his of her life savings into a leaky fishing boat when it was likely that it would then be destroyed by the U.S. Coast Guard and the refugee's family members eventually returned to the land of their persecutors?

[15] Nationals from Lebanon, Liberia, and Bosnia have been designated for TPS under the armed conflict category.

[16] Bill Frelick, *Haitian Boat Interdiction and Return: First Asylum and First Principles of Refugee Protection*, 26 CORNELL INT'L L. J. 675 (1993). Hiroshi Motomura, *Haitian Asylum Seekers: Interdiction and Immigrants' Rights*, 26 CORNELL INT'L L. J. 695 (1993); The Lowenstein International Human Rights Clinic, *Aliens and the Duty of Non-Refoulement*, 6 HARV. HUM. RTS. J. 1 (1993); Nasreen Margaret Kadivar, *Wrongful Treatment of Haitian Refugees: US Violations of Domestic and International Law*, 7 EMORY INT'L L. REV. 269 (1993); Arthur C. Helton, *The US Government Program of Implications and Prospects*, 10 N.Y. L. SCH. J. HUM. RTS. 325 (1993); Stephen H. Legomsky, *The Haitian Interdiction Programme, Human Rights and the Role of Judicial Protection*, INT'L J. REFUGEE L., Special Issue 181 (1990); Thomas David Jones, *The Haitian Refugee Crisis: A Quest for Human Rights*, 15 MICH. J. INT'L L. 77 (1993).

The U.S. Supreme Court eventually upheld the interdiction of Haitian refugees on the high seas. This decision was sharply criticized by the U.N. high commissioner for refugees as a "setback to modern international refugee law."[17] American policy in this situation was seen as particularly hypocritical because the United States was then pushing Asian countries to accept the Vietnamese boat people.[18]

In Europe, parallel developments have been taking place. Spain reached an agreement with Morocco in which Morocco agreed to step up its patrols in the Straits of Gibraltar to prevent Moroccans from leaving for Spain. Italy started patrolling the Adriatic Sea and interdicting Albanian boats. In 1991, without a hearing of their asylum claims, Italy returned 19,000 Albanians who fled the brutal conditions in their home country by boat.[19]

In response to domestic political pressures, many European states have sought to tighten their immigration procedures. In exchange for unrestricted movement for their nationals within the European Union, Greece, Italy, Portugal, and Spain were required to adopt stringent visa and external border controls.[20]

The deterrent regime adopted for foreigners makes no special provision for asylum seekers. The UNHCR has criticized the carrier sanctions (whereby the airlines are expected to ensure that each traveler has valid documentation to enter the EU) because they tend to increase the risk of refoulement and violate the basic principle of the Geneva Convention that a government agency should determine a refugee's needs of protection, not an airline. If a refugee manages to reach Europe, the immigration officials of the first country he or she arrive in will determine for all the other countries the refugee's eligibility; there will be no more "asylum shopping." This mutual agreement to be tough is in direct conflict with the duty of each state to implement its obligations under the refugee convention. In addition, the EU immigration ministers have agreed to exclude automatically from consideration for refugee status individuals who come from a country "in which there is generally no serious risk of persecution" and to adopt fasttrack procedures in other cases to avoid human rights–based scrutiny.[21]

[17] U.N. High Commissioner Responds to U.S. Supreme Court Decision in *Sale v. Haitian Centers Council*, 32 I.L.M. 1215, 1215 (1993).

[18] *Congress, Courts React to Presidential Order Turning Back Haitian Boat People*, REFUGEE REP. 13 (June 1992).

[19] Bruno Nascimbene, *The Albanians in Italy: Is the Right of Asylum under Attack?* 3 INT'L J. REFUGEE L. 714 (1991); Daniel C. Turack, *The Movement of Persons: The Practice of States in Central and Eastern Europe Since the 1989 Vienna CSCE*, 21 DENVER J. INT'L L. & POL'Y. 289 (1993).

[20] James C. Hathaway, *Harmonizing for Whom? The Devaluation of Refugee Protection in the Era of European Economic Integration*, 26 CORNELL INT'L L. J. 719, 724 (1993).

[21] AMNESTY INTERNATIONAL, EUROPE AND HARMONIZATION OF ASYLUM POLICY: ACCELER-

When confronted with the massive wave of Bosnian refugees, European countries have employed a concept of temporary protection similar to that used in the United States. Although most of the Bosnians would have qualified as convention refugees because they had a legitimate fear for their individual lives based on their religion or national identity, the European countries did not accept them as asylum refugees for domestic political reasons and to avoid being trapped in the lengthy process required to withdraw their asylum status. Instead, the rights of the Bosnian war refugees are only temporary; therefore they may be returned once the hostilities have ceased and it is "safe" to go home. The only problem is to where if their homes have been destroyed or are located in a hostile ethnic entity. The European countries are seeking to resolve the issue practically with a voluntary, phased repatriation program with options for resettlement. Instead, a number of states have amended their domestic legislation to allow nonconvention refugees to remain in the country of refuge until it is possible for them to return to their home country in dignity and without danger.

In general, the European states (and this applies equally to North American and Asian-Pacific states) seek to limit their obligations for accepting refugees and then providing for them. They do this primarily through legal and administrative measures that place tremendous burdens on the asylum seeker to prove the likelihood of persecution; torture; or cruel, inhumane, or degrading treatment if he or she is returned. Some countries even deny refugees access to administrative procedures, reject them at frontiers, detain them, and push them off without hearings in clear violation of the principle of non-refoulement.

There are, of course, real difficulties in identifying legitimate refugees and preventing illegal or unauthorized immigration. In fact, the distinction between a person fleeing persecution and one fleeing desperate poverty, hunger, or no economic prospects at home—which may be caused by discrimination against the group and even be the root cause of the conflict—is almost impossible to make. All these persons are often detained together in refugee centers, frequently near the frontiers, rarely given employment or training, and, if possible, passed to a third safe host country or back to the first country of asylum. In addition to the various measures adopted to prevent unauthorized immigration, such as complicated visa procedures and sanctions imposed on airlines and other carriers for transporting irregular migrants, the mechanisms for determination of refugee status are often deliberately clogged.

ATED PROCEDURES FOR MANIFESTLY UNFOUNDED ASYLUM CLAIMS AND THE SAFE COUNTRY CONCEPT (1992).

The delayed determination of refugee status can have the effect of inhumane or degrading treatment for a legitimate convention asylum seeker. Refugees, already the victims of torture, rape, or other forms of violence, are often subjected to a second round of ill treatment. If located in remote areas close to their country of origin, they may again be victims of the armed forces from the country they sought to flee, through banditry, robbery, organized rape, and the recruitment of men and even children into irregular forces.

In many cases, it may be unfair to blame the neighboring host countries for not providing asylum because they are often also in the war region and have their own displaced persons to assist. Croatia has, however, been condemned several times for making the distinction between ethnic Croat and Muslim refugees from Bosnia and for threatening to revoke refugee status for the latter. First asylum countries shelter the vast majority of the world's refugees, but they are also in many cases the least able to provide the material resources to maintain them. Pakistan has sheltered 3 million Afghanis, Malawi 1 million Mozambicans, Thailand nearly 1 million Cambodians, Kenya a half million Somalis, and now Zaire increasing numbers of desperate Rwandese. The least developed countries are in particular need of help to sustain the immediate additional costs of caring for these refugees. Thus, there is a clear need for greater burden sharing. States spared large influxes of refugees need to provide greater assistance to "first asylum countries" bilaterally or through international organizations. In addition, richer countries should accept and provide for more refugees instead of turning more and more refugees away.

Of course, the best method to prevent the massive movement of refugees is to deal with the causes of refugee flows. Resolving political grievances, ethnic disputes, or human rights abuses would in many cases solve the problem of masses of frightened refugees trying to flee their country and would also provide the necessary basis to return them to their homes. Thus, provisions for the repatriation of refugees in safety and dignity and the protection of minorities and human rights monitoring are included in the most recent peace agreements, which then provide a basis for international intervention. But in most cases, international law (the "sovereignty principle") still limits more forceful United Nations actions to redress human rights violations or to prevent the persecution of certain groups.[22]

The United Nations General Assembly, "deeply disturbed by the increasing scale and magnitude of exoduses of refugees," has recognized that human rights violations are one of the multiple factors causing mass exoduses.[23] It was particularly concerned by the increasingly heavy bur-

[22] Mary Ellen O'Connell, *Continuing Limits on UN Intervention in Civil War*, 67 IND. L. J. 903 (1992).
[23] G.A. Res. 48/139 (1993).

den being imposed upon developing countries with limited resources. The General Assembly had already endorsed the recommendations of the Group of Governmental Experts on International Cooperation to Avert New Flows of Refugees, which, inter alia, called upon all states to promote human rights and fundamental freedoms and to refrain from denying them on the basis of nationality, ethnicity, race, religion, or language.[24] At the same time, the secretary-general has stressed the need to develop the capacity of the Secretariat for early warning and preventive diplomacy. The U.N. Department of Humanitarian Affairs has been designated to monitor all potential refugee outflows and is the focal point for an interagency exchange of information and consultation with regard to appropriate actions to alleviate the possible causes of new flows of refugees. But even though the General Assembly has asked that "effective action [be] taken to identify human rights abuses that contribute to mass outflows," and even though the human rights rapporteurs pay attention to problems resulting in mass exoduses of populations, no mechanism has been established to follow up with appropriate political or other actions.

Similarly, little has been done to deal with problems facing internally displaced persons. The secretary-general's representative on internally displaced persons, Francis Deng, after reviewing the situation in Burundi, El Salvador, the Russian Federation, Rwanda, Somalia, Sri Lanka, Sudan, and the former Yugoslavia, concluded that consultations with the "pertinent circles in the international community" had convinced him that "the available options for improving protection of and assistance to internally displaced persons are clearly limited."[25]

In fact, he saw his own mandate as "an excuse for inaction by the international community."[26] Even when the U.N. Security Council did decide to declare the towns of Bihac, Gorazde, Srebrenica, Tuzla, and Zepa safe havens in Bosnia, this status did not prevent the towns from being attacked and in some cases overrun, for the simple reason that not enough soldiers were assigned to protect them. Tadeusz Mazowiecki, the special rapporteur of the Commission on Human Rights, who was examining the situation of human rights in the territory of the former Yugoslavia, resigned when the international community stood by and watched further ethnic cleansing (including the fall of Srebrenica) after he had documented glaring human rights abuses and had warned that more effective measures must be taken.

Admittedly, the situation of internally displaced persons is more complicated. The internally displaced do not qualify for international protection under the Geneva Convention. Yet they are the same kinds of people

[24] G.A. Res. 41/70 (1986).
[25] G.A. Doc. A/49/538, para 25 (1994).
[26] *Id.* para. 26.

(of the same ethnic group) who have fled their homes for the same reasons as international refugees—fear for their lives on account of race, religion, or membership in a particular ethnic group—and who tomorrow may *be* international refugees. UNHCR has taken the position that it would be morally untenable to provide humanitarian assistance to those who have managed to cross an international frontier but to deny assistance to those who have not. Therefore, UNHCR will help internally displaced populations to return to their homes along with groups of repatriated refugees, if they come from the same areas to which the refugees are expected to be repatriated. UNHCR will also provide assistance if the same causes have produced both internal displacement and international refugee flows or if there is a significant likelihood of crossborder movement.

The legal basis for international programs on behalf of people displaced within their own country is developing. In general, such programs can be undertaken only with the consent of the host government. It would, however, be desirable to have principles and norms equivalent to those in international refugee law that would prohibit forcible displacement and provide for the protection of those already displaced, norms that would extend well beyond the protection already provided by international human rights and humanitarian law. In addition, it is vital that existing standards be better implemented.

A preliminary compilation of existing norms has been undertaken by the Ludwig Boltzmann Institute for Human Rights, the American Society of International Law, and the International Human Rights Law Group for the Commission on Human Rights.[27] The report focuses on three sources of international legal standards—human rights law, which is applicable in all situations; humanitarian law, which is applicable in situations of armed conflict; and refugee law—that together might serve as a model for how certain issues could be dealt with in a future international instrument applicable to internally displaced persons. The experts who compiled the report make many specific recommendations for provisions to be included in any new instrument in order to deal with the special problems commonly faced by displaced persons. Among other things, such provisions would prohibit discriminatory violence, gender-specific violence, and the use of displaced persons as human shields. Nonetheless, much work remains to be done in order to clarify the rights of displaced persons with respect to detention in closed camps, forced labor, forcible recruitment into the armed forces, forced relocation, restitution for lost property, and the right to leave one's country during times of conflict.

For most displaced persons, however, legal issues are secondary. Instead, they are mainly concerned with finding food, shelter, medical assis-

27 E/CN.4/1996/52/Add.2 (1995).

tance, education for their children, and employment. To satisfy these needs, they need access to humanitarian assistance. A government may, however, be unwilling to accept international assistance. It can be argued that every state has an obligation to permit humanitarian assistance and to allow relief workers and their organizations access to the country under the International Covenant on Economic, Social, and Cultural Rights; the Fourth Geneva Convention; various General Assembly resolutions; and Article 1(3) of the U.N. Charter. But only in very exceptional cases, where the humanitarian crisis contributes to a "threat to peace," has the Security Council authorized such aid against a government's will, as it did in Iraq and Somalia. In most cases, however, the real problem is not government opposition to external assistance. Instead, insufficient aid is made available, and it is difficult to transport such aid to the often inaccessible displaced persons (who may be in hiding or surviving in difficult terrain).

One technique used in recent years to avoid or limit displacement has been to establish safe havens. In Bosnia, for example, the Security Council, acting under Chapter VII of the U.N. Charter, designated the besieged towns of Srebrenica, Sarajevo, Tuzla, Zepa, Gorazde, and Bihac as safe havens when it appeared that the Serbs would overwhelm these Muslim enclaves.[28] As a result, the rural population fled to them, contributing to the ethnic cleansing of the countryside. The problem was that unlike the "free cities" in World War II, around which the belligerents agreed to cease any military operations, the Muslims used the safe havens for the protection (and recuperation) of their troops and to launch military operations. The United Nations troops in Bosnia could do little in response because they had neither the mandate nor the means to disarm the armies in or around the safe havens. Bosnian Serbs therefore had reason to attack the safe havens. Unfortunately, the Security Council refused to provide the necessary resources to keep the havens safe from aggression. Indeed, the provision of a few hundred lightly armed soldiers in Gorazde, Bihac, and Srebrenica made a mockery of the concept itself, with predictable consequences.

A more successful safe haven was established for the Kurds in Iraq in the aftermath of the Gulf War. Although Saddam Hussein did sign a memorandum of understanding allowing United Nations guards and humanitarian personnel to protect and assist the Kurds, it was military pressure and economic sanctions that kept Iraq from crushing the quasi-Kurdish state in northern Iraq.[29]

[28] Christopher Tiso, *Safe Haven Refugee Programs: A Method of Combatting International Refugee Crises*, 8 GEO. IMMIGR. L. J. 575 (1994).

[29] Michael E. Harrington, *Operation Provide Comfort: A Perspective in International Law*, 8 CONN. J. INT'L J. REFUGEE L. 585 (1993).

Less well known but perhaps more workable precedents for providing protection for innocent civilians caught in ethnic conflict were the Open Relief Centers (ORCs) established by UNHCR throughout the war-torn countryside of Sri Lanka.[30] Some 50,000 Sri Lankans lived full time in ORCs while others fled to them whenever they felt threatened and returned home when the violence abated. Others resided on a semipermanent basis, leaving only for short periods to check on their property and cultivate their land. By providing these options, the ORCs prevented massive dislocation of people far from their homes.

At a recent symposium, "Refusing Refugees: Political and Legal Barriers to Asylum," held at the Cornell Law School, the chief of the Legal Advice Section of UNHCR urged that practical solutions be found for refugees fleeing persecution.[31] He accepted that temporary protection was the only viable instrument for those fleeing an armed conflict, even though such protection could be ended after the homeland was safe again.

But determining whether a country is peaceful and stable and whether the human rights of all of its citizens are being respected is difficult. UNHCR has taken a very conservative position and has only certified the cessation of refugee protection on a few occasions.[32] In general, UNHCR advocates that countries allow refugees to remain in the country of refuge for two years after an armed conflict or civil war ends. The high commissioner has asked host countries to have sufficient patience to allow adequate reconstruction to occur to make repatriation a viable and durable solution.[33]

UNHCR has promulgated certain criteria to help determine when it is appropriate to return refugees after the cessation of a conflict.[34] The high commissioner has always insisted that refugees should be able to return safely and with dignity to their homeland. Similarly, the drafters of the Refugee Convention envisaged that, before a refugee could be returned, three conditions must exist:

(1) the change in the refugee's home country must be politically significant, i.e. there must be a significant democratic reform of all elements of the state apparatus including free and democratic elections, a government com-

[30] See Bill Clarance, Protective Structure, Strategy and Tactics: International Protection in Ethnic Conflicts, 5 INT'L J. REFUGEE L. 585 (1993).

[31] Pierre Bertrand, An Operational Approach to International Refugee Protection, 26 CORNELL INT'L L. J. 495 (1993).

[32] Specifically, it has done so for refugees in Guinea-Bissau in 1975, for Zimbabweans in 1981, and for Argentinians in 1985.

[33] Sadako Ogata, Challenges of Humanitarianism in the 1990s, Address sponsored by the Asia Society (April 3, 1992).

[34] United Nations High Commissioner on Refugees, Handbook on Procedures and Criteria for Determining Refugee Status under the 1951 Convention and the 1967 Protocol (1988).

mitted to human rights and an independent judiciary able to provide a fair and open trial to accused persons and to prosecute human rights abuses effectively;

(2) change must be truly effective; and

(3) change must be durable.[35]

But in some cases, conditions for repatriation may never approach UNHCR's ideal. In such situations, the root causes of the exodus may never be completely eliminated, and the pressure to relieve the burden on the host country has led UNHCR to repatriate refugees even if their return was not voluntary. In fact, refugees may be returned to countries devastated by war (where their homes have been destroyed) even if the national reconciliation process is precarious. For this reason, UNHCR seeks assistance from the richer host countries to help with demining, provision of shelter, and resettlement grants. At the same time, UNHCR monitors the security of the returnees and assists with the reintegration process.

Although, in practice, ways have been found to provide some assistance to refugees fleeing armed conflict and civil strife, UNHCR still considers it desirable to elaborate a new convention to enhance the security and predictability of the protection now given to refugees.[36] In 1977, a United Nations plenipotentiary conference was organized to consider a draft convention on the subject. It failed miserably because the participants could only agree on four articles. Some observers felt the conference was badly prepared. Others felt that it represented a step backward with respect to the article on non-refoulement because the conference accepted that the prohibition of refoulement can be disregarded in cases of mass influx, an exception that has no parallel in the 1951 Refugee Convention.[37]

On the other hand, there were strong international protests when the Thai government wished to repatriate Kampuchean refugees and when Zaire threatened to return Rwandese refugees. The actions of the United States vis-à-vis Haitian refugees and the Europeans vis-à-vis Bosnian refugees have also been condemned.

The dual standards are so difficult to maintain because most of the countries that today advocate that others should open their doors have, in the past, admitted selected groups of people en masse or as a special category. As I have mentioned, the United States has been one of these countries, as evidenced by the 500,000 Vietnamese admitted after the end of the Indo-China War. It is natural that preferences willl be shown to

[35] JAMES C. HATHAWAY, THE LAW OF REFUGEE STATUS 199–205 (1991).

[36] Note on International Protection in Mass Influx, Submitted by the High Commissioner to the General Assembly, September 1995.

[37] INTERNATIONAL INSTITUTE OF HUMANITARIAN LAW, ROUND TABLE ON SOME CURRENT PROBLEMS OF REFUGEE LAW (1978).

former allies or to people affiliated in other ways. Nevertheless, the former colonial powers have great difficulty accepting the admission of all former subjects who seek peace and security in the motherland. Unfortunately, racism and rising xenophobia play a role in government decision making on whether to admit foreigners. It is the fundamental concept of the nation-state to be more or less homogeneous or at least not to be substantially changed by a massive influx of persons with a different culture, particularly when that influx may also prove to be a huge economic burden on the host state.

At present, there is no obligation for any state to open its doors to the homeless and poor of this world. The situation of the persecuted is, of course, different; at least temporary refuge or sanctuary should be given to them. Long-term solutions, however, have proven elusive; and even the UNHCR is moving away from traditional resettlement or integration solutions. UNHCR is recognizing instead that political solutions adopted before conflicts erupt are the only real means of preventing mass exoduses. The high commissioner has accepted that political compromises—particularly when bitter ethnic conflicts are involved—are imperfect. Often a careful balance of power must be arranged, which cannot be upset by addressing individual injustices; thus, there is often the need for a general amnesty. At other times, the power of certain groups must be suppressed in order to ensure peace. The prevailing philosophy now is that it is better to have an imperfect peace than a lingering war.

In the end, as we have seen in Croatia and Bosnia, effective assistance to refugees depends upon the will of the international community, which too often accepts or only condemns pro forma forcible expulsions or organized population exchanges. Many critics have accused the United Nations of assisting with ethnic cleansing and have argued that the Dayton peace accords have not only accepted the reality of separate ethnic entities in Bosnia but have entrenched ethnic politics. At a minimum, the real politik pursued in the Balkans has run roughshod over the rights of displaced persons, leaving smouldering embers of injustices that may ignite into acts of terrorism or full-scale war.

In this century, some refugee groups have been warmly accepted by other countries, but in many more instances the persecuted have struggled to survive on the borders of their countries or have been kept in closed camps in a neighboring host country. Treaties in the past have ratified boundary shifts that place an ethnic group in a different country by the stroke of a pen, and history is full of forced or voluntary migrations of defeated populations. Some states have provided autonomy or a large degree of self-government to certain ethnic groups. But the reaction of most countries when confronted with the survivors of the most heinous genocide openly committed upon any people in this century was not to open their doors. Under the Convention on the Prevention and Punishment of the Crime of Genocide, the contracting parties undertake to prevent genocide, which could be interpreted in part as requiring the provision of sanctuary to a persecuted people. But the Genocide Convention has not been ratified by all states and has not been so interpreted by many of the states that have ratified it. It is therefore difficult to imagine that anything better than temporary protection of a persecuted people will be accepted by most host countries or by the international community.

12

Citizenship and National Identity

Diane F. Orentlicher

For all but the first six years of her life, Yelena Permyekova had lived in Latvia, where her Russian parents settled in the mid-1940s. But after nearly half a century there, she was decreed an alien in 1991.[1] Soon after the Soviet Union fractured into fifteen states, the Supreme Council of Latvia proclaimed that only citizens of prewar Latvia and their descendants would be granted automatic citizenship in the newly independent state. With this, some half a million ethnic Russians in Latvia became instant aliens in the place they considered home.[2]

But if this seems insupportable, consider also Latvia's recent history: From 1918 to 1939, the Republic of Latvia was an independent state. Pursuant to a notorious secret protocol to the Soviet-German nonaggression pact of 1939, the Soviet Union annexed Latvia in violation of international law. Occupied by German forces from 1941 to 1944, Latvia reverted

I am grateful to participants in the Cornell Law School workshop on international law and ethnic conflict for helpful comments on an early draft of this chapter. I am also indebted to Susan Benda, Erika Schlager, and John Quigley for generously sharing information and insights about the subject of this chapter and to Michelle Domke, Ana Kocur, Rupal Kothari, and Mark Williams for excellent research assistance.

[1] Alessandra Stanley, *Divided Latvians Awaiting Clinton: Ex-Soviet Nation in a Battle Over Russian Citizenship*, N.Y. Times, July 6, 1994.

[2] At the same time, persons with few meaningful ties to Latvia were entitled to automatic citizenship. For example, Joachim Siegerist, who was entitled to Latvian citizenship because his father was Latvian, became a citizen in 1992 despite the fact that he had lived most of his life in Germany (and indeed was a member of the German parliament); did not speak Latvian; and had been convicted of hate crimes in Germany. Siegerist campaigned for the presidency of Latvia in 1995. Stephen Kinzer, *Fretful Latvians Turn to German with a Racist Past*, N.Y. Times, October 17, 1995, at A13.

to Soviet control in 1944. In the ensuing years Soviet authorities encouraged large numbers of Russian nationals to settle in Latvia and deported to Siberia thousands of Latvians who resisted Soviet policies. Under Soviet rule Russian was the lingua franca in Latvia, and in other consequential respects Russians enjoyed a privileged status while Latvian culture was repressed.[3] Yelena Permyekova's parents presumably were among those who settled in Latvia pursuant to Moscow's Russification policy.

That policy radically altered Latvia's demography: by 1991, ethnic Latvians made up less than 52 percent of the country's population—down from 75.5 percent in 1935.[4] Some 42 percent of the population were Russian speakers, most of whom settled in Latvia after World War II as a result of the USSR's Russification and Sovietization policies.[5]

Thus, just when Latvians regained their independence after half a century of annexation, they found themselves a bare majority in their own country. In response, the Supreme Council of Latvia acted to limit automatic citizenship in the revived state to those who had possessed Latvian citizenship as of June 17, 1940, and their descendants.

In the view of the Russian government, this was a sweeping infringement of the human rights of Russian nationals. With the proverbial stroke of a pen, a major portion of Latvia's population was denationalized. The Latvian government saw matters quite differently. In its view, Russian settlers could not lose a citizenship they never lawfully possessed: in the eyes of international law, their migration to Latvia was incident to an illegal occupation. Further, the long-term effects of Soviet policies on Latvia's demographic makeup presented a potent threat to its national identity—a precious resource for fostering civic loyalty to the newly independent state.

Similar concerns prompted neighboring Estonia to adopt a restrictive citizenship law in 1992 as it reclaimed independence following fifty-one years of Soviet rule. Like Latvia, Estonia, an independent state from 1918 to 1940, was annexed by the Soviet Union pursuant to a secret protocol to the 1939 Molotov-Ribbentrop Pact. During five decades of Soviet rule, Estonia's demographics changed dramatically as a result of Moscow's policies. While some 280,000 non-Estonians migrated to Estonia between

[3] Dzintra Bungs, *Latvia: Toward Full Independence*, RFE/RL Research Report 96, 98 (January 1993); Commission on Security and Cooperation in Europe, Human Rights and Democratization in Latvia 2 (September 1993).

[4] *Report of the Secretary-General on the Work of the Organization, The Situation of Human Rights in Estonia and Latvia*, U.N. Doc. A/47/748, Annex, at 3, para. 4 (1992) [hereinafter *U.N. Report on Latvia*]; Ruth Donner, The Regulation of Nationality in International Law 295 (2d ed. 1994).

[5] Bungs, *supra* note 3, at 98. The term *Russian speakers* refers to a group comprising mainly Russians, Belarusians, and Ukrainians. During the period of Soviet rule, less than one-quarter of these people learned the Latvian language. *Id.*

1944 and 1959, thousands of Estonians were deported to Siberia from 1944 to 1949,[6] and thousands of others were killed.[7] In 1939, ethnic Estonians constituted roughly 88 percent of Estonia's population, while approximately 8 percent were Russian. By 1989, ethnic Estonians had decreased to 61 percent of Estonia's population, with ethnic Russians constituting some 30 percent.[8] While most ethnic Estonians speak Russian, only 10 percent of the non-Estonian population learned to communicate in Estonian.[9]

Unlike Estonia and Latvia, the territory now constituting the Czech Republic did not endure a forcible dilution of its national identity by Soviet occupiers. Nevertheless, when it became an independent state upon its "velvet divorce" from Slovakia in December 1992, it, too, enacted a restrictive law excluding some long-term residents from citizenship.

The restrictive citizenship laws of Latvia, Estonia,[10] the Czech Republic, and other states raise profound dilemmas, implicating the deepest values of political community. These laws squarely present the question whether ethno-national models of citizenship comport with contemporary values of global society. The underlying policies raise the larger issue of how political communities *should* be constituted—a question that looms large at a time when popularly engineered rearrangements of territorial sovereignty seem the order of the day. May (should) states constitute their polity on the basis of explicitly national criteria? Even if national criteria generally may be used to define citizenship, do states nonetheless presumptively owe citizenship to persons who have long resided in their territory? Does the answer depend upon the circumstances surrounding their residence?

In light of the importance of these questions, it was inevitable that the restrictive policies of Latvia, Estonia, and the Czech Republic would provoke intense controversy. A raft of delegations from intergovernmental organizations, including the Council of Europe, the Conference (now Organization) for Security and Cooperation in Europe (CSCE/OSCE), and the United Nations, have visited these countries to assess their citizen-

[6] COMMISSION ON SECURITY AND COOPERATION IN EUROPE, HUMAN RIGHTS AND DEMOCRATIZATION IN ESTONIA 9 (September 1993).

[7] *Report of the Secretary-General, Situation of Human Rights in Estonia and Latvia*, U.N. Doc. A/48/511, Annex, at 6, para. 20 (1993) [hereinafter *U.N. Report on Estonia*].

[8] Riina Kionka, *Estonia: A Difficult Transition*, RFE/RL RESEARCH REPORT 89, 90 (January 1993).

[9] *U.N. Report on Estonia, supra* note 7, at 11, para. 48.

[10] In contrast to the restrictive policies adopted in Latvia and Estonia, most of the new states that emerged from the breakup of the USSR adopted a zero-option approach, granting citizenship to all persons living in their territory at the time of its independence or of the law's enactment. *See* HELSINKI WATCH, NEW CITIZENSHIP LAWS IN THE REPUBLICS OF THE USSR 2 (April 1992).

ship policies. Their assessments, summarized in this chapter, have laid bare a profound but heretofore largely subterranean shift in international legal doctrine governing matters of citizenship. Spanning a relatively short period, these assessments capture in microcosm the evolution across decades of legal paradigms governing citizenship determinations by states.

While evincing deep concern about the humanitarian implications of the restrictive citizenship policies described above, many of these delegations ostensibly reaffirmed international law's broad indulgence of state discretion in respect of citizenship. As a matter of law, they concluded, determinations of citizenship remain today, as in the past, largely the province of sovereign prerogative. This dimension of the legal assessments exemplifies the classic sovereign prerogative paradigm of citizenship, which largely denies international law the right to judge whether states' citizenship policies may be effective for purposes of municipal law.

Notably, however, this bottom-line judgment was overwhelmed by the reports' more resonant conclusions, whose basic thrust was radically to constrain states' discretion in respect of citizenship. The principal source of these constraints is the postwar law of human rights, which has progressively, indeed radically, diminished even this last great preserve of state privilege. This dimension of the various assessments is thus informed, above all, by a human rights paradigm.

Further, although human rights law generally permits states to deny full political rights to noncitizens, several of the reports suggested that the restrictive citizenship policies under scrutiny might run afoul of democratic principles. As I argue in this chapter, this strand of the experts' analysis, applying a democratic principles paradigm, presents an especially potent challenge to the discretion that states classically have enjoyed in respect of their citizenship policies.

A fourth and important theme in these assessments is their affirmation of a civic / territorial model of citizenship in preference to an ethnic model. This preference, I argue, has long been an influential subtext in various strands of international law concerning nationality. Significantly, however, two evaluations relating to the Czech law seemed to apply that preference as though it were a rule of international law—one that constrains governments in their fashioning of citizenship laws. In this and other respects, the recent assessments of the Czech law have been more forthright in recognizing profound doctrinal shifts, which had gone largely unnoted until the recent implosion of several multiethnic states placed the issue of restrictive citizenship policies squarely in the foreground of international concern.

I. Exclusionary Citizenship Laws

A. Estonia

The three Baltic states were recognized by the Soviet Union on September 6, 1991, and were admitted to the United Nations eleven days later. Because their decades-long incorporation into the Soviet Union had been in violation of international law, these states are regarded as reemerging or revived states rather than as successor states to the former USSR;[11] and the government of Estonia relied on this status when it enacted a new citizenship law. On February 26, 1992, the Estonian Supreme Council issued a decree reestablishing the 1938 Citizenship Law of the Republic of Estonia and specifying which categories of people would automatically be considered citizens of the Estonian state.

Among those excluded from automatic citizenship were all persons who were not Estonian citizens as of June 16, 1940, the date when the Soviet Union established control over Estonia, and their descendants. In this way, the Estonian government "recogniz[ed] the de jure continuity of Estonian citizenship."[12] In principle, the law did not denationalize any Estonian citizens; it resumed the state's suspended sovereignty by declining to recognize as citizens those who migrated to Estonia pursuant to an illegal annexation.

The 1992 law established a two-year residency requirement, commencing on March 30, 1990, followed by a one-year waiting period for naturalization. Further, the law established a requirement of minimum competency in the Estonian language as a condition of naturalization.[13] Pursuant to the 1993 Law on Aliens, noncitizens are required to obtain residence permits, work permits, and aliens' passports in order to remain in the country.[14]

Russians excluded from automatic citizenship in Estonia would not necessarily become stateless by virtue of this law. The Russian Federation has offered Russian citizenship to all former citizens of the USSR regard-

[11] *See* Donner, *supra* note 4, at 292.

[12] UBA/BATUN, The "Law on Aliens" Controversy in the Republic of Estonia 8 (August 7, 1993) [hereinafter UBA/BATUN Report].

[13] *See* Kionka, *supra* note 8, at 90; *Easier Language Test for Citizenship in Force since Beginning of New Year*, BBC Summary of World Broadcasts, January 9, 1997. The post-independence citizenship law was preceded by various enactments, beginning in 1988, aimed at establishing Estonia's independence from the Soviet Union and asserting the preeminence of Estonian culture within the state. These laws are summarized in a report by Raimo Pekkanen and Hans Danelius on *Human Rights in the Republic of Estonia* to the Parliamentary Assembly of the Council of Europe, Doc. AS/Ad hoc-Bur-EE (43) 2 of December 17, 1991, *reprinted in* 13 Hum. Rts. L.J. 236 (1992) [hereinafter *Pekkanen-Danelius Report*].

[14] Commission on Security and Cooperation in Europe, Report on the March 5, 1995, Parliamentary Election in Estonia and the Status of Non-Citizens 3 (May 1995).

less of their residence.[15] In practice, however, the law has resulted in large numbers of people becoming stateless because many ethnic Russians in Estonia have not opted for Russian citizenship.[16]

B. Latvia

Soon after Latvia regained independence, its Supreme Council enacted a resolution establishing principles governing citizenship while a draft law on the subject was being prepared. The resolution, adopted on October 15, 1991, provided: "Latvian citizenship belongs in principle only to those who held it on 17 June 1940 and their descendants, if they were resident in Latvia on 15 October 1991 and if they register before 1 July 1992; if they were not resident on 15 October 1991 or if they are citizens of another State, they may obtain it at any time on condition that they register and show proof of permission of expatriation."[17]

Proof of sufficient knowledge of the Latvian language was required of other categories of people who wished to be naturalized, including persons who would have been eligible for citizenship under Section 1 of the Latvian Citizenship Act of August 23, 1919, and their descendants.[18] For others, four further conditions to naturalization were imposed, of which a sixteen-year residency requirement proved to be particularly controversial.[19] Acquisition of citizenship by naturalization would, moreover, be limited by yearly quotas to be established by the parliament.[20] Several categories of people would be barred from acquiring citizenship, notably including members of the Soviet security forces.[21]

[15] Russian Federation Citizenship Law of February 6, 1992, art. 18, *cited in* UBA/BATUN REPORT, *supra* note 12, at 8.

[16] *See U.N. Report on Estonia, supra* note 7, at 9–10, para. 42. In addition, certain categories are excluded from applying for citizenship. These include foreign military personnel in active service, persons who have worked for the security and intelligence organizations of the Soviet Union, persons who have been convicted of serious criminal offenses, and persons lacking a steady income. *Id.* at 8, para. 34.

[17] Resolution Concerning the Restoration of the Rights of Citizens of the Republic of Latvia and the Fundamental Principles of Naturalisation, art. 2(1), October 15, 1991.

[18] *Id.* art. 3(3).

[19] *Id.* art. 3(4). The other conditions were familiarity with fundamental principles of the Latvian constitution, a loyalty oath to the Latvian Republic, and renunciation of previous citizenship. *See* Report by Jan De Meyer and Christos Rozakis on *Human Rights in the Republic of Latvia* to the Parliamentary Assembly of the Council of Europe, Doc. AS/Ad hoc.-Bur-EE (43) 4 of January 20, 1992, *reprinted in* 13 HUM. RTS. L.J. 244, 246, III, para. 3 (1992) [hereinafter *De Meyer-Rozakis Report*].

[20] *U.N. Report on Latvia, supra* note 4, at 4, para. 7.

[21] *See De Meyer and Rozakis Report, supra* note 19, at 246, III, para. 3. Dual nationality is not permitted. *See Latvia Replies to Human Rights Committee on Questions on Constitution, Citizenship, Legal Structure,* U.N. Information Service, HR/CT/418 (July 18, 1995).

On June 22, 1994, the Latvian parliament adopted citizenship legislation whose basic provisions were prefigured by this resolution. Apparently prompted by criticism from the Council of Europe and the OSCE, the president of Latvia returned the legislation to the parliament with recommendations for amendment; in response, the parliament amended the law to remove a harsh quota system for naturalization.[22] A new law was adopted on August 11, 1994,[23] and was amended in March 1995.[24] Under the new law persons not entitled to automatic citizenship—limited, as under the earlier resolution, primarily to persons who were citizens of Latvia as of June 17, 1940, and their descendants—must satisfy a five-year residency period beginning no earlier than May 4, 1990.[25]

While these laws seek to restore the ethnic preeminence of each country's titular national group, they do not explicitly adopt an ethno-national approach to citizenship. Among those entitled to automatic citizenship in both countries are ethnic minorities, including Russians, who lived in Estonia or Latvia on the relevant date in June 1940 or who are descended from such persons.

C. The Czech Republic

Under the Czech Law on Acquisition and Loss of Citizenship,[26] the initial body of citizens in the new state—those entitled to automatic citizenship as of January 1, 1993—comprised persons who had been citizens of Czechoslovakia and had been registered as having Czech nationality. This latter qualification referred to an internal designation of nationality established in 1968–69, when Czechoslovakia became a federation of the Czech and Slovak republics. Under this prior law, nationality was assigned principally on the basis of the federal republic in which a Czechoslovakian citizen was born. These nationality designations had no legal significance internally in Czechoslovakia; nor were they relevant internationally.[27] Yet they became largely determinative of automatic citizenship

---

[22] Timothy Morris, *Latvia Amends Citizenship Law to Meet Europe Pleas*, REUTERS, July 22, 1994.

[23] Citizenship Law, August 11, 1994, *reprinted in Law of the Republic of Latvia on Citizenship*, BBC SUMMARY OF WORLD BROADCASTS, August 18, 1994.

[24] The amendment provided for restoration of citizenship to women who, under the 1919 law, lost Latvian citizenship upon marriage to a person from another country as well as to the descendants of such women. *Latvian Parliament Passes Amendments to Citizenship Laws*, BBC SUMMARY OF WORLD BROADCASTS, March 8, 1995.

[25] Citizenship Law, *supra* note 23, art. 12(1)(1).

[26] Law No. 40/1992.

[27] *See Report of the Experts of the Council of Europe on the Citizenship Laws of the Czech Republic and Slovakia and their Implementation and Replies of the Governments of the Czech Republic and Slovakia*, Doc. DIR/JUR (96) 4, at 7, para. 3, and 10, para. 21 (April 2, 1996) [hereinafter *Council of Europe Report on Czech/Slovak Laws*].

in both the Czech Republic and Slovakia when the two states attained independence. Under this approach, someone born in the Slovak federal republic who had lived in the Czech federal republic for decades would nonetheless be deemed a Slovak national and hence ineligible for automatic citizenship in the newly independent Czech state.

Although provisions establishing a right of option mitigate the exclusionary effects of the Czech and Slovakian citizenship laws,[28] the Czech law qualifies this right by establishing preconditions, including a requirement that applicants for citizenship must not have been convicted of an intentional criminal offense within the previous five years. Scarcely remarkable in the context of established states' naturalization laws, this requirement has proved highly controversial because it effectively bars thousands of long-term residents of the territory now constituting the Czech Republic from becoming citizens there, even if they had been citizens of Czechoslovakia. In contrast, citizenship in the former Czechoslovakia is the only precondition to exercising the right of option under Slovakia's new citizenship law.[29]

II. INTERNATIONAL RESPONSES

The restrictive citizenship laws of Estonia and Latvia evoked profound anxiety among the states' Russian-speaking residents and elicited vigorous protests by Russian authorities. The Czech law also drew sharp criticism, including the charge that its restrictions disproportionately affected Roma who had been long-term—in many cases lifelong—residents of the territory. In response, each government invited certain intergovernmental bodies to assess its new or draft law in light of international legal standards; other bodies initiated their own inquiries, with which the governments cooperated.

Informed by human rights concerns as well as deeper assumptions about the nature of democratic societies, their assessments reflect an emerging trend favoring territorial/civic rather than predominantly ethnic models of citizenship. Above all, their conclusions signify how radi-

[28] Pursuant to this right, Slovak nationals could opt to become citizens of the Czech Republic, and Czech nationals could opt for citizenship in Slovakia.

[29] See Appendix II, Council of Europe Report on Czech/Slovak Laws, supra note 27, at 61, para. 243. For this reason, the new citizenship law of Slovakia has not been generally condemned and will not be addressed in this chapter. An amendment to the Czech citizenship law that entered into effect in May 1996 enables the minister of the interior on a discretionary basis to waive the clean-record requirement with respect to present or former Slovak citizens. See Talking Points of the Delegation of the Czech Republic on the Czech Citizenship Legislation, OSCE REF.PC/519/96 (August 22, 1996). Because this amendment did not eliminate the clean-record requirement, it has done little to blunt criticism of that requirement.

cally these doctrinal themes have circumscribed the province of state discretion in respect of citizenship determinations.

A. Council of Europe

The Council of Europe was among the first international organizations to assess the Baltic states' citizenship policies. When these states applied for membership in the council, they had to satisfy its requirements that they be pluralist, parliamentary democracies that respect human rights, including minority rights.[30] The council designated a two-person team to study the human rights situation in each of these applicant states and to report to the council's Parliamentary Assembly.

With evident reluctance, the first team concluded that the course on which Estonia had set itself was in principle consistent with its obligations under pertinent human rights instruments. Noting with concern that strict application of the language requirement "could exclude large numbers of persons belonging to the [Russian and other] minorities from citizenship,"[31] the report continued: "As regards the human rights aspect of this problem, it should first be noted that neither the European Convention on Human Rights nor any other international human rights convention recognises the right to a certain citizenship as a human right. Consequently, it must in principle be left to each State to determine the conditions for acquiring its citizenship."[32] Yet having found that Estonia was in principle free to deny automatic citizenship to resident minorities, the team proceeded to express concern lest Estonia in practice exclude large numbers of residents. Manifestly eager to identify legal principles that would confine Estonia's discretion in this regard, the report noted several.

The nondiscrimination norm, a central pillar of the postwar system of international human rights law, was the most important. While major human rights conventions permit states parties to discriminate between citizens and non-citizens in respect of political rights, they proscribe other forms of discrimination among persons subject to the jurisdiction of a state on grounds such as nationality. This nondiscrimination norm would be breached, the council report cautioned, if the denial of citizenship to large numbers of residents resulted in their being disadvantaged in respect of employment and the like.[33] Further, whatever freedom states enjoy to deny their citizenship to those who do not yet possess it, they may not deny it on grounds that discriminate among noncitizens. It was

---

30 *See* DONNER, *supra* note 4, at 293.
31 *Pekkanen-Danelius Report, supra* note 13, at 239, para. 34.
32 *Id.*, para. 35.
33 *Id.*, para. 37; *see also id.*, para. 28.

apparently with this in mind that the report asserted: "Human rights problems could arise if citizenship was refused to residents on the ground of their membership of a certain minority group and not on the basis of an examination of each individual case."[34]

While these observations highlighted the extent to which well-established postwar human rights norms now constrain states' discretion in respect of their citizenship policies, the council report suggested a more novel and potentially far-reaching constraint: "[I]f substantial parts of the population of a country are denied the right to become citizens, and thereby are also denied for instance the right to vote in parliamentary elections, this could affect the character of the democratic system in that country. As regards the European Convention on Human Rights, the question could be raised whether in such a situation the elections to the legislature would sufficiently ensure the free expression of the opinion of the people, as required by Article 3 of the First Protocol to the Convention."[35]

In effect, the report implied, a state's democratic character may be vitiated by denying full citizenship rights to habitual residents. In view of the distinction traditionally drawn in human rights conventions between citizens and noncitizens in respect of the right of political participation, this was a notable, indeed quite potent, claim, whose implications I explore in Part VI.

The team charged to assess the human rights situation in Latvia produced a sparser report, couching its conclusions regarding Latvia's October 1991 resolution less in terms of legal standards than of reasonableness. Applying this standard, the team affirmed Latvia's right to restrict automatic citizenship to those who possessed it in June 1940 and their descendants, while granting it to others only through naturalization.[36] Yet, the report continued, the team found the resolution "less reasonable in other respects." In particular, "[t]here is room for misgivings about the provisions which, for naturalisation purposes, require sufficient knowledge of the Latvian language and at least sixteen years' residence in Latvia, and perhaps also with the requirement that applicants for naturalisation must be familiar with the fundamental principles of the Constitution."[37] With the exception of the sixteen-year residency requirement, the other conditions about which the team expressed concern are scarcely uncommon

---

[34] *Id.* para. 37.

[35] *Id.* para. 36. Article 3 of the First Protocol provides in full: "The High Contracting Parties undertake to hold free elections at reasonable intervals by secret ballot, under conditions which will ensure the free expression of the opinion of the people in the choice of the legislature." European Convention for the Protection of Human Rights and Fundamental Freedoms, Protocol No. 1, March 20, 1952, 213 U.N.T.S. 262, E.T.S. 9.

[36] *De Meyer and Rozakis Report, supra* note 19, at 246, III, para. 4.

[37] *Id.*

conditions of naturalization. The report's misgivings about their reasonableness thus can perhaps best be explained as a reflection of the team's broader apprehension about Latvia's plan to exclude from automatic citizenship persons long resident there.

A team of experts representing the Council of Europe, who assessed the citizenship laws adopted by the Czech Republic and Slovakia, went farther in suggesting that international law now constrains governments' discretion regarding citizenship requirements in the context of state succession, even as their report ostensibly affirmed states' prerogatives in respect of citizenship. Echoing the council's assessments of the Baltic citizenship laws, the report affirmed that international law accords states "a wide-ranging power to decide who are, and who are not [their] citizens."[38] While regretting that neither the Czech Republic nor Slovakia had chosen to use the criterion of habitual residence to determine its initial body of citizens, the experts concluded "that the two States are not in breach of international law only for this reason."[39] Further, the experts opined that the two countries' "conditions for naturalisation are compatible with European legal standards in this area."[40] Yet the broad concessions thus made to the two states' discretion proved largely illusory in the context of state succession, as the experts' subsequent analysis made clear.

Their report noted that states' discretion in determining their initial body of citizens is "only limited in respect of protection of human rights . . . and by the principle of effective nationality according to which a nationality should be based on a genuine, effective link between the State and its citizens."[41] Focusing on the Czech Republic's requirement that applicants for naturalization have a clean criminal record for the previous five years, the experts drew a sharp distinction between states' discretion with respect to "real" foreigners and to long-term residents of the territory who possessed the predecessor state's citizenship.[42] Significantly, it framed its misgivings in terms of international law: "Admittedly, a State may decide who are its own citizens but it is doubtful whether, in a case of State succession, under international law, citizens that have lived for decades on the territory, perhaps are even born there, can be excluded from citizenship just because they have a criminal record."[43] The experts also found that the Czech law's requirement that applicants have a clean crimi-

---

38 *Council of Europe Report on Czech/Slovak Laws, supra* note 27, at 19, para. 45.

39 *Id.* para. 46.

40 *Id.* at 23, para. 67.

41 *Id.* (footnote omitted.)

42 *Id.* at 25, para. 79. *See also id.* at 42, para. 149 (concluding that "[a]cquisition and loss of citizenship and the status of aliens cannot be considered according to the same criteria in the case of State succession and in the case of ordinary immigrants taking up residence in a State and eventually applying for citizenship").

43 *Id.* at 25, para. 76.

nal record "is not proportional," thereby violating an element of the Rule of Law, "and could be considered discriminatory for this segment of the population which is already marginalized."[44] Further, the experts concluded that non-nationals who were citizens of Czechoslovakia on December 31, 1992, and who habitually resided on the territory of the Czech Republic "should have the right to permanent residence" there, without any further preconditions.[45]

B. United Nations/UNHCR

At the invitation of the Estonian and Latvian governments respectively, the United Nations sent delegations to each country to assess its citizenship policy. Both reports concluded that the basic approach adopted by the newly independent states was compatible with international law.[46] Yet in both cases, the assessments evinced profound discomfort with the scope of discretion thus left to these states and made clear the authors' hope that the governments would foster full integration of long-term residents into the political life of the countries.

For example, the report on Latvia asserted that it would be "desirable if Latvia, for humanitarian reasons, would extend its nationality to the majority of its permanent residents who express a desire to be loyal citizens of Latvia."[47] The report recommended that the final version of the citizenship law reduce the residence requirement for naturalization from sixteen to five years, arguing that this would "have a very positive psychological effect on non-Latvian minorities and would certainly contribute to the consolidation of inter-ethnic harmony."[48] Further, the report urged that residents over fifty should be exempted from the language requirement imposed as a condition of naturalization.[49] But while thus seeking to alleviate the hardship on elderly residents of Latvia, the report noted that the government's affirmative steps to promote the national language "go along with the respect of minority languages."[50]

[44] *Id.* para. 77.

[45] *Id.* at 31, para. 102.

[46] *See UN Report on Latvia, supra* note 4, at 4, para. 9 ("As to generally accepted principles of international law concerning the granting of citizenship, Latvia is not in breach of international law by the way it determines the criteria for granting its citizenship."); *id.* at 5, para. 13 ("The language law itself is not incompatible with international law nor with generally accepted human rights standards, even if they [sic] cause a degree of hardship or inconvenience to the non-Latvian speaking population."); *U.N. Report on Estonia, supra* note 7, at 16, para. 87 ("The citizenship and language laws examined are . . . compatible with general principles of international human rights law.").

[47] *U.N. Report on Latvia, supra* note 4, at 4, para. 9.

[48] *Id.* at 7–8, para. 26(b).

[49] *Id.* at 8, para. 26(e).

[50] *Id.* at 5, para. 13.

Similarly, the U.N.'s report on Estonia reluctantly affirmed the government's right to adopt its 1992 citizenship law[51] and the basic thrust of its language law.[52] Nevertheless, the report made clear the authors' hope that the government would facilitate the naturalization of long-term residents. To this end, they recommended that the government waive language requirements as a precondition of naturalization for persons sixty years old and older as well as for invalids and endorsed recent amendments to Estonia's citizenship law that lowered the language competency requirement of other applicants for naturalization.[53] Most tellingly, the report asserted that, although most of the stateless people residing in Estonia are eligible to acquire citizenship in another state, "they should not be encouraged to do so if they intend to remain as permanent residents of Estonia."[54] Instead, they "should be encouraged to learn the Estonian language and to apply for Estonian citizenship" because "[i]t is in the interest of Estonia to take all necessary measures to facilitate their integration so as to maintain and preserve its traditionally peaceful and tolerant multicultural society."[55]

The United Nations' principal inquiry into the Czech Republic's citizenship law was undertaken by the office of the High Commissioner for Refugees (UNHCR), which issued a highly critical analysis.[56] Where analyses of the Baltic laws had seemingly affirmed states' discretion in respect of citizenship policy (while circumscribing its exercise), the UNHCR report unambiguously condemned the Czech law as incompatible with international law.

At the heart of its analysis was the concept of a "genuine effective link" between individuals and a particular state. In the view of the UNHCR, individuals possessing such a link to a state—established principally by long-term residence in its territory—are entitled to become citizens of that

---

[51] *See supra* note 46. The study seemed to regret international law's dearth of standards regarding citizenship in the special context prevailing in Estonia: "International law has traditionally left the issue of citizenship within the realm of a State's jurisdiction. Although human rights declarations and conventions contain relevant provisions on citizenship or nationality, there remains a gap in international human rights law. Indeed, the specific factual situation of annexation accompanied by the influx of very large numbers of persons into a small State with a different ethnic origin, followed by 50 years of settlement and multi-ethnic coexistence, followed by the re-emergence of the original State as an independent entity, does not seem to have been envisaged by drafters of the relevant instruments." *U.N. Report on Estonia, supra* note 7, at 7, para. 28.

[52] "Since the national identity of Estonians is intimately linked to their language, which is not spoken anywhere else in the world," the report observed, "it is important and legitimate for Estonians to give a high priority to the active use of the Estonian language in all spheres of activity in Estonia." *Id.* at 10, para. 46.

[53] *Id.* at 16–17, para. 88.

[54] *Id.* at 17, para. 90.

[55] *Id.*

[56] The Office of the United Nations High Commissioner for Refugees, *The Czech and Slovak Citizenship Laws and the Problem of Statelessness* (February 1996) [hereinafter UNHCR Report].

state when it emerges as an independent sovereign from the breakup of a predecessor state. In its view, the Czech law "contradicts international legal principles" because it excludes "from the initial body of citizens . . . long-time permanent residents, who had a genuine effective link and who had indicated their social attachment through exercise of civil and social functions."[57] Use of the former internal Czechoslovakian law on nationality was not, in the view of the high commissioner, a permissible basis for establishing citizenship in the new state.[58]

C. CSCE/OSCE

Among the international organizations that have examined the Baltic states' citizenship policies, the CSCE/OSCE has been the most actively engaged, maintaining an ongoing dialogue with the Estonian and Latvian governments. The overwhelming thrust of its interventions has been to persuade these governments to facilitate naturalization of long-term residents who were denied automatic citizenship.

The organization's first recommendations were set forth in a January 1993 report by a delegation that visited Estonia, at the government's request, on behalf of the CSCE's Office of Democratic Institutions and Human Rights (ODIHR). The ODIHR report concluded that Estonian laws "meet the international standards for the enjoyment of human rights"[59] and that "no international human rights instrument recognizes the right to a nationality as a human right enjoyed by everyone."[60] The report elaborated: "Neither under Article 15 of the Universal Declaration of Human Rights nor under any of the CSCE documents is Estonia obligated to grant its citizenship to all residents without any preconditions."[61] Still, the report asserted a limited restraint on Estonia's discretion, relevant by virtue of its accession to the ICCPR: "However, international commitments flow from Article 24, paragraph 3, of the International Covenant on Civil and Political Rights, according to which every child has the right to acquire a nationality. By virtue of this provision, States are obligated to confer their nationality on any children who otherwise would remain stateless at birth."[62] This interpretation notably places a more exacting duty on states parties to the ICCPR than the text of Article 24(3) itself seems to mandate. While establishing a right on the part of children to acquire a nationality, the provision does not explicitly assure the right to acquire a

---

[57] *Id.* at 13, para. 53.

[58] *Id.*

[59] *Report of the CSCE ODIHR Mission on the Study of Estonian Legislation,* January 15, 1993, reprinted in 4 HELSINKI MONITOR 63, 74, para. 68 (1993) [hereinafter *CSCE ODIHR Report*].

[60] *Id.* para. 71.

[61] *Id.*

[62] *Id.*

particular country's nationality. Although the Human Rights Committee established under the covenant has implied that states parties should confer their nationality on children born in their territory who would otherwise be stateless, it has stopped short of proclaiming a duty in this regard.[63]

Despite its conclusions regarding Estonia's compliance with international standards, the report made clear its authors' belief that Estonia should aspire to "facilitate the integration of the large majority of the persons remaining in the country and to provide them with equal rights including citizenship as soon as possible."[64] Acknowledging that Estonia's requirements for naturalization might be considered "liberal under conditions of continue[d] statehood," the report suggested that these same requirements do "not fully meet the requirements of a society whose ethnic composition has dramatically changed during 50 years of Soviet rule."[65]

Without finding Estonia in breach, the report also suggested several ways in which the government *could* run afoul of international law. With no apparent sense of the irony that might have been warranted by Estonian history, the report noted in reference to the country's Russian-speaking minority: "It is of course clear that mass expulsions of population groups are prohibited" by international law.[66] Further, the report suggested that, to remain in compliance with international standards, Estonia must assure that its citizenship, naturalization, and related policies not be applied in a manner that interferes with CSCE standards relating to family unification, general international standards relating to freedom to leave one's country, and the cultural rights of minorities.[67]

Subsequent CSCE recommendations came from the organization's high commissioner on national minorities, the highly respected Max van der Stoel, whose appointment to this post became effective in January 1993. His recommendations made a forceful case for extending full citizenship rights to the two states' resident aliens and for facilitating their naturalization.

Echoing the ODIHR report, van der Stoel noted that "massive expulsion of non-Latvian residents"—an option the government was not considering—"would be contrary to international humanitarian principles even

---

[63] *See infra* note 90.

[64] *CSCE ODIHR Report, supra* note 59, at 74, para. 72.

[65] *Id.* at 66, para. 23. Buttressing this suggestion, the report urged lenient application of the language-proficiency requirement for naturalization: "It appears questionable whether this fairly high degree of language proficiency should be made conditional for naturalization under the circumstances prevailing in Estonia." *Id.* at 68, para. 34.

[66] The report hastened to make clear, however, that such expulsions "are certainly not contemplated in Estonia." *Id.* at 70, para. 48.

[67] *Id.* at 75, paras. 73–75.

more so because the overwhelming majority of the non-Latvians living in your country have not been actively engaged in oppressive practices during the years of the Soviet occupation of Latvia."[68] In effect, then, the vast majority of non-Latvian nationals in Latvia had a presumptive right to be permanent residents.

From this legal toehold van der Stoel bootstrapped a presumptive entitlement to acquire Latvian citizenship, even while implicitly conceding that non-Latvian residents were not legally entitled to automatic citizenship. "To deny citizenship to hundreds of thousands [of] non-Latvians residing in Latvia," he wrote, "is tantamount to refusing to grant them political rights. . . . If the overwhelming majority of non-Latvian[s] . . . is denied the right to become citizens, and consequently the right to be involved in key decisions concerning their own interests, the character of the democratic system in Latvia might even be put in question."[69] In this connection, van der Stoel referred to the 1990 CSCE Copenhagen Document, "which states that the basis of the authority and legitimacy of all governments is the will of the people."[70]

Not surprisingly, the OSCE has also condemned the Czech law on citizenship. During a September 1994 seminar on Roma, van der Stoel pressed the Czech government to amend its law, urging: "In no case should new citizenship laws be drafted and implemented in such a way as to discriminate against legitimate claimants for citizenship, or even to withhold citizenship from possibly tens of thousands of life-long and long-term inhabitants of the state, most of whom are Roma."[71]

D. Shifting Paradigms

These assessments capture in microcosm a profound shift in legal paradigms governing issues of citizenship—one that has emerged, almost imperceptibly, across decades of doctrinal development. Classically, few matters have been more emblematic of sovereignty than the right of states

[68] *Letter of CSCE High Commissioner on National Minorities to Georgs Andrejevs, Minister of Foreign Affairs of the Republic of Latvia,* December 10, 1993, *reprinted in* 4 HELSINKI MONITOR 109, 110 (1993).

[69] *Id.*

[70] *Id.* In his recommendations to Estonia, van der Stoel noted—and strongly disapproved of—the option of addressing citizenship by establishing a privileged position for each state's titular national group. Such a policy, he wrote, "would scarcely be compatible with the spirit, if not the letter, of various international obligations Estonia has accepted" and would "involve a considerable risk of increasing tensions . . . which, in turn, could lead to a destabilization of the country." *Recommendations by the CSCE High Commissioner on National Minorities, Mr Max van der Stoel, upon His Visits to Estonia, Latvia and Lithuania* (April 6, 1993), *reprinted in* 14 HUM. RTS. L.J. 216, 217 (1993).

[71] Statement by Max van der Stoel, OSCE High Commissioner on National Minorities, Human Dimension Seminar on Roma in the OSCE Region, *quoted in* UNHCR *Report, supra* note 56, at 2.

to determine the incidents of their nationality. Yet international law has gradually narrowed the compass of state prerogative in respect of citizenship. The postwar emergence of international human rights law in particular has significantly constrained governments' choices.

Increasingly, moreover, international law has subtly reinforced territorial/civic conceptions of nationality. By virtue of this trend, states now bear special responsibilities toward those who have meaningfully become part of their territorial communities. The recent emergence of a democratic entitlement has accelerated this trend and presents a potentially powerful assault on the distinction long recognized in human rights law between the political rights of citizens and of other long-term residents.[72]

III. The Sovereign Prerogative Paradigm

Notably, none of the analyses of the Baltic citizenship laws concluded that international law bars states from enacting legislation that excludes from automatic citizenship hundreds of thousands of long-term residents. This conclusion, reached with manifest reluctance by many of the interlocutors who assessed the Baltic laws, reflected a long-established principle of international law. "In the present state of international law," the Permanent Court of International Justice (PCIJ) advised in 1923, "questions of nationality are . . . in principle within [the] reserved domain" of the state.[73]

Control over matters of nationality has, in fact, long been regarded as "a concomitant of State sovereignty" itself.[74] Thus, successive editions of Oppenheim's classic treatise on international law reiterate, "It is not for International Law but for Municipal Law to determine who is, and who is not, to be considered a subject."[75] In practice, states have exercised this right by attributing citizenship at birth based on birth either within their territory (jus soli) or to parents who are nationals of the state (jus san-

---

[72] The phrase "democratic entitlement" was coined by Thomas Franck to describe an emerging trend in international law and state practice in support of democratic government. Thomas M. Franck, *The Emerging Right to Democratic Governance*, 86 Am. J. Int'l L. 46 (1992).

[73] Tunis and Morocco Nationality Decrees (Advisory Opinion), 1923 P.C.I.J., ser. B, no. 4, at 24. *See also* Nottebohm Case (*Liechtenstein v. Guatemala*) (Second Phase), 1955 ICJ Reports 4, 20.

[74] Paul Weis, Nationality and Statelessness in International Law 65 (1956) [hereinafter Nationality].

[75] I. Oppenheim, International Law 643 (8th ed. 1955). This rule has been codified in the 1930 Hague Convention on Certain Questions Relating to the Conflict of Nationality Laws (Hague Convention) (1937–38), 179 L.N.T.S. 89 (No. 4137), which provides that "[i]t is for each State to determine under its own law who are its nationals," *id.*, art. 1., and that "[a]ny question as to whether a person possesses the nationality of a particular State shall be determined in accordance with the law of that State." *Id.*, art. 2.

guinis),[76] or on some combination of these two principles,[77] as well as by conferring citizenship through naturalization.

There have always been exceptions to the principle that states are free to determine the incidents of their nationality, but classically these reinforced the state-sovereignty paradigm that supported the basic rule. For example, it has long been recognized that states may not impose their nationality through involuntary naturalization (though consent may be presumed in respect of certain types of automatic acquisition of citizenship, as, for example, through marriage to a national).[78] Although some writers have explained this rule in terms of individuals' freedom of choice, "[i]t is not the freedom of the individual whose nationality is at issue, but the rights of the State of which he is a national, that are the primary consideration in international law."[79] If a state imposed citizenship on a large number of foreign nationals, its action "must be regarded . . . as an unfriendly or even hostile act against the State of nationality comparable to a violation of the State's territorial jurisdiction: it constitutes a threat to peaceful relations and is as such illegal."[80]

In keeping with the logic of state sovereignty, international law was, until recently, concerned with nationality principally in the context of states' right of diplomatic protection. Thus, in the Nottebohm case, the International Court of Justice drew a sharp distinction between a state's broad discretion as a matter of municipal law to determine conditions of nationality on the one hand, and its right to confer its nationality for purposes of exercising protection on the international plane on the other hand. As to the former, the court found it unnecessary even to determine whether international law imposes any limitations; as to the latter, it found international law decisive. Because diplomatic protection and protection through international judicial proceedings "constitute measures for the defence of the rights of the State" vis-à-vis another state, international law could concern itself with the criteria used by states to establish a link of nationality with persons on whose behalf they espouse international claims.[81]

In keeping with the state-sovereignty paradigm, the effect of changes of territorial sovereignty on the nationality of inhabitants was governed principally by domestic law except to the extent that states entered into treaties governing this issue. In practice, upon a transfer of territorial

---

[76] See Report by Manley O. Hudson, Special Rapporteur, to the International Law Commission, Nationality, Including Statelessness, U.N. Doc. A/CN.4/50 (1952), 2 Y.B. INT'L L. COMM. 3, 7 (1952).

[77] See WEIS, NATIONALITY, supra note 74, at 97.

[78] See id. at 104–19.

[79] Id. at 115.

[80] Id. at 116.

[81] Nottebohm Case, supra note 73, at 24.

sovereignty by cession, habitual residents typically have acquired the citizenship of the new sovereign; but international law did not compel this result.[82]

The principal legal conclusion of the assessments of Baltic citizenship policies—that the restrictive approaches of the proposed / enacted laws were permissible—reflects the longstanding rule that matters of citizenship are, in the main, subject to the sovereign discretion of states. Yet the assessments are notable less for their avowal of that principle than for the extent to which that affirmation is eclipsed by the reports' overriding thrust in favor of presumptive citizenship for longtime residents. By the time the Czech Republic's citizenship law was assessed by international organizations—just a few years after the Baltic laws had come under critical scrutiny—this preference was cast as a rule of international law. The emerging doctrinal trend evident in these various assessments builds squarely on the foundation of postwar human rights principles.

IV. The Transition to a Human-Rights Paradigm: Reducing Statelessness

International efforts to reduce statelessness provide a conceptual bridge between the state-sovereignty paradigm of older law and the human rights paradigm that prevails in contemporary legal discourse. The first significant international effort to address the issue was undertaken at the 1930 Hague Codification Conference. Although the resulting conventions include provisions designed to avert statelessness—prefiguring subsequent assurances of a right to nationality—the 1930s-era treaties emphatically reaffirm the state-sovereignty paradigm of nationality.

For example, the 1930 Hague Convention affirms that "[i]t is for each State to determine under its own law who are its nationals."[83] And while the 1930 Protocol Relating to a Certain Case of Statelessness establishes an affirmative duty for states parties to confer their nationality on certain persons born in their territory,[84] the protocol affirms that this obligation

---

[82] D. P. O'CONNELL, THE LAW OF STATE SUCCESSION 245–47 (1956); see also WEIS, NATIONALITY, supra note 74, at 150–51. In the absence of municipal law to the contrary, international law presumes that successor states provide for acquisition of their nationality by such habitual residents. See id. at 151. For the view that international law has long required successor states to confer their nationality on inhabitants, see John Quigley, Wartime Mass Displacement and the Individual Right of Return (forthcoming). Cf. Yasuaki Onuma, Nationality and Territorial Change: In Search of the State of the Law, 8 YALE J. WORLD PUB. ORD. 1, 1–2 (1991) (from the seventeenth through early twentieth centuries, states consistently observed the principle that, upon change in territorial sovereignty, nationals of the predecessor state who habitually resided in the successor state automatically became nationals of the latter).

[83] See supra note 75.

[84] Article 1 provides: "In a State whose nationality is not conferred by the mere fact of

"shall in no way be deemed to prejudice the question whether [the princi-ples it embodies] do or do not already form part of international law."[85]

But the postwar emergence of human rights principles wrought a sig-nificant change in the discourse of international efforts to address state-lessness, reframing the issue in terms of individual rights rather than states' prerogatives. A significant benchmark of the conceptual transition can be found in Article 15(1) of the 1948 Universal Declaration of Human Rights,[86] which provides: "Everyone has the right to a nationality."

At least initially, however, the right to a nationality presented only a minimal encroachment on sovereign discretion. Notably, while the Uni-versal Declaration proclaims nationality as a fundamental right, no partic-ular state is required to guarantee that right, making the assurance essentially aspirational.[87] The entitlement recognized in Article 15(1) has, moreover, found its way into only one of the major human rights treaties adopted in the postwar years, the American Convention on Human Rights.[88] When the United Nations drafted treaties to give binding effect to the Universal Declaration, the assurance set forth in Article 15(1) was omitted. Although states were prepared to accept the sweeping incur-sions on domestic jurisdiction entailed in the International Covenant on Civil and Political Rights (ICCPR)[89] as a whole, they were unwilling to relinquish their sovereign right to determine conditions of nationality by their own lights. In the end, only children were given the right to acquire a nationality.[90]

Still, meaningful efforts to assure nationality can be found in both human rights instruments and treaties concerned specifically with nation-ality. Early efforts to reduce statelessness did so by prescribing circum-stances in which states should not denationalize individuals if it would

---

birth in its territory, a person born in its territory of a mother possessing the nationality of that State and of a father without nationality or of unknown nationality shall have the nationality of the said State." (1937–38) 179 L.N.T.S. 115 (No. 4138), art. 1.

[85] *Id.*, art. 2.

[86] G.A. Res. 217 (III) A, U.N. Doc. A/810, at 75 (1948) [hereinafter UDHR or Universal Declaration].

[87] *See* Paul Weis, *The United Nations Convention on the Reduction of Statelessness, 1961,* 11 INT'L & COMP. L.Q. 1073, 1075 (1962).

[88] *Opened for signature* November 22, 1969, 36 OAS T.S. 1, OAE/ser.L/V/II.23, doc. 21, rev. 6, 9 I.L.M. 673 (1970). Article 20(1) provides: "Every person has the right to a nationality."

[89] *Opened for signature* December 19, 1966, 999 U.N.T.S. 171.

[90] Article 24(3) provides: "Every child has the right to acquire a nationality." Interpreting this provision, the Human Rights Committee established to monitor states parties' compli-ance with the ICCPR has said that "it does not necessarily make it an obligation for States to give their nationality to every child born in their territory. However, States are required to adopt every appropriate measure, both internally and in cooperation with other States, to ensure that every child has a nationality when he is born." Human Rights Committee, *General Comment 17,* para. 8, Compilation of General Comments and General Recommendations Adopted by Human Rights Treaty Bodies, U.N. Doc. HRI/GEN/1 at 24 (1992).

result in statelessness.[91] Over time, efforts to reduce statelessness also defined circumstances in which states should affirmatively confer nationality on individuals while at the same time further constraining states' freedom to withdraw nationality from those who already possessed it. Notably, both of these doctrinal trends have increasingly been shaped by the discourse of human rights.

Exemplifying this trend, Article 15(2) of the Universal Declaration provides: "No one shall be arbitrarily deprived of his nationality nor denied the right to change his nationality."[92] Significantly, this provision protects individuals from loss of nationality even when they would not thereby become stateless. The 1961 Convention on the Reduction of Statelessness[93] similarly seeks to prevent arbitrary withdrawal of nationality and clarifies circumstances that constitute arbitrary deprivation of nationality. These include, inter alia, deprivation of citizenship without due process of law (even when withdrawal of citizenship is otherwise permitted).[94] The convention provides without qualification that states parties "may not deprive any person or group of persons of their nationality on racial, ethnic, religious or political grounds"[95]—a provision whose grim debt to Nazi history needs no elaboration.

While these provisions impose significant restraints on states' ability to withdraw nationality, they have little direct bearing on the citizenship policies of Latvia, Estonia, and the Czech Republic. None of the long-term residents who were denied automatic citizenship in these countries already possessed it; they were, of course, citizens of the now extinct USSR or Czechoslovakia. More relevant to their plight are international standards that seek to reduce statelessness by establishing affirmative obligations on states to confer their nationality on certain persons. Although few of these are legally binding on Latvia, Estonia, or the Czech Republic, the basic approach they incorporate pervades the critiques of those states' citizenship laws summarized in Part II.

Prefigured by earlier conventions, the 1961 Convention on the Reduction of Statelessness exemplifies contemporary treaty approaches to reduction of statelessness. The heart of the convention is a provision

---

[91] For example, the 1930 Convention on Certain Questions Relating to the Conflict of Nationality Laws contains various provisions designed to prevent loss of nationality through the operation of personal status laws that would render a person stateless. *See* (1937–38) 179 L.N.T.S. 89 (No. 4137), arts. 8–9. The 1930 convention did not address the problem of loss of nationality upon changes in territorial sovereignty, although that was the chief cause of loss of nationality at the time of the Hague Codification Conference, which produced the convention. *See* Johannes M. M. Chan, *The Right to a Nationality As a Human Right: The Current Trend towards Recognition,* 12 Hum. Rts. L.J. 1, 2 (1991).

[92] UDHR, *supra* note 86.

[93] (1975) 989 U.N.T.S. 175 (No. 14458).

[94] *Id.* art. 8(2).

[95] *Id.* art. 9.

generally requiring states parties to confer citizenship on persons born in their territories if they would otherwise be stateless.[96] The general duty is qualified by a provision enabling states parties to limit the grant of nationality based on birth in their territories to persons habitually resident there before the age of maturity.[97]

Most important for purposes of this analysis, Article 10 seeks to assure that changes in territorial sovereignty do not result in statelessness. While the first provision recognizes that questions of nationality arising by virtue of transfers of territory are often dealt with by treaty, the second paragraph seeks to prevent statelessness in the absence of treaty arrangements.[98] In the case of a new state formed on territory previously belonging to another, the new state "shall confer its nationality upon the inhabitants of such territory unless they retain their former nationality by option or otherwise or have or acquire another nationality."[99]

The 1961 convention can scarcely be seen to embody customary standards. It took fourteen years after its adoption for the convention to come into effect, and it has not been widely ratified.[100] But its core principle—the assurance that every person possess a nationality—had already gained widespread adherence through its incorporation in the 1948 Universal Declaration of Human Rights. Further, the obligations that the convention imposes to this end echo a persistent theme, evident in international legal responses to issues of nationality, which implicitly endorses a territorial/civic vision of nationality. It is that vision above all, I will argue in the following section, that has informed international responses to the Baltic and Czech citizenship policies.

V. TERRITORIAL/CIVIC NATIONALITY

Central to a territorial/civic model of nationality is the concept of a political community, defined in significant part by a particular bounded territorial space within which people obey the same political and legal authorities and that also demarcates the boundaries of their shared political loyalty. Its antonym is a predominantly ethnic model of citizenship, in which the political community is defined above all by common descent and culture.

---

[96] (1975) 989 U.N.T.S. 175 (No. 14458), art. 1.

[97] *Id.* art. 1(2)(b). Similar provisions are included in Article 6(2) of the Draft European Convention on Nationality, Council of Europe Doc. DIR/JUR (97) 2 (1997) [hereinafter Draft European Convention].

[98] Article 10(1) provides: "Every treaty providing for the transfer of a territory shall include provisions for ensuring that, subject to the exercise of the right of option, the inhabitants of that territory shall not become stateless."

[99] *Id.* art. 10(2).

[100] *See* Chan, *supra* note 91, at 4.

Neither of these models corresponds precisely to the jus soli and jus sanguinis bases for determining citizenship, though extreme forms of the jus sanguinis approach to citizenship may affirm an ethnic model.[101] For the most part, both the jus soli and jus sanguinis principles are ascriptive—that is, they ascribe citizenship based upon what might be viewed as an arbitrary circumstance rather than on affirmative consent to citizenship by either the individual on whom citizenship is conferred or by his or her political community.[102] When, however, either principle is combined with the further requirement of habitual residence in a territory as a condition of acquiring citizenship, the resulting criteria tend to support a territorial/civic model.

While international law has long been formally neutral on which criteria states may use to determine citizenship (within, of course, permissible limits), it has long subtly favored a territorial/civic model. For example, in the Nottebohm case the International Court of Justice found the links of the applicant state, Liechtenstein, and the individual on whose behalf it sought to espouse a claim, Friedrich Nottebohm, insufficient to entitle Liechtenstein to assert a judicial claim of protection against Guatemala that the latter was required to recognize. German by birth, Nottebohm had moved to Guatemala in 1905. Although Guatemala remained his home thereafter, Nottebohm possessed German nationality until 1939, when, shortly after Germany invaded Poland, he successfully applied for naturalization in Liechtenstein. Upon acquiring a Liechtenstein passport, Nottebohm returned to Guatemala. Based on these facts, the court found the link between Liechtenstein and Nottebohm inadequate to entitle the former to espouse the claim of the latter. The court reasoned:

> [N]ationality is a legal bond having as its basis a social fact of attachment, a genuine connection of existence, interests and sentiments, together with the existence of reciprocal rights and duties. It may be said to constitute the juridical expression of the fact that the individual upon whom it is conferred,

---

[101] Examples include Germany and Israel, which extend citizenship to all Germans and Jews, respectively, regardless of whether a prospective citizen's parents possessed the states' nationality. More commonly, countries that utilize the jus sanguinis principle confer citizenship on persons whose parents possess their nationality.

[102] See generally PETER H. SCHUCK & ROGERS M. SMITH, CITIZENSHIP WITHOUT CONSENT: ILLEGAL ALIENS IN THE AMERICAN POLITY 9–41 (1985) [hereinafter CITIZENSHIP]. As these authors note, both the jus soli and jus sanguinis principles may seem antithetical to an Enlightenment view that a government's legitimacy rests upon the consent of its citizens. For John Locke, the jus soli principle was even harder to reconcile with the principle of consent than the jus sanguinis approach. The latter could be reconciled with the principle of consent on the basis that parents, in Locke's view, possessed a right of tutelage over their children until the latter reached maturity, at which time they would freely chose their political allegiance. As a practical matter, persons reaching majority would generally elect the citizenship of their family. See id. at 23–26. Still, only citizenship through naturalization would be fully consistent with the principle of consent.

either directly by the law or as the result of an act of the authorities, is in fact more closely connected with the population of the State conferring nationality than with that of any other State. Conferred by a State, it only entitles that State to exercise protection vis-à-vis another State, if it constitutes a translation into juridical terms of the individual's connection with the State which has made him its national.[103]

Although the "genuine link" test thus articulated was explicitly limited to the context of states' espousal of claims on the international plane, the territorial / civic conception of nationality on which it is based has shaped more recent responses to issues of statelessness, responses that focus more on the rights of people than on the prerogatives of states. This is notably true of the 1961 Convention on the Reduction of Statelessness. As I have noted, the convention generally requires states parties to confer citizenship on persons born in their territories if they would otherwise be stateless. But states parties applying the jus soli principle may condition the acquisition of nationality on habitual residence before the age of maturity, in effect limiting the jus soli principle to persons who have established a meaningful membership in a state party's political community through habitual residence in its territory. This same approach governs the convention's treatment of changes in territorial sovereignty. As noted earlier, new states are required to confer their nationality on those inhabiting their territory unless they have or acquire another nationality.

Scarcely an innovation, this provision reflects a longstanding state practice in respect of transfers of territorial sovereignty. Treaties of cession have often provided for acquisition of the new state's nationality by citizens of the transferred territory, but these provisions have frequently sought to exclude people whose presence at the time of transfer was merely transitory. The most commonly used criterion for automatic citizenship in the new state has been habitual residence in the transferred territory,[104] and influential proposals for legal reform have endorsed this as the preferred approach.[105] Signifying the trend of international legal doctrine in this regard, a United Nations rapporteur has suggested that successor states may now

103 Nottebohm Case, supra note 73, at 23.

104 See International Law Commission, *First Report on State Succession and Its Impact on the Nationality of Natural and Legal Persons*, by Vaclav Mikulka, Special Rapporteur, U.N. Doc. A / CN.4 / 467, at 27, para. 74 (1995) [hereinafter *ILC Report*].

105 For example, the Harvard Research Draft on Nationality proposed that, in cases of partial succession, habitual residence should be the test for conferring the new state's nationality on persons in the transferred territory. 23 AM. J. INT'L L. 26 (1929). *See also* O'CONNELL, *supra* note 82, at 258 (expressing view that habitual residence is "the most satisfactory test for determining the competence of the successor State to impress its nationality on specified persons"). Many proponents of this approach add the qualification that habitual residents should possess a right of option with respect to another nationality.

have some duty under international law to confer their nationality on inhabitants who would otherwise become stateless.[106]

Notably, the UNHCR's assessment of the Czech citizenship law treated the genuine link test, applied by the ICJ as a rule governing states' relationships inter se, as though it were equally relevant in assessing internal laws on citizenship. Although the *Nottebohm* opinion had expressly confined the genuine link test to the court's assessment of a state's right to assert diplomatic protection on the international plane, the UNHCR invoked *Nottebohm* to condemn as incompatible with international law the Czech Republic's new law.[107] Similarly, the Council of Europe invoked the concept of a "genuine, effective link between the State and its citizens"[108] as a principle limiting the Czech and Slovak governments' discretion in determining criteria for citizenship.[109]

By applying the genuine link test in this fashion, the UNHCR and the Council of Europe transported a test that had been firmly rooted in the sovereign prerogative paradigm to a context that radically encroaches on states' prerogatives. In *Nottebohm*, the ICJ invoked the genuine link test to determine whether the manner in which Liechtenstein had naturalized Mr. Nottebohm gave it "a sufficient title to the exercise of protection in respect of Nottebohm as against Guatemala."[110] What was at stake was not Mr. Nottebohm's rights—which would have been better served had the court judged Liechtenstein entitled to espouse his claim—but those of Liechtenstein vis-à-vis Guatemala. The ICJ again affirmed the sovereign

[106] *ILC Report, supra* note 104, at 30–31, para. 87. More recently, a working group established by the ILC to identify issues relating to the impact of state succession on nationality has proposed that a future instrument should include a principle recognizing the "obligation of States concerned to avoid that persons who, on the date of the succession of States, had the nationality of the predecessor State and had their habitual residence on the respective territories of the States concerned, become stateless as a result of such succession." Report of the International Law Commission on the work of its forty-eighth session, U.N. GAOR, 51st sess., Supp. No. 10, para. 87, U.N. Doc. A/51/10 (1996). *Cf.* Draft European Convention, *supra* note 97, art. 4(d) and (g) (each state party to draft treaty "shall facilitate in its internal law the acquisition of its nationality for . . . persons who were born on its territory and reside there lawfully and habitually; . . . [and] stateless persons . . . lawfully and habitually resident on its territory"); *id.,* art. 19(1) (in matters of nationality in cases of state succession, principles contained in article 4 shall be respected); and *id.,* art. 2(b) (in that same context, each state party, in deciding on the granting or retention of nationality, should take particular account of, inter alia, "the habitual residence of the person concerned at the time of State succession").

[107] *See* UNHCR *Report, supra* note 56, at 6, para. 13; 18, para. 53.

[108] *Council of Europe Report on Czech/Slovak Laws, supra* note 27, at 19, para. 45.

[109] A Draft European Convention on Nationality similarly invokes the genuine link standard as a limitation on the nationality rules that states parties may adopt and enforce. *See, e.g.,* Draft European Convention, *supra* note 97, arts. 7(e) and 18(2)(b). The Czech government responded to the UNHCR and Council of Europe reports by asserting, inter alia, that nonapplication of the criterion of habitual residence is permitted by international law, which also does not normally link issues of citizenship to the context of state succession. *Position of the Czech Republic on the* UNHCR *Regional Bureau for Europe Document: The Czech and Slovak Citizenship Laws and the Problem of Statelessness* 4–5, 13 (April 1996); *Reply of the Government of the Czech Republic,* in *Council of Europe Report on Czech/Slovak Laws, supra* note 27, at 98–99, 106.

[110] Nottebohm Case, *supra* note 73, at 17.

prerogative paradigm by making clear that its ruling did not call into question Liechtenstein's sovereign right to confer its nationality on Mr. Nottebohm for purposes of its internal law.[111] Rather, the genuine link test was relevant only in respect of Liechtenstein's right to extend its protection to Mr. Nottebohm vis-à-vis Guatemala. This distinction, critical to the court's analysis in *Nottebohm*, was swept aside by the UNCHR and the Council of Europe.

VI. HUMAN RIGHTS RESTRAINTS ON NATIONALITY CRITERIA

The analyses summarized in Part II highlight the extraordinary degree to which international assurances of personal rights now circumscribe states' discretion with respect to citizenship determinations.[112] This is notably true, for example, of international legal guarantees of non-discrimination on such grounds as race, national origin, and gender.

For example, although the Convention on the Elimination of All Forms of Race Discrimination[113] permits some distinctions between citizens and noncitizens, it makes clear that states parties may not discriminate among noncitizens on the basis of race or nationality. Article 1(3) asserts that nothing in the convention "may be interpreted as affecting in any way the legal provisions of States Parties concerning nationality, citizenship or naturalization, provided that such provisions do not discriminate against any particular nationality." Article 5, the key provision prohibiting discrimination, reinforces this by requiring states parties "to guarantee the right of everyone, without distinction as to race, colour, or national or ethnic origin, to equality before the law, notably in the enjoyment of . . . (d)(iii) The right to nationality." Because this convention requires states parties to "nullify any laws and regulations which have the effect of creating or perpetuating racial discrimination,"[114] parties to the convention presumably could be in breach if their nationality laws had the effect of discriminating against persons of a particular national origin.

---

[111] *Id.* at 20.

[112] *Cf. Amendments to the Naturalization Provisions of the Constitution of Costa Rica,* Advisory Opinion, Inter-Am. Ct. Hum. Rts., No. OC-4/84, January 29, 1984, *reprinted in* 5 HUM. RTS. L.J. 161, 167, para. 32 (1984), in which the Inter-American Court of Human Rights proclaimed: "[D]espite the fact that it is traditionally accepted that the conferral and regulation of nationality are matters for each state to decide, contemporary developments indicate that international law does impose certain limits on the broad powers enjoyed by the states in that area, and that the manner in which states regulate matters bearing on nationality cannot today be deemed within their sole jurisdiction; those powers of the state are also circumscribed by their obligations to ensure the full protection of human rights." *See also id.* at 168, para. 38; *ILC Report, supra* note 104, at 30, para. 85 (1995).

[113] *Opened for signature* March 7, 1966, *entered into force* January 4, 1969, 660 U.N.T.S. 195 [hereinafter *Race Convention*].

[114] *Id.* art. 2(c).

Similarly, citizenship laws that discriminate on the basis of gender have been found incompatible with the prohibition against gender-based discrimination found in all major human rights conventions.[115] Further, several of the analyses discussed in Part II suggested that the Baltic states' new/proposed citizenship laws could run afoul of international standards if they were applied in a manner that interfered with international legal assurances of family unity and freedom of movement. One of the grounds on which the Czech Republic's law has been faulted is the claim that it violates international prohibitions of retroactive punishment.[116]

But if restrictive citizenship laws can founder on the basis of these and other human rights, it is not the sheer aggregation of internationally protected rights that has so substantially circumscribed states' discretion in respect of citizenship. Rather, human rights doctrine provides a deeper justification for international law's emerging affirmation of a territorial/civic model of citizenship.

The central idea is elegant in its simplicity: it is those states to whose (abuse of) power individuals are vulnerable that owe individuals an obligation to respect and ensure fundamental rights. This idea informs the entire body of postwar law protecting individuals against the abuse of state power; the scope of states' human rights obligations is, in the main, defined in territorial terms.[117] States are thereby held to account for their treatment of persons who are subject to their sovereign power—a power generally, but not exclusively, exercised on a territorial basis.[118]

---

[115] See *Amendments to the Naturalization Provisions of the Constitution of Costa Rica, supra* note 112. Both the Estonian and Latvian citizenship laws have been amended to eliminate distinctions based upon gender.

[116] As I have noted, persons who were citizens of Czechoslovakia but who did not possess what was formerly the equivalent of a federal-state nationality can be denied citizenship in the successor state of the Czech Republic based on a crime for which they have already been convicted. This, it has been urged, constitutes imposition of a further penal sanction in violation of the international proscription of retroactive punishment. *See* COMMISSION ON SECURITY AND COOPERATION IN EUROPE, *EX POST FACTO* PROBLEMS OF THE CZECH CITIZENSHIP LAW (September 1996).

[117] The predominantly territorial approach of human rights law is captured in Article 2(1) of the ICCPR, which provides: "Each State Party to the present Covenant undertakes to respect and to ensure to all individuals within its territory and subject to its jurisdiction the rights recognized in the present Covenant." The extension of states parties' obligations to persons subject to their jurisdiction even if outside their territory reinforces the principle underlying the basic approach of territorial responsibility: states owe human rights obligations to individuals who are vulnerable to their exercise of sovereign power.

[118] To be sure, treaties generally apply on a territorial basis. *See* Vienna Convention on the Law of Treaties, art. 29, May 23, 1969, U.N. Doc. A/CONF. 39/27 (*entered into force* January 27, 1990). Yet as I have noted, in the case of human rights treaties the scope of application is often more broadly defined to cover all *persons subject to the jurisdiction* of states parties. Notably, the International Court of Justice has found that states parties' duties under the Convention on the Prevention and Punishment of the Crime of Genocide, December 9, 1948, G.A. Res. 260 A (III) (*entered into force* January 12, 1951), to prevent and punish genocide are not territorially limited. Decision on Preliminary Objections, Case Concerning Application of

This idea, then, begins to explain why international law has moved in the direction of establishing a presumptive right to citizenship in the state of habitual residence. It is that state on whom individuals must depend for the effective assurance of fundamental rights. As the various assessments of the citizenship laws summarized in Part II reiterated, the effective realization of many internationally protected rights turns on full citizenship.

In larger perspective, citizenship in the state where one habitually resides is the only meaningful way to realize other values associated with self-government, an entitlement that received special attention in the assessments of European organizations not merely because of its instrumental value in securing other rights but because of its independent and singularly important value in the lexicon of international human rights assurances. To exclude longtime residents from citizenship, the European delegations' reports concluded, would vitiate the democratic nature of these countries.

This conclusion was surely the most legally innovative aspect of the assessments summarized in Part II; human rights instruments recognizing a right of political participation typically limit that right to persons already possessing citizenship.[119] If not clearly established by legal precedent, how, then, are the European delegations' conclusions to be explained? To put the question more precisely, in what way would a country's democratic nature be fundamentally subverted by denying full citizenship to longtime residents?

The answer lies at "the very heart of the democratic idea: that governmental legitimacy depends upon the affirmative consent of those who are governed."[120] Michael Walzer captures the point this way: "Men and women are either subject to the state's authority, or they are not; and if they

---

the Convention on the Prevention and Punishment of the Crime of Genocide (Bosnia-Herzegovina v. Yugoslavia), July 11, 1996.

[119] For example, while most of the rights recognized in the ICCPR apply to all persons in a state party's territory, rights relating to political participation are explicitly assured only in respect of citizens. Further, the International Convention on the Elimination of All Forms of Racial Discrimination, whose principal thrust is to prohibit racial discrimination, explicitly excepts "distinctions, exclusions, restrictions or preferences made by a State Party . . . between citizens and non-citizens." Race Convention, *supra* note 113, art. 1(2).

[120] Jamin Raskin, *Legal Aliens, Local Citizens: The Historical, Constitutional and Theoretical Meanings of Alien Suffrage*, 141 U. PENN. L. REV. 1391, 1444 (1993). In the 1809 Pennsylvania case of *Stewart v. Foster*, 2 Binn. 110 (Pa. 1809), Justice Blackenridge explained in clarion terms how this idea would be vitiated by denying resident aliens the right to vote in local elections: "The being an inhabitant, and the paying tax, are circumstances which give an interest in the borough. The being an inhabitant, gives an interest in the police or regulations of the borough generally; the paying tax gives an interest in the appropriation of the money levied. A right, therefore, to a voice mediately or immediately in these matters, is founded in natural justice. To reject this voice, or even to restrain it unnecessarily, would be wrong. It would be as unjust as it would be impolitic. It is the wise policy of every community to collect support from all on whom it may be reasonable to impose it; and it is but reasonable that all on whom it is imposed should have a voice to some extent in the mode and object of the application." *Id.* at 122.

are subject, they must be given a say, and ultimately an equal say, in what the authority does."[121] If taken seriously, this basic principle would sharply curtail states' discretion respecting criteria for naturalization with respect to long-term residents. Habitual residents of a state would enjoy a presumptive claim to full citizenship, a theme that pervades the European organizations' assessments of restrictive citizenship laws adopted by newly independent states.

More complex issues are raised by the question whether, or in what ways, democratic values constrain states' naturalization policies with respect to other categories of noncitizens—in particular, whether democratic values might be offended by naturalization policies that favor particular national groups. At least one important judgment has suggested that bonds of ethnic affinity may appropriately shape a state's naturalization laws. In a 1984 advisory opinion assessing the compatibility of a proposed Costa Rican citizenship law with the American Convention on Human Rights, the Inter-American Court of Human Rights concluded that proposed rules for naturalization that imposed less stringent residency requirements for Central Americans, Ibero-Americans, and Spaniards than for other foreigners were not impermissibly discriminatory. The court reasoned that such differentiation was reasonable because those who would benefit from the expedited procedures "objectively . . . share much closer historical, cultural and spiritual bonds with the people of Costa Rica. The existence of these bonds," the court continued, "permits the assumption that these individuals will be more easily and more rapidly assimilated within the national community and identify more readily with the traditional beliefs, values and institutions of Costa Rica, which the state has the right and duty to preserve."[122] Those same factors arguably facilitate the collective process of deliberation that is the warp and woof of self-government. On the other hand, though, concerned regard for co-citizens who belong to an "other" category is the hallmark of mature democratic deliberation.[123] But however

---

[121] MICHAEL WALZER, SPHERES OF JUSTICE: A DEFENSE OF PLURALISM AND EQUALITY 61 (1983). Pressing the cause further, Walzer argues that a place in which citizens govern over noncitizens is nothing less than tyrannical. *Id.* at 62.

[122] *Amendments to the Naturalization Provisions of the Constitution of Costa Rica, supra* note 112, at 173, para. 60. The Council of Europe's report on the Czech/Slovak citizenship laws sounded a similar note, but—inexplicably and regrettably—implied that the principle is equally valid in the context of state succession: "It is legitimate to make distinctions on the basis of language and, in so far as this denotes a better ability for integration into a country, on the basis of ethnic origin in giving citizenship to new citizens of a State, also in case of dissolution of a previous State. Such distinctions are not considered as discrimination and accepted under general principles of nationality law." *Council of Europe Report on Czech/Slovak Laws, supra* note 27, at 48, para. 184.

[123] I explore these issues in *Separation Anxiety: International Responses to Ethno-Separatist Claims,* 23 YALE J. INT'L L. 1 (1997). For a sophisticated analysis of the complex issues raised by political arrangements in democratic states that take account of national identity, see David Wippman's chapter in this volume.

perplexing these questions, their complexity should not obscure the principle recently affirmed in clarion terms: democratic values are deeply offended by the exclusion from citizenship of persons long resident in a political community.

Formerly subject to the sovereign discretion of states, questions of nationality are now extensively governed by human rights law. Ironically, at a time when human rights law has narrowed the gap between protections assured to citizens and noncitizens—and in that respect has diminished the importance *of* citizenship—that same law may be creating a new entitlement *to* citizenship. Above all, rights relating to participatory democracy establish a strong claim to citizenship on the part of persons long resident in a territory. The central importance of democratic values—values enshrined in all of the major human rights treaties—has thus wrought a radical reconception of the relationship between sovereign power and political community.

Conclusion: What Do International Lawyers Do When They Talk about Ethnic Violence and Why Does It Matter?

Tom Farer

The American minimalist Raymond Carver published a book of short stories called *What We Talk about When We Talk about Love.*[1] As I prepared to write this concluding piece, I recalled Carver's curiously evocative title. It was a natural connection, natural because one of the most intriguing features of this book is the ways in which the authors—luminaries in the field of public international law yet at the same time fairly representative of contemporary academic international lawyers, at least of the American species and the baby-boomer generation—write about the subject of ethnic conflict. As they define, diagnose, and prescribe in their various ways, no doubt illuminating many of the issue's facets, simultaneously they illuminate what international lawyers do (and what they generally do not do) when they talk about any contemporary world-order problem.

However intriguing international lawyers' talk may be to international lawyers, is there any reason why nonlawyers concerned primarily with stanching the gush of blood from riven polities should bother to reflect about the metes and bounds of that talk, its deep assumptions, its claims to relevance? I think there is at least one compelling reason, a reason applicable to the claims of all the disciplines that, without benefit of the laboratory conditions and associated techniques with which hard scientists test their intuitions about the nature and cause of things, attempt to construe an important part of reality and to make it more manageable. Until auditors grasp the assumptions behind the techniques various sorts

---

[1] RAYMOND CARVER, WHAT WE TALK ABOUT WHEN WE TALK ABOUT LOVE: STORIES (1981).

of social scientists employ, they cannot estimate the possible value of the resulting products to the mitigation of ethnic conflict or any other world-order task. Hence, before attempting to summarize the didactic and prescriptive elements in the essays integrated here, I feel the necessity of meditating first on what international lawyers can reasonably claim to be doing when they speak about world-order issues and why what they do could be useful.

I. Positivists and Realists

When I was in law school, a generation before most of the other authors, champions of two views of international law and the role of its practitioners struggled for preeminence in that insignificant province of law's empire to which their specialty had been consigned by general consensus of the academy and the bar. The Positivists insisted that, in the international as in the domestic sphere, law and politics were distinct realms of thought and action, that they called on different skills and depended on very different sources of legitimacy. The Positivists implicitly visualized the archetypical legal function as judging—that is, applying authoritative prescriptions to particular cases—whether prospectively (as where a lawyer advises a client about the legality of some proposed act) or retrospectively (as where a public official denominated a judge or justice decides in the face of behavior that has already transpired what consequences the law commands). They identified a sovereign state's manifestation of consent to be bound by some normative declaration as the sole source of all international legal obligation. In so doing, they were rejecting every sort of natural law claim, whether based on religious conviction (that obligation arose from divine will knowable through right reason) or secular premises about the necessity of a certain normative order (apprehendable through right reason) stemming from the nature of the human species and the resulting conditions for its minimum well-being.

Insistence on sovereign consent as the source of law stemmed from both the logic and the practical implications of an international political order constituted by territorial states formally equal and acknowledging no superior. It was logical because, under the shared understanding about the character of sovereignty, no source of authority superior to the sovereign state could exist. It was practical because, in the absence of centralized institutions for making, construing, and enforcing legal prescriptions, compliance with alleged obligations had to be largely voluntary. There remained, of course, the option of self-help; but its frequent exercise by self-judging actors would have undermined the system of sovereign states and greatly sapped the capacity of the legal order to facilitate cooperation and minimize friction, its raison d'être.

Again because of the accepted view of sovereignty and the practical necessities of the political order it constituted, consent was not to be presumed or casually established. On the contrary, states were presumed to exercise a plenary discretion in the formation and execution of public policy until their prior consent to restraint could be demonstrated persuasively. Consent could be manifested in formal agreement among two or more states or by implication through a pattern of acts (including declarations and explanations—that is, verbal acts) and acquiescences in the face of acts by other sovereigns. It followed that historical inquiry was the principal means for determining the validity of any claim about the existence of a legal norm and also its content. Had the governments of the relevant states consented? If so, to what did they intend to consent? On this view of the law, neither the contemporary context nor the material consequences of past, even ancient, manifestations of consent were more than marginally or occasionally relevant. If, for instance, the language of an old agreement were hopelessly ambiguous, then interpreters might consider which of the possible interpretations seemed likely in the present context to promote most efficiently the broad purposes of the parties that lay behind the specific agreement.

A determination to protect the discretion of states by tracing all legal obligations to a specific event or cluster of events in the past, and, most commonly, to a formal text (the agreement or treaty) could be effective only on the assumption that texts could be so drawn that they would speak clearly and consistently to successive generations of readers. One might then have expected that international legal positivism would find its friendliest reception in civil law countries. After all, classical civil lawyers began with the premise that all of the law was in formally enacted codes so clear and comprehensive that, once the facts of a given case were established, law appliers need only find the right code provision in order to reach the correct result.[2] Of course, the civil lawyers visualized the codes as a huge, tightly meshed net embracing the whole universe of human relationships in all their minute particulars. They assumed the existence of a provision designed to govern every possible human interaction.

The legal net of Positivist international lawyers had a very wide mesh indeed, wide enough so that much of state action passed back and forth virtually untouched. But in a sense they postulated a system as complete as the civil law one, a system that by its nature left little room for inter-

---

[2] *See* Burt Neuborne, *Judicial Review and Separation of Powers in France and the United States,* 57 N.Y.U.L. REV. 363, 378 (1982) (referring to classical civil law judges as "skilled mechanics operating a syllogism machine").

pretation because that whole terrain of state relations not governed by specific norms stemming from consent was governed by the grand norm of sovereign discretion: in other words, all that was not clearly forbidden was allowed. In this scheme of things, law was a matter of fact, not degree. An act was either legal (in the mild sense of being allowed or tolerated) or illegal. Hence, there was a bright line between law and politics, between the bounded realm of legal norms and the unbounded one of state discretion.

In fact, deep into the twentieth century, positivism found equal favor in common-law England.[3] Its appeal there probably had two roots. One was geopolitical and social: a conception of normative order emphasizing state discretion was very liable to charm the world's most powerful state, as the United Kingdom was for most of the nineteenth century. Then, as British power ebbed much faster than the valuable empire that it had produced, the second dimension of Positivist international law, its conservative emphasis on the sanctity of formal agreement and relative indifference to change in power, perceptions, or values would inevitably find favor. The other root was historical attachment to the idea of parliamentary supremacy, a supremacy unbridled by judicially enforceable constitutional restraints. If the governing establishment entrenched in Parliament accepted no unalterable domestic restraints on its discretion to define and pursue the national interest, its prior acceptance of international restraints was not to be presumed; on the contrary, the natural presumption lay in the other direction.

Nothing more sharply defines the difference between the Positivists and their opponents, the Realists or Contextualists, than this matter of the bright line between law and nonlaw, implying as it does a kind of objective or real character to legal norms. For the Realists, paradoxically, legal norms cannot have a real presence. Norms are rather a construct of widely shared subjectivities, namely the dual perceptions or beliefs that a prescription for which legal character is alleged issues from a source with the authority to prescribe and that it will probably be enforced or will otherwise induce compliance. Law, therefore, is necessarily a matter of degree, the degree varying with the breadth and intensity of the dual beliefs. Hence, international lawyers can never quite affect the imperious assurance of the Positivist's judge in answering the question, Is the proposed or consummated action unlawful? At best, lawyers can hypothesize

---

[3] Indeed, its clearest statement could be found in the writings of the English nineteenth-century jurisprude, John Austin. *See* LECTURES ON JURISPRUDENCE OR, THE PHILOSOPHY OF POSITIVE LAW, PART 1, LECTURE 6 (Robert Campbell ed., 1875–78) ("Every positive law [or every law simply and strictly so called] is set, directly or circuitously, by a sovereign individual or body, to a member or members of the independent political society wherein its author is supreme.").

that the stipulated actions will be widely perceived as lawful or unlawful. That estimate concerning the aggregate of judgmental response to the proposed action rests only in part on its surface compatibility or incompatibility with the text of a treaty or statutelike summations of state practice in widely read, unofficial texts. In greater part it must rest on the total context of the act seen in light of *contemporary* views of what is and is not permissible, including notions about conditions that radically mitigate if they do not entirely excuse state acts. Those views will be influenced by the texts of treaties and the consistent practice of states, Realists will concede, although less so, ceteris paribus, as their antiquity grows.

But neither text nor practice can by the nature of things be decisive. Why? In the case of texts, because their normative statements are largely contextless. In effect, they can be read as saying that under existing and foreseeable circumstances stipulated behavior is normally permissible or demanded because it will advance the collective ends that generated the agreement. The problem for practice claimed to have ripened into law is essentially the reverse, namely the complex, time-bound context of each of the precedents that constitute the practice. A new case is a unique pattern of facts (described in sufficient detail, of course, all cases are unique) arising in a new context; permissible behavior is the behavior that, given the context, will appear compatible with widely shared interests and values, particularly those of governing elites in important states and blocs. Where the Positivist saw *law*, the Realist saw *trends* in appraisal and decision. And while the Positivist looked to the past for guidance as to the permissibility of behavior, the Realist looked to the present for guidance in predicting both the normative judgments and the corresponding material reactions of other state elites. As judging was the archetypical legal act for Positivists, advising was archetypical for the Realist: the international lawyer as grand vizier.

Corresponding to the sum of these differences was a difference in the scope of matters deemed relevant to the professional activities of the international lawyer, a difference, we might say, in notions about what constituted relevant evidence. The classical Positivist was concerned primarily with texts: texts of treaties, unofficial texts summarizing practice, texts of government departments offering legal-sounding justifications of practice, and the texts of judicial and arbitral decisions interpreting all of the other texts. For the Realist, texts were just one among many means for getting a purchase on behavioral trends, including trends in evaluating the behavior of others. What states, in fact, did and the deep, often unstated, reasons for why they did things and the institutional arrangements that sometimes refracted their preferences and actions were equally or more important. So the lawyer had to appreciate and employ in his or her analysis and extrapolation of trends geopolitics, economics, compelling ideas about ethics and justice, and every other kind of material that persons trained or self-trained in international politics rather than law incorporated into judgments about how best to advance state interests.

The Realists' incorporation into their legal analysis of the materials and perspectives native to the traditional practitioners of statecraft led to the charge that they had obliterated the distinction between law and politics, that they had substituted Machiavelli for Grotius as their household god. However much this might be true of particular individuals, overall it was a misconception (although it did underscore a risk to which the Realist approach was vulnerable). Despite their differences, compared to Political Realists like Henry Kissinger, Legal Realists and Positivists were members of the same intellectual family. Both tended to see the system of sovereign states as one marked by strong elements of cooperation, of common interests, which coexist with the conflicts of interest and resulting fierce competition posited by the Machivellians. Both tended to see war as an anomaly rather than the appropriate and indeed inevitable arbiter of conflicts of interest. Both correspondingly visualized law—whether conceived in terms of consensual texts or as a process of authoritative decision—as more than an idiom for recording transient relationships of force. Instead, law reflects the long-term common interests of states fated to coexist; it expressed calculations of common interest made, normally, in a deliberate way and exercising a benign restraint on impulsive action in moments of perceived crisis or opportunity.

But while in comparison with the Machivellians, the champions of raison d'état, Realists and Positivists had strong family connections, in mutual comparison the connections were far from close. For when applied to particular cases, the method of Legal Realism does cloud the relationship between law and power. Rather than being fixed by a determinate text or a pattern of behavior that at some previous time solidified into a norm, the law is always in process of becoming more or less clear as decisions and associated subjectivities change. Moreover, powerful states, having more capacity and opportunity to take initiatives, have disproportionate means to shape perceptions of what is permissible just as, by their acts and acquiescences, they shape expectations about enforcement. In addition, the process of inquiry demanded by Realists—a minute study of an unending stream of state behavior of all kinds— inhibits the production of indisputable statements about the content of the substantive law. Finally, the very insistence of conceiving of law as a process rather than a fixed set of obligations could undermine its normative authority in the face of power. From the Realist perspective, these objections to Realist methods rest on the delusion that old texts (the law as a series of normative propositions contained in dusty books) can by themselves constrain the imperious, shifting demands of organized communities struggling to improve their security and welfare in the volatile conditions of contemporary life.

II. A GENERATION OF SYNCRETISTS

I recall this jurisprudential debate not to rehearse once again the relative merits of the two positions but to note its loss of salience for the generation of American academic international lawyers now on the threshold of preeminence, a generation represented in this volume by some of its leading lights. Hardly a hint of this old dispute appears in their essays, nor do we encounter any claim that unqualified references to "law" are problematical.[4] When these authors diagnose or prescribe with the aid of a legal lens, they do so in ways recognizably akin to the traditional fashion of treating authoritative texts as the point of analytical departure and the frame into which the author incorporates an assessment of political and human consequences and material possibilities. This is evident, for example, in Damrosch's chapter on genocide and ethnic conflict.

A couple of decades ago, when the postmodernist style of discourse first insinuated itself into legal academe, primarily through the channel of critical legal studies, one might have anticipated a contrary development because insistence on the radical indeterminacy of texts and the instability of interpretation seemed calculated to accelerate the erosion of Positivist discourse initiated by Realism. The survival of the core of traditional legal discourse stems at least in part, I suppose, from legal academia's institutional, intellectual, and personal connections to the working world—in the case of international law, still primarily the world of statecraft, although it now includes many actors in addition to state elites. These connections inhibit a sharp discontinuity of discourse between the academy and the makers and executors of policy for whom authoritative texts and settled practices provide both the framework of strategic calculation and vital tools for making cooperation routine. In a world where states are increasingly unable to pursue their national interests through unilateral initiatives, these tools and the related and essential beliefs about the distinctiveness and efficacy of legal epistemology accrue added value.

While the core of academic discourse about international law has not experienced root-and-branch change, it has hardly been immobile. Indeed, while most younger academics have eschewed the specialized vo-

---

[4] Anne-Marie Slaughter's essay is strikingly illustrative of this point. She writes, at 134: "[T]he shift from individual to group rights reflects the continuing expansion of the legal into the political, the legal colonization of ever-larger areas of political life." I cannot imagine a comparable observation appearing in the work of the classical international law Realists.

cabulary of the seminal international law Realists (Harold Lasswell and Myres McDougal of Yale and their emphasis on the process of law producing rather than the law produced), in terms of epistemology, the Yale paladins are parents to us all.[5]

At the Diplomatic Conference on the Law of Treaties in Vienna, McDougal led the American delegation in a furious assault on the Anglo-European position that the text was the principal means for its own interpretation. The interpreter, McDougal insisted, must interrogate every source of information about the purposes of the text's drafters and then, having ransacked the whole universe of relevant behavior before, during, and after the agreement, must choose for every disputed word and phrase the meaning most consonant with those purposes. As the traditionalists no doubt appreciated, so wide-ranging an inquiry subtly de-emphasizes the text and reduces its apparent certainties because the broader the inquiry, the more likely one is to find evidence of compromised, conflicting, and unresolved purposes and expectations and assumptions about the relationship between text and the affairs it was supposed to shape. In other words, the wider the range of inquiry, the greater the scope of plausible interpretation and hence the greater the ability to construe it in light of present desires, needs, expectations, and relations of power without conspicuous contempt for the anchor of original intent.

McDougal had to settle for a compromise weighted toward the Positivists. Interpreters were enjoined to consult the broad contextual setting of an international agreement and most other extratextual sources of intention only in the event the text is ambiguous or an interpretation consonant with its literal meaning would produce an obviously absurd result.[6] That injunction has manifestly failed to restrain this volume's authors. In their approach to interpretation, they are very much in the Realist tradition. But as I have already suggested, in their approach to international law as a whole, their work is a melding of traditions. For while their discourse implies a substantive no less than a procedural (and institutional) dimension to international law, in the policy centeredness of their inquiries and their emphasis on normative trends (particularly in the realm of human rights) subversive of strong conceptions of national sovereignty (as in Diane F. Orentlicher's essay on ethno-nationalist criteria

---

[5] Among the principal works applying and elaborating the jurisprudential views of the Yale School are M. S. McDougal & Associates, Studies in World Political Order (1960); M. S. McDougal & F. Feliciano, Law and Minimum World Order (1961); M. S. McDougal & W. Burke, The Public Order of the Oceans (1962); M. S. McDougal & H. Lasswell, The Interpretation of Agreements and World Public Order (1967); M. S. McDougal, H. Lasswell & L. Chen, Human Rights and World Public Order (1980).

[6] See Vienna Convention on the Law of Treaties, May 23, 1969, U.N. Doc. A/CONF.39/27, sec. 3, arts. 31–32.

for citizenship), one sees realism if not in the flesh than certainly in the spirit.

III. LAW AMONG THE POLICY SCIENCES, or WHAT LAWYERS BRING TO THE TABLE

One can also see the spirit of realism in the authors' implicit view of their vocation. Realists conceived of law as a policy science, a set of critically important techniques for the effective execution of policy. The lawyer was not a species of superior clerk producing decisions through the mechanical application of rules like a customs official checking a book to resolve your claim that the old cracked chamber pot you are importing from France is a nondutiable antique. Legal materials—whether texts or precedents—are sufficiently indeterminate to leave lawyers with space they can fill only through the exercise of judgment about what the law allows or requires, as the case might be. Judgment cannot be evaded; it is immanent in the vocation. And it has to be informed by a clear appreciation of the policies that normative materials serve. The lawyer, too, serves policy. Service is not merely an unavoidable obligation. It is the profession's reason for being; it was what makes it a calling, not simply work.

But just what do international lawyers bring distinctively to the world of policy? Certainly they bring neither an essentially deductive general theory of human behavior like public choice[7] nor an inductive one grounded in statistical manipulation of the variables that attend the translation of ethnic competition into violent conflict.[8] In fact, they bring no explicit theory or means for confidently predicting either the incidence of conflict or the impact of various palliatives.

One thing they carry with them and offer to consequential actors, what the lawyers have always offered when invited, is specialized historical knowledge: in this instance knowledge about previous efforts—expressed through formal rules and principles, institutions, and actions—to inhibit the eruption of intercommunal violence and to limit the destruction once an eruption has occurred and knowledge about the express or implied preferences of contemporary governments concerning relevant norms and behavior naturally incident to their enforcement.

Behind their offer lie four assumptions about its value. The first three are closely related and relatively uncontroversial. One assumption is that for any international political pathology, there is a finite number of treat-

---

[7] See JAMES M. BUCHANAN & ROBERT D. TOLLISON, THEORY OF PUBLIC CHOICE; POLITICAL APPLICATIONS OF ECONOMICS (1972).

[8] See, e.g., TED ROBERT GURR, WHY MEN REBEL (1970); TED ROBERT GURR & RICHARD C. HULA, POLITICS OF CRIME AND CONFLICT: A COMPARATIVE HISTORY OF FOUR CITIES (1977).

ments, the tangible remains of which are embedded in norms, institutions, and practices that it has been the academic lawyer's vocational necessity to record and conserve. By bringing this repertoire of techniques to the table so that they need not be reinvented, often under conditions of high stress, lawyers increase the efficiency of policy choice.

A second assumption is that, for all its local peculiarities, ethnic conflict has a finite number of causes and forms for which there are a correspondingly finite number of relevant responses. Third, and virtually a corollary of the second, is the assumption that, precisely because this is a family of conflicts with recognizable features, study of past efforts to manage and control the family will assist contemporary prediction about the efficacy and side effects of different measures.

The fourth assumption, international law's bedrock, is that international agreements originally intended by the parties to generate legal obligation and also the customary practices of states once they have been widely acknowledged to be obligatory strongly influence the policy choices of states and other consequential actors and thus increase the predictability of the behavior of national governments in their mutual relations. Law, in other words, is not simply an institutionalized means for recording decisions driven by real phenomena, whether it be the imperatives of capital accumulation or the international correlation of forces among sovereign states.

Several developments since World War II have reinforced this once heavily contested assumption to the point where it is almost anodyne. One is postmodernism's insistence on the role of ideas, not simply material factors, in determining what individuals perceive as reality and how they correspondingly behave.[9] While, of course, detecting power relationships behind conceptions of what is normal, prudent, tolerable, or even possible, postmodernism's high priests have nevertheless implicitly or explicitly imputed an autonomous force to social constructions of reality. Otherwise, what would be gained by Postmodernist efforts to reveal the edifice of hegemonic ideas constructed by the beneficiaries of hegemony? Indeed, were thought not capable of eluding such constructions, of slipping through their inevitable gaps and contradictions, the Postmodernist enterprise would be impossible. Thus, the rising ride of postmodernism has incidentally elevated the credibility of international law's background assumption that norms embedded in the routines and vocabularies of public officials and privileged by their formal discourse tend to structure, color, and limit their appreciation of policy options.

Postmodernism was created primarily by intellectuals working in the

---

[9] See JEAN BAUDRILLARD, SIMULATIONS (1983); PAULINE MARIE ROSENAU, POSTMODERNISM AND THE SOCIAL SCIENCES: INSIGHTS, INBOARDS AND INTRUSIONS (1992).

humanistic disciplines and traditions.[10] From the social sciences has come a second set of ideas and concerns beneficial to the legal project, namely regime theory.[11] The taproot of regime theory was a degree and persistence of interstate cooperation that could not be satisfactorily explained by reference to the force-correlation paradigm of Realists like Hans Morgenthau and Kissinger.[12] In its purest form, international relations realism imputed all state action to deliberate balance-of-power calculations.[13] It postulated a zero-sum game featuring rational, unitary decision making and the steep subordination of all other issues to omnipresent security and power-maximization concerns. Such iron assumptions left little room for the possibility of sustained, much less institutionalized, cooperation and none for bureaucratic alliances across national frontiers—left little or no room, then, for phenomena that became increasingly salient in the second half of the twentieth century. As the threat of external aggression diminished in much of the world, interdependence in economic and other issue areas intensified, and intergovernmental arrangements for managing interdependence proliferated, regime theory emerged to explain and clarify the operation of these increasingly developed systems of cooperation.

A regime, according to its leading theorists, is a cluster of norms, rules, principles, and decision-making institutions, regional or global in scope, that operates to stabilize the behavior of states in a given issue area.[14] In contrast to the Realists' view of issues as organized in an authoritarian hierarchy with security utterly dominant at its apex, regime theoreticians postulated a world in which different issue areas generally enjoyed a considerable degree of independence from the harsh imperatives of military security. They also rejected the idea of the state as a unitary decision maker, substituting instead the image of government factions struggling with each other over resources and policy priorities, often finding common cause with their counterparts in the governments of other states. Crossnational alliances stemmed also from the increasing technical complexity of issues that gave rise to counterpart communities of experts in

[10] Consider Jürgen Habermas, The Philosophical Discourse of Modernity: Twelve Lectures (trans. Frederich Lawrence, 1987). Consider also the work of Jacques Derrida and Michel Foucault.

[11] See Stephen D. Krasner, International Regimes (1983); Regime Theory and International Relations (Volker Rittberger ed., 1993).

[12] Hans Morgenthau, Politics among Nations: The Struggle for Power and Peace (4th ed. 1967).

[13] "The aspiration for power on the part of several nations, each trying either to maintain or overthrow the status quo, leads of necessity to a configuration that is called the balance of power and to politics that aim at preserving it." Id. at 161.

[14] See Krasner, supra note 12, at 2–5 ("Regimes can be defined as sets of implicit or explicit principles, norms, rules, and decision-making procedures around which actors' expectations converge in a given area of international relations".).

different countries, "epistemological communities" which made common cause to advance the ends (such as cleaner air or water) that made their knowledge relevant.[15]

Regime theory was not simply a deduction or an intuition. Beginning as an arresting, intuitive interpretation of available data, it has generated empirical research that has tended to confirm the theory's explanatory value. The emergence of regime theory coincided with, if it did not precipitate, a general flowering of interest among academics concerned with international relations in the function and force of rules and principles. Although initially the strict regime theorists showed little interest in distinguishing legal principles and rules from more informal understandings and practices,[16] their interest changed to such point that today it is sometimes difficult to tell whether one is reading the work of someone trained in political science or international law.[17]

Historians, too, contributed, albeit indirectly, to the legal project by reconstructing the behavior and perceptions of elites in periods when, as we can now easily see, the balance of power was, in fact, shifting. The resulting picture bore little resemblance to the Realist's unitary rational actor relentlessly calculating every shift in the balance and acting accordingly with monomaniacal energy and demonic indifference to personal or public sentiment or to conceptions of the public interest beyond the accumulation and preservation of state power.[18] If states were not efficient utility (defined in terms of power) maximizers, if there were an inevitable lag between impending shifts in the correlation of forces and a common perception of the problem within affected governments, and if, even thereafter, governments had difficulty in achieving agreement on how to respond, clearly there was room for other factors to play a role in the shaping of foreign policy—above all, perhaps, the inertial force of accumulated practices and commitments.

If political realism seems deficient as a comprehensive explanation of state behavior a century ago, when force remained an accepted (albeit increasingly challenged[19]) means for advancing national interests and

[15] See ERNST B. HAAS, WHEN KNOWLEDGE IS POWER: THREE MODELS OF CHANGE IN INTERNATIONAL ORGANIZATIONS (1989); Peter Haas, Introduction: Epistemic Communities and International Policy Coordination, 46 INT'L ORG. (Special Issue), 1–36 (1992).

[16] For a discussion of the relationship between regime theory and international law, see Andrew Hurrell, International Society and the Study of Regimes: A Reflective Approach, in REGIME THEORY AND INTERNATIONAL RELATIONS, supra note 12.

[17] Compare, for instance, Anne-Marie Slaughter's essay in this volume with those of Andrew Hurrell, id. at 49–72, and Friedrich Kratochwil, Contract and Regimes: Do Issue Specificity and Variations of Formality Matter? in REGIME THEORY AND INTERNATIONAL RELATIONS, supra note 12, at 73–93. See also Anne-Marie Slaughter, International Law and International Relations Theory, 10 AM. J. INT'L L. 717–43 (1995).

[18] See e.g., AARON L. FRIEDBERG, THE WEARY TITAN (1988).

[19] See RONALD VICTOR SAMPSON, THE DISCOVERY OF PEACE (1973).

hence governments had good reason to be obsessed with the balance of power, how much more partial it must appear as an explanation of contemporary statecraft. In some parts of the world—particularly in North America and Western Europe—a consensus against the use of force appears so strongly embodied in norms, institutional practices, and the expectations of governing elites as largely to eliminate concerns about the wholesale loss of territory and political independence. Even though security risks remain tangible in other parts of the world, the broad-based reaction to Iraq's attempted annexation of Kuwait resulting in the effective defense of the latter's sovereignty demonstrates an intolerance for classical forms of predation that can only have a dampening effect on expectations about the use of force.

A shift in perceptions about the use of force and generally about the absoluteness and permissible range of national discretion are no doubt symptoms of profound existential changes in global life, including the spread of weapons of mass destruction and the proliferation of means for delivering them, together with the explosive increase in other threats to national and human welfare that resist unilateral responses even by the most powerful states. Changes in the human condition have left powerful states with fewer opportunities to pursue their interests unilaterally. At the same time, the spread of education and the revolutionary easing of barriers to movement and communication and the triumph of the liberal economic paradigm have driven even fairly authoritarian regimes to incorporate the personal welfare priorities of ordinary people into the agenda of national interest.[20]

But while states are faced with reduced capacity to address their interests unilaterally as the number and variety of interests grow, changes in institutions and technology have given them greater opportunities for collective action. In addition to effecting a revolution in communications, technology has strengthened the possibilities of cooperation by increasing the transparency of states; now it is more difficult to cheat. Along with transparency and ease of communication from capital to capital, the proliferation of intergovernmental forums eases the negotiation of multiparty agreements and both accelerates and multiplies the normative evaluation of state practice.

The generality of authoritative rules and principles in national legal systems—that is, those embedded in constitutions, legislation, and administrative decrees—are no more linguistically precise than those declared in international agreements or implied in the patterned acts and

---

[20] Of course, some popular welfare concerns (air and water pollution are examples) would have reached the policy agenda even without popular pressure sharpened by democratic openings because to a considerable degree they are shared by governing elites.

acquiescences of states—that is, in their customary practice concerning matters of international concern. But to most people the former appear far more precise because courts with general and compulsory jurisdiction are available to construe them in the concrete circumstances of particular cases. While national legal systems retain a huge advantage in this respect, the gap between them and the international legal system progressively diminishes. It diminishes in part because, as I have already suggested, international forums of all kinds where the meaning and applicability, particularly of treaty provisions, can be examined have multiplied (the new World Trade Organization being one among so many citable instances). But it also diminishes because international law is increasingly applied by national courts. Opportunities for clarifying the substance of international law, much less using the enforcement mechanisms of national legal systems, obviously make its rules and principles appear far more important today than at any time since the modern state system emerged in the seventeenth century.[21]

In the realm of international law, private scholars, now situated primarily in universities, have played a singularly prominent role. Article 38 of the Statute of the International Court of Justice formally acknowledges their writings as one of the subsidiary sources to which the court will look for evidence of authoritative norms. In fact, the statute places distinguished scholars' summations of the controlling law on the same level, epistemologically, as the opinions of national courts and international tribunals.[22]

Scholars have, to a degree, filled the gap in the international legal order resulting from the absence of courts with broad, compulsory jurisdiction. While purporting and doubtless trying merely to describe the state of the law, even Positivist scholars, determined as they have been to honor without exception the intentions of state elites, have found themselves no more able than judges to avoid the exercise of discretion in choosing among competing interpretations of treaties and practice and in describing normative trends. In other words, one of the things legal scholars bring to the table of diplomacy is a quasi-judicial authority to confirm the applicable rules and principles and thus to affect the allocation of power that derives from being on the right side of the law.

[21] See, for instance, Anne-Marie Slaughter's reference to the interplay of national and international criminal jurisdiction with respect to gross violations of human rights in Bosnia and Rwanda. Slaughter at 137.

[22] "The Court, whose function is to decide in accordance with international law such disputes as are submitted to it, shall apply . . . judicial decisions and the teachings of the most highly qualified publicists of the various nations, as subsidiary means for the determination of rules of law." Article 38(1)(d) of the Statute of the International Court of Justice, June 26, 1945, 59 Stat. 1055, T.S. No. 993, 3 Bevans 1179.

IV. THE LAWYER AS PRACTICAL PHILOSOPHER

One can see the attempted exercise of that quasi-judicial authority in many of this volume's essays, but nowhere more clearly, I would argue, than in Fernando R. Tesón's critical appraisal of claims for the legal status of collective rights. But affirmation through interpretation of the governing law is not Tesón's only objective. Along with a number of other authors—obviously including Brilmayer, Orentlicher, and Wippman—he is also trying to winkle out of liberal philosophy moral criteria for assessing the claims of ethnic nationalists.

Practical moral philosophy is a peculiarly appropriate—indeed, an ineluctable—occupation for international lawyers in their quasi-judicial roles. Like judges, they must find outside their personal preferences criteria for resolving claims where the governing norms were never very clear or where, although clear in relation to the matter being contested, the norms are losing their authority in the face of an incipient shift in collective notions of value, interest, and efficiency. It is not enough that the standards be drawn from sources external to the scholar's personal conception of wise and decent ends and efficient means. They must as well be drawn, to the extent possible, from the very sources that generate the scholar's authoritative position in the international legal process, namely the consensus of governments. But what if, with respect to a given issue, one cannot induce a widely preferred outcome from treaty and practice and official texts of all kinds? What if there is, in fact, a broad and unbridgeable conflict of preferences among consequential participants in the international legal order? One move is to climb up the ladder of abstraction to the point where general agreement sets in. For example, while there probably is no demonstrable consensus that secession is justifiable where the group attempting to secede has experienced brutal repression and harsh discrimination, there is consensus that genocide violates fundamental norms and that all states have an interest in its prevention. Hence, possibly consistent with the interpretive role assigned to them, scholars might conclude that secession is legal as a last-resort remedial measure for groups threatened with cultural if not physical extermination.

This possible move at the international level is analogous although not identical to the one urged on national constitutional courts by Ronald Dworkin, the distinguished legal theorist.[23] He suggests that, when adopting governing norms, particularly open-textured constitutional provisions, legislators have several levels of intentions and expectations. Some are immediate and concrete. In the case of the Equal Protection Clause of the U.S. Constitution's Fourteenth Amendment, the immediate

---

[23] See generally RONALD DWORKIN, TAKING RIGHTS SERIOUSLY (1977).

purpose was to guarantee to the newly emancipated black population of the country both physical security and the opportunity to enter into enforceable contracts and to buy and sell property and thus to participate in the economy.[24] Almost certainly not included in those immediate intentions was desegregation of schools and other public facilities. But as Dworkin argues, the immediate, concrete purpose flowed from a deeper stream of purposes or values the concrete expression of which would necessarily vary with time and circumstance. At the time of the passage of the Fourteenth Amendment, public schooling was not compulsory and universal and not yet essential to a person's meaningful participation in American life either as a citizen or a factor of production. When it became so, it was necessary to forbid segregation of the schools in order to give effective expression to the underlying purpose of the amendment.

However meritorious as a contribution to the effective operation of a national legal system (in well-established states with strong civic cultures), this interpretative move is problematic for the international one. The paradigm nation-state, after all, is a group of people who imagine themselves as part of an enduring association—a historic, self-governing community that nurtures them, promises security to their progeny as well as themselves, infuses transient life with meaning, and will endure long after they are dead. People integrated into such a powerfully affective association will impute to it coherent, transgenerational purposes and immutable values. Constitutions in successful nations are not simply instrumental; they also are expressions of the community's ideal sense of itself.

Constitutional courts, one may reasonably claim, have not merely a license but an obligation to construe the constitution so as to sustain the community. Dworkin's move (that is, the coherent instantiation of collective purposes in a perpetually changing context) enables them to fulfill that obligation because a sense of shared values transcending the inevitable fault lines of class and generation (and often many others) is essential to the bridging of latent conflicts and hence to the community's long-term survival.

Of course, even if this view of the obligation and the means for its fulfillment were not controversial (and even if there were no strong dissident cultures within the community), its quotidian performance by fallible human beings would be precarious work. The best means for expressing communal values in a given setting will often be unclear. And although values cannot coexist over time if they are completely contradictory, cer-

---

[24] "No State shall make or enforce any law which shall abridge the privileges or immunities of citizens of the United States; nor shall any State deprive any person of life, liberty, or property, without due process of law; nor deny any person within its jurisdiction the equal protection of the laws." U.S. CONSTITUTION, Amendment 14, sec. 1.

tainly they can conflict at the margin. Moreover, if electorates and the average persons who compose them invariably appreciated and gave precedence to their ideals in any conflict with immediate interests and passions, we would have little need for the police and courts and none at all for moral philosophers. What sometimes makes it possible for constitutional courts to implement the logic of constitutional ideals in the face of hostile electoral messages is the prestige they enjoy by being themselves part of the constitutional fabric, expressions of the community's historic continuity. In any event, national constitutional courts can in the short term rely on the general conservative interests of the state bureaucracy and the political establishment in maintaining respect for the law.[25]

International society, if it can be so called, plainly lacks these institutional and affective buffers for interpretations of the law inconsistent with the demands and expectations of certain powerful members of that society. It is not a community in the same sense that successful nation-states are. In fact, their very sense of national community, because it requires a collective sense of the "other," the "alien," the "unincluded," obscures the vision of a global one. There are no centralized enforcement institutions with a vested interest in enforcing even decisions that many of their operatives dislike. The nub of the matter, then, is that because, as a coherent cluster of shared subjectivities—expectations and felt commitments—the international legal system remains primarily an instrumental association far closer in character to a business partnership than a community, independent interpreters of the law intent on maintaining their credibility and influencing state behavior need to be very cautious about constructing consent out of abstract declarations of normative ideals. Consciously or not, most of the authors in this volume seem to have accepted that dictum; they have, in other words, been ready to "acknowledge the limits of law."[26]

What they have not accepted is letting the extant law define the limits of their calling. That in itself is perfectly unremarkable; even Positivist international lawyers have, in the process of restating long-established authoritative norms, adverted to claims and emerging patterns of interest and preference that could augur a normative shift. What is, perhaps, slightly more notable is the straightforward move to moral philosophy not so much to anticipate the law to be as to illuminate the allegedly unsatisfactory quality of the law that is and promises to endure. "Law," Brilmayer

---

[25] When sending federal troops to enforce court-ordered desegregation in Little Rock Arkansas, President Dwight D. Eisenhower did not conceal his personal belief that the Supreme Court's decision requiring desegregation of the schools was erroneous. But the more important issue was the rule of law. The federal courts having decided, their decisions had to be enforced. *See* RICHARD KLUGER, SIMPLE JUSTICE: THE HISTORY OF BROWN V. BOARD OF EDUCATION AND BLACK AMERICA'S STRUGGLE FOR EQUALITY (1977).

[26] Slaughter at 134.

writes, "may, perhaps, make compromises with practicality, and in this sense it is not surprising that international law does not purport to grant strong entitlements to groups that challenge the statist status quo. But international morality should shoulder the job of identifying ideals. In the present context the ideal is to recognize and promote the cause of corrective justice. . . . Unless and until we are ready to abandon [that ideal] more generally, [it is the ideal] that we should turn to in evaluating the normative worth of nationalist claims."[27]

Who is the "we" to which Brilmayer refers? It is, I presume, the same moral community in which all of the authors appear to participate, the community of liberal idealists. It now extends far beyond its Western home, having insinuated itself into practically every national society,[28] although not establishing its hegemony in all cases.[29] For all their range and diversity, the preponderance of essays in this volume share a common concern: how to reconcile—or, if not to reconcile then at least to accommodate—liberal values and ethnic nationalism?

Behind this concern, I surmise, lies the assumption that international initiatives to preempt, mitigate, and terminate ethnic violence will come primarily from the nations of the West, where democracy and individual rights do enjoy hegemony within the civic culture, and that such reconciliation or accommodation is therefore necessary if they are to act coherently or even act at all because action apparently in conflict with civic culture cannot command popular support. Even Diane F. Orentlicher, while using a single case to support a pragmatic, context-sensitive, informal, problem-solving approach to ethnic conflict, implicitly concedes the pressure of a categorical normative perspective both by attempting herself to find a point of moral balance between the conflicting claims of ethnic Balts and Russian immigrants and by recounting with apparent approval the view of external monitors and mediators that human rights norms limit the right of the ethnic Balts, even when acting through the medium of sovereign states, to determine if not who shall be a citizen then at least the rights of resident noncitizens.

Judging from the differences among these authors and among others who have made the attempt, normative reconciliation is no easy task. Despite their diversity, the various efforts can be organized into four positions. One, exemplified here by Fernando R. Tesón, stands on the

[27] Brilmayer at 85.

[28] *Compare* EDWARD GIBBON, THE HISTORY OF THE DECLINE AND FALL OF THE ROMAN EMPIRE, chap. 15 (1880) ("While that great body [the Roman Empire] was invaded by open violence, or undermined by slow decay, a pure and humble religion gently insinuated itself into the minds of men, grew up in silence and obscurity, derived new vigor from opposition, and finally erected the triumphant banner of the Cross on the ruins of the Capitol.").

[29] LARRY DIAMOND, JUAN J. LINZ & SEYMOUR MARTIN LIPSET, DEMOCRACY IN DEVELOPING COUNTRIES: LATIN AMERICA XVII (1989).

proposition that the only rights legitimately recognizable within the liberal canon belong to individuals. It follows that ethnic nationalists who do not control a state can claim no more under the rubric of self-determination than the full panoply of human rights, including rights to equal treatment and to association for the purposes of expressing and fostering their culture. Secession is not a right but a last-resort remedy. The existing state has not only a right but an obligation to suppress operative elements of a minority culture that impinge on the individual rights of members of the minority or outsiders.

Tesón's position may rest ultimately on the belief that, whatever nationalists declaim about their right to political independence, they would normally be satisfied if only they actually enjoyed a full measure of individual human rights. In short, demands for secession spring from the state's failure to satisfy its obligations fully to protect individual human rights. For those people who, in a given case, are actually demanding more than that, the Tesón position is less a recipe for reconciliation of nationalism and liberalism and more a justification for suppression of the former.

A second position, summarized and apparently endorsed by Lea Brilmayer, starts from the conviction that the sense of belonging to a distinct community is profoundly human and essential to the individual well-being that is for liberals the highest good. Without shared practices and powerful cultural experiences, which a civic nationalism may not always provide, individuals can make no sense of their lives; therefore, even though the exercise of choice is unburdened by external constraint, choice is literally meaningless. Thus, community is liberalism's necessary complement. Without its shaping, animating force, the individual would be as free as the Determinist's donkey, starving to death because it is unable to choose between equidistant and equally succulent bales of hay. So when liberalism concedes the existence of collective rights and then ignores, within limits, coercive and discriminatory communal practices, it is not compromising expediently with an alien set of values; instead, it is acknowledging a necessary condition of its existence as an intellectual system for the organization of social life.

If we want to give it the nicest possible face, we might describe this second argument as the communitarian position. While it is not exactly a formula for reconciliation, it offers a conciliatory statement of parameters for negotiation.

Brilmayer, while appearing to accept the logic of the communitarian claim, cleverly absorbs it into a third position that, insofar as accommodation is concerned, seems even less promising than the first one if it were to stand alone. The trouble with the communitarian approach, she argues, is that it makes an awkward fit with the real world of nationalism. For bedrock nationalist claims are rarely about opportunities for equal treatment or cultural flowering.[30] They are about specific bits of land and a claim to it grounded in notions of corrective justice. Paradoxically, she cleverly notes, communitarian values may be invoked in defense of the existing distribution of sovereignty; for it provides the security, continuity, and exclusivity so important to the development of communal feeling. So the communitarian premise in itself provides no criteria for evaluating particular secessionist claims (as distinguished from claims to some form of autonomy or power sharing) and implies a form of discourse for the rivals and their allies that will be a dialogue of the deaf. The issue being one of corrective justice, it must be discussed and resolved precisely in those terms, drawing, one presumes, on general principles developed within national legal systems.

Brilmayer understands that the appraisal of corrective justice claims can be exceedingly difficult. She knows that virtually every state-building exercise is spotted with blood and seems to concede in passing that the passage of time can reduce the force of claims based on confiscatory acts. By insisting on corrective justice as the morally ideal optic for viewing nationalist claims, she offers a formula hugely difficult to apply and apparently hostile to the compromise of shared governance and partial autonomy, which, as David Wippman suggests in his essay on consociationalism, may often be the least worst solution. What Brilmayer would argue, I presume, is that compromise, if it is to endure, must grow out of a dialogue and that you cannot conduct one in terms that one of the parties does not accept. Moreover, conceptions of corrective justice are so widely shared that they may well appeal to both parties, however much they disagree on the application of corrective justice criteria to their particular case.

None of the essays really elaborates a fourth position, which, in that it draws bits and pieces from the first three, we might call the syncretic one. It is nicely exemplified by the philosopher Allen Buchanan's book on seccession.[31] The syncretists accept no single criterion as sufficient for the appraisal of nationalist claims. If oppression is the issue, secession is a last resort—similarly, if it is a matter of preserving group culture. Considerations of corrective justice are important but not decisive. What finally distinguishes the syncretic approach is its insistence on weighing in every case the interests of the dominant majority (except where they rest on predation), the aggrieved minority, and those of third parties as well. In moral tone it seems to me similar to just-war discourse, particularly to the

[30] Nationalist movements are not always culturally homogeneous; the anticolonial ones rarely were.
[31] ALLEN E. BUCHANAN, SECESSION: THE MORALITY OF POLITICAL DIVORCE FROM FORT SUMTER TO LITHUANIA AND QUEBEC (1991).

criterion of reasonable belief that action will produce more good than evil, good and evil being defined, at least for Buchanan, in terms that themselves balance a classical liberal emphasis on the individual and a Burkean conservative appreciation of the importance of community, stability, and order for the flowering of any values whatsoever, whether those of the individual or a group.

Because it recognizes and attempts to balance the interests of the contending parties consistent with the imperative of respect for basic human rights and, in effect, penalizes intolerance and intransigence, the syncretic position seems to me to offer a more useful normative framework for efforts to mediate ethnic conflict. Certainly I would argue that some normative framework is necessary even if one agrees that conflict prevention, mitigation, and termination will usually be approached most effectively in a flexible, mediatory posture rather than a rigorous, hierarchical, rule-directed one. Without such a framework, the antagonists could converse only in the grunt-and-click language of raw power, leaders would have no affective idiom for justifying compromises to their followers, and third parties would lack any principled basis for bringing power to bear when sweetness and reason fail, as they so often do in this less than perfect world.

Index